D0074994

CHATTEL OR PERSON?

Chattel or Person?

THE STATUS OF WOMEN
IN THE MISHNAH

JUDITH ROMNEY WEGNER

New York   Oxford
OXFORD UNIVERSITY PRESS
1988

Oxford University Press

Oxford   New York   Toronto
Delhi   Bombay   Calcutta   Madras   Karachi
Petaling Jaya   Singapore   Hong Kong   Tokyo
Nairobi   Dar es Salaam   Cape Town
Melbourne   Auckland

and associated companies in
Berlin   Ibadan

Library of Congress Cataloging-in-Publication Data
Wegner, Judith Romney.
Chattel or person?
Originally presented as the author's thesis
(Ph. D.)—Brown University.
Bibliography: p.   Includes index.
1. Women in rabbinical literature. 2. Mishnah—Criticism,
interpretation, etc. I. Title.
BM509.W7W44 1988   296.1′23′0088042   87-28305
ISBN 0-19-505169-6

The New JPS Torah translation (1962) is used by permission
of The Jewish Publication Society.

1 3 5 7 9 8 6 4 2

Printed in the United States of America
on acid-free paper

PREFACE

At the end of World War II, I was the only girl in a small class of twelve-year-olds in a synagogue Hebrew school whose enrollment was much depleted by the wartime evacuation of Londoners during the Blitz. Coaxing my privileged classmates to teach me the mysteries of Torah reading, as they practiced for bar mitzvah celebrations denied to me, I little dreamed that one day I myself should stand before a congregation and chant from the sacred scroll. Thirty years later, the first woman to read the Torah portion at New Year services in a prominent American Conservative synagogue knew she had not been the best girl in the boys' school for nothing!

When my parents sent me to Cambridge in the fifties—despite the prediction of a local Cassandra that I'd become a bluestocking and never marry, a fate worse than death for a nice Jewish girl—I should have liked to work toward a degree in Hebrew studies. Prominent scholars, escapees from the Holocaust, were then teaching Judaica at Cambridge and elsewhere. But Anglo–Jewry thought this was *nisht far yidishe kinder* ("no job for Jewish children"), not even for boys and certainly not for girls. So instead of talmudic law, I studied English law and, my courses duly completed, was called to the bar of Gray's Inn. I recall one student of Talmud in my Cambridge years, John Rayner, later to become senior rabbi of the Liberal synagogue. The shock of seeing him pore over his tractate *bareheaded* (a shameful desecration, so I thought then) remains a vivid memory recalled today with amusement as Yentl-like I don skullcap and prayer shawl and cradle the Torah in my arms.

Much later at Harvard, encountering Islamic law for the first time, I experienced a revelation and surrendered myself to researching the fascinating parallels between Islamic and talmudic jurisprudence, especially in the Muslim and Jewish laws governing marriage and divorce. Much soul-searching led me to renounce the world of legal practice and return to academe to earn a doctorate in Judaic studies. My road to Damascus had brought me back to Jerusalem.

These events coincided with the rise of Jewish feminism—a spinoff from the raised consciousness generated by the women's movement. So I wrote my dissertation on the status of women in mishnaic law. To this study, inspired by Simone de Beauvoir's claim that patriarchal cultures treat women as chattel, I brought a lawyer's question: Does the mishnaic system, in fact, perceive woman as a legal chattel or a legal person? I soon found that in the domain of private law the Mishnah treats all women as persons some of the time and some women as persons all the time. But then I had to reframe my question to ask when and why the sages reduced women to chattel. Thus recast, my investigation reaped dividends. I found that the Mishnah treats woman as chattel *only* when her biological function belongs to a specified man *and* the case poses a threat to his control of that function.

This insight was the result of a departure from the usual approach to the question of women's place in Judaism. Most such studies (including some that appeared while this book was in preparation) place primary emphasis on a critique of male perceptions of women's *role*, treating her legal *status* as merely an aspect of that role. This is understandable, given the andro-centric perspective of Genesis on woman as man's enabler and her conse-quent subservience to him. Scripture's stance (no less than feminist faith in "the Gospel according to de Beauvoir") begs the question of women's legal status. So Jewish feminists, like feminists in general, have ignored the need to investigate historical patriarchies to test blanket hypotheses about wom-en's status in such systems. Yet a number of ancient societies provide abundant textual evidence beyond Scripture. I am thinking in particular of legal rules. At least three lawbooks appeared during the late second century C.E.[1]: the *Laws of Manu* in India, the *Institutes of Gaius* in Rome, and the *Mishnah* in the Land of Israel.

The present study describes, analyzes, and interprets the mishnaic law concerning women's status. In this endeavor I try to avoid apologetics, on the one hand, and polemics, on the other. I steer a middle course between the orthodox view of Scripture and tradition as the word of God mediated through divinely inspired minds and the feminist claim that text and exegesis alike are the work of men whose self-interest dictated the subjection of women. But this raises a problem of methodology. If the text is the work of men, women must deconstruct it to expose the motivations that subordi-nate women to men's needs. If the text is the word of God, women must explore whether gynecentric exegesis yields results different from those obtained by androcentric interpretation.

My enterprise takes as raw material one basic text of Judaism, namely, the Mishnah, which for present purposes I treat as self-contained (that is, primarily to be analyzed and interpreted as it stands, without reference to later exegesis by rabbis of other times and places). This compendium of rules includes a large section on personal status, which focuses primarily on the status of women. Although the Division of Women forms the bulk of my material, I include other mishnaic rules that bear on my topic. I treat these texts as the work of men because the doctrine of the Mishnah's divine provenance first appears only in the Babylonian Talmud. Far be it from me to make for our mishnaic sages of blessed memory a claim they never made for themselves.

In exploring women's status in the mishnaic system, I go beyond earlier discussions of the place of women in rabbinic Judaism. My study is the first to treat women's status as an exercise in jurisprudence, exposing the legal theory that makes the system view woman variously as chattel and person. I hope my conclusions will not only shed light on women's status in Jewish law but will also contribute to the general understanding of the place of women in patriarchy.

This book is intended as more than an exercise in ancient history. Investigation of women's place in ancient cultures has relevance for the modern feminist enterprise. My analysis of the status of women in the mishnaic system may convince Jewish feminists that their best strategy is not to campaign aggressively for rights that were systematically denied to women but rather to argue for the restoration of women's personhood in Jewish law in accordance with basic mishnaic conceptions. By showing that the sages departed from their own view of woman as person only when their social system needed to reinforce male claims on woman's reproductive function or to allay male fears of women's sexuality, we pull the theological ground from beneath the feet of those who justify the *status quo* as Torah from Heaven.

I want to thank everyone who contributed to this enterprise: first, Professor Jacob Neusner, my dissertation director, who gave generously of his time and scholarship; then Professors Ernest Frerichs and Joan Scott who served as readers; next Professor Marvin Fox for his thorough critique of the final draft; Professor Ellen Umansky for her invaluable constructive comments, which have been incorporated at many points; and, finally, fellow students Roger Brooks, Howard Eilberg-Schwartz, Paul Flesher, and Louis Newman for their intellectual and moral support at all times. The textual interpretations offered here are, of course, my own.

Last but not least, I wish to record the contribution of my family, who coped with the domestic disruption caused by the return of a wife and mother to academic life by undertaking many chores that the framers of the Mishnah had allotted explicitly to me. My husband and sons thus became the enablers of a woman pursuing the life of the mind, reserved by the sages of old for men only. That is why this book is dedicated to Peter, Simon, Mark, Jeremy, and Michael.

Providence, Rhode Island   J.R.W.
Passover 5747/April 1987

CONTENTS

CHATTEL OR PERSON?

INTRODUCTION

The most important social revolution of the late twentieth century has been the rise of modern feminism. The raising of women's consciousness has, for the first time in recorded history, brought substantial numbers of men and women to understand how patriarchal culture constructed and maintained male dominance and female subservience, and how the restriction of women to the private realm of domesticity and their exclusion from the public domain of intellectual activity has systematically deprived women of the life of mind and spirit available to men (or at least to male elites) within patriarchal society.

The question of women's status has been much debated by feminists and others, and is now recognized as a problem by most educated people—apart from religious fundamentalists, who remain unshakably committed to the belief that woman's place was not assigned by man but ordained by God. But the wealth of theoretical discussion contrasts with a conspicuous dearth of historical studies to test the various global hypotheses on which feminist analysis has so far rested. Only recently have scholars begun to notice this lacuna and to call for such studies as essential to a fuller understanding of women's status today and of the possibilities for change. This book examines the image and status of women in one historical patriarchy, namely, the culture of a social group of Jews in Palestine of late antiquity, enshrined in the sacred text known as the Mishnah.

The Mishnah, a book of legal rules compiled by Jewish sages in second-century Roman Palestine, depicts a society whose central character is the free adult Israelite male. Possessor of wives, children, land, slaves, livestock,

3

and other chattels, he occupies a sociolegal status not unlike that of the Roman *paterfamilias*, his counterpart in the dominant culture of the day. The Mishnah's socioeconomic system, rooted in private property, considers people and things from the perspective of their relationship to the owner or master. The present study explores the place of women in that system.

The Mishnah as a Sociolegal Document

The Mishnah comprises sixty-three tractates arranged according to subject matter in six divisions (*sᵉdarim*) dealing with agriculture, holy days, family law, civil and criminal law, sacred objects, and cultic purity.[1] But the document is far more than a book of legal rules. To cultural anthropologists it is a model of sanctity, a blueprint for a way of life that expresses the worldview of the social group that produced it.[2] The emphasis on sanctity reflected a utopian vision of the people Israel, set apart by Yahweh from the nations of the world, as *"a kingdom of priests and a holy nation."*[3] For the framers of the Mishnah, Israel's service to God entailed endless repetition of an annual cycle of religious practices—reminiscent of Eliade's sacred "succession of eternities"[4]—performed in a state of cultic purity.

This stress on cultic purity extended to every detail of daily life; the sages aimed to preserve not only the sanctity of sacred space and time—the Land of Israel and the sabbaths and festivals ordained in Scripture—but also the purity of people, places, and objects involved in sacred rites. Crucial to the system was the preservation of sanctity in human relationships, above all in matters of family law. Cultic purity required the avoidance of illicit unions with women who belonged to other men. So the Mishnah focused on the sanctity of Israelite life at bed and board as well as in courthouse and marketplace, synagogue and study-house.

Most of the rules that govern women's status appear in *Seder Nashim* ("Division of Women"), one of two divisions that prescribe guidelines for the conduct of life in society.[5] The four remaining divisions largely deal with aspects of the Temple cult and related matters.[6] But when the Mishnah was completed at the end of the second century, the Temple, destroyed by the Romans in 70 C.E., had lain in ruins for more than a hundred years; so most of the contents of those four sections had no practical application at the time of their redaction. They may have constituted a blueprint for a utopian society, a messianic age in which the Mishnah's creators imagined the Temple restored. As for the rules set out in the Divisions of Women and Damages, we do not know how far the sages could enforce their view of the sanctified life in a Land of Israel groaning under the yoke of Rome. But even as a purely theoretical construct, the Mishnah repays investigation as the view of one group of second-century Jews about the ideal functioning of Israelite society. For the purpose of this study we shall assume that the Division of Women generally reflects the sages' conception of the place of women in their culture.

Besides being a blueprint for the conduct of a sanctified life, the Mishnah is also the first postscriptural collection of Jewish law. I use the word *collection* because it looks far more like a schoolbook or manual than an actual code of law.[7] A comprehensive code would have included basic rules of law as well as more complex provisions, but the Mishnah's framers often take the basic rules for granted, focusing instead on "hard cases" that threaten the smooth working of the system. The Division of Women primarily addresses situations in which an Israelite may impair his personal sanctity by having relations with a woman whose sexual and reproductive function belongs to another man. For example, tractate *Giṭṭin* ("Writs of Divorce,"), without even bothering to cite the basic rule (viz., that a husband divorces his wife by giving her a document with a specified form and content), plunges right into a discussion of errors that can invalidate the divorce. The sages' main concern is to avoid the cultic pollution that results when a man mistakenly contracts an unholy union with an invalidly divorced woman. Other tractates likewise focus on problems that arise from the application of clearly articulated principles to hypothetical hard cases. So the Mishnah is as much a casebook as a code of law. But, either way, it casts its framers' worldview in a quasi-legal form; so we may justly regard its rules as a legal expression of cultural norms.

At another level the Mishnah is preoccupied with taxonomy, with placing everything in an appropriate slot. The sages' worldview posits a close connection between human society and cosmic order—a phenomenon well documented by the social sciences.[8] Along with an insistence on order goes an abhorrence of the disorder caused by anomalies or ambiguities. As we might expect of a system designed by men, the Mishnah treats the male as the norm and the female, by definition, as an anomaly, a deviation from the norm. Woman as "other" automatically occupies a different category from man. Nonetheless, the sages do perceive woman as a human being, a creature similar to man in important ways. Hence she is both "like" and "not like" man, a point whose significance will become clear later on.

This ambivalent approach generates apparent inconsistencies in the Mishnah's treatment of women. On the one hand, the sages perceive women as sentient, intelligent beings whose reactions to real-life situations resemble those of men. On the other, they view women through the androcentric lens of a male-dominated culture, which sometimes turns woman into an object rather than a subject of the laws, makes her peripheral rather than central to the culture, and subordinates her to male jurisdiction—above all in those aspects of the female that hold most value for men. The Mishnah maintains strict control of women's activities, especially their sexual and reproductive role in the social economy.

A woman's biological and economic functions have intrinsic value in human society;[9] the Mishnah understands this very well. Thus, the sages require a man to take a second wife if the first remains barren for ten years; they endorse Scripture's levirate law that is aimed at producing a posthumous heir for a man who left no son; and in the economic sphere they specify precisely the wife's work norm for production of yarn or cloth. Women's importance in the mishnaic world is highlighted by the fact that the Mishnah's redactors (or some later editor) chose to name one of its six sections the Division of Women. (The absence of a corresponding Division of Men reflects the fact that in patriarchies men make rules about women, but women do not make rules about men.)

Despite their obvious importance, women do not play a central role in mishnaic culture; they occupy a marginal position that is restricted to the domain of private transactions. When it comes to public affairs, particularly communal religious practices, the sages expressly or implicitly bar women from active participation. Those exclusions involve sacrificial and other ministrations of the Temple cult—a purely hypothetical enterprise in the Mishnah's day—as well as religious exercises that were actually practiced by Jews in second-century Palestine. For instance, women may not lead a congregation of men and women in public worship even though the Mishnah explicitly requires them to recite prayers in private; and the sages discouraged or even forbade the convening of all-female congregations. Certainly they barred women from the most significant enterprise of their culture, the communal study of sacred texts—a religious observance that along with communal prayer came to replace the sacrificial cult after the destruction of the Temple. Denied access to the intellectual stimulation and spiritual satisfaction of Jewish communal religious expression, women were effectively excluded from the life of mind and spirit.[10]

Thus far my analysis of the mishnaic attitude toward women supports contemporary feminist interpretations of patriarchy—that is, the form of social organization in which the eldest male (usually the father) heads the social unit (family or household) and in which women, subject to male domination, automatically possess inferior legal status.[11] But close scrutiny of mishnaic texts yields some surprises: The Mishnah often treats women as virtually equivalent to men, ascribing to them the same rational minds, practical skills, and moral sensibilities. The sages acknowledge a woman's competence to own property, conduct business, engage in lawsuits, present legal testimony on specified matters, and (if autonomous) to manage her personal affairs, including her sex life, without male guidance or control.

These discoveries prompted a rethinking of my original formulation of the problem (Is woman chattel or person in mishnaic law?) as too simplistic. In fact, the assumption that it is possible to characterize women consistently as either chattels or persons, but not both, begs the question. It turns out that the Mishnah sometimes views women in one way and sometimes in another. Hence, the question required a different focus: When and why does the Mishnah treat women as persons and when and why does it treat them as chattels?

Why Chattel or Person?

Two considerations led me to pose the question in terms of *chattel* and *person*. First, this legal dichotomy puts matters into sharp relief. *Personhood* means the complex of legal entitlements and obligations that largely define an individual's status in society. The converse of *person* in this sense is *chattel*—an entity lacking powers, rights, or duties under the law. So it made sense to ask whether the mishnaic system perceived woman as a chattel or a person and, if the latter, to what degree?

Second, the form of the question was virtually dictated by the nature of mishnaic taxonomy, resting as it does on analogy and contrast.[12] The sages assume that everything can be classified in principle and that every category has a polar opposite. All objects placed in class *X* must by definition possess the attributes of that class; if excluded from class *X*, they must exhibit diametrically opposed qualities. But what about objects that do not fit clearly into a given category or its converse? Here the Mishnah's special brand of binary logic comes into play. Rather than conceding the viability of hybrid categories and thus permitting an unacceptable blurring of lines, the sages resort to describing problematic entities as "like *X*" in some respects and "not like *X*" in others. Then they assign the ambiguous object to category *X* for some purposes and to category *Y* for others.

Consider the following illustration. At one point the Mishnah discusses a certain animal, the *koy*. This creature, the mythical offspring of a goat and a gazelle,[13] poses a taxonomic conundrum: Should a cross between a domestic animal and a wild beast be classified as wild or domestic? The modern mind would find it logical to create a third category, the hybrid. But the sages, inhibited by a Hellenistic dislike of the excluded middle, analyze the creature thus: "The *koy* in some ways resembles a wild beast, whereas in other ways it resembles a domestic animal; and in some ways it resembles both a wild beast and a domestic animal, whereas in other ways it resembles neither a wild beast nor a domestic animal."[14] They then spell out in meticulous detail the cultic purposes for which the *koy* falls into one or another of these categories (M. Bik. 2:9-11). Thus, the *koy* resembles a wild beast in being subject to the rules of carrion (Lev. 7:24), but it is like cattle in that certain portions must be offered to the priest (Deut. 18:3). It resembles neither a wild nor a domestic animal in that it may not be yoked with either to pull a plough (Deut. 22:10), and it is like both in being subject to the laws of ritual slaughter (Deut. 12:21). This example nicely illustrates the mishnaic mode of thought, especially the process of analogy and contrast and the polarities of "sameness" and "difference"—a basic dichotomy of Western rational thought.

When faced with the need to classify women, the sages treat them very much as they treat the *koy*. They vacillate between defining woman as chattel and as person. For instance, tractate *Qiddushin* ("Espousals") opens by describing procedures for acquiring wives, slaves, cattle, land, and other chattels. The presentation of a list that groups women with property strongly implies that a woman is perceived as an object rather than a person when being acquired in marriage. This impression is reinforced by the discussion of the acquisition of wives in the same technical terminology as the acquisition of property generally, and by the fact that mishnaic law does not require the consent of a daughter married off by her father (which is the normal case). Yet in other contexts, such as responsibility for violations of criminal law, the sages place women in the same category as men, subjecting both to the same penalties—a procedure that clearly treats women as persons.

To the Mishnah's framers, then, woman presents an anomaly, a "legal hybrid" that defies logical classification. She is "like" a man, hence a person, in some ways, and "not like" a man, hence a nonperson, in others. As with the *koy*, the sages, unwilling to recognize an intermediate category, choose to split the woman into her "chattel" and "person" components, depending on context, and treat her accordingly.[15] This solution at once reflects and reinforces an ambivalent attitude toward women. In the language of structural anthropology and modern feminist theory, the sages sometimes perceive woman as Self (i.e., a being who shares a common humanity with man) and sometimes as Other (i.e. a creature that can legally be handled in ways not acceptable when dealing with men). The practical result, as we shall see, is that the sages sometimes treat women as the property of men—chattels possessing neither morality nor intellect— whereas at other times they view women as both moral and intelligent, hence as persons with legal rights, duties and powers. The scope of a woman's entitlements and obligations varies with her relationship to specified men or with the absence of any such relationship as well as with the nature of the case at hand.

In this study I spell out these variations in detail, analyze them, and isolate the factors that account for differential treatment of different classes of women in the private domain and for differential treatment of men and women in the public domain of mishnaic culture. The final chapter relates the findings of the study to recent developments in feminist analysis of the status of women in patriarchy.

Methodology

Finally, a methodological note. Many traditional students of Jewish law decline to consider any halakhic source in isolation from those which preceded and followed it; they prefer to treat the entire history of the Halakhah as a continuous unfolding of the divine Word received by Moses at Sinai, as claimed in the Babylonian Talmud (B. Ber. 5a). This essentially theological approach, however, disserves the historical enterprise of trying to understand the Mishnah on its own terms, as a document produced during the late second century c.e. by a social group (the tannaitic sages) whose worldview and idealized way of life it presumably represents. For the purposes of this study I treat the Mishnah as a text standing alone, in isolation from subsequent exegesis and later modifications of the rules it sets out. My analysis is concerned with a document that came to substantial completion about 200 c.e. (ignoring the problem of several aggadic or midrashic sections, like tractate *Abot* or the last half of tractate *Soṭah*, believed by modern scholars to represent later interpolations into the mishnaic text). Where appropriate—for instance, where a later commentary sheds light on an unclear or incomprehensible passage, or where a mishnaic rule was subsequently modified in the Talmud, medieval codes, or *responsa*—I refer either in text or notes to such later development. But where the Mishnah makes sense standing alone, or as elucidated by reference to other contempary legal systems of the Greco-Roman world, I have assumed, for the theory of mishnaic jurisprudence, that the relevant rules are those stated in the mishnaic text and not the rules of Halakhah as they exist today following later modification.

1

CHATTEL OR PERSON?

The problem of women's status in the Mishnah is multifaceted, having legal, theological, anthropological, psychological, and sociological dimensions. Though I shall touch on all of these aspects, the present study emphasizes a jurisprudential approach, which focuses on the specific question of women's personal status in the law of the mishnaic system. Central to the analysis are the basic legal concepts *person* and *chattel*. We must consequently begin with some definitions.

Definition of Personhood

What distinguishes a legal *person* from a legal *chattel*? *Personhood* means the legal status defined by the complex of an individual's powers, rights, and duties in society. An entity possessing no powers, rights, or duties is no person at all but merely an object or *chattel*. For instance, some slaveholding societies prescribe neither rights nor duties for slaves. If the law mandates no food ration and sets no limit to the work load, owners may treat slaves as they wish, even starve them or work them to death. The slave is a mere beast of burden, an animate chattel. Other cultures may legislate rights and duties for slaves, *pro tanto* recognizing their personhood. All societies have rules, whether customary or written, that define the relative status of men, women, and children as well as various subgroups within society. The ratio of an individual's entitlements to his or her obligations defines the level of personhood. So in order to assess the level of an individual's personhood in the mishnaic system, we must know the extent of his or her

10

powers, rights, and duties—and above all how his or her personal status sets legal bounds to them.

A legal *power* is the capacity to act in a way that produces a legal effect. Thus, a property owner can generally transfer his or her property to another person, but some people (e.g., minors and imbeciles) may lack that power. Sometimes the power of alienation is limited by another's right to intervene. Thus, the law may permit a wife to hold property in her own right yet forbid her to dispose of it without her husband's approval. Conversely, if a husband holds his wife's property in trust, the wife may have power to prevent him from alienating it without her consent. But even if the law requires a third party's consent to a transaction, the *inherent* capacity to own, buy, and sell property remains a substantial entitlement. Another important power is the capacity to make binding agreements such as a contract of marriage, or to obligate oneself by a unilateral stipulation, such as a religious vow. Age, gender, or subordinate status may limit the scope of a power. Again, a person may be competent to testify in a court of law (in all cases or only in some) or may lack competency because of age, gender, mental incapacity, or relationship to some party involved in the case. The possession of legal powers is obviously an important gauge of legal personhood.

A legal *right* is the entitlement to a specified benefit that some other person (or perhaps the social polity) is bound by law to supply. A wife may possess specified matrimonial rights against her husband—usually a right to maintenance, sometimes a right to inheritance. A husband may enjoy a reciprocal right to the wife's obedience in all respects or only in some. In monogamous societies each spouse has the legal right to an exclusive sexual relationship with the other; in polygynous societies, by contrast, the husband alone enjoys this exclusive right. A husband in patriarchal culture may have an unconditional right to restrain his wife from leaving the house; or that right may be subject to modifications, such as her right to visit her family at reasonable times. As with legal powers, the nature and extent of an individual's rights constitutes an important index of personhood.

A legal *duty* is something that a person is bound by law to perform. As such, a duty is always the obverse of a legal right. Thus, a wife's right to maintenance implies her husband's legal duty to maintain her. Conversely, a wife's duty to serve her husband reflects his right to receive such services. If a husband has an absolute right to conjugal relations, it is the wife's duty to submit at all times. Some systems, by contrast, assign the spouses reciprocal conjugal rights and duties. The possession of legal duties as much as the enjoyment of legal rights is a mark of personhood, because the imposition of duties implies that the bearer possesses the intelligence and morality to carry out such duties without physical compulsion. Suppose a man's household includes wives, slaves, and cattle. If the system assigns duties to the wives but not to the slaves or the oxen, then even though all three are set to work, only the wives count as persons. Slaves, like oxen, are chattels in that system—not because they lack morality and intelligence, but because the system chooses to ignore their possession of those faculties.

In a given society all who qualify as persons do not necessarily enjoy equal status. Different individuals, classes, or castes may enjoy different levels of personhood in the social hierarchy. Adults may rank higher than children, men than women, freemen than slaves, Brahmans than Untouchables, lords spiritual than lords temporal, priests than lay Israelites. The level of an individual's personhood, as we saw, depends on the ratio of powers and rights, on the one hand, to duties on the other. Those who possess more claims on others than others have on them enjoy higher status than those who owe many duties to others and have few claims against them. In some systems a gender-based classification gives male slaves less personhood than freeborn women. Sometimes gender and caste invoke similar disabilities, for example, when the Mishnah disqualifies women along with slaves, minors, and other marginal groups from participation in communal religious enterprises of Israelite society.

The level of a woman's personhood is governed not only by her gender, it depends also on her legal relationships to specified men or on the lack of such relationships. Thus a minor daughter is subject to her father and a wife subservient to her husband. The degree of subordination may vary; a father may have more control over his daughter than a husband over his wife. Or the converse may apply: An emancipated daughter who remains unmarried may enjoy higher legal status (though not necessarily social status) than a wife, for she has neither father nor husband to control her. In some systems a widow or divorcée, free of a husband's authority, may revert to her father's control; in others she may gain her independence. Some systems keep women under perpetual tutelage no matter what their age or personal status.[16] The theoretical options are unlimited; but in practice the laws reflect particular societal norms.

The Legacy of Scripture

The Mishnah's framers did not function in a social vacuum but in a patriarchal system. However, they operated under one very special constraint: the authority of the Hebrew Scriptures, especially the first five books of the Old Testament, known as the Torah. The Torah, understood by the sages as God's revelation to Moses at Sinai, constituted the written law of the people Israel; and the Mishnah's framers, centuries after the Torah's redaction, still took for granted its continuing applicability to Israelites of their own day. Though mishnaic sages rarely claim explicit dependence on those laws, their rules concede by implication (and sometimes by direct citation) the authority of Scripture.

Because the Torah contains a number of laws that affect women, we cannot fully understand the mishnaic view of women's status without taking Scripture into account. The Torah's prescriptions provide the rudiments of a theory of women's place in Israelite society. They show the impact on women of certain status relationships to men, notably those of father/daughter and husband/wife, as well as the effect of the absence of any such relationship, as in the case of widows or divorcees.

Scripture's laws about women display two distinct tendencies. Some deal with "women's rights." One rule (Exod. 21:10) speaks by implication of a wife's right to maintenance. Another (Num. 27:1–11) establishes a daughter's right to inherit from her father in the absence of sons. A third (Num. 30:2–17) specifies the varying capacity of daughters, wives, and unattached women to make binding religious vows. All of these provisions assign women certain rights or powers, hence they treat women as persons.[17]

Other biblical laws, by contrast, treat women as property. Most familiar is the Tenth Commandment, which forbids an Israelite to covet his neighbor's possessions: wife, slaves, cattle, or anything else that belongs to his neighbor (Exod. 20:14). The prohibition of adultery (Deut. 22:22) defines a married woman as *be'ulat ba'al*, which, though usually translated as "married woman," literally means a woman laid by a husband and also (as the word for husband, *ba'al*, is identical with that for master, or owner, of a domestic animal or for the possessor of an object or quality) bears the inescapable connotation of the property of an owner. A daughter is likewise perceived as the property of her father; he collects bride-price from the man who marries her or from one who seduces or rapes her (Exod. 22:15–16; Deut. 22:28–29) whether or not the violator marries the girl. The bride-price compensates for loss of the daughter's virginity, treated as the father's economic asset. It is this view of the minor girl as the father's sexual property that most likely accounts for the glaring omission of the daughter from the list of women with whom a man may not cohabit (Lev. 18:6–20, 19:10–21). Only *some* of these women are actual blood relatives of the man himself; but virtually *all* those listed are the sexual property of *other men*. The incest taboos thus protect private property as much as sexual propriety. Likewise, the law of adultery (Exod. 20:13; Lev. 18:20; Deut. 22:22) prohibits intercourse between a man and *another man's wife* but not between a *married man* and an *unmarried woman*. Scripture perceives adultery primarily as a violation of property and for this reason alone an offense against morality.[18] Again, the Torah's sole reference to the formalities of divorce (Deut. 24:1) describes a unilateral procedure in which the husband releases the wife; the possibility of a wife's divorcing a husband is not discussed. The conclusion that no such option existed in biblical Israelite society is admittedly an argument from silence; but we can see the logic of a system that permits a man to discard his property (i.e., his exclusive right to the wife's sexual function) but finds no way for that property to discard its owner. The levirate law (Deut. 25:5–10), permitting certain men to inherit their brothers' widows, likewise reflects a view of women as the property of men. So, too, does the ordeal of the suspected adulteress (Num. 5:11–31).

Biblical laws that govern women suggest that conflicting perceptions of woman as person and as chattel existed already in biblical Israel, centuries before the time of the Mishnah. The present study will show that, just as Scripture's view of women varies with context, the same is true of mishnaic treatment of women, which in many cases draws heavily on scriptural law. We therefore begin with Scripture's taxonomy of women and shall later demonstrate Mishnah's dependence on it.

Scripture's Taxonomy of Women

Scripture knows six distinct statuses for free women.[19] These constitute two main categories, each comprising three subclasses. The first category includes three kinds of dependent women; the second, their three autonomous counterparts. The dependent women are (1) the minor daughter, controlled by her father; (2) the wife, under her husband's authority; and (3) the levirate widow, whose husband's death without male issue transfers the widow to her husband's brother. My analysis matches these three women with three subclasses of autonomous women, each forming the mirror image of one of the dependent classes: (1) the legally emancipated daughter who has outgrown her father's jurisdiction; (2) the divorcée, no longer subject to her husband's authority; and (3) the normal widow whose husband left an heir and, thus, saved her from the automatic levirate tie.

This taxonomy of women has more than theoretical significance. A woman's status affects her legal entitlements. For instance, in describing the effect of a woman's personal status on her capacity to make binding vows, Scripture (Num. 30:2–17) deals with five of the six women in our list. All vows of a minor daughter and some vows of a wife require acquiescence by father or husband, respectively; but no one can countermand the vow of a widow or divorcée. The restriction of the father's authority to the case of a *minor* daughter necessarily implies a fifth category, the *emancipated* daughter, who ranks with widows and divorcées as a person whose vows no one can revoke. Thus, of the six categories I have identified, only the levirate widow is missing. But Scripture indicates elsewhere (Deut. 25:5–10) that such a widow ranks virtually as the wife of her levir; and the Mishnah, in specifying the levir's control of the vows of his brother's widow, merely makes explicit what Scripture already implies.

Mishnah's Taxonomy of Women

An important feature of the mishnaic law of women is the extent of its dependence on biblical rules. Like Scripture, the Mishnah discusses all three classes of women in whom some man has a legitimate sexual interest: minor daughter, wife, and levirate widow. As in Scripture, their counterparts are the emancipated daughter, divorcée, and regular widow. Further, in certain contexts the sages treat dependent women not as persons at all but rather as chattels of the men who control them. By isolating the factors that underlie these laws, we can understand why different women enjoy different levels of personhood in similar circumstances and why the same woman's level of personhood varies in different contexts.

Take, for instance, the minor daughter. Her father wields total authority over her and can treat her virtually as he pleases; he can legally refuse to maintain her, and up to the age of twelve he may sell her as a slave.[20] Most important, he owns her sexuality; he can dispose of her in marriage to a man of his choosing even without her consent. Her virginity is a marketable asset. Thus, a man who rapes or seduces a girl must pay her father a penalty equivalent to bride-price, for he has diminished her value on the marriage market.[21]

The Mishnah explicitly contrasts the status of the minor daughter with that of her sister who has reached her majority (i.e., twelve and one-half years and one day).[22] The minor daugher is mere chattel, but the adult daughter becomes *sui juris*, a person in her own right, for the father loses dominion over her at puberty. He can no longer bestow her in marriage; she is free to choose her own husband. Unlike her younger sister, she can make a religious vow without fear of her father's revoking it. She can manage her own property. She may even testify in court on matters peculiarly within the knowledge of women. In a word, the emancipated daugher enjoys total personal autonomy (at least in legal theory). However, the legal status of emancipated daughter is largely hypothetical; she is an exception to the general rule. Girls normally are married off at puberty and never attain autonomy unless divorced or widowed in later life.

This brings us to the second matched pair: wife and divorcée. A wife continues under male authority, for her father has transferred his dominion over her to the husband. This includes, in particular, the exclusive right to benefit from the bride's sexuality. A bridegroom can sue the bride's father if her virginity is not intact; a husband can divorce, with forfeiture of her marriage portion, a wife who commits adultery. Here, mishnaic law expands on Scripture's ruling; even if he merely *suspects* his wife's infidelity, a husband who has warned her before witnesses can divorce her without paying off her settlement. In addition he can first subject the wife to trial by ordeal—the *only* case of trial by ordeal known to scriptural or mishnaic law. A husband who dies without heirs continues to control his wife's reproduction function from the grave: she automatically falls by inheritance to his brothers, one of whom must marry her in the attempt to produce a posthumous heir for the deceased.

From the standpoint of women's personhood, the most conspicuous feature of these rules is their onesidedness. The wife's lack of corresponding rights against the husband reflects a polygynous system in which the wife is the husband's exclusive sexual property, but the reverse is not the case. Even the ceremonial formalities of marriage and divorce, expressing the husband's acquisition or disposition of the wife, emphasize the biblical-mishnaic view of the wife's sexuality as the husband's property. This explains why mishnaic rules that govern the wife's sexual function treat her as chattel.

In nonsex-related contexts the Mishnah's framers treat the wife quite differently, assigning her specific rights and powers as well as legal duties. Her right to maintenance is made explicit as is her husband's duty to provide for her. Her reciprocal duties toward the husband include specified household tasks and the spinning or weaving of a prescribed quantity of woollen yarn or cloth. The husband's rights to the proceeds of his wife's labor and to usufruct of her property, which he holds in trust during the marriage, are balanced by the wife's right to retain legal ownership of her property and to receive her agreed marriage portion on widowhood or divorce. Although the wife cannot dispose of her property without the husband's approval, neither can he sell it without her consent. In contrast to the case of father and daughter, a husband cannot revoke his wife's religious vows indiscriminately, but only if they are likely to impair conjugal relations. The sages' assignment of legal entitlements and obligations to the wife demonstrates their view of a woman as something more than the sexual property of her husband; she is also a person in her own right. *Indeed, it is only in matters involving her biological function, and in no other context, that we find the Mishnah treating the wife as her husband's chattel.*

The contrast between the wife and her counterpart, the divorcée, further demonstrates the pivotal nature of the woman's biological function. When a husband divorces his wife, he releases her from his control; specifically, he relinquishes ownership of her sexuality. The Mishnah highlights this by insisting that the essence of the writ of divorce lies in the phrase "Thou art now permitted to any man" and rejecting the formula "Thou art now permitted to any man except Simeon b. Jacob." Because mishnaic divorce frees the wife from the husband's sexual claims he cannot legally prevent another man from marrying her. More important, the divorcée herself becomes emancipated. For when her husband releases her, she does not revert to her father's jurisdiction. She may return to her father's house with his permission—perhaps out of economic necessity—or she may decide to live alone. She may bestow herself on a suitor or choose to remain single. The vows of the divorcée possess the same legal force as those of a man, for no one has power to revoke them. In addition she gains complete control of her property. All in all her new found autonomy invests her with the legal power to control both the sexual and nonsexual aspects of her life. The Mishnah treats her as a person in all matters of private law.

We come now to the third and last matched pair: the normal widow and the levirate widow. The Mishnah's differential treatment of these two categories reflects a difference in the perception of their biological role. The normal widow's position approximates that of the divorcée; she is *sui juris*, that is, with all the rights just described for the divorcée—and more. Her legal autonomy stands in sharp contrast to the status of the levirate widow, to whom Mishnah, following Scripture, denies those freedoms. The levirate widow falls automatically to the husband's brother, who may choose to consummate the union, thus gaining control both of her property and her person. Only if the levir rejects her may she select another marriage partner; if the levir fails to release her, she is tied to him for life—a problem that continues to afflict Jewish women to this day.

What accounts for Scripture's and Mishnah's harsh treatment of levirate widows? The answer once more lies in the woman's sexuality. The main point of levirate marriage is to supply the dead husband with the heir he lacked. If the expedient works, the firstborn son will be reckoned as the dead man's heir and inherit his property. So the levirate widow's biological function holds great importance for her husband's family; to the Mishnah's framers it is her only significant feature, a fact which leads them to treat her like chattel. This explains the glaring discrepancy between her legal status and that of the normal widow. The latter's biological function no longer matters: No man has a claim in it, hence the system grants her autonomy.

Ambiguity of Status: Effect on Woman's Rights

Besides her sexual function and its practical effects on her legal entitlements, another, more formal matter affects the woman in mishnaic law. We noted earlier the sages' insistence on classification and their discomfort with people or things whose status becomes unclear. Unfortunately for an Israelite woman, a taxonomical problem may arise at two points in her life: first, on her transfer as a young girl from her father's authority to that of her husband; second, on her release as a wife in the process of divorce. The Mishnah's framers feared that some error would allow these women to slip through the cracks while passing from one status to another. Fear of interstitiality and liminality (a phenomenon well known to anthropologists)[23] plays an obvious part here. The sages' reaction to the problem of the woman in transition is quite simple: The moment ambiguity sets in, they cease to view her as a person. Instead, they treat transitional women—whether entering or leaving the married state—as objects to be dealt with in summary fashion in order to ensure that the transition is accomplished without a hitch. This attitude and the notion of the husband's acquiring or discarding sexual property combine to produce the unilateral ceremonies of marriage and divorce noted earlier.

The substantive matter of the woman's sexuality joins with the formal problem of taxonomy to produce rules that treat the woman as chattel rather than person. Thus, if some formal error or uncertainty casts doubt on her precise marital status, the sages resolve matters by applying arbitrary rules that ride roughshod over her human rights. The need to reclassify her unambiguously outweighs all other considerations. Examples abound throughout the Division of Women. A woman whose divorce is invalidated by some technical error in the writ or the manner of its delivery incurs grave financial and other penalties if she mistakenly remarries. By contrast, the man responsible for the error—husband or scribe who made a mistake in the writ—goes scot-free.) A levirate widow who mistakenly thinks herself released from the levirate tie and marries another man is likewise severely penalized. So, too, with the putative widow whose husband returns from the dead after she has remarried in reliance on witnesses testifying to his death. All three of these women lose their matrimonial rights in *both* marriages. These examples suggest that as soon as her marital status falls into doubt, the sages cease to perceive a woman as a human being.

This response is generated not by the ambiguity alone. The sages are equally bothered by the fact that a woman's illicit union with a man not the owner of her sexual function will infect that man with cultic pollution.

Such contamination will disqualify him from engaging in any cultic activity until he abandons the illicit union and undergoes ritual purification. The unfortunate woman, now viewed solely as a source of pollution, loses all her personal rights and becomes mere chattel.

All cases of women's doubtful status addressed in the Mishnah have a single common denominator: They always involve the question, Who owns the right to a woman's sexuality? This is the crux of the matter in the Mishnah's approach to women. In essence, it is the woman's sexuality rather than some other aspect of her being that most troubles the men who created the Mishnah.

Exclusion of Women from the Public Domain

The sages' preoccupation with female sexuality affects women not only in the private sphere of family relations, but also in the public domain. Sexuality accounts for the deliberate exclusion of women from participation in those aspects of Israelite culture that take place in public forums. The underlying logic is easily seen: If a woman's sexuality can be misdirected through accidental failure of male-controlled *private* transactions, how much more dangerous must it be to let her mingle freely with men in the *public* domain. Far better to exclude her from communal enterprises than to run such risks!

In the public domain, moreover, we find a further development. It is not only the *dependent* woman (i.e., as the sexual property of a specific man) who presents problems for men in the public domain. Even an *autonomous* woman poses a danger if admitted into public forums, especially places where communal religious exercises take place. A woman's propensity to destroy the sanctity of the male is not neutralized merely because she is no man's sexual property and hence theoretically accessible to men at large. A second kind of peril lurks in female sexuality, the danger of pollution by contact with a menstruant. Such contamination, no less than that generated by illicit unions, disqualifies men from cultic activity. The menstrual taboo, which appears in many cultures, is a phenomenon well documented by anthropologists.[24] This makes it desirable to discourage the presence of women at public worship or communal study of sacred texts. The sages eliminate the potential hazard by the simple expedient of exempting—and ultimately barring—women from participating in such communal pursuits.

Two additional motives come into play. First, the sages' attempt to confine women to the domestic scene affirms Scripture's view of woman's essential function as man's enabler. For the Mishnah's framers (as in all patriarchal societies), a woman's domestic role is her principal *raison d'être*, hence her sphere of activity is appropriately limited to the private domain. Second, as proposed by recent feminist scholarship, we cannot discount the (probably subconscious) men's-club syndrome: Men create exclusive forums for male cultural activity in order to supply their psychological need for creativity, a need women largely satisfy through the natural mechanism of procreation.[25]

Chattel or Person? Sexuality as the Key

Early in my exploration of the mishnaic law of women, I began to discern a pattern that seemed to make sense of the data and allowed me to formulate a hypothesis about the significance of female sexuality. Because closer scrutiny has validated the hypothesis, let me state formally the two principal results of this investigation.

First, the key to differential treatment of women in Mishnah lies specifically in the sexuality factor. This works as follows: Whenever some man has a proprietary interest in the sexual and reproductive function of a specified girl or woman, the Mishnah's framers treat the woman as that man's chattel in all matters that affect his ownership of her sexuality; in all other contexts, the dependent woman is treated as a person. When, by contrast, no man has a legal claim on a woman's sexuality, the system always treats her as a person, both in sex-related and other matters. So when we seek the rationale of any rule about women, all boils down to *"Cherchez l'homme!"*: Which man owns the biological function of the woman at hand? For it is he who ultimately controls her life to a greater or lesser degree. Only when no such man exists does the woman control her own personal life.

Second, the differential treatment of women just cited refers only to transactions in the domain of private law, which defines the limits of women's participation in mishnaic society. Even for the autonomous woman, participation in society is heavily circumscribed. She has no more right than her dependent sister to function in the public cultural domain. Though her sexuality never gives grounds for treating her as chattel or for restricting her private activities so long as she retains her autonomy, it still justifies excluding her from the intellectual and spiritual pursuits of the androcentric Israelite community. These restrictions substantially diminish the quality of life and level of personhood of the Israelite female as compared with the Israelite male. Thus, in the last analysis, a woman's sexuality lies at the root of limitations on her personhood in both the private and public spheres of mishnaic culture.

2

THE MINOR DAUGHTER

The sexuality factor exerts a profound influence on the personhood of women in mishnaic law. By sexuality factor I mean the presence or absence of a relationship in which some man owns the exclusive right to the woman's biological function (using this term to include both the man's right to intercourse with her and his ownership of her reproductive capability).[26] If such a relationship exists, the woman is legally dependent on the man in question; if no such relationship exists, the system grants her autonomy. A woman's status of dependency or autonomy makes a considerable difference to the level of her personhood because it affects the scope of her legal rights and powers and hence the degree to which she controls her own life. We shall explore here (and in chaps. 3 through 5) the relationship between a woman's sexuality and her legal status of dependency or autonomy.

The Minor Daughter as Chattel

The dependent female with the lowest status in the mishnaic system is the minor daughter. Rules concerning her pay scant attention to her personhood, the sages viewing her first and last as a sexual chattel. They focus on such matters as the impact of virginity on bride-price, circumstances when a man can or cannot expect his bride to be a virgin, the bridegroom's right to redress if his bride is not intact, and the father's right to financial compensation from a man who violates his minor daughter. The young girl is little more than her father's marketable asset. The Mishnah's framers capture their perception of her in a graphic metaphor:

A. [27] The sages spoke [in] a parable concerning woman: [She is like] an unripe fig, a ripening fig, and a fully ripe fig.

B. "An unripe fig"—while she is yet a child [under twelve years and one day].[28]

C. "A ripening fig"—this refers to the days of her pubescence [twelve to twelve and one-half years and one day].[29]

D. In [the case of] both these girls [B and C], her father has the right to anything she finds, and to [the proceeds of] her labor [lit. the work of her hands], and [the power] to annul her vows.

E. "A fully ripe fig"—after she has become mature [at twelve and one-half], her father no longer has dominion over her. [*At this age the minor daughter still unmarried becomes legally emancipated.*]

M. Nid. 5:7

This parable states in microcosm just about everything the Mishnah has to say about the minor daughter.[30] The metaphor of a gradually ripening fruit (the analogy between food and sex seems to be a cultural universal) alerts us to the relationship between the daughter's developing sexuality and the scope and extent of the father's authority.[31] These two themes surface time and again in the sages' discussion. For them, the young girl possesses one salient characteristic: She is a sexual chattel. Nearly all references to the girlchild under twelve (*qeṭannah*) or the pubescent girl between twelve and twelve and one-half years (*naʿarah*)—unlike references to minor sons[32]—speak directly or indirectly of her sexuality, with particular emphasis on her virginity.

Virginity and Bride-Price

The Mishnah's framers, placing a premium on virginity, set the customary bride-price twice as high for virgins as for nonvirgins (M. Ket. 1:2). The bridegroom gives the bride a document, the *keṭubbah*,[33] that specifies he is paying her the "bride-price of virgins."[34] The commercial aspect of the transaction is underscored by the fact that the sages open their discussion of marriage contracts (tractate *Keṭubbot*) with a rule providing prompt legal redress for a bridegroom who claims the bride's father has deceived him. This lawsuit vindicates a man's scriptural right to receive a virgin in return for the bride-price (Deut. 22:13–21).[35]

A. A virgin is to be married by the fourth day of the week [*i.e., Wednesday*] and a widow by the fifth day [*i.e., Thursday*]

B. because courts of law sit twice a week in the towns, on Monday and Thursday,

C. so that if a husband has a complaint about [her] virginity, he can go at once [on Thursday] to court.[36] [*A widow, by contrast, need not be married before Thursday because, obviously, no virginity suit can be lodged against her.*]

M. Ket. 1:1

Having paid for his bride's virginity, an aggrieved bridegroom, just as any buyer of goods that fail to meet specifications, can bring suit. But he should not have paid bride-price unless he could reasonably expect the girl to be a virgin; so the sages make a point of telling him when this assumption is reasonable and when it is not:

A.   A virgin's $k^e tubbah$-money is two hundred [zuz][37]; a widow's, one *maneh* [one hundred zuz].

B.   [As for] a virgin who was widowed [*i.e., a betrothed girl whose fiancé died before espousal and consummation*], or divorced [after betrothal but before espousal], or released from the levirate tie [by the brother of a betrothed man who died before consummating the marriage in question], their $k^e tubbah$-money is two hundred [zuz]. [*Though technically married, such girls remain physical virgins. Hence, if they remarry, they qualify for the bride-price of virgins.*]

C.   And they are subject to virginity suits [if found on consummation to be nonvirgins.]

D.   [As for] female proselytes, captives, or slave girls who were ransomed, converted, or manumitted [as the case may be] at [the age of] less than three years and one day, their $k^e tubbah$-money is two hundred [zuz]. [*Even though these are presumed to have been violated, the sages believe the hymen of a girl under three will grow back (M. Nid. 5:4). Such girls count as virgins when they become brides and, like the girls at B, are entitled to receive the bride-price of virgins.*]

E.   *And they are subject to virginity suits* [*like the girls at B and C*].

M. Ket. 1:2

A.   [As for] virgin[s] [who married and later became] widowed, divorced, or released from the levirate tie after [presumed] consummation of marriage [though they retained their physical virginity, perhaps through the husband's impotence], their $k^e tubbah$-money is one *maneh*. [*Even though these women may through happenstance have retained their physical virginity, the fact that they were married and presumably consummated the marriage classifies them as nonvirgins.*]

B.   And they are not subject to virginity suits [*for the same reason as at A*].

C.   [As for] female proselytes, captives, or slave girls who were ransomed, or converted, or manumitted beyond [the age of] three years and a day, their $k^e tubbah$ is one *maneh*. [*Like the girls at M. Ket. 1:2D, these girls are assumed to have been violated; but as they were not rescued early, their hymens cannot have grown back. Hence they are classified as nonvirgins.*]

D.   And they are not subject to virginity suits [*because no one expects them to be virgins*].

M. Ket. 1:4

Curiously, the sages judge virginity not by direct examination of the girl herself, but by external cultural criteria. "Virgin" means any girl or woman *conventionally* presumed innocent of sexual activity. These fall into two groups: first, girls who have never been married, including those once betrothed but divorced by their fiancés before consummation of the marriage (M. Ket. 1:2B);[38] second, girls rescued before the age of three from an environment that had exposed them to sexual abuse (M. Ket. 1:2D). The latter qualify as virgins because the sages believe a hymen ruptured before the age of three will spontaneously regenerate if the girl is removed from the abusive environment.[39] Nonvirgins form the mirror image of these groups of virgins. Thus girls divorced after presumed consummation count as nonvirgins even if they somehow remain intact (M. Ket. 1:4A), whereas an irrebuttable presumption of nonvirginity applies to girls exposed beyond the age of three to a sexually vulnerable environment (M. Ket. 1:4C)—again without regard to their actual physical state at the time of betrothal.

In the mishnaic system, then, the legal definition of virginity rests solely on the sages' cultural assumptions about what has happened to the girls in question. Everyone "knows" that female slaves, female captives, and girls raised by gentiles have been subjected to sexual abuse—even those under the age of three; but everyone also "knows" that if ruptured before three years of age, the hymen will regenerate. Because cultural conventions about the condition of these girls leave no room for doubt, no one need examine the girls themselves. This approach places the girls in undifferentiated groups.[40] In other words, the sages refuse to consider them as individuals whose virginity could be determined by examination on a case-by-case basis.

Oddly, a girl's prior sexual activity seems to be irrelevant so long as she has (or can be presumed to have) retained her physical virginity. This emphasis on the *virgo intacta* shows that the sages regard virginity as a clinical phenomenon. They perceive the girl not as a human being possessing or lacking sexual experience, but as a chattel whose owner pays brideprice for an intact hymen—an attitude borne out by the casual assumption that men will routinely violate girls in their power, even those of tender years. As shocking as this seems,[41] its chief significance is the perception of the female as mere sex object.

Seduction and Rape: Criminal Penalties

The man who deflowers a virgin ruins a valuable asset and must compensate its owner (in this case, the father) for the damage. Just as a husband pays bride-price, so a rapist or seducer pays an equivalent penalty prescribed by Scripture.[42] This rule applies to a minor girl still living in her father's house and not yet betrothed. Normally, she would marry some man of her father's choice; but whoever destroys her virginity, whether by marriage, rape, or seduction, must pay bride-price or an equivalent fine to her father (Exod. 22:15–16; Deut. 22:28–29). The fine, however, applies only to girls conventionally presumed virgins; one who deflowers a presumed nonvirgin is exempt because she has already lost her market value.

A.   For which girls is there a fine ($q^e nas$) [*i.e., payable by the rapist or seducer even though these girls (listed at B) are ineligible to marry Israelites, to whom, therefore, their virginity does not matter*]?

B.   [A fine must be paid by an Israelite] who has intercourse with a *mamzeret*, or a *n^etinah*, or a Samaritan girl. [***These are lower castes who are ineligible to marry Israelites. Israelite girls are omitted from this list because the sages take for granted that everyone knows a fine is payable for their violation.***][43]

C.   [Also by] one who has intercourse with a female proselyte, or [former] captive, or [former] slave girl who were ransomed, or converted, or manumitted under [the age of] three years and a day. [***Though such girls are presumed to have suffered sexual intrusion, sages believe that their ruptured hymens will have subsequently regenerated, as explained at M. Ket. 1:2D, so that they once more qualify as virgins.***][44]

M. Ket. 3:1

A.   And for which [girls] is there no fine [whether they are Israelite or lower-caste girls]?

B.   [No fine need be paid by] one who has intercourse with a female proselyte, or [former] captive, or [former] slave girl who were ransomed, or converted, or manumitted beyond [the age of] three years and a day. [***Sages assume that such girls will have suffered sexual intrusion beyond the age at which their hymens can regenerate, hence they are not virgins.***]

C.   [But] R. Judah holds that a ransomed captive [remains] in her state of fitness [lit. sanctity] even though she is a grown girl. [***He deems such a girl to have retained her virginity despite the facts at B.***][45]

M. Ket. 3:2

The sages view the victim of rape or seduction from the father's economic standpoint. Defloration reduces her value by the same amount no matter how it happened; to compensate the father the Mishnah imposes exactly the same criminal penalty for rape as for seduction. This perception of the violated girl as damaged goods takes no account of her as person. Above all it ignores the greater heinousness of rape as compared with seduction; the suffering of the victim does not affect the criminal penalty.[46] Because the girl's virginity is an economic asset, the sages emphasize the damaged chattel rather than the human being who may have suffered a devastating trauma. An identical fine is incurred (M. Ket. 3:1B) regardless of the girl's caste (M. Ket 3:7; M. ʿArak. 3:4), reflecting the view that as sexual chattels all virgins look alike.[47]

The minor daughter's chattel status emerges even from exceptions to the rule that her violator must compensate her father. In the most important exception, the sages, endorsing Scripture's rule that lets a father sell his girlchild under twelve into slavery (Exod. 21:7), virtually force him to do so in order to recover his loss for her rape or seduction.

A.   In every case where there is a right of sale [of a girl by her father], there is no fine [for rape or seduction of such a girl]; and in every case where there is a fine, there is no right of sale.

B.   [Thus, as for] a girlchild [under twelve] (*q^eṭannah*), there is a right of sale with respect to her, and so there is no fine [for raping or seducing her]. [***Exod. 21:7 permits a father to sell his daughter under twelve as a slave. Because the father can recoup himself for her lost virginity by selling her, the sages inflict no fine on the violator.***]

C.   [And as for] a pubescent girl [aged between twelve and twelve and one-half years] (*na'arah*), with respect to her there is a fine but no right of sale. [*As the law does not permit the sale of a girl over twelve, the penalty for her violation remains in force.*]

D.   [However, as to] a mature girl [over twelve and one-half] (*bogeret*), with respect to her there is neither fine [levied against the violator] nor right of sale [on the father's part.][48]

M. Ket. 3:8

The sages interpret Scripture (Exod. 21:7) to permit a father to sell his girlchild into slavery.[49] Because he can choose to recoup himself in this way for his daughter's lost virginity, her rapist or seducer (at M. Ket. 3:8B) escapes the usual penalty. Deprived of the fine, the father must either sell her or absorb the loss himself.[50]

This equation of the girlchild with a slave is confirmed by its gratuitous appearance in a totally different context (M. Qid. 2:3, discussed later). There, the sages speak of a man who falsely claims to have "a *daughter* or *slave woman* who is a hairdresser." The casual choice of this illustration (in a context unrelated to M. Ket 3:8) offers psychological insight into their attitude toward the minor girl. Perhaps they equate her with the slave woman because her father could, in fact, sell her as a slave, if he chose. Scripture's lack of any law permitting a man to sell his minor *son* reinforces Mishnah's view of the lesser personhood of the female.

Seduction and Rape: Civil Damages

Besides the biblical fine (a quasi-criminal penalty), the violation of a virgin incurs civil damages in tort. But these damages, too, go to the father, not to the girl. Plaintiffs generally receive compensation for physical disfigurement, pain and suffering, medical expenses, time lost from work, and insult or disgrace (M. B.Q. 8:11). The Mishnah's framers apply some of these categories of damage to seduction and rape. But the rapist incurs two further penalties decreed by Scripture (Deut. 22:29); he must marry the girl and forfeit the normal right of an Israelite husband to divorce his wife at will.

A.   The seducer pays [compensation under] three heads, and the rapist [under] four.

B.   The seducer pays [damages for] disgrace, and disfigurement, and the fixed penalty; the rapist pays more than [the seducer], for he pays [also] for [the victim's] pain and suffering.

C.   What is [the difference] between the rapist and the seducer?

D.   (1) The rapist pays for pain and suffering, whereas the seducer does not pay for pain and suffering;

E.   (2) The rapist pays at once [*i.e., even though he must marry the girl, he must pay the penalty, equivalent to bride-price, beforehand (Deut. 22:29)*], whereas the seducer pays when he lets her go [*i.e., if he marries her, he pays the bride-price only when he dies or divorces her in the normal way; and if the father decides not to give her to him, he pays the bride-price to her father only when the latter makes that decision].*

F.   (3) The rapist must drink from his earthen pot [*see M. Ket. 3:5*], whereas the seducer [should he in fact marry her], if he [later] wishes to divorce her, he may divorce her.

M. Ket. 3:4

A.   What is the meaning of "He must drink from his earthen pot"? [He can be forced to marry her, and may never divorce her] even if she is lame, even if she is blind, and even if she is plagued with skin disease.[51]

M. Ket.3:5

Besides the fixed criminal penalty, rapists and seducers must pay for the blemish (lost hymen) and the disgrace; but they incur no liability for cost of healing or time lost from work. The sages assume that the wound will heal naturally while the girl continues with her normal household chores. That assumption is not unreasonable; but it takes no account of the psychological trauma of the rape victim.[52] True, the sages distinguish between a seduced girl and a rape victim by awarding pain and suffering to the latter; and they force the rapist to marry his victim (Deut. 22:29)—unlike a seducer, who may do so only at the father's option (Exod. 22:16). (Although this solution may seem repugnant to us, it at least ensures the girl a husband despite her misfortune.) But these measures do not necessarily reflect a concern with the victim's *personal* rights. All scheduled payments, including pain and suffering for rape, go to the victim's father (M. Ket. 4:1), thus identifying *the father* (not the girl) as the injured party; the requirement that the rapist marry the victim probably stems more from a wish to spare the father the trouble of finding her another husband than from any concern with the girl herself.

In assessing damages the sages evaluate the blemish by comparing the girl with a slave woman put up for sale before and after the injury; more significantly, they calculate the disgrace according to the father's station in life, explicitly treating the humiliation as *his* rather than *hers*.

A.   What is [the compensation for] disgrace? Everything follows [the social standing of] the man who inflicts the disgrace and the man [*i.e., the girl's father*] who suffers it. [*The term* mitbayyesh *appears in the masculine form, and hence must refer to the father rather than the girl.*][53]

B.   [And what is the compensation for] blemish? We view her as though she were a female slave about to be sold. How much was she worth [before] and how much is she worth [now]?

C.   [But] the penalty [prescribed by Scripture (Exod. 22:16) for seduction and (Deut. 22:29) for rape] is the same for everyone. [*It does not vary with social standing because it represents the bride-price of virginity, which is the same for all girls, regardless of class or caste (M. ʿArak. 3:4)*].

D.   And whatever incurs a fixed penalty [prescribed] in the Torah is the same for everyone.

M. Ket. 3:7

A.   [As for] a girl who was seduced, [the damages for] her disgrace, her disfig-
     urement and her fine go to her father.
B.   And likewise the [damages for] pain and suffering of a rape victim [go to her
     father].

M. Ket. 4:1

The father collects damages for the daughter's reduced value as though
she were his slave injured through someone's negligence (M. Ket. 3:7B).[54]
Even in a rape case, the compensation for pain and suffering goes to the
father, not the girl. Furthermore, it is not the *girl's* embarrassment or
humiliation that counts, but that of her father (M. Ket. 3:7A). The same
point is made in another ruling.

A.   It is all one whether [a man] has raped or seduced a girl of the highest
     priestly stock or of the lowest stock in Israel—
B.   he pays [a flat rate of] fifty *sela*ᶜ—
C.   but as for the disgrace and the blemish, all depends on [the relative social
     standing of] the man who inflicts the disgrace and the man who is dis-
     graced.

M. ᶜArak. 3:4

Here we find a curious discrepancy between Scripture's rules about
bride-price and compensation for rape and the Mishnah's rules on these
same points. The sages endorse Scripture's view that the penalty for destroy-
ing a girl's virginity goes to the father. But this rule conflicts with their own
ruling about bride-price on marriage, which, by mishnaic times, no longer
went to the father but to the bride herself as part of her marriage portion
payable on divorce or widowhood (M. Ket. 4:2). Why do the sages not assign
the penalty for violation to the girl in the same way? I suggest the following
answer. Scripture nowhere states explicitly that bride-price in the normal
case *must* go to the father rather than the bride; the text merely implies
this.[55] But in violation cases, Scripture explicitly requires payment to the
father (Deut. 22:29 read together with Exod. 22:16). Though willing to
disregard Scripture's *implied* intention and assign bride-price to the bride
herself, the sages refuse to ignore an *explicit* scriptural directive on who
receives the fine-money for rape or seduction. This nicely illustrates the
constraints placed on Mishnah by Scripture. Sages may occasionally circumvent Scripture when the text leaves room for maneuver; but they will
not defy a clear directive, even when this produces an anomalous result.
Scriptural constraints sometimes force the sages to make rulings that conflict with the viewpoint underlying their own directives made elsewhere.[56]
The sages' perception of the young girl as sexual chattel and her virginity as her father's property probably has ancient, prehistoric roots. A clue to
the antiquity of this notion lies hidden in Scripture's glaring omission of
the daughter from the long and detailed list of females with whom a man is
forbidden to cohabit (Lev. 18:6–20, 20:10–21)—a lacuna faithfully reflected
by the Mishnah's omission of the daughter from the list of incestuous
relationships that incur the penalties of extirpation (M. Ker. 1:1), stoning

(M. San. 7:4) or scourging (M. Mak. 3:1). This list, generally perceived as a list of incest taboos, includes mainly women who are not actually consanguineous with the man forbidden to touch them *but who are, more significantly, the sexual property of other men*. The daughter's absence from the list reflects the fact that her sexuality belongs to her father in the most literal sense.[57] Theoretically he could choose whether to make use of it himself, sell it to another man, or even give it away, as with Lot's daughters and the Sodomite mob (Gen. 19:8). Granted, by mishnaic times, relations with one's daughter were explicitly forbidden on pain of death by burning (M. San. 9:1); though it is noteworthy that the sages, finding no direct scriptural support for their ruling, had to base it on a forced construction of Lev. 18:17.[58] But the rulings just discussed make it clear enough that the sages continue to view the daughter's sexuality as the father's valuable asset. Indeed, they scarcely notice her in any other context.

Ambiguity of Status: Effect on the Minor Daughter

What happens to the minor daughter if doubt arises concerning her precise marital status? Such doubt can occur when a father who betrothed his daughter in infancy later forgets to whom he has promised her or when a man with many daughters fails to recall which one he has promised to the man who claims her at puberty. Or some other circumstance may create ambiguity.

A.   [If a father said,] "I gave my daughter in marriage, but I know not to whom I gave her," and a man came and said, "It was I who espoused her," he may be believed.

B.   If one man said, "It was I who espoused her," and another said, "It was I who espoused her," both of them must give [her] a writ of divorce.

C.   Or, if [the two men] so desire, one may give [her] a writ and the other may consummate [with her].

M. Qid. 3:7

A.   If a man gave authority to his agent to give his daughter in marriage, and [meanwhile] went himself and espoused her [to a different man],

B.   If his own [disposition] came first, his disposition creates a [valid] espousal;

C.   but if [the disposition of] his agent came first, [the agent's] disposition creates a [valid] espousal.

D.   But if it is not known [which came first], both [of the putative husbands] must give [her] a writ of divorce;

E.   or, if [the two men] so desire, one may give [her] a writ and the other may consummate [with her].[59]

M. Qid. 4:9

These rules solve the problem of ambiguity—but at the girl's expense. In the first case (M. Qid. 3:7), she was espoused in infancy, which may account for the father's later uncertainty about the matter. Here, the proposed solutions completely ignore the girl's desires. Either both men must divorce her—leaving her without a husband—or they may settle by a gentlemen's agreement which one shall have her. The girl herself is treated like a piece of livestock that men haggle over.

Why does the Mishnah pose such strange hypothetical cases? The answer lies in the sages' abhorrence of uncertainty, above all when it comes to the ownership of a woman's sexuality. A woman's marital status must always remain crystal clear for two reasons. First, a girl or woman who mistakenly consummates marriage with one man when she is promised to another counts as an adulteress, and her children will be illegitimate.[60] Second, and worse still, she cultically pollutes the man who has intercourse with her, however innocently, thus disqualifying him from performing any act of religious worship that demands a state of cultic purity.[61] Therefore, a girl or woman who may have become espoused to a given man cannot marry another until the first man divorces her. Even though the marriage was not consummated, she still needs a writ of divorce from the putative husband, who only thus yields his (possible) claim on her.[62]

The ultimate absurdity is the man who cannot remember which of his many daughters he has given in marriage.

A. If a man has two sets of daughters from two wives, and he said: "I gave my eldest daughter in marriage [to a specified man], but I do not know whether [it was] the eldest of the older set, or the eldest of the younger set, or the youngest of the older set, she being older than the eldest of the younger set,"
B. all these [girls] are forbidden [to marry any other man without a writ of divorce from the putative husband, or to marry a *kohen* even if they receive such a writ], except the youngest of the younger set [*who clearly cannot qualify as any kind of "eldest daughter"*]. So rules R. Meir.
C. But R. Yose rules that they are all permitted [to marry someone else], except the eldest of the older set.
D. [If a father said,] "I gave my youngest daughter in marriage, but I do not know whether [it was] the youngest of the younger set, or the youngest of the older set, or the eldest of the younger set, she being younger than the youngest of the older set,"
E. all these [girls] are forbidden [as aforesaid], except the eldest of the older set [*who clearly cannot qualify as any kind of "youngest daughter"*]. So rules R. Meir.
F. But R. Yose rules that they are permitted [as aforesaid], except the youngest of the younger set.

M. Qid. 3:9

It is difficult to decide which amazes us more: the mental gymnastics required to set up this problem or the mind-set that can conceive of a father who forgets which daughter he has promised in marriage.[63] But here, as before, the underlying motive is clear enough. The Mishnah's framers wish to prevent the girl from contaminating an Israelite man by marrying him without obtaining a divorce from the man who may be her legal spouse (though no one knows for sure). In this ambiguous situation, Meir would play it safe by maximizing the class of ineligible brides. In so doing he places all but one daughter under a cruel disability. Except for the girl whose status is not in doubt (M. Qid. 3:9B and E), none of them can marry until the putative husband takes the trouble to give her a precautionary divorce in case she is the one earlier espoused to him. (Yose's solution, less drastic, disqualifies only one girl in each case—but still with no assurance that she is the girl who was actually pledged.)

The sages do not seem to care that their solution renders innocent girls unmarriageable for lack of a writ of divorce. The girls' basic human rights fall victim to the more important goal of ensuring that no Israelite man mistakenly marries a woman who is pledged to another; the preservation of male sanctity and cultic purity takes precedence over all else. Furthermore, the very contemplation—even as a hypothetical question—of a father who cannot recall which daughter he has given away typecasts minor daughters as nonpersons. Like the virgins and nonvirgins discussed earlier (M. Ket. 1:2, 1:4) they are an undifferentiated group, all looking exactly alike.[64]

Another type of ambiguity involves the vows of a betrothed maiden. This girl, aged between twelve and twelve and one-half, is old enough to make valid religious vows but still young enough to fall under her father's jurisdiction. But because she is betrothed, her husband-to-be also has a legitimate interest in her vows. Yet, until she enters his domain to consummate the marriage, he does not gain sole control of her. The interstitial status of the girl could cause serious problems. Suppose, for instance, a girl on the point of marriage abjures sexual intercourse, and her father unaware of her vow fails to revoke it before transferring her. The new husband cannot revoke a vow made by his wife while still in her father's house, and thus the purpose of marriage would be defeated. But the Mishnah finds a way.

A. [As for] a betrothed maiden, her father and her [prospective] husband may annul her vows [together].
B. [If] the father annulled [a vow] but the [prospective] husband has not annulled [it] [or if] the [prospective] husband annulled [it] but the father has not annulled [it], [the vow] is not annulled.
C. And it goes without saying that [if] one of them has confirmed [it], [the vow cannot be annulled].[65]

M. Ned. 10:1

A. [If] the father dies, the [sole] right [of annulment] does not [thereby] pass to the husband; [but if] the husband dies, the [sole] right reverts to the father. In this respect, the father's power surpasses the power of the husband.
B. In another matter, the husband's power surpasses that of the father; for the husband can annul [the vows] of an adult [wife], whereas the father cannot annul [the vows] of an adult [daughter].

M. Ned. 10:2

A. [If a maiden] vowed while betrothed, was divorced on the same day, was betrothed [again] that same day, even a hundred [times], her father and her latest husband can annul her vows [together].

B. This is the general principle: [Concerning] any woman who has not attained autonomy for a single day [lit. hour], her father and her latest husband can annul her vows [together].

M. Ned. 10:3

A. [This was] the practice of disciples of sages:

B. Before his daughter went out from his house [to consummate marriage with the chosen husband], [the father] would say to her, "All vows that thou has vowed in my house, lo, they are annulled."

C. And likewise, the husband, before she entered his domain, would say to her, "All vows that thou hast vowed before entering my domain, lo, they are annulled" [endorsing the father's declaration at B].

D. For after she has entered his domain, he can no longer annul [vows she made before she entered his domain].

M. Ned. 10:4

To revoke the vows of a betrothed girl, father and husband must act in concert (M. Ned. 10:1); but what happens if one of them dies during the betrothal period (M. Ned. 10:2)? It is vital that the locus of authority always remain clear. If the prospective husband dies, full authority reverts to the father because the girl remains in his house. But if the father dies, control cannot pass to the prospective husband, for the girl has not yet entered his domain. M. Ned 10:3 presents the exceptional case of the youthful divorcée who, though still under age, becomes legally *sui juris* (M. Qid. 1:1; see p. 42). She is called "an orphan in the father's lifetime" (M. Yeb. 13:6) because even though he still lives, she does not revert to his jurisdiction. But the father can keep control of her by summary betrothal to another man on the very day of her divorce. If the period of autonomy lasts less than a day, it does not vest, and she remains under the jurisdiction of her father and her new husband-to-be. Finally (M. Ned 10:4), a father and husband well versed in the law can ensure that the girl enters her new husband's home free of any vows not previously annulled.

These rules tell us something else: The Mishnah's framers dislike interstitiality as much as they abhor ambiguity. They worry not only about *who* controls the girl, but also about ensuring that *someone* controls her at all times, so as to avoid any gap in authority and responsibility. When a girl is transferred from her father's domain to that of her new husband, the sages specify the precise moment at which the father's control ceases and the husband's takes effect.

A. [A minor girl] is always in the domain of her father until she enters the domain of her husband for consummation of marriage.

B. [If] the father has handed [her] over to the husband's agents, she is in the husband's domain.

C. [If] the father went with the husband's agents or the father's agents went with the husband's agents [to escort her to the husband's house], she [remains] within the father's domain [until she enters the husband's house].

D.   [If] the father's agents have handed [her] over to the husband's agents, she is in the husband's domain.

M. Ket. 4:5

Normally, an Israelite female remains under continuous male control for most of her life. In the ideal situation at M. Ket. 4:5A, the pubescent girl passes directly from the status of daughter to that of wife. One of the most interesting aspects of this situation lies in a phenomenon we noted earlier. The sages' Hellenistic logic cannot tolerate hybrid categories that accommodate the excluded middle. So their only way to discuss the vows of the "daughter-wife" (the espoused girl not yet transferred for consummation), is to claim that for the purpose at hand she is both wife and daughter at once. In so doing they treat her much like the *koy* ("goat-stag"), which for certain purposes "resembles both a wild beast and a domestic animal" (M. Bik. 2:8).

From the standpoint of women's personhood, the rules just discussed illustrate a fundamental difference between Israelite sons and daughters. The girl, normally betrothed in childhood and transferred for consummation at puberty before she can escape her father's control by reaching twelve and one-half years (M. Nid. 5:7), rarely attains the autonomy that routinely accrues to her brother on reaching the age of thirteen (M. Nid. 5:6). Only if her father fails to marry her off beforehand, does the Israelite daughter become *sui juris* at puberty.[66] Generally, an Israelite woman never gains autonomy unless her husband either divorces or predeceases her (M. Qid. 1:1). But those eventualities are beyond the woman's control. She may not gain her freedom until she grows old. Indeed, she may never gain it at all.

Minor Daughter's Lack of Basic Rights

The sages' intense preoccupation with the girlchild's sexuality is matched only by their profound lack of interest in anything else about her.[67] Not only do they treat her as a nonperson, they actually make a special point of the fact that the minor daughter lacks even the basic rights of personhood. Her chattel status is reflected both in the absoluteness of her father's authority and in her lack of entitlement to maintenance.

A.   The father has legal power over his [minor] daughter to give her in marriage [whether] by money, by writ, or by intercourse [*the three modes of espousal prescribed in M. Qid. 1:1. The father may marry her off with or without her consent, in contrast to a minor daughter married off by her mother or brothers after her father's death (M. Yeb. 13:2).*]

B.   And he has the right to anything she finds, and to [the proceeds of] her labor [lit. the work of her hands], and [the power] to annul her vows [M. Ned. chap. 11].

C.   And he receives her writ of divorce [if her betrothed husband divorces her before actual consummation of marriage]. [*After consummation, the daughter even if under age would keep her own writ of divorce as she then becomes* sui juris (*M. Qid. 1:1*); cf. *M. Ket. 4:2 with respect to the k^etubbah of a minor girl divorced after betrothal and one divorced after consummation.*]

D. But he does not have usufruct [of her property inherited from her mother while she was still a minor] during her lifetime [though he does inherit if she dies while still a minor.] [*The reason is that the minor girl herself does not actually acquire her inheritance until she comes of age, so the father cannot benefit from something she herself does not yet fully own.*]

E. [When] she marries, her husband has one advantage [over her father] in that he does have usufruct [of her property during her lifetime].

F. But [in contrast to the father], [the husband] is liable for her maintenance and for her ransom [if she is kidnapped] and for [the costs of] her burial.

G. R. Judah holds [with respect to a wife's burial] that even the poorest man in Israel must [hire] no fewer than two flutes and one keening woman [for the wife's funeral].

M. Ket. 4:4

The father's most important power over his daughter is his control of her marriage (M. Ket. 4:4A). That her consent is not required may be deduced from the Mishnah's explicit statement that the right of refusal belongs only to a girl whose mother or brothers arrange her marriage after her father's death.

A. Which is the girlchild who can [lit. must] exercise [the right of] refusal [*in order to avoid marrying a husband selected for her during her childhood*]?

B. Any [girlchild] who was married off by her mother or her brothers with her consent [given before reaching the age of puberty]. [*Such a girl, in contradistinction to one married off by her father, can avoid an undesired marriage by refusing in the presence of two witnesses to go through with it. Her power to avoid this marriage indicates that her mother or brother (who have tried to marry her off because her father died before he could do so) do not possess the same unlimited dominion over the girl as did her father.*]

M. Yeb. 13:2

As powerful as the father seems in dictating his daughter's choice of husband, the minor daughter's lack of control over her marriage is not the most shocking feature of her powerlessness. The fact is that she has no rights at all against her father—not even the elementary human right to minimum subsistence. Even though he gets the benefit of her labor (M. Ket 4:4B), he has no legal obligation to feed or clothe her. This point (implied at M. Ket. 4:4F) is spelled out in the following rule, justified by an egregiously casuistic argument:

A. The father is not liable for the maintenance of his [minor] daughter. This is an interpretation expounded by R. Eleazar b. Azariah before the sages in the vineyard of Yavneh.[68]

B. "Sons shall inherit and daughters be maintained [out of my estate after my death]." [*Eleazar recites here a Hebrew version of the Aramaic k^etubbah formula found at M. Ket. 4:10–11. See also M. B.B. 9:1.*]

C.   [This means that] just as sons do not inherit until after the father's death
      [*necessarily implied at M. Ket. 4:10*], so daughters need not be main-
      tained until after the father's death [*at which point they are automatically main-
      tained out of the inheritance that falls to the sons. Eleazar imputes this into
      M. Ket. 4:11 (discussed later) by analogy with the implication at M. Ket.
      4:10, though there is no such necessary implication at M. Ket. 4:11.*]

                                                                    M. Ket. 4:6

This rule exempts a father from any duty to feed his daughter. Certainly
the Mishnah contains no such exemption with respect to a son (just as it
contains no parallel, for sons, to the rule allowing a father to sell his
girlchild as a slave). Although we should not make too much of an argument from silence, [69] neither should we ignore the speciousness of the sages'
reasoning here. Contrary to their assertion, inheritance and maintenance are
not analogous in principle. A man must by definition die before his sons
can inherit; but no logic dictates that he must die before his daughters can
qualify for maintenance!

Why, then, do the sages indulge in this logic chopping? Probably they
wish to legitimate an existing social norm: People place less value on
daughters than on sons. Yet, shocked as we are by the notion that the
mishnaic father need not feed his daughters, we should not forget that the
dominant surrounding cultures placed even less value on girlchildren, even
to the point of permitting female infanticide.[70] By contrast, nothing in the
Mishnah (or for that matter in Scripture) suggests that Israelites practiced
infanticide at all.[71] If the father fails to provide for her, the girl presumably
subsists on scraps of the food and clothing produced by her mother (M. Ket.
5:5, 5:9).

The Minor Daughter as Person

What we have learned so far leads us to wonder whether the sages perceive a
young girl as even a *potential* person. To answer this question we must
recall the distinction between a girlchild under twelve (*qᵉṭannah*) and a
pubescent girl (*naᶜarah*) between twelve and twelve and one-half. The sages
recognize the fact that the *naᶜarah* is chronologically close to legal adult-
hood (and generally also to marriage) by assigning her more rights than her
younger sister.

The Pubescent Girl as Potential Woman

We have already noticed some respects in which the *naᶜarah* does better than
the *qᵉṭannah*. For instance, although mishnaic law permits a father to sell
his girlchild into slavery, he loses this power as soon as she reaches the age
of twelve. Likewise, though daughters have no legal right to maintenance,
we find one interesting exception made for a *naᶜarah*. When the time comes
to transfer a girl from father to husband, the father must provide a trousseau

(or the means to buy one) befitting the dignity of a bride unless the bride-groom agrees to take care of this.

A.   One who transfers his daughter [to her new husband] "as is" [*i.e., without providing a trousseau*], must give her not less than fifty *zuz*.

B.   But if he stipulated to bring her in [to the husband's house] naked (*pasaq lᵉhaknisah ᶜarumah*),

C.   the husband may not say, "When I bring her into my house, I shall clothe her in garments [belonging] to me,"

D.   but he must clothe her while she is still in her father's house.

E.   And likewise, one who gives an orphan girl in marriage must give her not less than fifty *zuz*.

F.   If there are [sufficient funds] in the poorbox, they should furnish her according to her father's station in life.

M. Ket. 6:5

A young girl about to enter marriage—even a lowly orphan—must be treated with respect; she may not be transferred to the husband in a shameful manner. These rules foreshadow the improvement in status that will accompany her transition from daughter to wife. So long as she is merely a daughter, her father, as we saw, can refuse to clothe her (M. Ket. 4:6). But once she becomes a bride, her husband must do so (M. Ket. 4:4F). The sages solve the problem of this girl's interstitiality by insisting that she be treated with the dignity that befits this important rite of passage.[72] This solution symbolizes the transformation of the young bride, so recently her father's chattel, into a legal person.

The Girlchild as Potential Adult

At one point the Mishnah recognizes even a girlchild as a potential person. For instance, even through her father can sell her as a slave (M. Ket. 3:8), we know this expedient is only of temporary duration; she cannot be sold permanently, but must be redeemed at puberty unless she is married into her purchaser's family (Exod. 21:7ff.). In the same way a father has no power to dedicate his girlchild (i.e., her value as set down in Lev. 27:1ff.) as an offering to the Temple because she is not his permanent, absolute property.

A.   [As for] one who dedicates his son or his daughter, or his Hebrew bondman or bondwoman, or a field he has acquired,

B.   they are not [validly] dedicated

C.   because one cannot dedicate a thing that does not [totally] belong to him. [*The foregoing are not a man's property in an absolute sense.*]

M. ᶜArak. 8:5

Scripture permits an Israelite to devote or dedicate his chattels to the Temple for divine service or other cultic purposes (Lev. 27:28). But the items listed (M. ᶜArak. 8:5A) are not a man's absolute property; the boy will become an independent person at the age of thirteen years, the Hebrew bondman goes free after six years' service (Exod. 21:2), and the field bought for money (as opposed to one that is inherited) must revert to the original owner or his heirs in the jubilee year (Lev. 25:10). Similarly with the minor daughter, Scripture itself hints at the limits of a father's power when it prohibits him from selling her into slavery beyond the age of puberty. Because the girlchild is not her father's property in perpetuity, he cannot dedicate her or her value to the use of the Temple priesthood.

The Mishnah's framers likewise acknowledge the girl's potential personhood when discussing the physical and intellectual development of boys and girls. The girlchild (*qeʿtannah*), like the minor boy under thirteen (*qaṭan*), is considered a legal infant. Neither is bound by the laws of the Torah, so they cannot be punished for transgressions. Both lack legal capacity: For instance, neither can make a contract. But when it comes to religious vows, the sages consider whether a child close to maturity may have sufficient intelligence to understand the meaning of a vow. They prescribe a test that makes an interesting distinction between boys and girls.

A.   [As for] a girl aged eleven years and a day, her vows must be examined. [*If the girl understands what she is doing, her vow may stand unless her father revokes it, even though her general obligation to obey the precepts of Scripture does not accrue until the completion of her twelfth year.*]

B.   At twelve years and a day, her vows stand [without examination]. [*At that age there arises an irrebuttable presumption that she knows what she is doing. We recall, however, that between twelve and twelve and one-half, the father retains the right to revoke his daughter's vows (Num. 30:4–6; M. Ned. 10:1–4).*]

C.   But one must examine [her vows] throughout her twelfth year. [*Between eleven and twelve years her vows are valid only if she knows what the vow entails.*]

D.   [As for] a boy aged twelve years and a day, his vows must be examined.

E.   At thirteen years and a day, his vows stand. [*Because a boy matures, both physically and mentally, more slowly than a girl, his age of majority is set at thirteen rather than twelve.*]

F.   But one must examine [his vows] throughout his thirteenth year.

G.   Before that time [*i.e., before the age of twelve or thirteen, respectively*], even if [these children] say, "We know to whom we have vowed [meaning God]" or "[We know] to whom we have consecrated [an offering]," their vows are not [valid] vows, and their act of consecration is not a [valid] act of consecration.

H.   After that time, even though [these children] say, "We do not know to whom we have vowed" or "[We do not know] to whom we have consecrated [an offering]," their vows are [valid] vows and their act of consecration a [valid] act of consecration.

M. Nid. 5:6

Although for most purposes the age of majority depends on the appearance of signs of puberty (M. Nid. 6:11), legal responsibility here depends on the child's capacity to understand the meaning of its actions. The sages set the age of majority for a girl (M. Nid. 5:6B) earlier than for a boy (M. Nid. 5:6E). This difference, obviously reflecting the earlier onset of puberty in girls, also demonstrates the sages' belief that girls mature mentally—as well as physically—earlier than boys. Because intelligence is an important part of personhood, the sages are saying that a girl *intrinsically* becomes a person earlier than a boy.

This strong theoretical statement, however, would have little practical effect; for though the girl comes of age at twelve, she remains subject to her father's authority until age twelve and one-half. By that time most girls will have become subject to another man—the husband—for the foreseeable future. And even the unmarried daughter emancipated at twelve and one-half will find her life options severely limited outside the domestic sphere. The mishnaic system knows no *public* calling for women except that of prostitute—the sages allude to this with surprising rarity, either from lack of interest or, more likely, from a deliberate decision to ignore the phenomenon, since Israelite women are not supposed to function in the public domain.[73] An adult daughter will probably be forced for socioeconomic reasons to choose marriage and thus surrender her freedom. The young Israelite male, by contrast, moves automatically from dependence to full legal autonomy as soon as he turns thirteen. Unlike his sister he passes through no transitional status of *na'ar*, for no such category exists in mishnaic law. Mere passage of time will always bring the boy to full personhood; this hardly ever happens with his sister.

This brief excursus into the topic of religious vows forms a fitting conclusion to our discussion of the minor daughter. For it is in precisely this context that the sages highlight a girl's dependence on her father by listing nine exceptions to the rule that a father can revoke his daughter's vows.

A. [There are] nine classes of daughter-at-home (*na'arah*)[74] whose vows stand firm:

1. A woman of full age [who makes a vow and] who was [previously rendered] an "orphan [in her father's lifetime]." [*This technical term denotes a girl who was married and then widowed or divorced while still a minor. Such a girl does not revert to her father's domain despite her youth because her widowhood or divorce has rendered her* sui juris *in accordance with M. Qid. 1:1E, p. 42.*]

2. A *na'arah* who [vowed and then] came of age and who was an orphan [in her father's lifetime when she vowed].

3. A *na'arah* [who vowed and] who has not yet come of age but is an orphan [in her father's lifetime].

4. A woman of full age [who vowed and] whose father has [since] died.

5. A *na'arah* who [vowed and then] came of age and whose father has died.

6. A *na'arah* [who vowed and] who has not yet come of age and whose father has died.

7. A *na'arah* [who vowed and] whose father [then] died and who came of age after he died.

8. A woman of full age [who vowed and] whose father is [still] alive.

9. A *na'arah* [who vowed and] who has come of age and whose father is [still] alive.

B.   And R. Judah rules [that this list includes] also [the case in which a man]
      married off his infant daughter [under twelve] and she was widowed or
      divorced and returned to his domain and is still a *na'arah*.

                                                                M. Ned. 11:10

The nine classes listed here specify the three events that can emancipate a
girl or woman: becoming an orphan in the father's lifetime (classes 1–3);
becoming a genuine orphan through the father's actual death (classes 4–6);
and attaining her majority (classes 7–9). Girls who become *sui juris* through
any of these contingencies enjoy greater legal capacity, hence a higher level
of personhood, than girls under paternal control. The binding nature of her
vows serves, here as in Scripture, as a metaphor for her autonomy.

Summary

The minor daughter is completely under her father's authority. He has
the exclusive right to arrange her betrothal and marriage—with or without
her consent. If he dies without doing so while she is still under age, her
mother or brothers may betroth her—but the marriage can be consummated only with her consent. This subtle distinction reflects the most
significant aspect of the father/daughter relationship: As sole owner of her
sexuality, he alone has an unqualified right to dispose of it as he pleases.
The father's ownership is also manifest in other mishnaic rules that involve
the daughter's sexuality. Any man who rapes or seduces her, thereby reducing her value on the marriage market, must compensate the father. Not by
accident, the fine of two hundred *zuz* corresponds to the sum payable by a
bridegroom to a virgin bride. In awarding the fine to the father, the sages are
constrained by Scripture. But their own expansion of Scripture's rule endorses its underlying rationale: They award the criminal penalty and civil
damages for rape or seduction alike to the father—and in an amount that
depends on his social standing. That it is the father rather than the girl
who receives damages for the pain and suffering of the rape symbolizes a
total disregard of the daughter as person. The same is true of rules that
absolve the father from liability to maintain her and even permit him to sell
her as a slave. On balance, the girl's status is barely distinguishable from
chattel.

At the same time the sages recognize the minor daughter as a person *in
potentia*. Granted, her father will almost certainly have married her off
before she attains her majority and the status of wife will continue to limit
her personhood in many ways, but even so, a wife enjoys far more personhood than a daughter. Moreover, the daughter may (theoretically) remain
unmarried beyond the age of twelve and one-half years. In that case, she will
become *sui juris*, an autonomous person in the private sphere of Israelite
life. Her gender will still limit her options for self-expression in the public
domain, but she will enjoy many legal powers (e.g., to make religious vows

that no one can revoke, to own and dispose of property, to conduct business, to engage in litigation, and most important to choose her own husband from among her suitors). That potential occasionally leads the Mishnah's framers to recognize the minor daughter as an incipient person. For the most part, however, the men in her life—above all, those who make the laws—contemplate her simply as a sexual chattel to be exploited on the marriage market.

3

THE WIFE

When the Israelite daughter leaves her father's house for that of her husband, she exchanges subjection to one man for subservience to another. But something else changes, too. As her father's daughter she was a virtual chattel, lacking almost all the rights, duties, and powers we earlier defined as indicators of personhood. In advancing from the status of daughter to that of wife, she becomes a person, that is, she acquires numerous legal entitlements and obligations. Marriage transforms the girl into a woman in more ways than one, for besides fulfilling her biological destiny it brings her into a relationship marked by a reciprocal nexus of spousal rights and duties that clearly defines her as a person in the mishnaic system.

Even so, the wife never enjoys equality with her husband but always remains his subordinate. Her prescribed duties confine her largely to the home, setting bounds to her personal freedom. In return for her maintenance she owes her husband specified domestic and economic chores; her vows are subject to revocation by her husband if they are inimical to the conjugal relationship; she cannot dispose of her property without her husband's approval; and so on. Because the wife must defer to the husband far more than he to her, her level of personhood (as defined in chap. 1) is clearly lower than his.

One aspect of the husband's dominance stands out in particular: the sexuality factor. The husband's vested interest in the wife's biological function takes precedence over any competing interest, including the rights of the wife herself. This parallels the sages' view of the minor daughter; just as her sexuality belonged to her father, making her his chattel, so the wife's biological function belongs to her husband and makes her his chattel with respect to all matters affecting that function.

The Wife as Chattel

Mishnaic laws governing the matrimonial bond, particularly those involving conjugal relations, have one common denominator—an underlying perception of the female as a sexual chattel whose biological function may be acquired, controlled, and disposed of by the male for his own advantage. This does not mean that the sages regarded women as nothing but objects to be exploited by men for sexual gratification or for the economic and social prestige that accrues to a man with many wives and children. But they did see the wife primarily as a vehicle for a man's fulfillment of Scripture's command to *be fruitful and multiply* (Gen. 1:28).[75]

A. No man is exempt from the duty to *be fruitful and multiply* unless he [already] has children (*banim*).

B. The school of Shammai says [this means] two sons. [*The Hebrew term* banim *can mean either children in general or sons in particular.*]

C. The school of Hillel says [this means] a son and a daughter, as it is stated in Scripture, "Male and female created he them." [*Hillelites here choose to cite the version found in Gen. 5:2* (zakar u-neqebah bera'am) *rather than Gen. 1:27* (zakar u-neqebah bara' otam). The reason will become clear at G and H.]

D. If he married a woman, and lived with her ten years and she did not bear [a child], he is not permitted to be exempt [but must take a second wife in the attempt to fulfill his scriptural duty (M. Yeb. 6:6)]. [*The term of ten years reflects the story of Abraham, who took a second wife only after Sarah had remained barren for ten years following their settlement in the Land of Canaan (Gen. 16:3).*]

E. If he divorces [the first wife], she may be married to another [man], and the second [husband] is permitted to live with her for ten years [*because if her earlier barrenness stemmed from the sterility of her first husband, she may yet produce children with the second*].

F. If [the wife] miscarried [during the ten-year period], she may count [ten years] from the time she miscarried.

G. [Only] the man is commanded to be fruitful and multiply, but not the woman.

H. [But] R. Yohanan b. Baroqa says, "Of both of them [Scripture] says: *Be [ye] fruitful and multiply*" (Gen. 1:28). [*The Hebrew formula,* peru u-rebu, *appears in the grammatical plural, thus including both the man and the woman. Yohanan here cites the continuation of the verse normally adduced for the proposition "Male and female created he them," Gen. 1:27). He implies that the Hillelites, by citing Gen. 5:2 rather than Gen. 1:27, deliberately divert attention from Gen. 1:28, where the command to "be fruitful and multiply" couched in the plural clearly applies to man and woman alike.*]

M. Yeb. 6:6

Like Yoḥanan b. Baroqa (M. Yeb. 6:6H), we wonder at the sages' assertion that the commandment of procreation was directed solely to the *man*. The Mishnah offers no explanation,[76] but whatever its motivation, this interpretation of Scripture distorts the plain grammatical sense in claiming that only the man, not the woman, incurs the duty of procreation. The only reasonable interpretation is that the sages perceive woman in this context not as a person subject to a duty, but simply as a baby-incubator, a vehicle for the man's implementation of the divine command.[77]

This interpretation of the commandment of procreation gives us a clue to the sages' thinking as they formulate a whole corpus of rules to control women's sexual function. These include procedures for acquiring or disposing of a wife, for ensuring that the wife reserves her sexuality to her husband alone, and for precluding her use of her legal powers in any way that might impair conjugal relations. The rules that follow, designed to ensure that a wife's sexuality remains her husband's private preserve, are further buttressed by extraordinarily punitive sanctions against a wife who forms an illicit sexual union. When this happens, even through reasonable mistake, we shall find that the penalties imposed are out of all proportion to the offense.

Marriage: Acquisition of a Wife

The procedure for acquiring a wife (set forth in tractate *Qiddushin* ["Espousals"]) treats marriage as the formal sale and purchase of a woman's sexual function—a commercial transaction in which a man pays for the bride's virginity just as for any other object of value. The wife heads the mishnaic catalogue of transferable property. This, in turn, rests squarely on Scripture and follows the list found in the Tenth Commandment (Exod. 20:14) that defines the contents of a man's household as wives, male and female slaves, large and small cattle, and other property. The framers' opening statement, "A wife may be acquired in three ways . . . by money, by deed, or by intercourse," draws a gratuitous (hence deliberate) analogy between women and other forms of property.[78] In effect the Mishnah prescribes the same modes of acquisition for wives as for Canaanite slaves and real property—"by money, by deed, or by usucaption." In the case of a wife, intercourse constitutes usucaption.

A. A wife may be acquired (*niqneit*) in three ways[79] and acquires her autonomy [lit. acquires herself] in two ways.

B. She may be acquired by money, by deed,[80] or by intercourse.[81]

C. By money the school of Shammai holds "By a *dinar* or *a dinar's* worth," whereas the school of Hillel holds "By a *peruṭah* or a *peruṭah's* worth."

D. And how much is a *peruṭah*? One-eighth of an Italian *issar*.

E. And she acquires her autonomy by a writ of divorce or by the death of the husband.

F. A levirate widow is acquired by intercourse [with her late husband's brother] and acquires her autonomy by *ḥaliṣah* release[82] or by the death of the levir.

M. Qid. 1:1

A. A Hebrew bondman may be acquired (*niqneh*) by money or by deed and acquires his freedom [lit. acquires himself] by [six] years of service [Exod. 21:3], or by the advent of the jubilee year [Lev. 25:39], or by [payment of] a reduced [purchase] price [reflecting the slave's reduced value as the year of release approaches].

B. A Hebrew bondmaid has an advantage over him in that she [also] acquires her freedom by the onset of puberty [Exod. 21:7, as interpreted].

C. A slave whose ear is pierced is acquired by the piercing ceremony [Exod. 21:6] and may acquire his freedom by the advent of the jubilee year or by the death of the master.

M. Qid. 1:2

A. A Canaanite [*i.e., non-Israelite*] slave may be acquired (*niqneh*) by money, or by deed, or by usucaption.[83]

B. And he acquires his freedom by money [paid] by others or by a note of debt [executed] by himself. So holds R. Meir.

C. But sages [in general] hold [that he acquires his freedom] by money [paid] by himself or by a note of debt executed by others [*so long as the money to be paid belongs to others.*]

M. Qid. 1:3

A. Large cattle are acquired (*niqneit*) by the act of delivery and small cattle by the act of lifting-up. So hold R. Meir and R. Eliezer.

B. But sages [in general] hold that small cattle are acquired by the act of drawing [them toward oneself].

M. Qid. 1:4

A. Real property [lit. property subject to mortgage] may be acquired (*niqnin*) by money, or by deed, or by usucaption.

B. And personal property [lit. that which is not subject to mortgage] is acquired only by an act of drawing [it toward oneself].

C. Personal property acquired together with real property may be acquired by money, by deed, or by usucaption.

D. And the said personal property invokes the requirement of an oath concerning the real property also.

M. Qid. 1:5

The sages here equate the wife to chattel in several ways. First, they use the same technical term *q-n-y* ("to acquire ownership") as for other forms of property.[84] Second, the same three modes of acquisition apply to wife, Canaanite slave, and real property. In the case of the wife, intercourse (M. Qid. 1:1B) actually constitutes usucaption (M. Qid. 1:3A, 1:5A) because intercourse is the specific form of usucaption that applies to a wife. Third, after setting out the list, the Mishnah's framers drop the subject of property; espousal of wives occupies the entire tractate.[85] Obviously the sages list all these kinds of property along with the wife to suggest both a formal and a substantive analogy between acquiring a wife and acquiring a chattel.[86] At the same time the inclusion of the wife does not necessarily imply that she is the husband's property in all respects. As we shall see, this is true only of her biological function (just as with the Hebrew bondman, only his labor, not his person, is the householder's property).[87]

The view of woman as chattel is highlighted by the unilateral nature of the espousal ceremony, in which the man recites a formal declaration to which the woman makes no reply. Even if she were to speak, her words would have no effect. For as the Tosefta[88] points out, the formula of espousal can be recited only by a man, not a woman. Although the bridegroom can validly declare, "Lo, thou art espoused to me," the bride would create no legal effect by saying, "Lo, I am espoused to thee" (T. Qid. 1:1); formally it is *he* who acquires *her*, not *she* who gives herself to *him* (though, if of full age, she must have consented to be his wife). In other words a bride cannot execute the transaction on the groom's behalf. Likewise in discussing conditional espousals, the Mishnah's framers insist that if a condition fails, the transaction cannot be saved by the bride's willingness to waive the condition.

A.　[If he said, "Be thou espoused to me] provided that I am a *kohen*," when he is in fact a *levi*,[89] or "a *levi*" when he is in fact a *kohen*, or "a *natin*" when he is in fact a *mamzer*, or "a *mamzer*" when he is in fact a *natin*, or "a townsman" when he is in fact a villager, or "a villager" when he is in fact a townsman;

B.　or "provided that my house is near a bathhouse," when it is in fact far off or "far [from a bathhouse]" when it is in fact nearby;

C.　or "provided that I have a daughter or slave woman who is a hairdresser," when [in fact] he has not or "provided that I have not [the aforesaid]" when [in fact] he has;

D.　or "provided that I have no children," when [in fact] he has or "provided that I have [children]" when [in fact] he has none.

E.　In all these [cases], even if [the prospective bride] said, "It was my intention [lit. in my heart] to become espoused to him notwithstanding [the failure of the stated condition]," she is not [validly] espoused.

F.　And likewise [in a case where] she misled him [she is not espoused].

M. Qid. 2:3

Espousal can result only from a man's unilateral action; however, the woman (here assumed to be of full age) must previously have signified her consent. Here, a woman who wants the man even if the condition fails (M. Qid. 2:3E) has no power to save the transaction by waiving the condition. Nor (as indicated by T. Qid. 1:1 earlier) can she simply declare herself unconditionally espoused to him. Furthermore, the framers' insistence (M. Qid. 2:3F) that the espousal likewise fails if the woman misleads the man creates the false impression that man and woman are equally powerless to save the situation. This is not the case. A woman's misdescription of herself invalidates the espousal only because the *bridegroom* has chosen to make her self-description a condition of the marriage. But unlike the woman, the man has an easy remedy: He can always waive her failed conditions, just as he can withdraw his own false stipulations simply by repeating the espousal formula without them. She, by contrast, can do nothing about the failure of either his or her conditions. The sages' apparent evenhandedness here is utterly spurious. In sum the mishnaic law of espousal treats the man as a person acquiring a chattel, and the woman as the chattel he acquires.

In its insistence that the essence of marriage is the transfer of an object, namely, the woman's biological function, the law of espousal constitutes a paradigm for much else in the mishnaic law of women; we shall find that whenever a man owns, acquires, or disposes of a woman's sexuality, the law treats the woman as chattel for that purpose. This holds true for rules governing marriage, divorce, wife's suspected infidelity, wife's vows that impair conjugal relations, levirate widowhood—in short, for any situation that involves a man's legal claim on a woman's sexuality. In all such cases the man's claim overrides the woman's rights of personhood. The corollary holds equally true: When something other than ownership of her sexuality is at stake, the law treats the woman far more like a man, namely, as a person. Chapters 2 through 4, which deal with dependent women, and chapter 5, which discusses autonomous women, analyze in detail the effect of the sexuality factor on the level of a woman's personhood.

Divorce: Disposition of a Wife

The salient feature of mishnaic divorce is its unilateral form. A husband has legal power to divorce his wife, but a wife has no power to divorce her husband. The Mishnah's rules for disposing of a wife thus correspond to the procedures for acquiring her. As the woman's part in espousal is one of passive acquiescence, so too in mishnaic divorce. The examples that follow will make this clear.

Mishnaic divorce law (set forth in tractate *Giṭṭin* ["Writs of Divorce"]), rests on the sole pentateuchal allusion to divorce procedure:

> 1. *A man takes a wife and possesses her. She fails to please him because he finds something obnoxious about her, and* he writes her a bill of divorcement, hands it to her, *and sends her away from his house; 2. she leaves his household and becomes the wife of another man; 3. then the second man rejects her, writes her a bill of divorcement, hands it to her, and sends her away from his house; or the man who married her last dies. 4. Then the husband who divorced her first shall not take her to wife again, since she has been defiled—for that would be abhorrent to the LORD.*

> Deut. 24:1–4 (emphasis added)

The sages interpret Scripture as permitting a man to divorce his wife unilaterally by giving her a document of release or dismissal called a *geṭ*, here translated as "writ of divorce."[90] Their interpretation generates a dispute about the preparation of the document. They analogize divorce (as they analogize espousal) to other transactions that involve chattels.

A.   He who writes out forms for writs of divorce need [merely] leave a space for the man, a space for the woman, and a space for the date.

B. [Likewise, with] writs of indebtedness, he need [merely] leave a space for the lender, a space for the borrower, a space for the amount, and a space for the date.

C. [Likewise with] deeds of sale, he need [merely] leave a space for the buyer, a space for the seller, a space for the price, a space for the field [being sold], and a space for the date.

D. [The foregoing procedure is permitted] because of the convenience [*of having standard documents on hand for use as needed*].

E. R. Judah rules all of the above invalid [*because they were not prepared expressly for the transaction in which they will be used*].

F. But R. Eleazar rules them all valid, except forms for writs of divorce, [which he rules invalid] because Scripture says, *"And he shall write for her"* (*w^ekatab lah*, Deut. 24:1), [that is to say] *expressly* for her.

M. Giṭ. 3:2

For reasons of convenience (M. Giṭ. 3:2D), sages in general permit the use of standard forms, prepared ahead of time, for any property transaction that requires a writ or deed, including divorce. They reject Eleazar's minority view (M. Giṭ. 3:2F) that Scripture intended the writ of divorce to be written specifically for the woman to whom it relates.[91] The majority view conforms with that expressed at M. Qid. 1:1-5. Just as there the man acquires the exclusive right to the woman's sexuality, so here the divorcing husband transfers it back to her. Since Scripture (Deut. 24:1) requires documentary evidence of this particular transaction, the sages' equation of women with property logically dictates that rules for the document's preparation match those for any other property transaction.

Moving from formal details of writ preparation to matters of substance, we encounter a far more important dispute. The schools of Hillel and Shammai, although agreeing that divorce is a unilateral transaction, differ on the scope of a husband's grounds. The controversy stems from ambiguity in Scripture's allusion to grounds for divorce, namely, the term *'erwat dabar* in Deut. 24:1. Hillelites and Shammaites disagree on the meaning of this obscure term, which may connote a *specific* impropriety or impropriety *in any matter*. May a man divorce his wife only for sexual impropriety or may he do so for any misconduct whatsoever? The Mishnah records three views:

A. The school of Shammai holds that a man may not divorce his wife unless he has found in her a matter of sexual impropriety (*d^ebar 'erwah*), as stated in Scripture [Deut. 24:1]: *"because he found in her impropriety* in a [specific] matter (*'erwat dabar*)." [**Shammaites stress the sexual connotation of the word 'erwah, literally "nakedness".**]

B. But the school of Hillel holds [that he may divorce her] even if she [merely] burned his dinner, as it is stated: "because he found in her impropriety *in [any] matter.*" [**Hillelites stress the word dabar ("matter"), thus taking 'erwah ("nakedness") in the metaphorical sense of impropriety.**]

C. R. 'Aqiba holds [that he may divorce her] even if he [merely] found another woman fairer than her [and the wife is without fault of any kind], as Scripture states [in the very passage forming the basis of the rule]: *"If she fails to please him"* [Deut. 24:1].

M. Giṭ 9:10

In this dispute concerning grounds for divorce, the common denominator is that all three views treat the wife as chattel. The Shammaites perceive the essence of marriage as a husband's exclusive right to his wife's sexuality; so he can divorce her only if some other man has had sexual relations with her. This approach treats the wife as chattel when her sexual function is in issue, but it protects her when she is without moral fault. The school of Hillel, by contrast, permits her husband to divorce her for the least infraction of her duties toward him, even in matters totally unrelated to her sexual function.[92] The example given here, "even if she burned his dinner," reflects a broader view of a husband's rights over his wife: Her role is to serve him generally. If she falls short, whether in matters sexual or merely culinary,[93] his right to divorce her comes into play. In the latter case the gross disparity between infraction and penalty downgrades the woman's personhood by denying any meaningful equivalence between her rights and her responsibilities. ʿAqiba goes further still; he treats the wife as no person at all, permitting the husband to discard her without even the flimsiest excuse— for instance, if she is entirely faultless but he has taken a fancy to another woman. But the really important point here is not the scope of grounds for divorce, but the unilateral exercise of the husband's power, which stems from the fact that divorce, like marriage, represents a disposition of a man's exclusive right to a woman's sexual function.

The majority opinions (represented by Hillel and ʿAqiba) dissociate the husband's right of divorce from the wife's moral responsibility. Instead of grounding the power of divorce on breach of the reciprocal matrimonial rights and duties set out in tractate *Kᵉtubbot* (discussed later), they treat it as a unilateral power of the husband, permitting him to discard the wife like an old shoe. The redactor's decision to make this view the bottom line of tractate *Giṭṭin* underscores the basic premise of the whole tractate: A wife may be discarded at the husband's whim.

Inherent in this rule is its corollary: Just as a wife cannot *resist* divorce, so she cannot *compel* it, for she has no reciprocal power to dissolve the matrimonial bond. If her husband suffers a serious impairment, such as imbecility, which destroys his mental capacity to divorce her, she is left without a remedy. The sages spell out unequivocally the double standard that operates here.

A.   A male deaf-mute who married an unimpaired woman or an unimpaired man who married a female deaf-mute may divorce her at will or retain her at will.

B.   [For] just as he can marry her by making signs, so he can divorce her by making signs. [*The formalities of divorce require no spoken word, for Scripture speaks only of a writ.*]

C.   An unimpaired man who married an unimpaired woman, who then became a deaf-mute, may if he wishes divorce her, or if he wishes, retain her. [*Her loss of speech and hearing is irrelevant because the transaction is performed by the husband, and even a deaf-mute woman can be made aware of what is happening.*]

D.   [However] if she became an imbecile, he may not divorce her [*because, as stated in M. Giṭ. 6:2, a woman who is incapable of taking care of her writ of divorce cannot be divorced.*]

E.   If [the husband] becomes a deaf-mute or an imbecile [after marriage], he can never divorce her. [*A deaf-mute's legal transactions are defective, hence invalid in pentateuchal law. However, sages treat them as having limited effect. In particular, a deaf-mute can execute a divorce only in respect of a marriage entered by him as a deaf-mute (see A and B), but not where he is stricken after the marriage. An imbecile totally lacks the mental capacity to carry out the divorce procedure. So a husband who becomes insane cannot release his wife.*]

F.   Said R. Yohanan b. Nuri, "How is it that a woman who becomes a deaf-mute [after marriage] can be divorced, whereas a man who becomes a deaf-mute [after marriage] cannot divorce [his wife]?" [*If his supervening disability precludes him from divorcing her, how come hers does not have this effect?*]

G.   They said to him, "The man who divorces is not like the woman who is divorced, for a woman can be divorced with or without her consent, whereas a man cannot [effectively] divorce her without his own consent." [*Since divorce results from a man's unilateral act, only the man's state of mind matters here. Just as at F, the husband cannot divorce his wife if he lacks legal capacity, but he may do so despite her disability, so here he cannot divorce her if he lacks the will to do so but he may do so despite her wishes.*]

                                                                      M. Yeb. 14:1

The most important statement here occurs at M Yeb. 14:1G: *Divorce occurs solely at the husband's option.* This should not surprise us; after all, unilateral divorce is the logical corollary of unilateral espousal. Even with a woman of full age who has chosen to accept the man, the formal act of acquisition remains unilateral, for the only proof of her prior consent rests on the *husband's* declaration to that effect in the *ketubbah*. In divorce as in marriage, the wife's role is passive; her husband need not consider her desires in the matter.[94] Worse yet, if the husband succumbs to insanity or other mental impairment (M. Yeb. 14:1E), the wife may be chained to him for life. Yet in the reverse situation, where the wife loses her faculties (M. Yeb. 14:1C), the husband may generally discard her at will.[95] The double standard reflects the discrepancy between the sages' perception of the status of man and woman in the formalities of marriage. In this context he is a person, she an object; and whereas an owner can give up his property, property cannot abandon its owner.

In the law of divorce one very interesting set of rules illustrates the sages' occasional difficulty in reconciling their insistence on the chattel status of woman in the sexual context with their equally firm recognition of her personhood in other respects. The case at hand involves the law of agency. In the mishnaic system a woman, just as a man, has the legal power to appoint an agent to handle her affairs. Because agents may execute the formalities of divorce, there arises the theoretical possibility that a wife may be able to determine the precise moment of her divorce through an act of her agent. This makes the sages unhappy. Suppose, for instance, that a husband decides to divorce his wife who is living apart from him in a distant town. He can, of course, send his agent to deliver the writ. But if his wife sends her agent to receive the writ on her behalf, she will be free as soon as her husband places the document in her agent's hand—that is, sooner than the husband may have intended. The sages find a way to restore the husband's control.

A.   [In the case of] a husband who says [to his agent], "Receive this *get* for my wife" or "Take this *get* to my wife," if [the husband] wishes [subsequently] to retract [before the *get* actually reaches his wife], he can retract. [*Here, the agent's physical receipt of the document does not constitute legal delivery to the wife, for he is the husband's agent, not the wife's, and can be appointed only as agent for delivery, not receipt. Hence the wife will not be free until the agent hands her the writ.*]

B.   [But if] the wife said [to her agent], "Receive my *get* for me," [then] if [her husband] wishes to retract [after handing the *get* to her agent, but before the latter delivers it], he cannot retract. [*Here, the husband's handing the document to the wife's agent constitutes legal delivery to the wife; hence, she is immediately released and he can no longer retract.*]

C.   This being so [how can the husband retain his right of retraction]? If the husband said to [the wife's agent], "It is not my wish that thou receive it on her behalf, but [instead] take it and deliver it to her," [then] if the husband [subsequently] wishes to retract [after handing the document to the agent, but before the agent delivers it], he can retract. [*Here, the husband has effectively turned his wife's agent into his own agent. By countermanding her appointment, he puts himself into the same original position as at A, that is, he retains his right to retract the writ until it actually reaches his wife.*][96]

M. Giṭ. 6:1

In principle, the husband's control of divorce gives him the right to dictate the precise moment of his wife's release; normally this occurs when he or his agent hands her the writ. But the rule at M. Giṭ. 6:1B gives the wife some say in the matter, for she can either wait until her husband's agent delivers the writ or send her own agent to intercept him en route. In the latter case she actually expedites her release from the marriage, which could be important if, for instance, she plans to remarry at the first opportunity. This outcome conflicts theoretically with the husband's unilateral power to call the shots in divorcing her. The sages, seeking to neutralize her power to use the law of agency, find a neat solution: they simply empower the husband to countermand the wife's appointment of her agent. As divorce amounts technically to the husband's ceding control of his wife's sexuality, the Mishnah is wholly consistent here; as always in such matters, it does not hesitate to suspend a woman's normal legal powers. The husband, once more empowered to delay the wife's release until the writ reaches her hand, retains ultimate control.

This case illustrates nicely how the sages' handling of the woman's hybrid character as chattel and person at once matches their treatment of the hybrid attributes of the *koy*, discussed earlier in the Introduction. Here, they treat the woman as both a chattel and a person, just as the *koy* was treated for some purposes as "both a wild beast and a domestic animal" (M. Bik. 2:8). Although the solution is elegant in its simplicity, the method produces logical confusion and cognitive dissonance; it treats the woman as person and chattel in the same transaction, contrary to the law of the excluded middle, which denies that a thing can be *X* and not-*X* at once. This response exemplifies the problems encountered by systems that reject hybrid categories in principle. The conflict between woman-as-chattel and woman-as-person can be resolved only by temporarily suspending either the one aspect or the other. In the last analysis the sages choose to treat the wife as chattel here in order to retain the unilateral character of divorce that Scripture, on their interpretation, requires.

But the one-sidedness of mishnaic divorce law does not stem merely from the sages' dependence on Scripture, for Scripture does not conclusively supply the details of divorce procedure. The sole discussion occurs in the passage from Deuteronomy cited above. Because the actual focus of that passage is a *substantive* rule of divorce law (Deut. 24:4), the purely incidental reference to *procedure* (Deut. 24:1) need not have been taken as a comprehensive statement of divorce law. In fact, Scripture nowhere explicitly denies a woman's power to divorce her husband; that assumption is at best an argument from silence. Indeed, a contrary argument might be made from the levirate law (Deut. 25:5–10, discussed in a more detail later), which recognizes a woman's intrinsic capacity to carry out a procedure of release from a conjugal tie—the ceremony following the levir's rejection of his brother's widow is performed entirely by the woman.[97] Here, then, the Mishnah's framers are making a choice not necessarily dictated by Scripture. That choice expresses their independent belief that a wife should not have the legal power to divorce her husband. This view is consistent with their position that once a man has a legitimate claim on a woman's biological function, control over that function remains with him until he chooses to give it up; and it supports my assertion that where a man's rights over a woman's sexuality are at stake, the Mishnah will systematically deprive the woman of her personhood.

Reserving control of divorce to the husband meets yet another need of the Mishnah's framers. They desire, above all, to maintain order in their cosmos, for order preserves sanctity whereas disorder pollutes.[98] Women cannot be allowed to destabilize the system by arbitrarily releasing themselves from the husbands who selected them. The Israelite *paterfamilias* must retain authority over his subordinates. The hybrid woman must remain divisible into her component parts of chattel and person so that the system can retain control by treating her as chattel whenever necessary.

The "Straying Wife" as the Husband's Sexual Property

Perhaps the most graphic depiction of a wife as her husband's sexual property appears in the Mishnah's elaboration of the scriptural law of jealousy (Num. 5:11–31). To understand the sages' interpretation of this law, we need to look closely at Scripture.

11. The LORD spoke to Moses, saying: 12. Speak to the Israelite people and say to them: If any man's wife has gone astray and broken faith with him 13. in that a man has had carnal relations with her unbeknown to her husband, and she keeps secret the fact that she has defiled herself without being forced, and there is no witness against her— 14. but a fit of jealousy comes over him and he is wrought up about the wife who has defiled herself; or if a fit of jealousy comes over one and he is wrought up about his wife although she has not defiled herself— 15. the man shall bring his wife to the priest. And he shall bring as an offering for her one-tenth of an ephah of barley flour. No oil shall be poured upon it and no frankincense shall be laid on it, for it is a meal offering of jealousy, a meal offering of remembrance which recalls wrongdoing. 16. The priest shall bring her forward and have her stand before the LORD. 17. The priest shall take sacral water in an earthen vessle and, taking some of the earth that is on the floor of the Tabernacle, the priest shall put it into the water. 18. After he has made the woman stand before the LORD, the priest shall loosen the hair of the woman's head and place upon her hands the meal offering of remembrance, which is a meal offering of jealousy. And in the priest's hands shall be the water of bitterness that induces the spell. 19. The priest shall adjure the woman, saying to her, "If no man has lain with you,[99] *if you have not* gone astray in defilement while under [the authority of] your husband,[100] *be immune from this water of bitterness that induces the spell. 20. But if you have gone astray* while under [the authority of] your husband *and have defiled yourself, and some man other than your husband* has placed his seed in you"[101]— *21. Here the priest shall administer the curse of adjuration to the woman, as the priest goes on to say to the woman, "may the LORD make you a curse and an imprecation among your people, as the LORD causes your thigh to sag and your belly to distend; 22. may this water that induces the spell enter your body, causing the belly to distend and the thigh to sag." And the woman shall say, "Amen, Amen!" 23. The priest shall put these curses down in writing and rub it off into the water of bitterness. 24. He is to make the woman drink the water of bitterness that induces the spell, so that the spell-inducing water may enter into her to bring on bitterness. 25. Then the priest shall take from the woman's hand the meal offering of jealousy, wave the meal offering before the LORD, and present it on the altar. 26. The priest shall scoop out of the meal offering a token part of it and turn it into smoke on the altar. Lastly, he shall make the woman drink the water. 27. Once he has made her drink the water—if she has defiled herself by breaking faith with her husband, the spell-inducing water shall enter into her to bring on bitterness, so that her belly shall distend and her thigh shall sag; and the woman shall become a curse among her people. 28. But if the woman has not defiled herself and is pure, she shall be unharmed and able to retain seed. 29. This is the ritual in cases of jealousy, when a woman goes astray while married to her husband and defiles herself, 30. or when a fit of jealousy comes over a man and he is wrought up over his wife: the woman shall be made to stand before the LORD and the priest shall carry out all this ritual with her. 31. The man shall be clear of guilt; but that woman shall suffer for her guilt.*

Num. 5:11–31 (emphasis added)

The sages devote an entire tractate, Soṭah ("The Straying Wife"), to the ritual of the ordeal. A jealous husband who suspects his wife's fidelity, but lacks the eyewitness proof needed to convict her of adultery, can subject her to an ordeal designed to protect his sexual rights. Like marriage and divorce, this is a unilateral procedure, which cannot be invoked by a wife against her husband, for although she is *his* exclusive sexual property, he is not *hers*. Scripture makes the point explicit by naming the ritual the "law of jealousy" (*torat ha-qᵉna'ot*, Num. 5:29), thus emphasizing the husband's desire to jealously guard (*q-n-'*) property he has acquired (*q-n-y*). Obviously the substitution of trial by ordeal for normal due process (conviction by the testimony of two witnesses, as required by Deut. 19:15) rides roughshod over the accused wife's personhood. Yet paradoxically, in adopting the biblical ordeal, the Mishnah's framers change its name in a way that significantly recognizes the wife as a person. In calling it the "law of the straying wife" (*parashat soṭah*, M. Soṭ. 7:1), they build in an implication of moral guilt.[102] Moral guilt is the quality of a person, not of a chattel. We can only surmise the sages' reasons here; perhaps they choose to assume the wife has, indeed, committed the suspected offense in order to lend moral justification to a barbaric procedure.

Reduced to bare essentials, the ordeal works like this: At the husband's instigation, a priest forces the suspect wife to drink a bitter potion, composed mainly of dirt from the floor of the tabernacle and supposed by a kind of sympathetic magic to produce horrible physical effects: *"Her belly shall distend and her thigh shall sag"* (Num. 5:27). This last phrase suggests that if the wife has conceived through adultery, the fetus will abort.[103] If, on the contrary, the wife is innocent, Scripture promises that *"she shall be unharmed, and able to retain seed* (Num. 5:28)—presumably meaning that if she has conceived by her husband and not by a lover, the fetus will survive.

Scripture's view of the wife's sexuality as the husband's private preserve is more than endorsed by Mishnah. The latter's insistence that the husband's property rights override the wife's personal rights is aggravated by the double standard of sexual morality that characterizes the ordeal. For the sages use the ordeal, just as Scripture prescribed it, only for a straying *wife*. No corresponding ritual exists for an errant *husband*, because Scripture and Mishnah agree that adultery can be committed only by a wife (and her lover) against a husband, not by a husband against his own wife. A married man incurs no penalty for extramarital relationships unless his mistress happens to be another man's wife. Moreover, the ordeal of the straying wife is discriminatory in another respect, it is the *only* instance of trial by ordeal and the *only* case that circumvents the normal rules of evidence that appears in either Scripture or Mishnah. The double standard of due process superimposed on the double standard of morality speaks for itself.

An interesting feature of Mishnah's elaboration of the law of the straying wife (tractate Soṭah chaps. 1 through 6) is the way it separates the wife's sexuality into two aspects. By paying bride-price the husband acquired both the sole right to intercourse with her and (still more important to the sages) the sole right to utilize her reproductive function. Though these may look like two sides of a single coin, the sages treat them as separable. Consequently, although wives who cannot become pregnant by their lovers are exempted from the ordeal, they still forfeit their marriage settlements if divorced on suspicion of adultery. Why this ambivalent approach? I believe it stems from the fact that the sages interpret the ordeal as having two distinct purposes. The main goal is to protect paternity. A literal reading of Scripture's language—*"if . . . some man other than your husband has placed his seed in you [wayyitten 'ish bak et sheᶜkobto]"* (Num. 5:20)—restricts the ordeal to women who are physically capable of conception and childbirth. But the other side of the coin—the husband's exclusive right to intercourse with his wife alluded to in the preceding verse—*"if no man has lain with you [shakab 'otak]"* (Num. 5:19)—leads the sages to penalize the exempted wife by forfeiting her marriage portion on divorce even if she could not possibly have conceived from the lover.

A. [A wife] pregnant by another man [*e.g., her previous husband who has died or divorced her*] or [a wife] nursing a child by another man [*and who during the period of gestation or lactation has married a man who now accuses her of infidelity*] do not [have to] drink. [*I.e., such women are not required to submit to the ordeal. This is because an existing state of pregnancy or (so the sages believed) lactation prevent a woman's impregnation by the suspected lover.*]

B. But [such wives] do not collect [their] marriage portion [if the husband chooses to divorce them because of his suspicions]. [*Normally, a husband divorcing his wife without proof of misconduct must pay her the sum agreed in the marriage settlement. But here, the husband can avail himself of a technicality, namely, the rule that a pregnant or nursing mother may not remarry until the child is born and/or weaned[104] and hence should not have married him. The jealous husband, who cannot put his wife to the ordeal because of the exemption at A, can use this technical excuse to divorce her without paying off her settlement.*] So holds R. Meir.

C. But sages [in general] rule that he can divorce her and remarry her after the [prescribed] time. [*The husband should divorce the wife and remarry her after the weaning period, so Maim.,* Commentary, ad loc.]

D. A barren woman, an old woman [past menopause], or any woman unable to bear children does not have to] drink [*i.e., need not undergo the ordeal*]; but [if the husband divorces such a wife on suspicion] they do not get [their] marriage portion. [*Such women, like those at A and B, forfeit their marriage settlement because they have wrongfully prevented the husband from fulfilling Scripture's command to "be fruitful and multiply" (from which no man may abstain, M. Yeb. 6:6). Thus, although the wife's barrenness precludes the jealous husband from putting her to the ordeal, his suspicions permit him to divorce her, contrary to the usual practice, without paying her off.*]

E. R. Eliezer rules that [he may not divorce her without paying her, for even though she is barren] he has the legal power to marry another woman and *be fruitful and multiply* through her. [*For Eliezer, the marriage to the woman at D was valid despite her barrenness, hence she cannot be penalized in this way.*]

F.   [But] all the other women [mentioned] must either drink [*i.e. submit to the ordeal*] or they do not collect [their] marriage portion [if their husbands divorce them on suspicion].

M. Soṭ. 4:3

Because they see the ordeal as chiefly designed to protect paternity, the sages exempt women who cannot possibly become pregnant through an illicit union (M. Soṭ. A and D). But if a husband cannot threaten his wife with the ordeal, how else can he control her sexual behavior? Without two witnesses, he cannot divorce her for adultery; yet if he divorces her without proof of fault, he must hand over her marriage portion in the normal way. The sages refuse to make this man choose between two evils: retaining a suspected wife or paying a price to be rid of her. Instead, they let him divorce her without payment (M. Soṭ. 4:3B) on the rather lame excuse that marriage with a woman who cannot be impregnated should never have taken place (M. Soṭ. 4:3D). The threatened loss of her marriage portion may ensure the wife's fidelity even where paternity is not at stake.[105]

Before leaving the straying wife, we should note a statement in M. Soṭ. 9:9 to the effect that "when adulterers became numerous, the [rite of] bitter waters ceased." The Mishnah claims that Yoḥanan b. Zakkai banned the ordeal on the basis of a proof text (Hos. 4:14) because it was unfair to subject wives to the ordeal when Israelite husbands themselves were habitually resorting to prostitutes. However, T. Soṭ. 14:2 offers a more prosaic explanation: "For the [rite of] the bitter waters is performed only in cases of suspected [but unprovable] adultery, whereas now there are many who fornicate in public [i.e., before witnesses]." In such cases the ordeal was inapplicable because a regular trial for adultery would be appropriate. Clearly at some point in Israelite history the ordeal was abandoned. One supposes it became obsolete with the destruction of the Temple in 70 C.E., which fits the claim that it was banned by Yoḥanan b. Zakkai. But we cannot judge whether M. Soṭ. 9:9 reflects merely the cessation of the practice or the sages' rejection of the ordeal in principle (particularly as many scholars regard the chapter as a postmishnaic addition to the tractate). We certainly cannot assume that it constitutes a rejection of the double standard that assigned women far less sexual freedom than men.

Wife's Vows Inimical to Conjugal Relations

Earlier, when discussing the minor daughter, we spoke of the biblical and mishnaic restrictions on a woman's right to make a religious vow. An important proof of a man's ownership of his wife's sexuality is his power to revoke some—though not all—of her religious vows. Here, the sages manipulate Scripture's provisions to suspend a wife's votary powers when her vows may impair (directly or indirectly) her husband's right to conjugal relations. We begin with Scripture:

*2. Moses spoke to the heads of the Israelite tribes, saying; This is what the LORD
has commanded: 3. If a man makes a vow to the LORD or takes an oath imposing
an obligation on himself, he shall not break his pledge; he must carry out all that
has crossed his lips. 4. If a woman makes a vow to the LORD and assumes an
obligation* while still in her father's household by reason of her youth, *5. and her
father learns of her vow or her self-imposed obligation and offers no objection, all
her vows shall stand and every self-imposed obligation shall stand. 6. But if her
father restrains her on the day he finds out, none of her vows or self-imposed
obligations shall stand; and the LORD will forgive her, since her father restrained
her. 7. If she should marry while her vow or the commitment to which she bound
herself is still in force, 8. and her husband learns of it and offers no objection on the
day he finds out, her vows shall stand and her self-imposed obligations shall stand.
9. But if her husband restrains her on the day that he learns of it, he thereby annuls
her vow which was in force or the commitment to which she bound herself; and the
LORD will forgive her.* 10. —The vow of a widow or of a divorced woman,
however, whatever she has imposed on herself, shall be binding upon her.—
11. So, too if, while in her husband's household, *she makes a vow or imposes an
obligation on herself by oath, 12. and her husband learns of it, yet offers no
objection—thus failing to restrain her—all her vows shall stand and all her self-
imposed obligations shall stand. 13. But if her husband does annul them on the
day he finds out, then nothing that has crossed her lips shall stand, whether vows
or self-imposed obligations. Her husband has annulled them, and the LORD will
forgive her.* 14. Every vow and every sworn obligation of self-denial may be upheld
by her husband or annulled by her husband. *15. If her husband offers no objection
from that day to the next, he has upheld all the vows or obligations she has
assumed: he has upheld them by offering no objection on the day he found out.
16. But if he annuls them after [the day] he finds out, he shall bear her guilt.
17. Those are the laws that the LORD enjoined upon Moses* as between a man and
his wife, *and* as between a father and his daughter while in her father's household
by reason of her youth.

Num. 30:2-17 (emphasis added)

The Mishnah, tractate *N^edarim* ("Religious Vows"), following Scripture
(Num. 6:2, 30:4) takes for granted a woman's intrinsic power to make a vow.
Israelite women, like Israelite men, may use the vow to devote objects or
their monetary value to the use of the Temple (Lev. 27:1-33), or to forgo
some personal benefit by voluntary self-denial (Num. 30:14), or to devote
themselves to God's service as Nazirites (Num. 6:1-8).[106] The right to vow
lets an individual control his or her life in meaningful ways. In mishnaic
society, where people's activities are strictly circumscribed, the religious
vow is among the few forms of self-expression available to the average
person. In conceding a woman's right to vow, the Mishnah acknowledges
both her right to this self-expression and her moral and intellectual capacity
to understand the meaning of a vow and the obligation to fulfill it. Because
this essentially cultic act takes place in the private domain, they see no
reason to debar women in principle (in striking contrast to their ban on
women's *public* performance of cultic rites discussed in chap. 6).

At the same time the Mishnah, taking its cue from Scripture, places certain restrictions on a woman's right to vow. Unlike a man's vows, which are fully binding as soon as uttered (Num. 30:3), a woman's are often revocable by the man who has jurisdiction over her. We saw earlier that a father could countermand any vow of his minor daughter (Num. 30:6); and if she was betrothed, her prospective husband had some say in the matter too (M. Ned. 10:1–4). Far more interesting, however, is the case of the wife. For when we analyze the basis and scope of a husband's control of his wife's vows as defined in the Mishnah, we find that, in effect, the sages empower a husband to revoke any vow that directly or indirectly impinges on the quality of their conjugal relations.

Scripture empowers a husband to annul any vow of his wife that qualifies as a *"vow . . . of self-denial"* (Num. 30:14)[107] *and* that affects the relationship *"between a man and his wife"* (Num. 30:17). But the sages deliberately distort the meaning of Scripture in order to produce a somewhat different limitation on the wife's freedom to vow. To see how Mishnah modifies Scripture we begin with a dispute among sages about the meaning of a *"vow . . . of self-denial"* in Num. 30:14.

A. And which are [a wife's] vows that [a husband] can annul? [Vows concerning] matters that involve self-denial.

B. [I.e., "I vow to abstain from . . . (some specified benefit)] if [ever] I bathe [again], but if I never bathe [again], [I need not abstain from . . . (such benefit)" or "I vow to abstain from . . .] if [ever] I adorn myself [again], but if I never adorn myself [again], [I need not abstain from . . .]." [*Such vows being vows of self-denial, the husband may annul them if he chooses.*]

C. [But] R. Yose rules that these are not vows of self-denial [so the husband may not annul them].

M. Ned. 11:1

A. [*continuing Yose's opinion*]—Then which are vows of self-denial?

B. [I.e., if a wife] said, "Qonam be to me the fruits of the world!"[108] the husband can annul [this vow]. [*This is because the wife's vow amounts to a hunger strike, is totally self-denying, will incapacitate her (impairing her sexual performance), and ultimately will kill her.*]

C. [But if she said] ". . . the fruits of this province," he can [easily] bring her [food] from another province [and therefore may not annul her vow]. [*Here, the wife's vow, though partially self-denying, will not produce the same results as the vow at B. In particular, it will not impair her sexual performance.*]

D. [If she said] ". . . the fruits of this stallkeeper," he may not annul [her vow];

E. but if [the husband's] food comes only from that man [*perhaps because no other convenient source of supply exists or because no one else will extend credit to the husband*], this [husband] can annul [this vow]. [*This is because otherwise he cannot feed the wife, with the same results as at B*]. So holds R. Yose.

M. Ned. 11:2

Here R. Yose (M. Ned. 11:1C, 11:2) takes Scripture literally. A husband cannot annul his wife's vow unless it is one of *total* self-denial. So long as she has not abjured all food (M. Ned. 11:2B), or unless her vow effectively prevents her husband from supplying any at all (M. Ned. 11:2D), he cannot interfere with her vow. For Yose, the fear of loss of consortium that could result from the wife's incapacitating herself by starvation lies at the heart of the husband's power to countermand the wife's self-denying vow.

The same rationale holds good for sages in general, though most interpret vows of self-denial in a slightly different way: that is, to mean those in which both the *condition* of the vow and its *substance* consist of an act of self-denial (M. Ned. 11:1B). Significantly, the mishnaic examples involve conduct (like abstention from bathing or self-adornment) that will make the wife sexually unattractive. Perhaps, indeed, these vows are motivated by her disenchantment with her husband and represent a deliberate attempt to discourage his advances. In any event the Mishnah's choice of illustrations is no accident. For the sages' agenda diverges from that of Scripture in a material particular. They deliberately conflate Scripture's two distinct conditions requiring the wife's vow to be *both "self-denying"* (Num. 30:14) *and* relevant to the relationship *"between husband and wife"* (Num. 30:17) before the husband may revoke it. The wife's *self*-denying vow, as interpreted by sages, turns into a *husband*-denying vow, namely, one that prevents or impairs the quality of conjugal relations. It is precisely this kind of vow that the Mishnah permits a husband to revoke. We see once more a familiar pattern: the arbitrary suspension of a wife's rights of personhood when the husband's sexual claim on her is at stake. She may not use her votary powers to interfere with his conjugal rights in any way.

My interpretation is supported by an explicit statement in Tosefta that indicates the primary consideration is not the self-denying character of the vow as such, but whether it affects relations between the spouses.

A.   Any matter involving self-denial, whether [concerning something] between him and her or [something] between her and others, he can annul.

B.   [But as for] a matter *involving no self-denial* [if it is] between him and her, he can annul [it], [whereas if it is] between her and others, he cannot annul [it].

T. Ned. 7:1 (emphasis added)

The Tosefta rules, in effect, that if the vow involves the husband's rights, he can annul it whether self-denying or not. This is precisely the implied stance of the Mishnah's framers, though they seem to have balked at rejecting the self-denying rule of Num. 30:14 quite as blatantly as did the authors of Tosefta.[109]

Further support for the view that the sages care about a wife's vows primarily when these may directly or indirectly impair conjugal relations appears in tractate *Nazir*, which discusses the husband's right to veto a special kind of vow made by his wife, namely, the Nazirite vow. This is a

vow of self-dedication, which Scripture explicitly permits women as well as
men to make (Num. 6:1–21). Here, too, the sages develop rules that permit
the husband to revoke his wife's Nazirite vow. Analysis discloses that the
underlying rationale once more involves the question of impairment of
conjugal relations.[110]

The scope of the husband's detriment as the criterion for annulment is
somewhat expanded in the concluding units of tractate *N^edarim*. There, the
sages establish a husband's right to revoke a wife's vow that tends to deprive
him of some benefit that would otherwise accrue to him through the
marriage, whether involving the conjugal relationship specifically or of a
more general nature.

> A.   [If a wife said to her husband]: *"Qonam!* I shall accept no benefit from my
>   father . . ."* or "from thy father, if I work for thee" [*i.e., for her husband*]
> B.   or ". . . I shall accept no benefit from thee [*i.e., neither food, clothing, nor
>   conjugal rights (Ex. 21:10)]* if I work for my father" or "thy father."
> C.   [A vow like] this [the husband] can annul.

> M. Ned. 11:11

As expressed, the vow at M. Ned. 11:11A will become binding "if" the
wife works for her husband. But a wife is bound by law to work for her
husband (M. Ket. 5:5). She must, therefore, fulfill the condition that invokes
her vow. This, in turn, will prevent her from accepting benefit from her
father or father-in-law. Not only is this vow inherently self-denying, it will
also deprive her husband of a potential economic advantage—the usufruct
of gifts made to the wife by third parties, which by law (M. Ket. 4:1; M. Ned.
11:8) would normally accrue to him. Clearly, the vow at M. Ned 11:11A
may cause the husband economic loss; hence the sages empower him to
revoke it. The vow at M. Ned. 11:11B addresses the conjugal relationship
more directly. If the wife does work for her father or father-in-law, her vow
will preclude her from receiving any benefit from her husband. This includes food, clothing, and conjugal visitation, all of which Scripture requires him to provide (Exod. 21:10, as interpreted). Not only will she
thereby prevent him from performing his divinely prescribed duties toward her, but she will also disrupt the marriage by refusing the husband's
sexual advances. Hence the sages let him revoke the vow at M. Ned 11:11B.
Once more we see how the husband's detriment, above all in matters sexual,
takes precedence over the wife's personhood.[111] (It goes without saying that
a wife has no power to revoke her husband's vows inimical to conjugal
relations; at most, should he persist, she may have a moral right to request a
divorce.)

Finally, the Mishnah records an interesting historical development in
the rules that require men to divorce wives who have taken a certain kind of
vow or oath. At first sight the cases seem unrelated, but closer scrutiny
reveals their common denominator: All three involve a wife's (possibly
deliberate) evasion of sexual contact with her husband—conduct that by law
requires him to divorce her.

A. In former times, [the sages] used to rule that three women must be divorced [lit. go forth] but collect their *ketubbah*-money:

B. She who says, "I am defiled for thee [because another man has violated me]." [*This applies to a priest's wife, who must be divorced if someone has raped her (Lev. 21:7)*];

C. [she who says] "Heaven [knows what occurs] between me and thee" [*a euphemism for the husband's impotence;*]

D. [and she who says] "I am removed from [sexual contact with all] Jews" [*thus refusing to have intercourse with her husband.*]

E. [But later] the sages reversed themselves, to rule [*as follows*],

F. lest a wife cast her eyes upon another man, and destroy [her relationship] with her husband [*by making one of the aforesaid declarations*].

G. [We rule] rather, that she who says "I am defiled for thee" must bring proof of her words.

H. [and if she says] "Heaven [knows what occurs] between me and thee," they should deal with the problem by cajoling [her] [*they beg her to put up with her husband's impotence to avoid embarrassing him*];

I. [and if she says] "I am removed from [sexual contact with all] Jews," [the husband] may annul the portion [of the vow] pertaining to himself, and she must have intercourse with him; but [let the rest of the vow stand firm so that] she may remove herself from [all other] Jews. [*I.e., should she subsequently become widowed or divorced, she may by all means choose not to remarry.*][112]

M. Ned. 11:12

These rules constitute an egregious reduction of the wife from person to chattel. The women at M. Ned 11:12B through D possess both the knowledge and the initiative to exploit loopholes that circumvent the wife's powerlessness to divorce her husband. They can virtually force their husbands to divorce them without forfeiture of marriage portion. The wife at M. Ned 11:12B knows her claim of rape will force her husband (a member of the priestly caste) to divorce her in accordance with Lev. 21:7. The wife at M. Ned 11:12C knows that the court will pressure an impotent husband to divorce his wife (if only so that some potent man can utilize her sexual function rather than wasting it). The wife at M. Ned 11:12D, claiming that before marriage she vowed to abstain from intercourse altogether, gives the husband (who cannot revoke her vows made before marriage) no choice but to divorce her (in which case, she will forfeit her marriage portion, M. Ket. 7:7, but apparently she thinks her freedom worth the financial sacrifice). All three women, then, are smart enough to manipulate the law to gain release from marriages they no longer want or possibly never desired.

Now, these vows are hardly self-denying on the *woman's* part; so a strict interpretation of Scripture would prevent the husband from revoking them. How do the Mishnah's framers handle these uppity women? They simply refuse to let a wife impede her husband's right to use her sexual function. In any case they suspect (at M. Ned. 11:12F) that these women are lying to extricate themselves from unwanted marriages in order to marry other men. So they amend the rules (M. Ned 11:12G through I) to foil the women's strategies. The woman at M. Ned. 11:12G must prove her claim of defilement by rape. The woman at M. Ned 11:12H is pressed to desist from requesting a divorce on grounds of her husband's impotence or sterility, especially since (as discussed earlier) she is not personally bound by the commandment of procreation (Gen. 1:28). The example at M. Ned 11:12I) gives particularly vivid expression to the sages' rationale; the husband can sever the wife's vow of sexual abstinence into two parts, annulling it insofar as it affects him but confirming her rejection of other men if her marriage should ever end in widowhood or divorce. Here, the husband not only asserts his sexual claims on his wife during the marriage, but by confirming her vow with respect to other men actually forecloses her from remarriage if he dies or divorces her.[113]

The sages conclude the tractate in this manner to make a specific point: They wish to underscore their view that the essence of marriage is a man's unimpeded access to his wife's sexual and reproductive function. As the husband's sexual chattel, a wife cannot be allowed to do anything that will negate the paramount purpose.[114]

Ambiguity of Status: Effect on the Wife

As noted earlier, one of the Mishnah's salient features is its framers' abhorrence of uncertainty in the classification of persons and things. The sages' tendency to ignore a woman's personhood when dealing with ownership of her sexual function is exacerbated when doubt creeps in; not only do they resolve the doubt at her expense, they also punish her in a manner that strikes us as cruel and unusual—in other words, excessive. Suppose, for instance, doubt arises about an espousal. In discussing the father who did not know to whom he had promised his daughter and the father who had married his daughter off twice and could not say which transaction occurred first, we saw the sages' reaction to a dispute about male ownership of a woman's sexuality. Her marital status must remain crystal clear at all times lest an illicit union impair the sanctity of the man or men involved; furthermore, a woman who mistakenly consummates marriage with one man while still legally bound to another counts as an adulteress (despite her innocent intent), thus rendering illegitimate any children of the second union. Consequently, the mere possibility that a woman is tied to a particular man requires a writ of divorce from the putative husband before she can marry anyone else. This rule applies even when the doubtful marriage has not yet been consummated.

A. Where a man authorized his agent to give his daughter in marriage and [meanwhile] he himself went and espoused her [to a different man]
B. if his own [disposition] came first, his act of espousal creates a [valid] espousal;
C. and if [the disposition of] his agent came first, [the agent's] act of espousal creates a [valid] espousal.
D. But if it is not known [which came first], both [of the putative husbands] must give [her] a writ of divorce;

E. or if [the two men] so desire, one may give [her] a writ and the other may consummate [with her].

F. And likewise, where a woman authorized her agent to effect her espousal and [meanwhile] she went and espoused herself [to a different man]

G. if her own [disposition] came first, her act of espousal creates a [valid] espousal;

H. and if her agent's [disposition] came first, his act of espousal creates a [valid] espousal.

I. But if it is not known [which came first], both [of the putative husbands] must give her a writ of divorce;

J. or if [the two men] so desire, one may give her a writ and the other may consummate [with her].

M. Qid. 4:9

At first glance the symmetry between the solutions at M. Qid. 4:9E and J seems to flow naturally from the similarity in circumstances; but a second look reveals that the Mishnah's framers have ignored a material distinction between the facts at M. Qid. 4:9A through E and the facts at F through J: The first case involves a minor girl, whereas the second concerns a grown woman. In the case of the girl, whose consent is not required in the first place to a marriage arranged by her father,[115] we should hardly expect her wishes to be consulted here. But (as we know from M. Qid. 2:1 and as M. Qid. 4:9 clearly assumes) a woman of full age arranges her own marriage and (except for levirate widows) cannot normally be forced to take a husband against her will. So why do the sages treat this woman exactly like the minor girl?[116] The answer lies in their overriding concern with the resolution of ambiguity. Only one man can have sexual rights over a given woman at one time, and it is essential that everyone know precisely who he is. So the sages deprive her of a right they themselves accorded her (to select her own husband), and they let the two men fight it out. (This despite the fact that the scenario makes it clear which man she herself prefers!) This classic example shows how doubt about the ownership of a woman's sexuality can suspend her normal personal rights and reduce her to a virtual chattel.

The even graver question of doubtful divorce exercises the Mishnah's framers in much the same way. A putative divorcée whose marital status is unclear, because no one knows whether she is bound by a subsisting matrimonial tie or free to remarry, loses her rights of personhood until the question of her status has been firmly resolved. In addition, however, the woman who remarries following a dubious divorce receives even harsher treatment than the woman doubtfully espoused; she loses all the matrimonial rights that would have accrued had her status been clear.

What circumstances generate doubt about whether a woman is validly divorced? First, inherent ambiguity in the divorce formula itself.

A. [If a sick man said to his wife:] "This is thy writ of divorce if I should die," [or] "This is thy writ of divorce if I should die of this [present] sickness," [or] "This is thy writ of divorce after my death," he has said nothing. [*His*

declaration has no legal effect, for it implies that the divorce is to take effect
only the moment after he dies; but in that case, his death renders his wife a
widow, after which divorce becomes impossible.]

B.   [But if he said, "This is thy writ of divorce] as of today, if I should die" [or]
      as of now, if I should die," this is a [valid] writ of divorce [*because it is*
      retrospective to a time when he was still alive].

C.   [If he said] "As of today and after my death," it is a [valid] writ and it is not a
      [valid] writ. [*"As of today" takes effect immediately; "after my death" is*
      ineffective. So the combined result is ambiguous and the wife cannot know
      whether she becomes a widow or a divorcée on his death.]

D.   [Thus,] if he dies [without a male heir], she must perform ḥaliṣah release [in
      case she is a levirate widow rather than a divorcée], and she must not
      consummate the levirate union [in case she is a divorcée rather than a
      levirate widow]. [*A man may marry his brother's widow for levirate pur-*
      poses, but he may not marry his brother's divorcée, who falls within the
      prohibition of the brother's wife (Lev. 18:16).]

E.   [If he said] "This is thy writ of divorce as of today if I die of this sickness,"
      but he recovered and went about in the marketplace, and [again] fell sick,
      and [then] died, they must size [things] up.

F.   If [it seems to have been] from the first sickness [that] he died, this is a [valid]
      writ of divorce. [*The condition that he die of this sickness has been ful-*
      filled.]

G.   But if not, it is not a [valid] writ. [*Hence on his death without male issue the*
      wife becomes a levirate widow rather than a divorcée].

                                                                      M.Giṭ. 7:3

A.   [His wife] may not remain alone with him [*after receiving the writ men-*
      tioned at M. Giṭ. 7:3B, C, or E through G] except in the presence of
      witnesses. [*This is because until the specified condition (i.e., the husband's*
      death) either occurs or fails, no one knows whether the wife was retrospec-
      tively divorced from the moment he gave her the writ. So in case he has,
      indeed, divorced her, propriety demands that they not remain alone to-
      gether.]

B.   Even a male or female slave [will suffice as a witness]

C.   except for the wife's slave woman, for the wife will be overbold before her
      slave woman. [*The presence of a slave will not deter the wife from having*
      intercourse (cf. T. Giṭ. 5:4, which claims that the presence of her minor son
      will likewise not deter her).]

D.   What is her status during those days [*between the issue of the writ and the*
      death of her husband]?

E.   R. Judah holds [that she is] as a man's wife in all matters affecting her.

F.   [But] R. Yose holds [that she is as though] divorced and not divorced [*This*
      ambivalence generates the results stated at M. Giṭ. 7:3D.]

                                                                      M. Giṭ. 7:4

    As M. Giṭ. 7:3D makes clear, the husband's motive here is to protect his
wife's freedom to remarry if he dies without male issue. Ordinarily in such
cases the widow must marry her husband's brother (Deut. 25:5–6); at any
rate she needs a release from him before she can marry someone else (Deut.
25:7–10). But the husband must take care to use the correct formula (M. Giṭ.

7:3B); otherwise his well-meaning attempt to preserve his wife's freedom of action will fail. If he merely uses the wrong formula, at least the position will be clear—if he dies without heirs, his wife becomes a levirate widow with both the advantages and drawbacks of that status. If, however, the husband uses ambiguous language (M. Giṭ. 7:3C), a disorderly situation arises at his death: Is his wife his widow or is she his divorcée? A divorcée is always free to remarry because her sexuality is at her disposal. But the levirate widow can never remarry unless released by her levir. This doubt about who owns the woman's sexuality leads the sages to deal severely with the woman; she ends by losing the rights and benefits of both statuses. On the one hand, they forbid the levir to marry her in case she is a divorcée; on the other, they require her to obtain a release, in case she is a widow. The woman's normal rights, already limited, become still more restricted. A levirate widow can at least hope that her husband's brother will either offer her the protection of levirate marraige or release her to marry at will; but the woman at hand loses both the economic protection of levirate marriage and the right of a free widow to remarry without hindrance. Worse yet, if her levir (now relieved by law of the obligation to marry her), simply defaults on the necessary ḥaliṣah release, he chains her to him for life.[117] The sages' compromise solution thus places the woman in the worst of all possible worlds.

Even where the husband has used the correct formula, a problem still remains. Unfortunately, the use of the effective formula at M. Giṭ. 7:3B, "This is thy writ of divorce *as of today*, if I should die from my present illness," makes it impossible for the wife to know until the husband either dies or recovers whether she is still his wife or has been divorced. What is the result? As long as the husband lives, the wife's entitlements fall victim to the sages' mania for correct taxonomy—the ambiguity deprives her of her normal conjugal rights (M. Giṭ. 7:4). Uncertainty whether the husband will live or die creates a nontrivial period during which no one knows whether the wife is retrospectively divorced or not. The sages' solution, by forbidding conjugal relations between the parties, deprives the wife of a valuable entitlement—without, of course, depriving the husband, who may well have other wives (and can also take unmarried concubines if he so chooses). Moreover, in the cases at M. Giṭ. 7:3C and E, where the husband lacks male heirs, the ban on intercourse actually deprives the wife of her last chance to conceive a son and thus avoid the levirate tie if the husband should die later of some other cause (M. Giṭ. 7:3F). The sages, however, simply ignore her plight, for in this context they view her as mere chattel.

A second and more common doubt afflicts the wife of a missing husband whose death cannot be proved; she is perpetually barred from remarriage by the possibility (no matter how remote) that her husband is still alive. The problem typically arises when a man undertakes a perilous journey or goes off to war and disappears without trace. Lacking eyewitnesses to his death, his wife can never remarry unless the husband previously gave her a writ of divorce conditioned on his failure to return by a stated time.[118] Once more, a husband's humane attempt to save his wife from becoming an ʿagunah (chained wife) expresses his concern for her as a person. But the sages, as always, care only about resolving ambiguities that may taint this woman's marital status. Suppose, for instance, the husband dies after sending the writ by an agent and no one can tell whether his death occurred before or after the writ reached his wife.

A. [If a man said to his agents], "If I do not return between now and twelve months' time, write and deliver a *get* to my wife." If they wrote the *get* within twelve months and delivered it after twelve months, it is not a [valid] *get*. [*The husband had conditioned both the writing and the delivery on his failure to return within twelve months.*]

B. [Or if he said], "Write and deliver a *get* to my wife if I have not returned between now and twelve months' time." If they wrote [it] within twelve months and delivered it after twelve months, it is not a valid *get* [*for the same reason as at A*].

C. [But] R. Yose holds that [a *get*] like the latter [*i.e., case B*], is a [valid] *get*. [*The writ takes effect only on delivery, by which time the condition of twelve months' absence has been fulfilled and the case at B can be construed to mean "Write a* get *now, and, if I have not returned, etc., deliver it."*]

D. If they wrote [it] after twelve months and delivered it after twelve months, and the husband [at some point] died,

E. if [delivery of] the *get* preceded the death, this is a [valid] *get* but if the death preceded [delivery of] the *get*, it is not a [valid] *get*.

F. And if it is not known [which event preceded which], this is the woman concerning whom [sages] have held that she is "[both] divorced and not divorced."

M. Giṭ. 7:9

For the most part, there is no doubt about the validity of the writs described here (ignoring R. Yose's minority opinion at M. Giṭ. 7:9C).[119] But the ambiguous case at M. Giṭ. 7:9F poses a serious problem; no one can say whether the husband died before or after delivery of the writ. Is the surviving wife a widow (assuming her husband died earlier) or a divorcée (supposing he died later)? Here, as before, the sages resolve the problem by treating the woman as "both divorced and not divorced," with the same results (M. Giṭ. 7:3D). Once again, the sages' dislike of ambiguity concerning ownership of the woman's biological function takes precedence over the woman's personal rights.[120]

Punishment of the Wife Who Remarries in Error

A related problem arises with a putative divorcée who remarries after receiving an invalid writ of divorce and with a putative widow who hears that her husband has died beyond the seas. If the latter woman remarries on the strength of witnesses' reports and her first husband later returns, she suddenly looks like the wife of two men at once. This is totally unacceptable to a system that forbids polyandry and equally intolerable because of the cultic defilement of the two men involved and the impermissible blurring of distinct categories. So what happens if a woman, reasonably but mistakenly thinking herself free, remarries following an invalid divorce or on receiving plausible reports of her husband's death? The short answer is that the sages take no account of extenuating circumstances. They refuse to exonerate a wife who has relations with another man while her sexuality belongs to a husband who is still alive and has not released her. That the wife could not possibly have realized the error makes no difference. The mistake has a devastating effect on her matrimonial entitlements, above all on her right to collect the marriage portion normally accruing to a widow or divorcée. In fact, she loses all her matrimonial rights in both marriages.

A. If [the husband or his scribe] wrote [the writ of divorce] specifying the date of] an inappropriate dynasty [*i.e., he dated the writ by a dynasty not in power at the time and place of the divorce*], [such as] the dynasty of the Medes or of the Greeks, or [if he wrote] specifying "so-and-so many years after the building of the Temple" or "after the destruction of the Temple [*these last two datings fail to specify a ruling dynasty*],

B. [or] if [the scribe] was in the East [i.e., Babylonia] and [erroneously] wrote, "in the West," or in the West [i.e., the Land of Israel] and he wrote "in the East," [the following results ensue]:

C. [The wife who remarried on the strength of the invalid *geṭ*] must leave both men. [*Her first husband must divorce her for her technical adultery, and her second "husband," now recognized as her paramour, must likewise send her away.*]

D. And she requires a writ of divorce from both men. [*She needs a writ not only from the genuine husband, but also from the spurious "husband" for the sake of appearances.*]

E. And she is not entitled to [collect] *ketubbah*-money [from either man]. (*She cannot collect from the first because her technical adultery forfeits her right to her marriage portion, and she cannot collect from the second because she was never validly married to him at all*].

F. Nor [is she entitled to] usufruct [*the accumulated interest on her property administered by the husband during the marriage*].

G. Nor [may she receive] maintenance [any longer from either man] [*because she is no longer married to the one and was never married to the other*].

H. Nor [may she receive indemnity for] depreciation [on her property]. [*This refers to property administered by the husband during marriage on condition that on divorce or widowhood she receive indemnity for any loss in value while the property remained in his hands*]

I. [She cannot claim the aforesaid entitlements] from either husband. [*She loses these rights against the first husband because the sages regard her as an adulteress. As for the second man, because she was never his legal wife, he never owed her these things in the first place.*]

J. If she has taken [any of the aforesaid entitlemments] from either man, she must restore [them, for she had no right to them].

K. And any child [of hers] by either man is illegitimate (*mamzer*). [*Any child of the second "husband" as well as any child she may bear to her first husband if she illegally returns to him on discovering her mistake will have the caste status of a* mamzer.]

L.   And neither man may incur cultic pollution on her account. [*If either man happens to be a member of the priestly caste and the woman dies, the husband may not contract cultic impurity by burying her corpse even though priests normally have a dispensation from this rule on the death of close relatives (Lev. 21:2).*]

M.   And neither man has a right to what she finds or to [the proceeds of] her labor, nor [has he the power] to annul her vows. [*Just as the woman loses her rights against both husbands, they lose their normal rights over her as wife. These, of course, are normally far fewer in number and value than the rights lost by the wife.*]

N.   If she is an Israelite's daughter, she is disqualified from [subsequent] marriage into the priestly caste. [*A member of the priestly caste may not marry a divorcée or an adulteress (Lev. 21:7).*]

O.   [If she is] a Levite's daughter, [she is disqualified] from eating tithe-food [if she returns to her father's house]. [*This penalty is imposed by the sages by analogy with (M. Giṭ. 8:5P) but, without any basis in Scripture.*]

P.   [If she is] a *kohen's* daughter [she is disqualified] from eating *t^erumah*-food (heave-offering) [should she return to live in her father's house]. [*Normally the daughter of a* kohen *who becomes widowed or divorced may return to her father's household and partake of priestly rations donated by Israelites to the priestly caste (Lev. 22:13). But this woman's "adultery" has "profaned" her father's holiness, so she loses the privilege (Lev. 21:9).*]

Q.   And her heirs [begotten] of either man cannot inherit her *k^etubbah*. [*If she dies before the two men divorce her, her children by both men lose their right to inherit her marriage portion on the father's subsequent death in the normal way (M. Ket. 4:10).*]

R.   And if either man dies [without male issue before divorcing her], his brother must release her [by *ḥaliṣah*] and may not consummate levirate union [with her]. [*i.e. if either man dies before giving the woman a writ of divorce, she is in the status of divorced-and-not divorced and subject to the same rules as the doubtful widow discussed earlier.*]

S.   If [her husband] had altered his name or her name or the name of his city or her city [in the writ of divorce], she must [likewise] leave both [*the first husband and also the second if she has remarried in error not realizing that the* geṭ *was invalid*] and all of these [foregoing] conditions [apply] to her.[121]

M. Giṭ 8:5

A.   A woman whose husband went overseas [and disappeared], and to whom [witnesses] came and said, "Your husband has died,"

B.   and who remarried, and whose husband thereafter returned,

C.   must leave both [the second spurious "husband" and the first, genuine husband]. [*See M. Giṭ. 8:5C.*]

D.   And she requires a writ of divorce from both men [*See M. Giṭ. 8:5D.*]

E.   And she is not entitled to [collect] *ketubbah*-money [from either man]. [*See M. Giṭ E*].

F.   Nor [is she entitled to] to usufruct. [*See M. Giṭ. 8:5F.*]

G.   Nor [may she receive] maintenance [any longer from either man]. [*See M. Giṭ. 8:5G.*]

H.   Nor [may she receive indemnity for] depreciation [on the wife's property administered by the husband during marriage]. [*See M. Giṭ. 8:5H*]

I. [She cannot claim the aforesaid entitlements] from either husband. [*See M. Giṭ. 8:5I.*]

J. If she has taken [any of the aforesaid entitlements] from either man, she must restore [them]. [*See M. Giṭ. 8:5J.*]

K. And any child [of hers] by either man is illegitimate (*mamzer*). [*See M. Giṭ. 8:5K.*]

L. And neither man may incur cultic pollution on her account. [*See M. Giṭ. 8:5L.*]

M. And neither man has a right to what she finds or to [the proceeds of] her labor, nor [has he the power] to annul her vows. [*See M. Giṭ. 8:5M.*]

N. If she is an Israelite's daughter, she is disqualifed from [subsequent] marriage into the priestly caste. [*See M. Giṭ. 8:5N.*]

O. [If she is] a Levite's daughter, [she is disqualified] from eating tithe-food [if she returns to her father's house]. [*See M. Giṭ. 8:5O.*]

P. [If she is] a *kohen's* daugher [she is disqualified] from eating *t^erumah*-food (heave-offering) [should she return to live in her father's house]. [*See M. Giṭ. 8:5P.*]

Q. And her heirs [begotten] of either man cannot inherit her *k^etubbah*. [*See M. Giṭ. 8:5Q.*]

R. And if either man dies [without male issue before divorcing her], his brother must release her [by *ḥaliṣah*] and may not consummate levirate union [with her]. [*See M. Giṭ. 8:5R.*]

S. [But] R. Yose [*dissenting from M. Yeb. 10:1E*] rules that her *k^etubbah* [is a lien] on her first husband's property [*because the first marriage remains valid until dissolved and the wife's honest mistake does not forfeit her right or that of her heirs to receive this money*].

T. And R. Eleazar [*dissenting from M. Yeb. 10:1M*] rules that the first [husband] has a right to what she finds, and to [the proceeds of] her handiwork, and to annul her vows [*because the first marriage remains valid until divorce and the true husband should not lose his rights in it*].

U. R. Simeon [*dissenting from M. Yeb. 10:1R*] rules that [with respect to the true husband, the rules of levirate marriage remain in force, so that] her intercourse [to consummate levirate union] or her *ḥaliṣah* release by the first husband's brother [if her returned husband now dies without male issue before divorcing her] exempts her co-wife [from levirate marriage and from *ḥaliṣah*]. [*This is so because, in Simeon's view, the first marriage remained valid, so she is a true levirate widow, and the levir's action in either marrying or releasing her exempts her co-wives by virtue of M. Yeb. 4.11*].

V. And [R. Simeon further rules that] any issue from [the returned husband, before he divorces her] is not illegitimate (*mamzer*) [despite the intervening union that she has contracted with the levir.][122] [*Again, this is because Simeon considers the first marriage valid unless and until the first husband divorces her.*]

W. And [furthermore, in Simeon's view], if she remarried without [asking] permission [of the court] [*i.e., in reliance on the testimony of two witnesses, so that the court's permission was not needed*], she is permitted to return to him [*i.e., to the first husband. Simeon would restrict the penalties listed at A through R to a wife who, having only one witness to the husband's death, sought and received the court's permission to remarry on the strength of the single witness' testimony. Even though the court gave its permission, that*]

woman (Simeon concedes) is more at fault than the woman who followed
normal procedure in waiting for the testimony of two witnesses before
remarrying. Therefore, the first woman alone must leave both husbands;
whereas, in Simeon's view, the other, less culpable woman may return to
her true husband.]

M. Yeb. 10:1

This catalogue of penalties incurred by two women who made reasonable mistakes (the one thinking herself validly divorced, the other believing
herself a widow) appalls the modern mind. How can the Mishnah's framers
inflict such severe punishment on someone who has committed no moral
wrong? It is, of course, not unreasonable that the wife in each case should
lose her matrimonial rights against the *second* man whose legal wife she
never was. But to deprive her of all these rights with respect to the *first*
husband seems excessive; after all, she was (and is, until he divorces her) his
wife. So how do we account for this?

We see here, in part, the influence of Scripture as interpreted by the
Mishnah's framers. Deuteronomy 24:1–4, as we know, forbids a man to take
back his divorced wife who was subsequently married to and then divorced
or widowed from another man. The sages simply extend Scripture to cover
the present case. In M. Giṭ. 8:5, the first husband has "divorced" his wife
(even though the divorce turns out technically invalid). She has "married"
another man (even though the marriage turns out to be spurious). The true
husband may not impair his sanctity by taking back a wife who has had
sexual relations with another man. He must now divorce her for her unwit-
ting adultery; this automatically forfeits her rights in the first marriage.[123]
In addition she is forbidden to the spurious second "husband" who must
likewise "divorce" her. The same reasoning, *mutatis mutandis*, applies to
the woman at M. Yeb. 10:1 whose husband, still alive, never even tried to
divorce her. Here, too, the penalties visited on the unfortunate wife seem
disproportionate to her mistake. This is especially true when compared
with the outcome for the "other man" in each case. The latter, acting on the
same mistake as the woman, has participated equally in the illicit "remarriage." Yet he suffers no punishment beyond the loss of the woman's wifely
duties (M. Giṭ. 8:5H; M. Yeb. 10:1H). Meanwhile, the woman loses all her
entitlements from both marriages.

Even granting that the wife's spurious "remarriage" makes her a technical adulteress, we still wonder why the sages penalize her as though she had
committed a deliberate offense. Moreover, we find a double standard operat-
ing here; if the case were reversed and a man whose wife had disappeared
took another wife, the Mishnah's tolerance of polygyny would exempt him
from any penalty at all.[124]

But there is more here than mere dependence on Scripture. These cases
actually highlight three features of the mishnaic system. First, they illustrate
what happens to women perceived primarily as sexual chattels. Because a
wife's sexuality belongs exclusively to her husband, her bestowing it—even

by mistake—on another man violates the husband's sacred right; in consequence the wife's personhood is suspended and the law treats her as chattel. Second, and perhaps more basically, the sages' passion for taxonomy spells disaster for the woman. Her ambiguous position as the apparent wife of two men at once misplaces her; to the Mishnah's framers, a misplaced woman is a misplaced *object*. They react by treating the woman who appears to be the wife of two men as though she were the wife of neither, unfairly depriving her of her rights against the true husband as well as the spurious one. Third and last, these woman have violated the Mishnah's system of holiness, which aims first, last, and always to preserve the Israelite male's sanctity, above all in his sexual relations. To have intercourse with a forbidden woman generates contamination, specifically of a kind that disqualifies a priest from serving in the Temple (M. Bek. 7:7). The sages make no allowance for the fact that this cultic pollution stems from an innocent error. They see the woman not as a person whose intentions (good or bad) might have some relevance, but merely as a polluting object. As such, no less than as sexual chattel, she loses her rights of personhood.

We close our discussion of the wife as chattel with a rule that shows how far the sages will go in ignoring a woman's personhood in case of doubt about her marital status. In deciding such cases the Mishnah's framers totally disregard the woman's own *knowledge* of her circumstances. They prefer to rely on what people in the community *believe* about her. If local gossip claims she is married, the sages deem her so; if people think she is divorced, she is treated as such. Thus, a woman's reputation in the community may determine her status along with all its attendant rights or restrictions. In what follows, the man alleged to have married or divorced the woman in question has either died or disappeared; otherwise, he himself could testify to the facts. In his absence the sages must find some other way to establish her status. People need to know whether she is a divorcée (ineligible to marry a *kohen*), or a widow (perhaps subject to a levirate tie), or the wife of a missing person (not free to remarry at all). To settle these matters the Mishnah's framers choose to rely on the woman's local reputation rather than ask the woman herself.

A. If [a woman's] reputation has gone forth in the city as "an espoused woman," she is [deemed] espoused. [*Hence she is not free to remarry if the man reputed to be her husband has disappeared without divorcing her and she may be subject to a levirate tie if he has died*].

B. [If a report circulates that] she is divorced, she is [deemed] divorced [*and hence ineligible to marry a* **kohen**].

C. [This is the rule] so long as there is no [plausible] explanation [as to how the report arose in error].

D. What [would consitute] a [plausible] explanation?

E. [For instance,] if a certain man had divorced his wife subject to some condition [that has not been fulfilled]. [*In that case she is not deemed divorced despite reports to that effect.*]

F. Or if [a man] had thrown her a token of espousal [for the purposes of

espousal by money (M. Qid.1:1) and] there was doubt [whether it fell] nearer
to her or nearer to him [*cf. the writ of divorce in M. Giṭ. 8:2; see app. 6*], this
would be a [plausible] explanation [of how the report arose that she was an
espoused woman]. [*People recall that some man performed the ceremony of
espousal, but they do not realize it was invalid because of ambiguous
delivery of the token. Here, sages do not deem the woman married despite
reports to that effect.*]

M. Giṭ. 9:9

The sages want very much to know whether this woman is wife, widow
or divorcée—yet no one thinks of asking *her*. The gossip of talebearers takes
precedence over the woman's own knowledge. Important repercussions on
her rights thus hinge on the opinion of people who may have no real access
to the facts. True, these reports may be rebutted by contrary testimony, but
this must come from competent witnesses. It cannot come from the woman
herself because, with rare exceptions (discussed in chap. 5), a woman is
incompetent to testify in mishnaic law. Either way, her own knowledge is
ignored.

This rule carries to extremes the tendency to downgrade a woman's
personhood in cases of doubt. The Mishnah's framers, eager to classify this
woman by hook or by crook, will accept the views of third parties who may
know far less than the woman herself. Usually mishnaic actors in an
ambiguous situation have at least some connection with each other, for
instance, the husband, his wife, and the "other man." But here, a woman's
right to control her life can be negated by the intervention of total strangers.

The cases discussed thus far establish a crucial fact: Whenever a wife's
sexual role or reproductive function is at stake, the sages treat her as a chattel
whose sexuality is her husband's property. Any challenge to his proprietary
right generates a knee-jerk response that subordinates the woman's normal
rights of personhood to the husband's rights of ownership. To that extent, my
analysis has supported the general assumption that patriarchal cultures treat
women as the property of men. But the whole story is not yet told.

The Wife as Person

The mishnaic system, patriarchal though it is, does not regard the wife
as the husband's chattel in all respects. The framers assign her a large
number of rights, duties, and powers of the kind that we earlier defined as
marks of legal personhood. Most important of all, a wife has a right to
maintenance by her husband, who must supply food, clothing, and rights of
conjugal cohabitation. In addition, she enjoys other valuable entitlements,
chief among them the right to recover her marriage portion if her husband
should choose to divorce her without fault on her part. Besides these tangible property rights, she possesses equally important intangible rights. Her
husband must treat her humanely in specified ways, for example, permitting her to visit her parents from time to time, to eat her favorite foods, and

to wear her favorite ornaments; otherwise he is guilty of cruelty, and must release her and pay off her marriage settlement. Still more significant for her personhood, a wife enjoys important legal powers beyond her basic human rights. Many of these powers are roughly equivalent to those of her husband: she has the capacity to appoint an agent, to function as her husband's agent or bailee, to own and dispose of property, to bring or defend a lawsuit (though generally not to testify in person). The wife's personhood emerges also from her legal duties. She must perform prescribed household and other economic tasks in return for her maintenance, and she must observe many rules of biblical and mishnaic law—particularly where her non-observance will prejudice her husband's conjugal rights or impair his cultic sanctity. Finally, many of the wife's entitlements and obligations listed in tractate *K^etubbot* ("Marriage Settlements") are formally incorporated, either in writing or by irrebuttable presumption of law, in the settlement negotiated by the bridegroom with the bride's father (or with the bride herself if she is of full age) before the marriage takes place.

Possession of such entitlements and obligations makes an important statement about the wife's status: *she is no chattel.* Otherwise the Mishnah's framers would neither have granted her those entitlements nor imposed those obligations, and her personal status would have been far closer to that of a slave or minor daughter (of whom the Mishnah clearly states that a man has no legal obligation even to feed them). The scope of a wife's rights and duties that we shall now explore constitutes the clearest proof that she possesses a measure of personhood in mishnaic society that ranks her far higher than a slave or a minor in the Israelite social scale. Moreover, the reciprocal character of a wife's rights and duties *vis-à-vis* her husband suggests that although the sages do not regard her in all respects as his legal equal, they do perceive a certain equivalence or complementarity between spouses that enhances the personhood of the wife.

The Wife's Rights in Customary Law

The status of wife carries with it certain customary rights, normally stipulated in a marriage settlement, that the court will enforce even if the husband wrote no *k^etubbah* for her, or omitted them by accident or design. These rights bear the stamp of preexisting customary law incorporated in the mishnaic system. These "conditions enjoined by the court" include the customary bride-price; the wife's lien on her husband's property for payment of her *k^etubbah* on widowhood or divorce; the husband's duty to ransom a kidnapped wife;[125] the wife's assurance that if she predeceases her husband her *k^etubbah* will pass at his death to the sons she bore him, and daughters (who cannot inherit in the presence of sons, Num. 27:8) will be maintained out of their father's estate until they marry or come of age; and, finally, her right to maintenance as her husband's widow so long as she chooses to remain in his house or until his heirs decide to pay off her marriage settlement and let her go.

A.   [Even] if he had not written a k^e*tubbah* for her, [a wife who married as] a virgin collects two hundred *zuz* and [one who married as] a widow [collects] one *maneh* (one hundred *zuz*)

B.   because this is a condition enjoined by the court.

C.   [If] he had assigned her a field worth [only] one *maneh* in place of two hundred *zuz* but had not stipulated to her, "All property that I own is charged [with a lien] for thy k^e*tubbah*-money," he is [nonetheless] liable [for the full two hundred *zuz* (cf. *M. Ket. 8:8)]*

D.   because this is a condition enjoined by the court.

M. Ket. 4:7

A.   [Even] if he had not stipulated to her, "If thou art taken captive, I shall ransom thee and restore thee as my wife,"

B.   or—for a priest's wife—"I shall [ransom thee and] send thee back to thine own province" *[Scripture (Lev. 21:7) forbids a priest to retain a wife who has been raped—the presumed fate of any kidnapped woman],*

C.   he is [nonetheless] liable [to ransom her]

D.   because this is a condition enjoined by the court.

M. Ket.4:8

A.   If she is taken captive, he must ransom her,

B.   and if he says, "Here are her *get* and her k^e*tubbah*-money, let her ransom herself," he has no right [to do this]. *[He cannot evade responsibility by availing himself of the rule (M. Git. 9:10) that permits a man to divorce his wife at will. This is because the entire obligation to ransom her accrues as soon as she is kidnapped, namely, while she is still his wife.]*

C.   If she falls ill, he must [pay to] heal her [as long as she remains his wife].

D.   [But] if [contrary to C] he says, "Lo, here are her *get* and her k^e*tubbah*-money, let her heal herself," he has the right [to do this]. *[At A and B, because she was kidnapped while married to him, the obligation to ransom her accrues at once. Hence he cannot evade this by divorcing her, for instance, by sending an agent to deliver a get to her in prison. At C and D, by contrast, her medical bills constitute an ongoing expense that is part of the maintenance a man need provide only so long as the marriage subsists. Hence, if he divorces her, he ceases to be liable for medical expenses.]*

M. Ket. 4:9

A.   [Even] if he had not stipulated to her, "The sons that thou shalt have of me shall inherit thy k^e*tubbah*-money [if I outlive thee and become thy legal heir (*M. B.B. 8:1)*], in addition to their portion [which they will inherit from me] along with their brothers [after my death],"

B.   he is [nonetheless] liable [*i.e., his estate must pay his wife's marriage portion to her sons*]

C.   because this is a condition enjoined by the court.

M. Ket. 4:10

A.   [Even if he had not stipulated to her,] "The daughters that thou shalt have of me shall remain in my house [if I die before marrying them off] and shall be maintained out of my estate until they marry husbands,"

B.   he is [nonetheless] liable [*i.e., his estate must support minor daughters[126] as described at A (see also M. B.B. 9:1) because daughters do not inherit except in the absence of sons (Num. 27:8; M. B.B. 8:2; see M. B.B. 9:7) and would therefore be left destitute but for this provision]*

C. because this is a condition enjoined by the court.

M. Ket. 4:11

A. [Even if he had not stipulated to her, "If I predecease thee,] thou shalt continue to dwell in my house and be maintained out of my estate so long as thou dost spend thy widowhood in my house,"

B. he is [nonetheless] liable [to maintain her as stated at A]

C. because this is a condition enjoined by the court.

D. Thus used the people of Jerusalem to stipulate.

E. The people of Galilee used to stipulate like the Jerusalemites;

F. but the people of Judaea used to stipulate; "[Thou shalt be thus maintained] until [my] heirs are willing to give thee thy *k^etubbah*-money." Thus, if the heirs so desire, they can pay off her *k^etubbah*-money [at any time] and dismiss her.

M. Ket. 4:12

All these laws illuminate a single principle: A wife's status automatically endows her with certain customary rights of which the husband's failure (accidental or deliberate) to observe due formalities cannot deprive her. These rights do not depend on written agreement but arise automatically from the parties' relationship.[127] Furthermore, the law forbids a husband to evade his responsibilities toward his wife by simply exercising his power to divorce her at any time for any reason. Thus a husband must ransom his kidnapped wife (M. Ket. 4:9A and B) rather than divorce her and force her to ransom herself out of her own marriage portion. In this instance the Mishnah's framers curtail the husband's normal power of divorce to prevent his frustrating the wife's customary rights. Finally, the status of wife invests her with support rights during the widowhood that she may well experience at some point (given the likely age difference between a twelve-year-old bride and a bridegroom old enough to have amassed the necessary bride-price). The sages' insistence on the absolute character of a wife's rights of status, which her husband cannot abridge, emphatically endorses her personhood.

It is highly significant that all the rights protected by M. Ket. 4:7–12 directly involve a wife's *property* entitlements: bride-price, maintenance, ransom money, marriage portion. In general the Mishnah holds property rights sacrosanct; indeed, the equilibrium of the entire system rests on that foundation.[128] This attitude prevails even when the owner is a woman, including one subject to a husband's authority.

The sages' obvious concern with protecting a wife's customary rights contrasts strangely with the cavalier manner of her treatment discussed earlier in this chapter. What accounts for the discrepancy between their respectful attitude to the wife in the laws we now discuss and the disregard for her personhood we encountered before? The answer lies in a crucial difference between the thrust of these two sets of laws. The rules treating the wife as chattel had a common denominator: all involved *the protection of a*

husband's exclusive claim on his wife's sexuality. None of the regulations
we now address involves that claim; unless the wife challenges her husband's ownership of her sexual function, the sages invariably treat her as a
person in all matters of private law.

The Wife's Right to Maintenance

Marriage carries with it reciprocal rights and duties so well known that the
k^etubbah itself merely incorporates them by allusion. One such right is the
wife's scriptural entitlement to maintenance, implicit in the statement, *"If [a
man] marries another [woman], he must not withhold from [the first one] her
food, her clothing, or her conjugal rights"* (Exod. 21:10).[129] In the traditional
k^etubbah formula (dating probably from premishnaic times),[130] the husband
promises to supply his wife's "food, clothing, and [sexual] needs."[131] As to the
first two items, the Mishnah's framers specify precisely the minimum level of
food and clothing a husband must supply. Moreover, if he fails in his duty,
the wife may support herself from the proceeds of her labor instead of handing
these over to the husband as the law generally requires.

A. One who maintains his wife at the hands of a steward must assign her not
    less than two *qabs* of wheat or four *qabs* of barley [per week.][132]
B. Said R. Yose, "It was only R. Ishmael who measured out [double] barley for
    her because he lived near Edom [where barley was more plentiful than
    wheat]."
C. And he must give her [each week] half a *qab* of pulse (legumes), and half a
    log of oil, and a *qab* of dried figs or a *maneh* of pressed fig cake.[133]
D. And if he has none [*i.e., no dried fig products*], he must furnish in their
    place fruit [of an equivalent quantity] from somewhere else [or of some
    other kind].
E. And he must give her a bed, a reed mattress, and a rush mat.[134]
F. And he must give her a cap for her head, and a girdle for her loins, and
    sandals at each appointed feast [*i.e., Passover, Weeks, and Booths*], and
    garments to the value of fifty *zuz* every year.
G. And one may not give her new [clothes] in the summer season and worn
    [clothes] in the winter (lit. rainy season); rather, he must give her fifty *zuz*-
    worth of clothes in the winter, and she may wear the worn garments in
    summer; and the rags belong to her.

                                                                    M. Ket. 5:8

A. He must give her a silver *ma^cah* for her needs [*i.e. for her minor weekly
    expenses*],[135]
B. and she may eat with him each Sabbath [i.e., Friday] night.
C. And if he does not give her a silver *ma^cah* for her needs, [the proceeds of] her
    labor belong to her [*rather than accruing to the husband in accordance
    with M. Ket. 6:1*].[136]

                                                                    M. Ket. 5:9

The sages' careful specification of the wife's maintenance rights suggests
considerable respect for her. If a husband declines to lodge his wife at his

own house (in polygynous cultures a husband often houses his wives in separate locations), he must maintain her elsewhere, supplying a specified minimum amount of food, clothing, and bedding (M. Ket 5:8A through F). In addition she is entitled to spend the Sabbath with him—an implied reference to conjugal rights—though if he has several wives, she may have to share the Sabbaths in rotation with her rivals.[137] A husband must see that his wife receives her annual clothing allowance for the winter season—when new warm clothes are most needed—rather than supplying cheaper garments in summertime and forcing her to make do with the worn rags in winter (M. Ket. 5:8G). Again, he must give her a weekly allowance for incidental expenses, granting her some freedom to buy personal items (M. Ket. 5:9A). The painstaking detail of these rules of maintenance highlights a significant difference between the position of a wife and that of a slave: The Israelite householder has no obligation to feed his slave (M. Git. 1:6),[138] so the Mishnah prescribes no minimum food allowance for slaves. The law likewise points up the difference between the status of wife and that of minor daughter; the latter, we recall, resembles a slave in lacking the right to maintenance (M. Ket. 4:6). The wife clearly is far more of a person than either daughter or slave in mishnaic society.

Highly significant here is the rule (M. Ket. 5:9C) that if the husband fails to supply pin money (and *a fortiori* maintenance), the wife may legally withhold the proceeds of her labor—cloth she has woven or yarn she has spun (M. Ket. 5:5), which normally accrues to her husband in return for her support (M. Ket. 6:1). This rule demonstrates the perceived reciprocity of the wife's duty to work for her husband and his duty to maintain her—the more so as the sages (as we shall see) spell out precisely how much cloth she must produce. This mutual arrangement, by highlighting the interdependence of the spouses, explicitly recognizes husband and wife as persons of an equivalent order though not of equal status.

The Wife's Matrimonial Duties

In defining personhood as the aggregate of an individual's legal entitlements and obligations assigned by society, we observed that the allocation of duties, no less than the conferral of rights, implies some degree of personhood. An ox has no *duty* to pull the plough, a cow no *duty* to give milk; these creatures are simply *instruments* of economic value. When it comes to the wife, by contrast, the Mishnah's framers define her duties with as much precision as her rights. They list most of the entitlements and obligations of both spouses in a single chapter (tractate K*e*tubbot, chap. 5)—a redactional arrangement that reflects the inherent reciprocity, whereby a wife's rights correspond to a husband's duties and a wife's duties to a husband's rights. Yet the sages' perception of the two spouses as commensurable entities whose mutual relationship expresses a certain equivalence, or at least complementarity, does not imply total equality. On the contrary, we find an explicit double standard that gives the husband more rights and fewer duties than the wife. This built-in inequality means that although the wife's rights and duties clearly define her as a person, her personhood always remains lower than that of her husband.

The sages spell out the nature and quantity of the wife's domestic chores and economic work load.

A. These are the tasks a wife must perform for her husband:
B. [She must] grind grain and bake and launder;
C. [she must] cook [his food] and nurse her child;
D. [she must] prepare the bed and [she must] work at [spinning and weaving] wool.
E. If she brought him [as dowry] one slave woman, she need not grind, bake, or launder [*as the slave can do these chores*];
F. [if] two, she need not cook nor nurse her child [*this assumes the second slave woman is a wet nurse*];
G. [if] three, she need not prepare his bed nor work in wool [*the third slave can take care of these tasks*];
H. [if] four, she may lounge in a chair [all day].
I. [But] R. Eliezer rules [that] even if she brought him a hundred slave women, he can compel her [to work] in wool; for idleness leads to lechery [*and he may take any steps necessary to prevent her dallying with other men*].
J. [And] R. Simeon b. Gamaliel rules [that] one who has vowed that his wife shall do no work must divorce her and give the *keᵗubbah*-money to her, for idleness leads to dull-wittedness [*and the husband's vow constitutes cruelty to the wife*].

M. Ket. 5:5

D.¹³⁹ And what [quantity of] work must she produce for him?
E. [either] five *selaᶜ*-weight of warp thread in Judaea, which equals ten *selaᶜ*-weight of warp thread in Galilee, or ten *selaᶜ*-weight of woof thread in Judaea, which equals twenty *selaᶜ*-weight in Galilee.
F. But if she is nursing a baby, one reduces her work norm and increases her food allowance.
G. To whom do these rules apply? To the poorest in Israel.
H. But with wealthy folk, all is [calculated] according to [economic] standing.

M. Ket. 5:9

These rules tell us two important things about the wife. First, she is no slave forced to perform any kind of labor at the master's whim; the sages specify both the nature and the size of her work load, which is carefully adjusted to several factors, including the wealth she brings to the marriage in the form of slave women (M. Ket. 5:5E through H) and the husband's social class (M. Ket. 5:9H). A poor woman may have to work harder than a wealthy one (judging by M. Ket. 5:5A through G—a wife lacking slaves must do the work of three!), but this does not discriminate against the wife as a *woman*, it is simply a class distinction found in any stratified society. Again, the sages allow for the special needs of a nursing mother, who gets more food although doing less work (M. Ket. 5:9F). Even a wife's psychological needs are recognized. Eliezer (M. Ket. 5:5I) would compel her to work at spinning or weaving in order to make sure she has no time for dalliance, and Simeon b. Gamaliel (M. Ket. 5:5J) would preclude a man from forbidding his wife to work, lest enforced idleness dull her wits. These rulings implicitly acknowledge that a woman, like a man, has a mind that needs to be occupied (if only with mundane tasks) as much for her psychological health as to protect the husband's interests.

Second, these rules adumbrate the importance of women in the mishnaic economy. Beyond her domestic chores, a wife is expected to occupy herself with wool production.[140] The sages hint at a division of labor between the sexes in their agricultural/pastoral society. The wife is specifically required only to process the grain and wool (tasks that can be performed in the home), but not to plant, harvest, or tend sheep. Presumably those were men's tasks. Such a division of labor between spouses suggests a view of the family as an economic unit in which husband and wife play complementary roles, he supplying the raw material for food and clothing (either by producing them himself or, if he is a merchant or artisan, by buying them from a producer), she processing them at home. This economic interdependence, like the reciprocity of rights and duties just discussed, reflects an equivalence between the roles of husband and wife necessarily implying a view of the wife as person.

At the same time the prescribed wifely duties illustrate the different quality of personhood of men and women. The wife's life is far more severely circumscribed. The duties of a woman, especially of the poorer class, leave her with little leisure or choice of how to spend her day. The poorest of husbands, by contrast, enjoys some flexibility of occupation, at least within the limits of the economy. Even in the leisured classes, the wife is virtually a prisoner in her own home; the best the sages can offer her is the right to "lounge in a chair all day" (M. Ket. 5:5H). Even the wealthiest woman is confined willy-nilly to the domestic scene.[141]

These reflections hint at an aspect of personhood not yet discussed. We here consider a woman's status only in terms of her rights and duties in the private sphere of the family. We now perceive that participation in activities of the public domain, above all in the cultural life of the mind, was not available to women. A man's world might range far beyond the home; as we shall see (M. Ket. 5:6D), a man of leisure could legally leave his family for thirty days, even against his wife's will, in order to study Torah with other men at the feet of sages. But this opportunity to enter the world of ideas was reserved to men alone.

It is highly significant that in describing women's work the sages tell us nothing of women's group cultural activities. Later we shall find that they actually forbid the formation of women's fellowships (M. Pes. 8:7).[142] If sisterhoods existed, they were ignored by the Mishnah's framers. Probably such groups were unknown and the creative life of the mind was, indeed, for men only. Thus, even though the mishnaic system clearly treats a woman as a legal person in the private domain, it never lets her operate in the public domain. We revert to this topic in chapter 6, which discusses how women's exclusion from society at large stems at least in part from male fear of female sexuality.

Reciprocity of Conjugal Rights and Duties

The reciprocal nexus of rights and duties so far described does not address the important topic of conjugal relations. When we turn from the wife's general entitlements and obligations to the conjugal relationship in particular, we are in for a surprise. With the unilateral acquisition of wives and the husband's exclusive claim on the wife's sexuality in a polygynous culture that gives her no corresponding claim on him, we naturally anticipate that the wife will be subject to conjugal *duties*, that the law will require her to submit to her husband's sexual demands—as, indeed, it does, within reason. But we hardly expect that the wife might possess conjugal *rights* whereby the law requires the husband to satisfy *her* needs too. Yet it turns out that the mishnaic rules that govern conjugal rights rest on an obscure technical term in Scripture ('onah, in Exod. 21:10), which the Mishnah's framers interpreted to mean that a husband must supply his wife not only with food and clothing, but also with regular conjugal visitation.[143] In other words, the sages treat intercourse as primarily a wife's right and a husband's duty (rather than the reverse, as in most legal systems throughout history).

The wife's scriptural right, as understood by the Mishnah's framers, combined with their own cultural image of a wife as her husband's sexual property produces an interesting reciprocity of conjugal rights and duties. The sages supply detailed guidelines for performance of the conjugal duty, which varies with the husband's occupation—the more time he spends at home, the more he must attend to his wife. But his legal duty to cohabit is matched by her corresponding duty to consent; nonperformance by either spouse incurs penalties.

A.   [As for] one who forswears sexual intercourse with his wife,

B.   the school of Shammai rules [that he may keep his vow for] two weeks.

C.   The school of Hillel rules, one week [only]. [*If the husband persists beyond these limits, his wife may petition the court to order him to release her from the marriage and hand over her marriage portion.*]

D.   Disciples [of sages] may go away to study Torah for thirty days without consent [of their wives].

E.   Laborers [may absent themselves] for one week.

F.   The [wife's] conjugal right decreed in the Torah ('onah at Exod. 21:10) [is as follows]:

G.   Unemployed husbands (lit. strollers) [must pay conjugal visits] every day; laborers, two [visits] per week; mule drivers, one [visit] per week; camel drivers, one [visit] per month; sailors, one [visit] every six months—so holds R. Eliezer. [*Scholars are not mentioned here; but D indicates that a thirty-day interval is permitted for Torah study, otherwise a wife could expect to spend the night with her husband at least once a week (M. Ket. 5:9 discussed earlier).*]

M. Ket. 5:6

A.   [As for] the wife who rebels against her husband [*i.e., a refractory wife who will not submit to intercourse*],

B.   one may deduct from her *k^{e}tubbah*-money seven *dinars* per week; R. Judah rules, seven *tropaics* (= 3.5 dinars).

C.   How long may he [continue to] deduct [for her continued refusals]? As long as her *k^{e}tubbah*-money lasts [*after which, if he so chooses, he may divorce her without paying her anything*].

D.   R. Yose rules [that] he may keep on reducing it continually; thus, if an inheritance falls to her from elsewhere, he may claim against this [too].

E.   And likewise, [with] one who rebels against his wife [*i.e., withholds intercourse from her*],

F.   one must increase her *k^{e}tubbah*-money by three *dinars* per week; R. Judah rules, three *tropaics*.

M. Ket. 5:7

The most interesting feature of these rules is that even though they deal with the sexual relationship, they do not treat the wife as mere chattel, but primarily as a person subject to reciprocal rights and obligations. Yet this is not inconsistent with the thesis I have advanced. The framers of M. Ket. 5:6–7 deal not with the wife as the husband's exclusive sexual property (a claim she does not challenge), but with the scriptural rule that (so they think) gives the wife an absolute *right* to intercourse with the husband (Exod. 21:10). The issue in M. Ket. 5:6 is not her performance of her duty to her husband but his implementation of his duty toward *her*.

At M. Ket 5:7 the sages redress the balance of M. Ket. 5:6 by insisting on the wife's corresponding duty to the husband. The reciprocal network of sexual entitlements and obligations places the spouses in a complementary relationship, though not on a precisely equal footing.[144] Moreover, the framers' perception of intercourse as a wife's *right* (M. Ket. 5:7E) and not merely her *duty* negates any view of the wife as a mere vehicle for the satisfaction of the husband's sexual needs. To the contrary, the sages emphasize her right to have him spend as much time with her as his occupation permits. Furthermore, in penalizing husband and wife alike for neglecting their marital duties, the sages indicate that the wife is no mere chattel even in the context of conjugal relations. This raises an obvious question: On what basis do the sages distinguish the present case from those we discussed earlier concerning woman's sexuality? The answer is not far to seek. The earlier cases pitted one man against another—father and husband, two suitors, husband and lover. But the case before us involves no "other man" and thus poses no threat to the husband's exclusive claim on the wife's sexual function. The refractory wife does not challenge the husband's *legal* ownership of her sexuality any more than the reluctant husband challenges her *legal* right to receive his attentions. The only issue here is the extent of the reciprocal rights and duties. This is merely a domestic squabble, to be resolved by the imposition of an *ad hoc* penalty.

Yet the personhood of the wife always remains less than that of her husband. Symbolically, the sages here establish the ultimate double standard: The fine imposed for a wife's wilful refusal is more than double that imposed on the husband (M. Ket. 5:7B and F). Tempted though we are to suggest that the discrepancy reflects the greater value of the wife's services as compared with those of the husband, the true explanation is that in penalizing the refractory wife more severely than the reluctant husband, the sages value the woman's rights (hence her personhood) below those of a man. Despite the strictures of Exod. 21:10, they maintain that the woman's sexuality, when the chips are down, really belongs to the husband.

Spouses' Rights and Duties with Respect to Divorce

Although the *legal* power to divorce resides solely in the husband, who may theoretically exercise it at any time for any reason, the Mishnah's framers also consider the *moral* right of the husband to give or the wife to receive a divorce for good cause. Bound by their interpretation of scriptural law, the sages could not actually prevent a man's divorcing his wife at whim any more than they could force him to release her. But they did set forth their view of appropriate grounds for divorce based on unacceptable conduct by either spouse.

In recognizing the wife's moral entitlement to divorce in certain cases, the sages create an interesting paradox. The notion of a wife's moral entitlement to divorce contemplates her as a person, yet the formalities discard her like a piece of property. In mandating a wife's release in certain cases, the sages can enforce her rights as a person only by urging the husband to use a procedure that treats her as chattel. So here the sages treat the wife as chattel and person at once, reminding us again of the hybrid *koy*.

Cases Entitling a Wife to Divorce with Ketubbah

Mishnah, following Scripture (Deut. 24:1), permits a husband to divorce his wife at any time for any reason (M. Git. 9:10) provided he pays off her marriage settlement. Occasionally, however, the sages go beyond Scripture and actually *require* a man to divorce his wife and hand over her marriage portion regardless of his personal wishes. The sages list three types of case in which the court will (theoretically) compel a husband to divorce his wife[145] and pay off her settlement because he has placed her in a situation unbecoming the dignity of a wife. He may have done this either by neglecting his basic obligation to maintain her, or by tormenting her with petty tyrannies that restrict her unreasonably, or by being so repulsive that no woman should have to endure him.

A basic obligation of marriage is the husband's duty to maintain his wife. In the following case the husband vows that his wife shall derive no benefit from him, including maintenance; the sages consider how long a husband may persist in this conduct before his wife becomes entitled to her release.

A.   [Concerning] one who enjoins his wife by vow[146] from deriving any benefit from him [*i.e., she must forgo her rights to food, clothing, and conjugal visitation*],

B. [if the vow was for] less than thirty days, he [may fulfill his vow, but] must appoint a steward (*parnas*) to provide for her. [*He must maintain her by proxy during the period of the vow; he cannot evade the basic obligation of maintaining his wife.*]

C. [If the vow is to persist] longer than that, he must divorce her (lit. let her go forth) and pay off her *ketubbah*.

D. R. Judah rules [that] in the case of an Israelite, [if the vow was] for one month, he may continue [the marriage], but [if] for two months, he must divorce her and pay off her *ketubbah*.

E. whereas in the case of a *kohen*'s wife, [if the vow was] for two months, he may continue [the marriage], but [if] for three months, he must divorce her and pay off her *ketubbah*. [*The difference between D and E takes account of the fact that whereas an Israelite may remarry his wife after divorcing her, Scripture forbids the* kohen *to do so in those circumstances (Lev. 21:7). Hence a longer grace period is provided in the hope that divorce may be avoided.*]

M. Ket. 7:1

These rules assert the wife's personhood in two ways: First, the Mishnah's framers protect her right to maintenance; second, they protect her dignity by appointing a steward to furnish her supplies during the thirty-day grace period (M. Ket. 7:1B). If the wife's dignity is indeed the sages' motive,[147] they concern themselves not only with her tangible entitlements, but also with her intangible right to respectful treatment, for the appointment of a proxy avoids the appearance of abandoning the wife.

A husband who exercises petty tyranny by dictating what his wife may eat or wear, by unreasonably restricting her freedom to leave the house for legitimate purposes, or by forcing her to reveal intimate bedroom secrets or perform unseemly acts, must release his wife and return her marriage portion.

A. One who enjoins his wife by vow from eating a particular kind of food[148] must divorce her and pay off her *ketubbah*.

B. R. Judah rules [that] in the case of an Israelite, [if the restriction was] for a single day, [the husband] may continue [the marriage], [but if] for two days, he must divorce her and pay off her *ketubbah*.

C. whereas in the case of a *kohen*'s wife, [if the restriction was] for two days, he may continue [the marriage], [but if] for three days, he must divorce her and pay off her *ketubbah*. [*R. Judah once more takes account of the difference between a* kohen *and an Israelite as at 7:1D and E.*]

M. Ket. 7:2

A. One who enjoins his wife by vow from adorning herself with a particular kind of adornment must divorce her and pay off her *ketubbah*.

B. R. Yose rules [that] in the case of poor women, [this rule applies only] if [the husband] set no time limit [*to the restriction because poor women are less concerned with wearing finery*],

C. whereas in the case of rich women [the rule applies if he set a time limit of more than] thirty days [*because rich women are accustomed to wear their finery all the time*].

M. Ket. 7:3

A.   [As for] one who enjoins his wife by vow from going to [visit] her father's house,

B.   in a case where [the father] is with her in the [same] city, [if the restriction was] for one month, [the husband] may continue [the marriage], but [if] for two months, he must divorce her and pay off her $k^e tubbah$.

C.   And in a case where [the father] is in another city, [if the restriction was] for one festive season, [the husband] may continue [the marriage], [but if] for three [*i.e., for the entire annual cycle of festivals*], he must divorce her and pay off her $k^e tubbah$. [*The wife at C as at B has a right to visit her parents, but because they live in a distant city, she cannot reasonably expect to visit them as frequently.*]

M. Ket. 7:4

A.   One who enjoins his wife by vow from going to a house of mourning or to a house of feasting [*when a neighbor holds such a gathering*] must divorce her and pay off her $k^e tubbah$

B.   because he closes doors against her [*barring her from legitimate social contact with other women*].

C.   But if he claims [that he acted thus] on account of another matter [*i.e., a valid reason for forbidding her, for instance, that disreputable persons will attend the gathering*], he is permitted [to preclude his wife] and need not release her from the marriage.

D.   [If] he said to her, "[I vow] that thou shalt tell so-and-so the things that thou sayest to me," or ". . . things that I say to thee," or "[I vow] that thou shalt fill [the vessel] and empty it onto the dungheap" [*possibly a euphemism for some contraceptive technique (see B. Ket. 72a)*], he must divorce her and pay off her $k^e tubbah$.

M. Ket. 7:5

These rules are clearly designed to protect the wife's dignity. A husband may not subject his wife to petty tyrannies (M. Ket. 7:2-3). The sages take account of small satisfactions that enliven a wife's circumscribed existence, and they forbid the husband to deprive her of these without just cause (M. Ket. 7:4-5). They even make allowance for class differences (at M. Ket. 7:3B and C), thereby acknowledging the individuality of the women for whom they legislate. A husband may not restrict his wife's social contacts more than is customary (M. Ket. 7:4-5). She has a right to visit her parents and to attend weddings or to comfort mourners according to custom, lest her failure to appear at such gatherings cause neighbor women to dislike or despise her.[149] The husband may not degrade his wife for his own entertainment or convenience (M. Ket. 7:5D). These rules protect the wife's right, as a human being, to make some personal choices and maintain reasonable social contacts, thereby respecting her personhood; and the sages' restraints on the husband's use of the religious vow to control his wife reflect their view of a wife's freedom of decision in all matters not affecting conjugal relations. Just as the husband cannot revoke her vows in general, he cannot force her to vow away her privileges, nor may he abjure them on her behalf.

Finally, the sages require a husband to release his wife if he suffers from an offensive condition or serious mutilation. They will compel divorce if a husband develops a serious impediment after marriage; and they do so even where the blemish preceded the marriage if it is so inimical to conjugal relations that the wife cannot reasonably be expected to put up with it. But they argue about whether the wife must endure such defects if she agreed to this before marriage or whether she may later complain that she cannot, after all, bear to live with her husband.

A. [As for] a man in whom defects arise [after his marriage], [the court] does not compel him to divorce [his wife].

B. Said Rabban Simeon b. Gamaliel, "To what [defects] does this rule apply? To minor defects: But for major defects [blinding or loss of limb (so T. Ket. 7:10)], [the court] does compel him to divorce [her].

M. Ket. 7:9

A. And who are they whom [the court] compels to divorce [their wives]:

B. one smitten with boils, or having a polypus [*a stinking tumor*], or who collects [dog droppings], [*used in leatherwork (so T. Ket. 7:11 A and B; B. Ket. 77a)*], or a coppersmith, or a tanner.

C. [Such men must release their wives] whether [those defects] existed before they married [their wives] or whether [the defects] arose after they married.

D. And concerning all of these [defects], R. Meir rules [that] even if he stipulated with her [that she marry him despite the defect], she has the legal power to say, "I thought I could take [it], but now [I find] I cannot take [it]."

E. But sages [in general] rule that [*if she had previously agreed to such a condition*], she must accept it willy-nilly,

F. except for [the case of] one smitten with boils, because [in his case] she will enervate him [*by intercourse, which will produce a feeble child (so B. Ket. 77b)*].[150]

M. Ket. 7:10

If a husband develops an offensive disease or condition that makes it unreasonable to expect the wife to remain with him against her will, the only remedy is for him to release her (M. Ket. 7:9B). The principle is clear; only the extent of its application is in dispute. How serious must the defect be before a wife can no longer reasonably be expected to put up with it? If she agreed before the marriage to tolerate an existing defect, she may have committed an error of judgment: Should she be bound by her stipulation and hence denied relief (M. Ket. 7:10D)? The mere raising of such questions, whatever their resolution, treats the wife as a person with rights and responsibilities. On the one hand, she has a right to request release from a physically unendurable tie. On the other hand, she has a responsibility to live up to her word, on which the husband relied when he married her. We note as before that even though the wife's inability to endure close contact with her husband affects conjugal relations, she has not challenged the husband's exclusive *legal* right. Therefore, just as in the earlier case of the spouses' mutual rights to conjugal relations, the sages are willing to treat the wife as a person here.

The preceding examples have two significant features in common: None involves a challenge to the husband's exclusive ownership of the wife's sexuality, and all treat the wife as a person with human rights. The first feature is what makes the second possible; it is precisely the irrelevance of the sexuality factor that lets the Mishnah's framers treat the wife as a person with a moral right to release from the marriage in these situations.

Cases in Which a Wife Forfeits Her Ketubbah

Having specified when a man must divorce his wife and pay back her marriage portion, the Mishnah's framers consider the other side of that coin. If the fault lies with the wife rather than the husband, they permit him to divorce her without paying off her marriage settlement. This rule treats the wife as equivalent to the husband. Of course, the situation lacks total equality, for a wife still cannot actually divorce an errant husband. Nonetheless, the sages distinguish his legal right to discard her *at will*—like a worn-out chattel—from his moral right to divorce her *for cause*, which contemplates her as a person. In divorce at will the wife has done nothing to merit rejection, so the husband must compensate her by returning her marriage portion, which he has been holding in trust during the marriage. In divorce for cause, by contrast, the wife has behaved badly; consequently, she should expect to be penalized by the loss of her settlement.

A husband may divorce his wife without returning her marriage portion if she transgresses Mosaic law or contravenes established norms, thus violating her duty to observe Jewish law and custom; or if she has concealed from her husband blemishes or other impediments that would have made him think twice before marrying her.

A. These women are subject to divorce (lit. go forth) without $k^e tubbah$-money:

B. She who transgresses the law of Moses and [she who violates] Jewish custom ($y^e hudit$).

C. And what constitutes [transgressing] the law of Moses?

D. If she feeds [her husband] untithed [food] [*in violation of Num. 18:21*], or if she has intercourse with him while in a state of menstrual uncleanness [*in violation of Lev. 18:19*], or if she fails to set aside dough offering [*in violation of Num. 15:18ff*], or if she makes a vow but does not fulfill [it] [*in violation of Num. 30:3*].

E. And what constitutes [violating] Jewish custom?

F. If she goes out with her hair unbound, or spins in the marketplace, or speaks with any man.

G. Abba Saul rules [that she likewise violates custom] who curses [her husband's] progenitors in his presence.

H. R. Tarphon rules [that] also the loudmouthed woman [violates custom].

I. And who is a loudmouth? [This] refers to when she speaks inside her house and her neighbors can hear her voice.

M. Ket. 7:6

A. [Concerning] one who espoused a woman of full age (*'ishshah*) on condition that she was subject to no vows and vows are found incumbent on her, she is not [validly] espoused.

B. If he consummated with her unconditionally and vows are found incumbent on her, she may be divorced (lit. go forth) without *k^etubbah*.

C. [If he espoused her] on condition that she had no blemishes and blemishes are found in her, she is not [validly] espoused.

D. If he consummated with her unconditionally and blemishes are found in her, she may be divorced without *k^etubbah*.

E. All blemishes that disqualify priests disqualify wives. [*Lev. 21:18–21 specifies blemishes that preclude a priest from offering sacrifices; the same blemishes in a woman are subject to the condition at C or lead to the penalty at D.*]

M. Ket. 7:7

Responsibilities as much as rights mark an individual as a person. A woman no less than a man must abide by the law and must keep her personal commitments, otherwise she will be liable for breach of duty just like a man. The wife must conduct herself according to Israelite laws and norms, for her failure to observe the rules will embarrass her husband and may place him in a state of sin (M. Ket. 7:6D). A wife has the same duty to preserve the husband's dignity as he to respect hers. Beyond her general obligation to observe the laws of Moses and the customs of Israel, the sages expect a woman to behave with integrity in her private transactions (M. Ket. 7:7). Thus on becoming betrothed, she must honestly disclose any impediment to her performance of the wifely role (such as a vow to abjure intercourse or a physical blemish that might preclude or impair conjugal relations). Concealment of impediments constitutes a breach of duty to her husband and she must suffer the penalty of divorce with forfeiture of settlement. These rules, incidentally, tell us that a woman, no less than a man, is expected to speak truth and avoid deception—a requirement that assumes she has the same moral and intellectual qualities as a man. We revert to this point later in discussing a woman's right to manage her own property and the sages' treatment of women's testimony (when admissible).

Betrothed Woman Entitled to Divorce: A Rare Exception

One unusual case presents in microcosm the nub of the conflict between a wife's rights as a person and her status as her husband's sexual chattel. This is the rare case of a betrothed woman whose marriage never takes place because her father cannot come up with the promised dowry. Theoretically her fiancé need neither marry nor divorce her, but can leave her in limbo for life—an extreme instance of how a man's exclusive right to a woman's sexuality (even before he has married her) can empower him to treat her like a chattel. But the Mishnah's framers record an attempt to save her from this miserable fate:

A.   [Concerning] one who promised to give [dowry-]money to his [prospective] son-in-law and then reneged on the deal [*i.e., went bankrupt or disappeared (lit. stretched out the leg, showed a clean pair of heels)*],

B.   [the prospective bride] may sit until her hair turns gray [*i.e., no one can force her fiancé either to marry her or to divorce her*].

C.   [But] Admon rules that she has the [legal] power to say, "If I myself had made the promise [and failed to fulfill it], I would [be willing to] sit until my hair turned gray, but as father promised for me, what can I do? Either consummate marriage with me or release me!"

D.   Said Rabban Gamaliel, "I concur with the words of Admon." [*Admon and Gamaliel implicitly view the woman as a person entitled to what we should call the elementary human right to marry and have a family.*][151]

M. Ket. 13:5

The anguished plea of the jilted bride speaks for itself. But Admon's ruling finds an *ad hoc* solution to a particular case that illustrates the general phenomenon we know so well: When it comes to ownership of her sexuality, mishnaic law treats woman as chattel. It takes a special dispensation to combat the injustice that can result from this basic assumption. Even then, Admon's ruling is possible only because the prospective husband has not actually consummated the marriage, that is, he has not yet performed the act that symbolizes his ownership of the woman's sexuality. In this unique instance a woman is empowered to effect dissolution of her own marriage by uttering a formula that amounts to a legal ultimatum. But this case represents the exception that proves the rule.

To recapitulate: When it comes to the rights of the spouses in the termination of marriage, the sages present two sides of a single coin. A husband who mistreats his wife is penalized by losing her and the income from her marriage settlement; a wife who is at fault loses her husband and her marriage portion. The apparent correspondence of penalties, like the reciprocity of rights and duties discussed earlier, seems to treat both spouses evenhandedly, implying equivalence in their personhood. However, this formal equality overlooks one important point: The husband always retains control of divorce procedure. The sages' insistence on leaving the husband in ultimate control frustrates their own attempts to equate the position of the spouses as far as possible. An injured husband can divorce his wife and keep her marriage portion; but a wronged wife must rely on the court's good offices to gain her rights. Divorce procedure thus enshrines a basic lack of reciprocity between the spouses. If, indeed, the wife has mistreated her husband, his right to divorce her is not unreasonable. But where the husband is the wrongdoer, it is grossly unfair that she cannot divorce him in the same way. This represents the most serious limitation placed by mishnaic law on the personhood of the wife. It belies the equivalence implied in the sages' formulation of reciprocal obligations of the spouses. Despite their best efforts to treat the wife as a person, the Mishnah's framers are defeated in the end by their interpretation of a scriptural rule that they cannot or will not circumvent. This basic contradiction underscores the ambivalence of the sages toward the personhood of the wife.

The Wife as Owner of Property

Property ownership, with the economic power it confers, is a major mark of personhood in any society. An owner of property can make various dispositions—sell the property, give it away, use it to buy other assets, and in most legal systems (though not in mishnaic law, which follows biblical rules of inheritance) bequeath or devise it by will. How does ownership of property affect the personhood of women in the mishnaic system?

Any woman of full age has the intrinsic capacity to own property. She may acquire things in many ways: by gift, by inheritance, by finding a valuable object, by selling her work product. Taking all this for granted, the sages consider a wife's right to control and dispose of her assets. An emancipated woman—whether spinster, divorcée, or widow—may do so at will, but a married woman's property is subject to restraints on alienation. This reflects the general difference between the personal status of dependent and autonomous women. An independent woman may do as she pleases, but a wife can dispose of her property only with her husband's approval and cooperation. But not all of a wife's property falls under her husband's control; this depends on the time and manner in which she acquired it.

A woman of full age (over twelve and one-half years) can not only own property,[152] but if autonomous, she may deal with it as she pleases. A wife's property acquired before marriage remains at her disposition (unless she designates it as part of her dowry, which subjects it to her husband's control for the duration of the marriage); but her property acquired after marriage automatically falls under her husband's control. The following rules reflect the sages' view of a husband's legitimate expectations concerning what his wife brings to the marriage. Some items accrue to the husband outright; some remain the wife's property, though subject to the husband's control; and some never become his property at all.

A. Anything found by a wife and [the proceeds of] her labor [accrue] to her husband;
B. and [as for] her inheritance [from her father or mother], he has usufruct during her lifetime [*but the property passes to her heirs at her death*].
C. [But damages for] indignity or disfigurement [occurring] to her [through injury inflicted by a third party] are hers.
D. R. Judah b. Bathyra [taking a different view] rules [that] when [the injury occurs] to a hidden part [of her body], two-thirds [falls] to her and one-third to him; [whereas] when [the injury occurs] to a visible part [of her body], two-thirds [falls] to him and one-third to her.
E. His [share] should be given [to him] directly; but [as for] hers, land should be bought with it, and he has the usufruct.

M. Ket. 6:1

These rules divide a wife's acquisitions during the marriage into three types: what she acquires by her own actions, what accrues to her by inheritance, and what falls to her as compensation for personal injury. The sages dispose of these items in different ways. Anything that the wife finds or earns, that is, anything that comes to her by her own act, accrues to the husband (M. Ket. 6:1A). This disposition reflects the reciprocity, discussed earlier, between the husband's duty to maintain his wife and her duty to work for him. The value of her work—whether household chores, child care, or economic product—is set off against the husband's cost of maintaining her.[153] But even so, she is better off than the minor daughter, whose earnings accrue to a father not even required to maintain her at all (M. Ket. 4:4, 4:6, discussed earlier)—a striking illustration of the contrast between the personhood of the wife and the chattel status of the daughter. The second type of property, falling to the wife by inheritance (M. Ket. 6:1B), comes to her from her family, so the sages treat it like other property brought to the marriage as dowry; the wife remains owner, but the husband manages it and collects its yield for his pains. The wife's ownership of property is an important right of personhood, but the husband's entitlement to control it places significant restraints on that right.

As for the last and most interesting item, damages for personal injuries inflicted on the wife by a third party (M. Ket. 6:1C through E), the sages record a dispute. The majority treat the wife as a person: As it is she who has suffered the embarrassment of indignity and disfigurement, she is the one who should collect damages. This points up another contrast between wife and daughter: If a man's daughter is raped, all damages, including compensation for pain, disfigurement, and indignity, accrue to the girl's father, not the girl herself (M. Ket. 3:7) because the sages view the daughter as her father's property, not as a person in her own right. Here, by contrast, they award damages for personal injury not to the husband but to the wife herself; she is her own person. (Judah b. Bathyra's view that a husband should receive most of the damages for a visible disfigurement does seem to reduce the wife to the level of a fine piece of furniture whose owner may claim compensation for the loss of its perfection. So Judah views the wife almost as chattel in this context—a comment on the sex object as status symbol. But this is a minority view, not representative of the attitude of sages in general.)

One interesting set of cases bases the husband's right to control his wife's property strictly on the time of its acquisition.

A. [Concerning] a woman to whom property fell [by inheritance or gift], before she became betrothed,
B. the school of Shammai and the school of Hillel concur that she may sell [it], or give [it] away, and [her disposition] stands.
C. [But if the property] fell to her after she became betrothed,
D. the school of Shammai rules [that] she may sell [it], but the school of Hillel rules [that] she should not sell [it]. [*Shammaites hold that property she acquires during the betrothal period does not fall under the prospective husband's authority; Hillelites take the opposite view.*]

E. [But where the betrothed woman has gone ahead and sold such property, contrary to the Hillelite ruling], both of these [schools] concur that, if she has [in fact] sold [it] or given [it] away, [her disposition] stands. [*I.e.,* **Hillelites would not give such permission** ab initio, **but if the woman has already sold the property in question, they legitimate the transaction** ex post facto.]

F. Said R. Judah, "[Sages] inquired before Rabban Gamaliel, 'As [the betrothed husband] has acquired legal rights in the woman, does he not [thereby] acquire legal rights in the property [she inherits after betrothal]?'" **[If so, how can her disposition stand?]**

G. He said to them. "Concerning after-acquired property [*i.e., property acquired by the wife after actual consummation of the marriage*], we are [already] embarrassed [*by the lack of precedent in the form of scriptural or other authority for the view that the husband has a right to control such property*],

H. and [will] you bother us with [the problem of the wife's] prior acquisitions [also]?" [*I.e., if we can find no rationalization for a husband's control of property the wife acquires after marriage, how can we possibly justify such control with respect to property she owned beforehand?*]

I. [If property] fell to a woman after she was married,

J. both of these [schools] concur that if she [then] sold [it] or gave [it] away, the husband can take [it] away from the purchasers.

K. But [as to property that fell to her] before she was married and then she was married,

L. Rabban Gamaliel rules [that] if she sold [it] or gave [it] away, [her disposition] stands.

M. Said R. Hanina b. ʿAqabya, "[Sages] inquired before Rabban Gamaliel, 'As [the husband] has acquired legal rights in the woman, does he not [thereby] acquire legal rights in the property?'"

N. He said to them, "Concerning after-acquired property, we are [already] embarrassed [see G],

O. and [will] you bother us with [the problem of] prior acquisitions [also]?"

M. Ket. 8:1

A. R. Simeon distinguishes between [one kind of] property and [another kind of] property.

B. Property known to the husband, she may not sell, and if she has sold [it] or given [it] away, [the disposition] is void;

C. property unknown to the husband, she may not sell, but if she has sold [it] or given [it] away, [the disposition] stands.

M. Ket. 8:2

The dispute here presented (M. Ket. 8:1D) is less interesting than the underlying assumption: Not only does a woman possess an intrinsic capacity to own property (based on her scriptural right to inherit if she has no brothers, Num. 27:8), but even more important, some women may do as they like with their property. All depends on the personal status of the woman. A married woman's property falls under her husband's control, but that of an unmarried woman is administered by herself alone. The power to dispose of property is worth more than the bare right of ownership and enhances the

owner's personhood accordingly. Furthermore, the willingness of the sages
to entrust a woman with the handling of property attests their recognition
of her mental and moral capacity to transact business with the same intelligence and honesty they would expect of a man.

But if a wife retains legal ownership of her property, why limit her
power to control it at all? The restriction is all the more surprising as sages
themselves note their "embarrassment" at the lack of authority for this rule
(M. Ket. 8:1G and N). The answer must be that the wife has voluntarily
surrendered her right to control the property. A woman of full age has freely
consented to marry her husband in the knowledge that this involves ceding
control of her property during the subsistence of the marriage. To reserve
her free power of alienation would defeat the husband's entitlement to the
usufruct of his wife's property (M. Ket. 4:4, discussed earlier). Most significant is the difference between a married woman and one who is merely
betrothed. The status of the married woman is clear, but the betrothed
woman occupies a transitional position between her past independence as
an emancipated woman and her future subjection to a husband's authority.
Hillelites offer a solution typical in such ambiguous cases: Just as in the
doubtful divorces earlier discussed, they treat the woman as both dependent
and independent. On the one hand, she ought not to sell property acquired
during her engagement, for her future husband has certain claims on it
(spelled out in M. Ket. 9:1, App. 7); on the other hand, if she does sell it prior
to marriage, her independence prevails and the disposition stands. In terms
of my thesis this solution is possible only because the case involves the
betrothed woman's *property* and not her *sexuality*. We may contrast the
disposition of the betrothed woman's property with the case adjudicated by
Admon (M. Ket. 13:5) which required a special dispensation to permit a
betrothed woman to bestow her sexuality elsewhere when her fiancé refused
to go ahead with the marriage.

Simeon's theory (M. Ket. 8:2) holds particular interest. His criterion for
letting a wife control her property looks not to when she acquired it, but to
whether her husband knows of it: the husband can control only those items
of whose existence he is aware. Simeon presumes that the man married this
particular woman partly in consideration of his right to usufruct. Naturally
he cannot argue this with respect to property he knows nothing about.
Furthermore, "property known to the husband" means, specifically, property the bride (a woman of full age) has chosen to entrust to him by listing it
in the marriage settlement. Thus, the husband's control depends on the
contract between husband and wife. Such an arrangement, by assuming the
woman's capacity to contract and her ability to understand the transaction,
clearly treats the wife as the husband's equal, hence a person.

A wife's property controlled by the husband cannot be alienated without
the latter's consent as this would deprive him of his right to usufruct. So the
sages take pains to spell out the procedure for selling a wife's property.
Although they endorse a husband's right to control the disposition, the
Mishnah's framers recognize the need to protect a wife whose unscrupulous

husband may force her to sell her property against her will. The procedure thus protects the rights of both spouses.

A. If [a man] bought [a wife's field] from her husband and [then] repeated [the transaction] and bought [it] from the wife, his purchase is void. [*This is because the husband, having sold his wife's field, may have subsequently coerced the wife to collaborate in the transaction.*]

B. [But if he first bought it] from the wife and [then] repeated [the transaction] and bought [it] from the husband, his purchase stands. [*Here, it is presumed that the wife desired to sell, and her husband simply approves the sale as required by law.*][154]

M. Giṭ. 5:6

Both husband and wife must cooperate in the sale of a wife's property. Both have an interest—she as owner of the principal and he as beneficiary of the usufruct. If either spouse alone were to sell the property, this would infringe on the other's interest. So it must be clear that both spouses desire to sell and, in particular, that the husband has not coerced the wife. The rules here balance the husband's right to control his wife's property against the wife's right to protection from abuse. In thus limiting the husband's authority, the sages tacitly acknowledge that a woman—even a married woman—retains legal rights and powers similar to those of a man.[155]

The net effect of the mishnaic rules that govern a wife's property is this: Any woman of full age has the capacity to own property. Marriage does not extinguish a wife's ownership, but merely holds its full exercise in abeyance; though the wife's rights are subordinated to her husband, they remain potentially intact. In other words just as a husband does not acquire the person of his wife outright, but only a carefully defined use of her body during marriage, the same is true of her property. The husband possesses, at most, the right to manage her property and enjoy its usufruct; he never acquires title to the property itself. In fact, as we shall see, the wife's property reverts to her control on widowhood or divorce, underscoring once more the connection between property ownership and personhood.[156]

The "Straying Wife" Revisited

In describing the ordeal of the straying wife, I called it "the most graphic depiction of a wife as her husband's sexual property." One would hardly expect a wife subjected to the ordeal to retain a shred of personhood. Yet it turns out that even a suspected adulteress retains significant rights as a property owner. If her husband divorces her without actual proof of misconduct, she is entitled to recover the whole of her marriage settlement. But the biblical ordeal contemplates precisely the case of a man who cannot produce eyewitnesses to the wife's adultery. Thus if he divorces his wife following the ordeal, he lacks the requisite proof to deprive her of her marriage portion. The Mishnah's framers, great respecters of private property, forbid the husband to withhold the marriage settlement without due process; he must produce witnesses.

How do the sages solve this dilemma? They modify Scripture by refusing to put a wife to the ordeal unless the husband has first warned her in the presence of witnesses that he suspects her association with a named man. This preliminary precaution permits him later to use these witnesses to divorce his wife without returning her marriage portion. In that way the denial of due process that marks the ordeal will not taint the mishnaic provisions for forfeiture of the wife's property.

A.   [Concerning a husband] who invokes [the law of] jealousy against his wife,
B.   R. Eliezer rules that he can invoke [the law of] jealousy against her [only] on the testimony of two [witnesses, who will testify that he warned her not to seclude herself with a specified man], but [thereafter] he may make her drink [the bitter potion] on the testimony of a single witness or [even] on his own testimony [that she did so seclude herself].
C.   [But] R. Joshua rules that he may invoke [the law of] jealousy against her [only] on the testimony of two [witnesses to the warning] and may [thereafter] make her drink [only] on the testimony of two [witnesses that she did so seclude herself].

                                                                    M. Soṭ. 1:1

A.   How does he invoke [the law of] jealousy against her? If he [had merely] said to her before two witnesses, "Do not speak with so-and-so!" and she spoke with [that man], she remains permitted to her husband (lit., to her house), and permitted to eat priestly rations [if she is the wife of a *kohen*].
B.   [But] if she accompanied [that man] into a secluded place and remained with him long enough for defilement [to occur], she is forbidden to her husband and [if she is the wife of a *kohen*] forbidden to eat priestly rations [until after she has survived the ordeal of the bitter potion]. [*This is because the ordeal may "prove" her adultery, in which case she will have lost her entitlement to the privileges of the priestly caste from the time at which she consorted with the other man.*]
C.   And if [her husband] died without issue [before she undergoes the ordeal, so that she becomes a levirate widow], she must perform the release procedure (*ḥaliṣah*) and may not marry her levir. [*Her doubtful status as a putative adulteress disqualifies her from marrying the levir, just as though her husband had divorced her for adultery before he died.*].

                                                                    M. Soṭ. 1:2

Mishnah's rules mitigate the harshness of Scripture in two ways: The husband must prove through witnesses that he has warned the wife of his jealousy (M. Soṭ. 1:1), and the wife's conduct after the warning must be sufficiently compromising to invoke the ordeal (M. Soṭ. 1:2). Mere conversation with the suspected paramour does not suffice, someone must have seen her go off with him. Moreover, Joshua (M. Soṭ. 1:1B and C) insists on two witnesses to the assignation (where Eliezer's reliance on the husband's word alone would largely negate the protection afforded by the requirement of a witnessed warning).

Here, we have an attempt to circumvent Scripture and place the ordeal on the same footing as other trial procedures that require two witnesses. But in so doing the sages draw an interesting distinction between the wife as sexual property (whose rights of personhood can be arbitrarily suspended) and the wife as property owner (who cannot be deprived without due process). In a rare departure from the normal practice of stating rules without explanations, the Mishnah spells out the purpose of the witness requirement.

A. And which are [the women] whom the court must warn [of the husband's jealousy]?

B. She whose husband has become deaf-mute or insane or is confined in jail [and consequently cannot warn her himself].

C. It was not for [the purpose of] forcing her to drink that [the sages] ruled thus, but for [the purpose of] forfeiting her marriage settlement [should the husband subsequently recover and divorce her]. [*Sages thus preserve the husband's right to divorce her without payment when he recovers or comes out of jail and discovers she has been playing around.*]

D. R. Yose holds that [the court's warning to the wife is intended] also to make her drink [*i.e., to subject her to the ordeal*]. When her husband comes out of jail, he can make her drink.

M. Soṭ. 4:5

Following Scripture, the Mishnah could have dispensed with the requirement of two witnesses for the ordeal. But if the wife's suspected misconduct leads the husband to divorce her, he would have to pay her marriage portion in the usual way, for lack of witnesses to her adultery. The rule of prior warning represents a compromise between preserving the husband's exclusive sexual claim and protecting the wife's rights of due process as property owner.[157] Again the sages treat the woman like the hybrid *koy*—she is chattel and person at once.

The Nazirite Vow and the Personhood of the Wife

Mishnah, following Scripture, recognizes the woman's intrinsic capacity to take a religious vow and acknowledges her capacity to understand its moral significance. That power constitutes an important expression of personhood. One special kind of vow is the Nazirite vow whereby a woman, no less than a man, can dedicate herself to the service of God in accordance with Scripture (Num. 6:1–21, as discussed by the sages in tractate *Nazir*, "Nazirites"). Self-dedication requires the votary to abstain from wine, refrain from cutting the hair, and avoid contamination by contact with dead bodies (Num. 6:3–6). Though the *nazir* is not required to abjure sexual activity, the Mishnah permits a husband to annul the wife's Nazirite vow on the ground that her shaving her head as required at the end of her period of dedication would make her physically repulsive to him (M. Naz. 4:5) and also because Nazirites tended to abstain from intercourse to avoid the temporary pollution this causes.[158]

The sages consider what happens to a wife who breaks her Nazirite vow when, unknown to her, her husband has already revoked it, so that she incurs no legal liability.

A.   A woman who vowed to become a Nazirite and then went and drank wine or
     defiled herself [by contact] with dead bodies [thus breaking her vow], incurs
     the forty [stripes] [*the penalty for transgressing a scriptural prohibition
     (M. Mak. 3:4)*].

B.   [But] if her husband had annulled her vow and she did not know that her
     husband had annulled her vow and she went and drank wine or defiled
     herself [by contact] with dead bodies, she does not incur the forty [stripes].
     [*This is because her vow was no longer in force when she "broke" it.*]

C.   [However,] R. Judah rules that [even] though she does not incur the forty
     [stripes for breaking the vow], she does incur stripes for rebellion. [*A person
     who acts with intent to violate a scriptural injunction incurs a rabbinical
     penalty for rebellion against God's laws.*]

                                                                    M. Naz. 4:3

Two points are of interest here. First, the woman who breaks a binding
Nazirite vow suffers the same penalty as a man in similar circumstances.
This reminds us that the force of a woman's obligation to observe biblical
precepts is considered equal to that of a man (cf. M. Qid. 1:7, discussed in
chap. 6). Second, we have the implied dispute at M. Naz. 4:3B and C. If the
woman's husband has annulled her vow, all agree that she escapes the legal
penalty as the vow is no longer in force. Nor will sages in general (M. Naz.
4:3B) hold the woman liable for the intention to violate her vow even
though she has committed the very act that would have constituted the
violation. But Judah (at M. Naz. 4:8C) thinks that she ought to suffer for her
moral lapse. Judah's view implicitly treats a woman as a person in matters
of moral responsibility; both her actions and her intentions, that is, her
mental processes, have for him the same value as those of a man.

A final comment on the personhood of a wife emerges from the following rules in which the sages explicitly compare and contrast the legal status
of a wife with that of a gentile or slave.

A.   Gentiles have no [power of self-dedication by a] Nazirite vow [*because the
     wording of Num. 6:1-2 seems to limit that power to Israelites alone*].

B.   Women and [Israelite] bondmen have [power of self-dedication by] a Nazi-
     rite vow. [*Num. 6:2 expressly mentions a woman; the bondman's power
     derives from his Israelite birth.*]

C.   [On the one hand, the Nazirite law is applied] more strictly to women than
     to bondmen, for [a man] may compel his bondman [to break a vow],
     whereas he may not compel his wife [to break her vow]. [*However, he can
     simply revoke it, as at D.*]

D.   [On the other hand, the Nazirite law is applied] more strictly to bondmen
     than to women, for [a man] can annul the vows of his wife, whereas he
     cannot annul the vows of his bondman. [*Scripture provides for the former
     procedure (Num. 30:11-16), but not for the latter. But, as we just saw,
     Mishnah's framers permit the master simply to force the bondman to break
     his vow.*]

E.   If a man annulled [the Nazirite vow] of his wife, he has annulled it perman-
     ently. [*Therefore, if she becomes emancipated by widowhood or divorce, the
     vow does not revive.*]

F.   [But] if he [purported to] annul [the Nazirite vow] of his bondman [thus preventing his bondman from performing it], if [the bondman] is [subsequently] set free, he must fulfill his Nazirite vow. [*The vow remains in force, and by freeing the slave, the master has given up his legal power to force compliance with the master's will.*]

G.   If [the bondman] has left his [master's] presence, R. Meir rules that he may not drink [*i.e., he must abstain in accordance with his vow because the master can compel him only when he is physically present*], whereas R. Yose rules that he must drink [*i.e., his master's right of compulsion persists even when the master is not physically present*].

M. Naz. 9:1

These rules capture the ambivalence of a woman's status in mishnaic society. On the one hand, she enjoys more personhood than a gentile freeman, for she has something he lacks, namely the power of an Israelite to dedicate herself to God by taking a Nazirite vow. On the other hand, a wife has less personhood than an Israelite bondman; for Mishnah (following Scripture) expressly permits a man to annul his wife's Nazirite vow, whereas no one can revoke the vow of a male Israelite. However, Mishnah goes beyond Scripture in letting a master force his bondman to break the vow that the master cannot revoke; thus he can compel his bondman in ways that he cannot compel his wife. In the final result the sages virtually equate the wife and the bondman in holding that the Nazirite vow of either can somehow be negated if inimical to the interests of the husband/master.

Here, we have an exercise in juggling the many factors that affect an individual's level of personhood in Israelite society: race, sex, marital status, and autonomy. An Israelite woman inherently ranks higher than a gentile man, who stands completely outside the society; a freeman or autonomous woman ranks higher than a married woman or slave. But a male Israelite slave possesses more *potential* personhood than a wife, as will at once appear if slave and wife become emancipated (he by manumission and she by widowhood or divorce). For the slave's Nazirite vow will remain in force; no man, not even his master, could effectively revoke it. But the wife's vow does not revive, for her husband's power of annulment has obliterated it. Within Israelite society, then, maleness in the last analysis carries the most weight among the factors that determine an individual's level of personhood. We shall return to this topic in chapter 6, when we discuss the ultimate limitations of gender on a woman's personhood in mishnaic society.

Summary

Let us now summarize the wife's position as chattel in some contexts and as person in others. When a wife's sexuality is uppermost in the minds of the Mishnah's framers, they treat her not as a person, but as a chattel—a valuable object whose biological function belongs exclusively to her husband. As chattel, she plays little or no part in the formalities of her acquisition as wife, and divorce likewise takes the form of unilateral release at the husband's option. The husband can revoke a wife's vows inimical to conjugal relations. Mere suspicion that a wife has bestowed her sexual favors on another man suspends her normal rights of due process and invokes the ordeal. Whereas the suspected adulteress loses important personal protections, the proven adulteress (including a woman who forms an illicit union with another man in the reasonable belief that she is widowed or divorced) loses valuable property rights by forfeiting both marriage portions when the mistake is discovered. In all of the foregoing cases, the wife's personhood is held in abeyance because her value as sex object and brood mare reduces her to virtual chattel.

We also demonstrated the corollary: In nonsexual contexts the sages endow the wife with a high degree of personhood. She participates in the reciprocal nexus of rights and duties incidental to her wifely status. As a person in mishnaic society, the wife possesses valuable property rights, both tangible and intangible, set forth in her marriage settlement or granted by customary law. Even in the context of conjugal relations, so long as the case poses no challenge to the husband's exclusive rights over her sexuality, the Mishnah treats her as a person. In the law of divorce the sages distinguish between the formalities, which treat the wife as chattel, and the substance of the matter, in which husband and wife alike may have a moral right to terminate the marriage—a clear equation of the spouses as persons. She may freely make religious vows that do not impair conjugal relations. But perhaps the most significant mark of a wife's personhood lies in the legal protection she enjoys as property owner. Here, the paradigmatic case is that of the wife suspected of infidelity, who as sexual chattel can be put to a barbaric ordeal without evidentiary proof, but as owner of a valuable marriage settlement cannot be deprived of her property without due process. Finally, the sages affirm the wife's personhood by pointing out that the system assigns her rights and powers denied to the non-Israelite male. The wife, unlike the gentile, is an outsider who despite her limitations, possesses a defined status within Israelite society.

4

THE LEVIRATE WIDOW

The third kind of dependent woman in the mishnaic system is the levirate widow. When a woman's husband dies without male issue, Scripture requires her to marry her husband's brother in the hope that the union will produce a surrogate son and heir to the dead brother, so that his name *"may not be blotted out in Israel"* (Deut. 25:6). This consideration is so compelling as to override Scripture's explicit directive forbidding a man in normal circumstances to marry his brother's widow (Lev. 18:16).[159] Like the minor daughter and the wife, then, the levirate widow is defined by her relationship to a man who has an exclusive claim on her biological function; and, as with those other women, the sexuality factor diminishes her personhood. For just as the daughter's sexuality belongs to her father and the wife's to her husband, so the levirate widow is the sexual property of the levir; and, as with the first two women, the levirate widow's potential as a brood mare reduces her to the status of chattel when this function is paramount in the minds of the sages.

However, the levirate widow differs from other dependent women in one respect. Whereas the daughter was born into dependency and the wife (or her father on her behalf if she is a minor) accepts dependency when she enters a marriage, the levirate widow's situation results not from human action but from the operation of divine law; her dependency arises automatically on her husband's death without heirs. The levirate widow's position is anomalous: Most widows enjoy autonomy and a considerable degree of personhood, but the husband's death without heirs turns the widow into a sexual chattel inherited by the levir along with the deceased's estate. In the

97

Mishnah an interplay of conflicting factors is reflected in rules that treat the levirate widow sometimes as chattel and sometimes as person, depending on context.

The Scriptural Law of the Levirate

The rules of tractate Y^ebamot ("Levirate Widows") elaborate the scriptural levirate law, which is crucial to the system of holiness embodied in the mishnaic rules of marriage. The eligibility of the levirate widow (y^ebamah) to remarry in accordance with Scripture turns mainly on whether the levir ($yabam$) has released his sister-in-law from the automatic marriage bond to him.[160]

To understand the status of the levirate widow, we must begin with Scripture:

> 5. *When brothers dwell together and one of them dies and leaves no son, the wife of the deceased shall not be married to a stranger, outside the family.* Her husband's brother shall unite with her and take her as his wife, *performing the levir's duty. 6. The first son that she bears shall be accounted to the dead man,* that his name may not be blotted out in Israel. 7. *But if the man does not want to marry his brother's widow, his brother's widow shall appear before the elders in the gate and declare, "My husband's brother refuses to establish a name in Israel for his brother; he will not perform the duty of a levir." 8. The elders of his town shall summon him and talk to him.* If he insists, saying, "I do not choose to marry her," 9. *his brother's widow shall go up to him in the presence of the elders,* pull the sandal off his foot, *spit in his face, and make this declaration: Thus shall be done to the man who will not build up his brother's house!"* 10. *And he shall go in Israel by the name of "the family of the unsandaled one."*

Deut. 25:5–10
(emphasis added)

The thrust of the law is clear enough. The brother of a man who dies without male issue has a legal duty to marry the widow in the hope of producing a posthumous heir for the deceased.[161] But if he declines to shoulder that responsibility, Scripture thoughtfully provides a procedure for evading the law. The levir (husband's brother)[162] takes part in a special ceremony to release the brother's widow from the levirate bond known as *ziqqah* ("attachment," from a root meaning "shackled" or "chained"). This ritual is called *ḥaliṣah* ("release"), from the Hebrew term used in Deut. 25:9 meaning to "pull off" or "loosen" the sandal—the symbolic act whereby the widow gains her freedom.

The biblical levirate law incorporates two conflicting views of the personhood of women. On the face of it, the law treats the levirate widow as property in three ways. First, she falls automatically to her husband's brother, who as nearest agnatic kinsman is the deceased's legal heir.[163] That the levir actually *inherits* his brother's widow is clear from the automatic formation of the bond on the brother's death. Unlike marriage, this bond requires no act of betrothal or espousal by the levir; and should he reject the union, his mere refusal to consummate it does not suffice to free the widow. She must be released by *ḥaliṣah*—in effect a form of divorce.[164] Second, the levirate law treats the widow as chattel by viewing her as a potential brood mare who may still produce an heir for her dead husband by accepting the levir as a surrogate stud. Third, throughout the entire process, the levirate widow has no option but to comply with the will of the levir; as his chattel, her normal personhood is held in abeyance.

Yet if the levir decides to release her, the procedure involves a curious reversal: The rite of release treats the levirate widow very much as a person. It is she and not the levir who plays the *active* role. She, not he, initiates the ritual by publicizing his refusal to marry her. Still more surprising, it is she who actually performs the ceremony, drawing off the levir's shoe, spitting in his face, and declaring his shameful refusal to build up his brother's house.[165] This ceremony, adopted in minute detail by the Mishnah's framers, (and still required by Jewish law before a *yᵉbamah* may remarry),[166] affords a striking contrast to the mishnaic rites of marriage and divorce discussed earlier. There, the man played the active role, the woman a passive role. Here, the woman takes the initiative in a rite expressing communal outrage at the levir's antisocial behavior. The sages, like the Deuteronomist, cast the widow as spokesperson for the community. In so doing, they endorse Scripture's dichotomous perception of the widow's personhood, for the levirate widow appears as chattel and person at once, reminding us once more of the hybrid *koy*. I shall show later how this apparent anomaly fits my analysis of the sexuality factor.

The levirate law, when implemented rather than evaded, may have had significant social value in ancient Israel. Moreover, as one scholar has argued, it may be viewed as removing an anomaly—a barren widow of childbearing age—because it restores her to a normal place in society while helping to maintain the stability and order of Israelite social structure.[167] One could equally argue, of course, that when the levir rejects the union, the release produces a restitutive effect by restoring the woman's normal eligibility for remarriage like any widow or divorcée.

The Levirate Widow as Chattel

Following Scripture, the levirate widow is transferred to her husband's brother in the hope that he may engender a son to perpetuate the dead man's name. But the levir consummates the union, or releases the widow, at his option; the woman has no say in the matter. In this context the man is a person and the woman is his sexual property, to be retained or discarded at will, as in the law of divorce.

The chattel status of the levirate widow is borne out even more clearly by the fact that levirate union differs from marriage in dispensing with the marriage ceremony of *qiddushin*. The levir need not recite the formula, "Lo, thou art espoused to me according to the law of Moses and [the law of] Israel" as required in regular marriage, because the transfer of rights over the widow occurs automatically by operation of the laws of inheritance.

In exploring the ramifications of the levirate law, we find the sages not content merely to adopt Scripture's general purpose. They elaborate the law in ways that reflect peculiarly mishnaic concerns. But female sexuality as an object for male exploitation clearly underpins their modifications, all of which address some man's right, actual or potential, to acquire a particular woman as his sexual property.

Mishnaic Expansion of the Levirate Law

The Mishnah's framers expand the levirate law in ways that aggravate the status of woman as property. In setting out the rules for levirate marriage and release, Scripture spoke of only *one* surviving brother; but the sages extend the law's application to all brothers, substantially reducing the likelihood of the widow's release.

A. The duty of levirate union [rests first] on the eldest [surviving brother].
B. [If] he does not wish [to marry the widow], the duty devolves (lit. they go around) on each brother [in turn].
C. If [all the brothers] decline [to marry her], the duty reverts (lit. they go back) to the eldest, and they say to him, "The duty is yours—either release [her] or consummate [with her]."

M. Yeb. 4:5

Because Deuteronomy mentioned only the deceased's brother (in the singular), the Mishnah could have chosen to limit the impact of the law by applying the rule literally to one brother alone. Should he reject the widow, he would simply submit to *ḥaliṣah* as provided by Scripture, thus releasing the woman to remarry at will (or not at all if she so chooses). By granting her the most freedom compatible with Scripture, sages could have respected the woman's personhood as far as possible. Instead, they adopt an interpretation far more restrictive of the widow by imposing the levirate duty, and with it the power to compel the widow, on all survivors in turn. This maximalist interpretation cares more for the personhood of the dead man (as expressed in the persistent attempt to secure him a surrogate son) than for the living woman's freedom to control her life.

These constraints on the levirate widow contrast starkly with the freedom of widows in general to control their own sexual choices. What accounts for this difference? An answer suggests itself. Like the daughter and the wife, the levirate widow is sexual property; she is indispensable to the production of a surrogate son for the deceased. A normal widow by definition has already produced the desired son and is no longer needed for reproductive purposes. Instead, she becomes a liability to the heirs, who must by law maintain her as long as she chooses to remain in the matrimonial home (M. Ket. 4:12; see p. 73). So the sages have no reason to restrict a normal widow's freedom—on the contrary, the sooner she leaves home, the better for all concerned. This difference between the levirate widow, an *asset* to her husband's heirs, and the normal widow, a *liability* to those same heirs, explains the sages' strict control of the former as opposed to the latter. My argument is buttressed by the fact that the Mishnah's framers specifically exempt a sterile woman from the obligation of levirate marriage (M. Yeb. 8:5); useless for the prescribed purpose, she may go her way.

Another facet of the levirate widow as property appears in the rule that the brother who unites with her acquires title to his dead brother's entire estate. Only if all brothers reject her and the eldest releases her is the estate shared out among the brothers according to the normal rules of inheritance (Num. 27:9).

A.   [Concerning] one who releases his brother's widow [from levirate marriage], he becomes equivalent to the surviving brothers [with respect] to inheritance. [*He remains entitled only to his normal share of the dead brother's estate, which passes to the surviving brothers in the absence of issue.*]

B.   However, if there is a father [still living], the estate falls to the father [of the dead and surviving brothers]. [*This accords with M. B.B. 8:2, though Scripture does not specify that the deceased's father precedes his brothers in the line of succession (Num. 27:8ff.).*]

C.   [But] one who consummates levirate marriage with his brother's widow [thereby] acquires the legal right to the [entire] estate of his brother.[168]

M. Yeb. 4:7

In linking the disposition of the deceased brother's estate to the inheriting of his widow, the sages clearly treat her as a form of property. We learned (at M. Yeb. 4:5) that the brothers inherit the widow collectively, just as they jointly inherit the dead brother's estate (Num. 27:9). However, as Scripture and Mishnah forbid polyandry, only one brother can actually take the woman. The brother who fulfills the duty of *yibbum* is rewarded with the entire estate; the property goes with the widow and the widow with the property. Furthermore, the passing of the estate to the deceased's male agnates highlights the fact that a widow lacks the right of inheritance even where there are no children. If perceived as a person, she would surely inherit at least a portion of her husband's estate in the absence of lineal descendants; instead, we find her lumped together with the property and forming part of the estate. We have here yet another double standard; though a wife never inherits from her husband, a husband may inherit from his wife (M. B.B. 8:1)—and this despite the lack of any scriptural basis for that rule, an innovation of the Mishnah's framers.

The character of levirate widows as property appears likewise in the rule that if several brothers die without male issue, each leaving a widow, any surviving brother may take *all* the widows if he so chooses and those ahead of him have rejected them.

A.   [If] four brothers had married four women, and they [the four brothers] died [without male issue],

B.   if the eldest among [the surviving brothers] desires to perform the levirate duty with them all [*i.e., with all the widows*], the legal right is his.[169]

M. Yeb. 4:11

Each brother in turn enjoys an exclusive right to take *all* the widows even though the levirate purpose would probably be better served by distributing them among the surviving brothers (some of whom may be more fertile than others). To match each widow with one levir would also be more humane, for it would avoid turning four matrons from different households into rivals in a single home. Yet the sages choose to treat these widows not as individuals but as a generic class because (like a herd of cows) all serve an identical purpose.[170]

Control of a Levirate Widow's Property

The rules governing a levirate widow's property pending her union with the levir recognize the ambivalence of her position. How close is her link to a levir who has not yet decided whether to take or release her? If he decides to take her, he also acquires the right to control her marriage settlement until he himself dies, at which time she collects it like a normal widow (or it goes to her sons if she predeceases the levir, by virtue of M. Ket. 4:10; see p. 72). But how much control may the undecided levir exercise over her marriage portion or her after-acquired property (both of which reverted to her on her husband's death)? The Mishnah's framers consider whether a levirate widow can validly dispose of her property while awaiting her levir's decision, as well as who inherits her property if she dies before consummation.

A.   [Concerning] a widow awaiting the levir [who has not yet claimed her], to whom there fell an inheritance,

B.   the school of Shammai and the school of Hillel concur that she may sell [her inheritance] or give it away and [the transaction] stands. [*Here all the sages analogize the tied levirate widow to the betrothed woman in M. Ket. 8:1, whose disposition of her property was likewise valid.*]

C.   [But] if she died [while awaiting levirate marriage], what should one do with her $k^e tubbah$-money [from her deceased husband] and with property that comes in and goes out with her [*i.e., her dowry from her father, which reverts to her estate upon her death*]? [*The property listed in C, unlike the inheritance at A, was "tied" to the levir, that is to say, it would have passed automatically to the levir had he married her. But what happens if she dies before he consummates the union?*]

D.   The school of Shammai rules [that] the heirs of her [deceased] husband share [equally] with the heirs of her [deceased] father.

E.   But the school of Hillel rules [as follows], the property [goes] according to the [original] title; [namely], the $k^e tubbah$-money [from the deceased husband] falls to the heirs of the [deceased] husband and the property that comes in and goes out with her [which she brought from her father's house] falls to the heirs of the father.

M. Yeb. 4:3

A. But if [the levir] had consummated with her [*i.e., with the levirate widow*], she [counts] as his wife in every respect, except that her k^e*tubbah* [is a lien] on the property of her first husband. [*If her levir, after marrying her, predeceased her, her* k^{e}tubbah-*money comes from the first husband's property, not that of the second*].

M. Yeb. 4:4

The disposition of the waiting widow's property depends on whether she is her own mistress or subject to some man's authority—if the latter, which man? This widow (M. Yeb. 4:3 A and B) is not yet under the levir's full control, so she can dispose of her own property like any independent widow or other woman of full age, including a betrothed woman (see M. Ket. 8:1, p. 89, and M. Ket 9:1, app. 7). But if she dies before consummation, a different question arises: Who inherits her settlement from the prior marriage? Normally a wife's property reverts to her on her husband's death. But here the property remains in limbo, as her levirate status keeps it in the husband's family pending the levir's decision. Had the latter claimed her, he would have inherited everything if she predeceased him without heirs (M. B.B. 8:1); had he released her, her own family would have inherited everything in the same way. But if she dies before he marries or releases her, where do matters stand?

Here the sages view the y^e*bamah* purely in terms of men's proprietary claims on her: Is she more closely connected to the family of her dead husband or to her own family (i.e., her father and his heirs)? If she is reckoned in her husband's family (because her levir did not actually reject her before she died and may have intended to claim her), her marriage portion and other property would remain in the family of the husband and at her death would devolve on his heirs (in this case, the levir and his brothers). If she is deemed an independent widow (the levir who had not claimed her may have intended to release her), her property would become hers outright and, hence, descend to her own family (her father's heirs). In this equivocal situation, both Hillelites and Shammaites (each using a different formula) divide the loot between the two families. But all agree that the woman must be defined with reference to some man or other in order to determine the descent of her property.

The resolution of this question highlights a basic disparity between the rules of inheritance for women and for men. Had this childless woman died first, her husband would have inherited all her property (M. B.B. 8:1) and on his later demise without issue, it would have passed automatically to his brothers in accordance with the law of agnatic succession (Num. 27:9). The question of its going to his late wife's family would never have arisen. Yet in the converse case, where the childless husband predeceases the wife, he rules her even from the grave, preventing her family from inheriting her *ketubbah*-money (in the Hillelite view) or half the total property (in the Shammaite view). This discrepancy demonstrates that a woman is always defined with respect to her husband, whereas the reverse is never the case.

Annulment of a Levirate Widow's Vows

Our earlier discussion of the vows of a daughter or wife showed how the power of revocation belonged to father or husband, respectively (though a husband could revoke only vows affecting the conjugal relationship). The Mishnah's framers now consider the special case of the levirate widow. Does her levir (or levirs, if more than one man is eligible in principle) exercise control over her vows? If so, we see yet another contrast between the freedom of the autonomous widow, whose vows no man controls (Num. 30:10), and the shackles of the levirate widow. On the sages' interpretation of Scripture, the levirate widow is tied equally to all of her husband's brothers until one of them actually consummates the union or releases her. The question whether any single levir (even one who has actually bespoken the widow) can have sole control of her vows, when all levirs actually have equal rights in her, generates a three-way dispute.

A.　[As for] a woman awaiting the levir [*i.e., waiting for him to consummate the union*],

B.　whether [there exist] one levir or two levirs, R. Eliezer rules that [a levir who has bespoken her] may annul [her vows that would impair conjugal relations].

C.　R. Joshua rules [that this is so in the case of] one levir but not [in the case of] two.

D.　R. ʿAqiba rules [that this is so] neither [in the case of] one nor [in the case of] two.

E.　Said R. Eliezer, "Just as [in the case of] a wife he has acquired for himself he may annul her vows, [then in the case of] a wife transferred to him by heavenly action, is it not logical that he should [be able to] annul her vows?"

F.　Said to him R. ʿAqiba, "No! Though thou so rulest regarding a woman he has acquired for himself, over whom others have no control, dost thou so rule regarding a woman transferred to him by heavenly action, over whom others [*i.e., the levir's brothers*] do have some control?"

G.　Said to him R. Joshua, "ʿAqiba! Thy words apply to [the case of] two levirs, [but] what sayest thou about a sole levir?"

H.　He answered him, "The levirate widow does not belong so completely to the levir as does the betrothed woman to her [prospective] husband." [*Hence on ʿAqiba's view even a sole levir, unlike the normal prospective husband, cannot annul the vows of a levirate widow made prior to consummation of the union.*]

M. Ned. 10:6

The sages' dispute (A through F) is less significant than their consensus: Limitations on the right of a levir to revoke the vows of the levirate widow stem from the rights of *other men* in relation to this woman, not from any rights of the woman herself.[171] Because the levirate widow is, after all, a *widow*, we might suppose her vows would be immune from revocation, following biblical law (Num. 30:10), which makes no explicit distinction between levirate and other widows here. But the sages see things differently. For them, the biblical term *almanah* ("widow") does not include the case of a *yᵉbamah* ("levirate widow"). The latter, tied to the levir by divine law the minute her husband dies without male issue, never becomes a normal autonomous widow (cf. M. Qid. 1:1).

The levirate widow's lack of control over her vows emerges from the following discussion of a levirate widow who, before or after attaining that status, forswears any benefit from the man who is or may one day become her levir.

A. [Concerning] a woman who forswears any benefit from her levir [*thus abjuring sexual relations with him*]:

B. [If she vowed thus] during the lifetime of her husband, [the court] should compel the levir to release her [if her husband dies without male issue]. [*This vow was made when she was not under the control of the husband's brother, therefore not only can he not annul it, but he cannot insist on his right to marry her, as this would force her to break her vow by accepting the benefit of marriage with him.*]

C. [If she vowed thus] after the death of her husband, [the court] should [merely] request him to release her. [*As the timing of her vow indicates that the widow was deliberately trying to escape marriage with her levir, the court cannot compel him to release her. However, because the levirate law does not absolutely require him to marry her, they can ask him to exercise the option of release.*]

D. But if she intended this [avoidance of marriage with the levir], then even [if she made this vow] during the lifetime of her husband, they [cannot compel him, but may merely] request him to release her.

M. Yeb. 13:13

The fine distinctions drawn here nicely illustrate our thesis concerning control of a woman by the man who owns her sexuality. The first two cases (M. Yeb. 13:13B and C) turn on the presence or absence of the levirate relationship at the time the vow is made. If the man is not yet her levir, he cannot countermand her vow to derive no benefit from him; if he is already her levir, he can. The most interesting case appears at M. Yeb. 13:13D, where a woman vows deliberately to circumvent the levirate law, but the sages will not permit her to preempt a man's God-given right to possess her. So her vow made with that intent does not suffice to compel the levir to release her; she has no more power to neutralize his sexual claim than the wives in M. Ned. 11:12 (see p. 59), who could not circumvent their husbands' unilateral right of divorce by setting up scenarios to compel their release. These cases afford an interesting contrast to that of the dying man (M. Qid. 3:8, app. 10) whose declaration that he has sons (even if no one can locate them) deprives his brother of sexual rights over his widow. Though a *man's* action can sometimes alter the status of others, a *woman's* never can—a point to which we return in chapter 5.

There are two reasons why the law controls the levirate widow so strictly in the cases just discussed. First, her automatic inheritance by the levir(s) places her in the category of a chattel. Second, her chattel status is aggravated (M. Ned. 10:6) by uncertainty as to which of several levirs may eventually consummate the union. As always, doubt or ambiguity regarding reproductive function increases the tendency to treat a woman as chattel. Here, the levirate widow is a sex object awaiting the outcome of competing claims. As with the betrothed girl whose vows could be annulled by father and husband acting in concert (M. Ned. 10:3; see p. 31), the man's rights are defined in relation to the rights of rival males, but not limited by any rights of the woman. The reason is obvious: As potential husbands of this woman, all the levirs have a stake in her sexuality. The sages worry only about the possibility that these men may infringe each other's rights regarding her. She, by contrast, has no rights capable of infringement where the issue directly involves ownership of her biological function.

Incapacity of a Levirate Widow to Initiate Release

The same double standard we saw in the law of divorce (M. Yeb. 14:1) also precludes the levirate widow from dissolving the levirate bond against the will of the levir. Here again, the discrepancy highlights the lesser quality of a woman's personhood.

A.[172] [In a case where] two brothers, one deaf-mute and one unimpaired, married two unimpaired women who are strangers [in blood] [*i.e., not close kin to each other and hence not precluded by Lev. 18:18 from becoming co-wives if a Levirate situation should arise*],

B. if the deaf-mute husband of the unimpaired wife died [without male issue], what must the unimpaired husband of the unimpaired wife do? [*He is now the widow's levir. How should he proceed with respect to levirate marriage?*]

C. He may either carry out *ḥaliṣah* [releasing the widow] or consummate the levirate union. [*This is a normal levirate situation with no impediments.*]

D. If the unimpaired husband of the unimpaired wife died [without male issue], what must the deaf-mute husband of the unimpaired wife do?

E. He must consummate [the levirate union] and can never divorce [the levirate wife]. [*The deaf-mute levir cannot perform ḥaliṣah, for this requires recitation of a formula, "I do not choose to marry her" (Deut. 25:8). So there is no way he can release the levirate widow. He can, however, consummate the levirate union simply by having intercourse with the widow, for which Scripture requires no recitation. But he cannot subsequently release her by divorce because a deaf-mute can execute a divorce only by virtue of a scribal amendment, which does not suffice to terminate a marriage imposed by pentateuchal law. So Albeck 1958 ad loc.*]

M. Yeb. 14:4

Here the sages contrast the normal case of an unimpaired levir (M. Yeb. 14:4B and C) with the problematic case of a deaf-mute levir (M. Yeb. 14:4D and E). The difficulty arises from Scripture's insistence that a levir who wishes to release his brother's widow must recite a formula. As the deaf-mute cannot utter the words, the sages rule that he has no choice but to marry his brother's widow. The widow, a normal woman, cannot escape the impaired levir. Even if willing to release her, he cannot; nor is there any way she can release herself.[173]

Like mishnaic divorce, levirate union is a unilateral transaction executed at the man's option without regard to the woman's wishes (Deut. 25:7). On the one hand, the woman cannot untie the levirate knot without the man's concurrence; on the other, if he rejects her when she might prefer the economic protection of this marriage, she cannot resist the release. This double standard in levirate marriage as in divorce underscores once more the inequality of man and woman in cases that involve a man's ownership of a woman's sexuality.

Ambiguity of Status: Effect on the Levirate Widow

As with the invalidly divorced woman and the putative widow discussed earlier (M. Git. 8:5; M. Yeb. 10:1), the Mishnah's framers visit dire punishment on a levirate widow who remarries in the mistaken belief that she is free to do so. Normally she must marry her husband's brother unless he chooses to release her. Sometimes, however, the law exempts the levir from both requirements, that is, he need neither marry the widow nor release her. For instance, a levir who is too closely related to her by blood or affinity may not marry her. The paradigmatic case occurs when the levirate widow is the sister of the levir's existing wife (Lev. 18:18 bars a man from marrying two sisters). Again, where a man marries his niece (a union not forbidden by Lev. 18), if he dies his wife cannot marry the husband's brother, who happens to be her father. In these and other cases enumerated in M. Yeb. 1:1 (see app. 10), because the levirate tie cannot be formed in the first place, the widow requires no release. But the sages go even further: Whenever consanguinity precludes her levir from marrying her, they extend the prohibition to her co-wives (if any) even though these are not barred by personal consanguinity or affinity with the levir. Such co-wives are exempt both from marrying the levir and from obtaining a release before remarriage. But a co-wife who remarries in reliance on this extended exemption may be taking a grave risk.

A. [Concerning] all consanguineous women [*whose relationship to the levir or his wife precludes the levir from marrying them*], of whom [the sages] have ruled [M. Yeb. 1:1] that their co-wives are [likewise exempt from the levirate tie and hence] permitted [*to remarry like normal widows without first obtaining a release from the levir*],

B. [if] any such co-wife went and married [a man of her choice] and any such [aforesaid consanguineous woman who has exempted her co-wives as stated] is [later] found to be sterile [*and hence could not have married the levir even had she not been consanguineous (M. Nid. 5:9)*],[174]

C.   [any such co-wife who remarried without a levirate release] must leave both men [*i.e., her new "husband" must divorce her and the levir must release her*] and all the aforementioned conditions [*listed in M. Git. 8:5*] apply to her.

                                                                                    M. Git. 8:6

A.   [As for] a man who consummated levirate union with his brother's widow, and [thereafter] her co-wife [another widow of the deceased] went and married another man [*believing herself released from the levirate tie because the levir has now married one of his dead brother's widows*],

B.   if the first widow [who married the levir] is [later] found incapable of conception [so that her marriage to the levir is void by virtue of M. Nid. 5:9], the second widow [who meanwhile married another man] must leave both men. [*She never was released from the levirate tie because the levir's consummation with the first widow turns out to be retrospectively invalid. Therefore, when she remarried without first obtaining her release she became an adulteress. Hence the new "husband" must divorce her and the levir may not now marry her but must release her, just as in the cases previously discussed.*]

C.   And all the [aforementioned] conditions [apply] to her.

                                                                                    M. Git. 8:7

In the complex hypothetical case at M. Git 8:6, a man has died without sons, leaving a number of widows. One widow is exempt from the levirate tie because of consanguinity to the levir or his wife (as explained above), hence she need neither marry the levir nor obtain a release. The law extends her exemption to her co-wives also (even though they are not consanguineous with the levir). Suppose such a co-wife, relying on her extended exemption, goes and marries some man of her choice. Later, it transpires that the consanguineous widow who exempted the co-wife was actually sterile. This fact rendered her ineligible to marry the levir in the first place (M. Nid. 5:9), so there was no need to invoke her consanguinity. Hence, in retrospect, that blood relationship did not function to release her co-wives from the levirate tie. All of them remain shackled to the levir until he either consummates with one of them or grants them individual releases. This he has obviously not done as no one thought it necessary at the time. In consequence, the co-wife who actually remarried was not free to do so—though she had no way of knowing this.

     This poor woman's innocence, alas, does not excuse her. Her remarriage makes her appear tied to two men (the levir and the new husband) at once—an ambiguity that we know the sages will not tolerate. Her relationship with the new "husband" being adulterous, she loses her rights both against him and against the levir. That is, she forfeits her marriage settlement and all other benefits of the new marriage and at the same time loses her right to marry the levir; for now he may not consummate the marriage (she being an adulteress with respect to him) but must instead release her. Even then, she may not continue in the second marriage. Once more a blameless woman is treated like an object and penalized through the confusion of categories by events she cannot control. The case of the widow at M. Git. 8:7 is similar; morally blameless, she suffers for her technical adultery because of the sages' horror of ambiguity.

The Levirate Widow as Person

There is very little to say about the levirate widow as a person in the mishnaic system. In this respect she resembles the minor daughter. The sages' obliviousness to the personhood of the levirate widow stems from the fact that her social value, like that of the minor daughter, resides in her reproductive function. Just as the daughter was valued for the bride-price her sexuality could command, so too, the levirate widow is prized for her potential incubation of a son to perpetuate the name of the dead. Even so, as with the minor daughter, the sages perceive that the levirate widow possesses dormant personhood, which will emerge most prominently in the ḥaliṣah ritual of release.

The Levirate Widow's Part in the Rite of Release

Following Scripture, the mishnaic rite of release calls for the woman rather than the man to take the active part.

A. The religious duty of ḥaliṣah [is carried out as follows]:
B. He [the levir] and his brother's widow come to the court, which offers him the counsel that is proper for him,
C. as it is written [in Scripture]: *"The elders of the town shall then summon him and talk to him."*
D. Then she says, *"My husband's brother refuses to establish a name in Israel for his brother; he will not perform the duty of a levir."*
E. And he says, *"I do not choose to marry her."*
F. And they used to say this in the Holy Tongue [*i.e., the language of Scripture*].
G. Then *"His brother's widow shall go up to him in the presence of the elders, pull the sandal off his foot, spit in his face"*—spittle that can be seen by the judges—
H. and she shall answer and say, *"Thus shall be done to him who will not build up his brother's house!"*

M. Yeb. 12:6

Once the levir has indicated his intent to reject his brother's widow (Deut. 25:7), the initiative in the entire ritual rests with her. As the man's rejection of the union has theoretically released the woman, all that remains is for the parties to carry out the prescribed ceremony symbolizing that release. But how do we explain the fact that, in contrast to the marriage and divorce ceremonies described earlier, the levirate widow plays the leading role in that ceremony?

In adopting Scripture's procedure down to the last detail, the Mishnah's framers underscore their own view of the woman's hybrid character as both chattel and person simultaneously. This anomaly fully conforms to my earlier analysis of the effects of the sexuality factor. The *yᵉbamah* is chattel only because her importance to the levir lies precisely in her reproductive potential. As soon as he rejects her, he yields his right to exploit that function and she recovers the autonomous status of a normal widow. The levirate knot must still be symbolically cut, but the widow's autonomy, which imbues her with the same power as a man to conduct private legal transactions, lets her take the active part in her own release.

The Levirate Widow as Property Owner

Even before the levir expresses an intention to release the widow, the sages respect her rights in one very important matter—ownership of property. We recall the case of the woman who came into an inheritance before her levir had consummated with her.

A.   [Concerning] a widow awaiting the levir [who has not yet claimed her], to whom there fell an inheritance,

B.   the school of Shammai and the school of Hillel concur that she may sell [her inheritance] or give it away and [the transaction] stands. [**Here all the sages analogize the tied levirate widow to the betrothed woman in M. Ket. 8:1D and E, whose disposition of her property was likewise valid**].

M. Yeb. 4:3

As with a betrothed woman, the levirate widow's bond rests on the sexuality factor; levir and prospective husband alike have exclusive claims on these women. But neither man has yet exercised his right. So the sages rule that the levir, by analogy with the betrothed husband, lacks control over the woman's property, until he actually asserts his claim on his sexual chattel.

Even so, a subtle dispute between schools distinguishes the levirate widow from the betrothed woman as property owner. The sages were not unanimous about the property rights of the betrothed woman. Hillelites (M. Ket. 8:1D; see p. 88) denied the *ab initio* power of a betrothed woman to sell her property (presumably because the right to its usufruct was an element in her selection by the prospective husband); nonetheless, both schools agreed (M. Ket. 8:1E) that if she had, in fact, disposed of the property, the transaction was valid *ex post facto*. But the unclaimed levirate widow actually retains more personhood than the betrothed woman; neither school disputes the widow's right to go ahead and sell her own property (excluding property tied up in her marriage settlement, which must await the levir's decision). This status distinction between a betrothed woman and an unclaimed levirate widow, we recall, appears at the end of the sages' discussion of the levir's right to annul the vows of his levirate widow.

G.   Said to him R. Joshua, "'Aqiba! Thy words apply to [the case of] two levirs, [but] what sayest thou about a sole levir?"

H.   He answered him, "The levirate widow does not belong so completely to the levir as does the betrothed woman to her [prospective] husband." [*Hence on 'Aqiba's view even a sole levir, unlike the normal prospective husband, cannot annul the vows or property transactions of the levirate widow made prior to consummation of the union.*]

M. Ned. 10:6

Why should a prospective husband have a stronger claim on his bride than a levir on his brother's widow? The Mishnah does not spell out the basis of this distinction. 'Aqiba's judgment may perhaps rest on the following analogy: Scripture imposes the death sentence on one who violates a betrothed girl (Deut. 22:23–25) but no penalty is prescribed for a man who has intercourse with an unreleased levirate widow (even though Scripture expressly forbids her to remarry without a release, Deut. 25:7–10). Nor does Scripture specify a levir's right to annul the vows of his unclaimed widow, as it does for a betrothed husband (Num. 30:7–9).[175] The levirate widow's greater independence may stem from the fact that although the prospective husband presumably intends to marry his betrothed, one cannot be *sure* that a levir plans to claim his brother's widow until he actually consummates the union. In that sense the levir's claim on the widow's sexual function is weaker than that of the betrothed husband on his bride. With both women, however, the Mishnah makes the same distinction we have seen throughout: If the matter concerns her sexuality, she is chattel; if her property, she is person.

The Levirate Widow's Right to Reject a Repulsive Levir

Finally, let us take a second look at the circumstances under which a wife might ask the court to make her husband divorce her, specifically the case of the man suffering from an unpleasant disease or body odor. The last part of the unit (not presented earlier) considers whether the widow of a tanner (an occupation producing a foul body odor) can be forced to marry her husband's brother, likewise a tanner. Here, the sages treat the *yᵉbamah* with a degree of humanity that surprises us, especially as their ruling contravenes Scripture.

G.   It happened in Sidon, that a certain tanner died [without male issue] leaving a brother [who was likewise] a tanner [*and who must comply with the levirate law by marrying his brother's widow*].

H.   The sages ruled [with respect to the levirate tie, that] she had the legal power to say, "I was able to endure thy brother [*i.e., because I loved him*], but thee I cannot endure." [*Contrary to the general rule, this widow can reject her levir.*]

M. Ket. 7:10

Here, the sages on purely humanitarian grounds permit the levirate widow to flout scriptural requirements by rejecting the levir. Perhaps this case represents an extension of ʿAqiba's distinction between the betrothed woman and the levirate widow. In that case the levir did not own the widow as completely as the prospective husband owned his bride; in this case the levir does not own his levirate widow as completely as a husband owns his wife. For we recall that a wife who agreed to put up with an unpleasant physical feature of her husband was held to that promise (M. Ket. 7:10E); but here, a woman who married a tanner in the first place, thus demonstrating her willingness to tolerate him, cannot be forced to accept his brother who follows the same calling. The sages' readiness to make such distinctions attests their recognition of the levirate widow as intrinsically a person so long as her sexual function is not the sole issue. This widow did not voluntarily undertake to live with this particular tanner; so they distinguish her present situation from her former position as a wife who made that promise to her husband. This ruling also resembles the case of the woman allowed to release herself from a prospective husband who abandoned her when her father failed to come up with the dowry (M. Ket. 13:5), where the exception likewise turned on the fact that the woman had not made the promise herself.

Summary

For the Mishnah's framers, the levirate widow possesses one important feature—her reproductive potential. As part of the deceased's property, she is inherited by his nearest kinsman along with the estate. The sages expand scriptural law to give *all* levirs the right to marry her before any can offer to release her. Even when they exempt certain women (see app. 10), this is to make them available to *kohanim*, who may not marry women classified as divorcées through levirate release. Most significant of all, just as a wife cannot institute divorce proceedings, the levirate widow cannot institute release proceedings (unless her levir has indicated his intent to reject her); like the wife whose huband lacks the mental capacity to divorce her, the levirate widow may be tied for life to a levir unable to recite the required formula. Until her levir expressly rejects her, she remains his inheritance from his brother; and if she mistakenly remarries thinking herself exempt from the law, the sages visit her with the same penalties they inflict on the wife who thought herself free to remarry. Even more than the minor daughter, the levirate widow (precisely because she is no child but a grown woman) constitutes the ultimate example of the Mishnah's treatment of woman as chattel when her biological function is uppermost in the sages' minds.

As with the minor daughter, the sages have little to say about the levirate widow as person. Although she retains some important marks of personhood until her levir actually claims her (he cannot annul her property transactions or [generally] revoke her vows), she moves from the status of sexual chattel to that of autonomous woman only if her levir signals his intention to release her. Once bespoken, however, her personhood approximates that of a wife, as reflected in her right, for instance, to reject a repulsive levir. In both cases, of course, the woman's freedom depends on the man's compliance with the required formalities.

In chapters 2 through 4, I have analyzed the effect of the sexuality factor on the personhood of three categories of dependent woman: minor daughter, wife, and levirate widow. I pinpointed the basis of the treatment of these women as chattels rather than persons; it was inherent in their legal subordination to men possessing an exclusive claim on their sexuality. In every case the woman's sexual function clearly accounted for her legal dependence on a given man and for the scope and extent of that man's authority. At this point we can assert with confidence that legal control of the minor daughter, wife, and levirate widow stems directly from the entitlement of the father, husband, or levir to the exclusive benefit of these women's sexuality. But the law permits these men to treat their women as chattel *only* in matters pertaining to ownership of their biological function.

5

THE AUTONOMOUS WOMAN

Women defined as autonomous in mishnaic law comprise three subclasses: the emancipated daughter, the divorcée, and the widow. These three groups (explained in chap. 1) form mirror images of the three dependent subclasses discussed in chapters 2 through 4: the minor daughter's counterpart is the unmarried woman, whose coming of age at twelve and one-half years automatically emancipates her from her father's jurisdiction; the divorcée—counterpart of the wife—is released from her husband's authority by receiving his writ of divorce; and the levirate widow's counterpart, the normal widow, escapes control by her husband's brother because her husband produced an heir before he died.

The essential feature that distinguishes the autonomous woman from her dependent sister and accounts for her higher legal status is none other than the sexuality factor I isolated in chapter 1. Just as male authority over dependent women was grounded in ownership of their biological function, we now find the corollary: *A woman's freedom from male authority rests precisely on the fact that no man can lay claim to her sexuality*. Consequently, autonomous women remain legal persons even with respect to ownership of their sexuality, that is, in the very context that reduces dependent women to the level of chattels.

The proof of this proposition lies in laws permitting autonomous women to dispose of their own sexuality. They can decide whether or not to marry (or remarry) and select their own partners from among their suitors. This power *ipso facto* raises autonomous women to a higher status than their dependent counterparts. But the personhood of autonomous women

114

extends far beyond control of their biological function. The sages' interest in women focuses on those who have legal relationships to men; they have no stake in controlling the private lives of autonomous women, who in consequence have a great deal of freedom in private legal transactions of all kinds. In short, in the private domain the Mishnah's framers *always* treat autonomous women as persons, *never* as chattels.

The full significance of this fact is grasped when we recollect that the autonomy of women in legal systems need not rest exclusively on the sexuality factor. Some cultures of antiquity kept women under guardianship throughout their lives regardless of their age or matrimonial status. For instance, Roman law (the law of the dominant surrounding culture of the Mishnah's day) kept women in perpetual tutelage "on account of their instability of judgment."[176] So legal systems do not inevitably grant autonomy to women if no man owns their biological function. The mishnaic system, however, does just that; and the question is, why?

The answer lies partly in the fact that the autonomy of emancipated daughters, divorcées, and widows rests on scriptural foundations that the Mishnah's framers cannot ignore. The sages derive it from the paradigm of the biblical law of vows (Num. 30:2-17), which I analyzed in chapter 3. Recall that a father may annul any vow of his minor daughter, but not those of a daughter no longer living "in her father's house by reason of her youth"; a husband may revoke any "self-denying" vow of his wife that impairs relations "between a man and his wife," but he cannot control her other vows; and no one can countermand the vow of a widow or divorcée. The only subclass of women[177] not named explicitly in the biblical law of vows is the levirate widow. Though not actually falling under the scriptural rubric of widow—the Hebrew terms for widow (*almanah*) and levirate widow (*yᵉbamah*) are etymologically distinct—she is, in fact, a widow whose automatic bond to the levir makes her the dependent counterpart of the autonomous normal widow. Thus Scripture's law of vows forms the paradigm for Mishnah's taxonomy of women. In this chapter, we discuss the three autonomous subgroups: the emancipated daughter, the divorcée, and the widow.

The Emancipated Daughter

The Mishnah seldom mentions the emancipated daughter, and such references are mostly tangential to discussion of the minor daughter. Thus, in contrast to the minor daughter, a woman of full age arranges her own marriage, whether by herself or through an agent (M. Qid. 2:1).[178] A man cannot legally revoke the vows of his grown daughter (M. Ned. 10:2, 11:10; M. Nid. 5:7)—a rule extrapolated from Scripture's limitation of that power to the case of a daughter still *"in her father's household by reason of her youth"* (Num. 30:17). As for penalties and damages for rape or seduction, the sages specify that the father receives no fine in the case of a mature daughter (M. Ket. 3:8), whose sexuality the father no longer owns; by contrast, the case of the autonomous orphan girl (M. Ket. 3:6, app. 2) implies that a grown woman collects her own damages for rape (though not if she permits a man to seduce her).

Whether the Mishnah's rules about women reflect a real or an imagined society, the paucity of references to the emancipated daughter suggests that she is not very important in the mishnaic scheme. Concerned mainly with women's impact on men who own their biological function, the sages display far more interest in the minor daughter because of the value of her virginity to her father. At the same time it is clearly no accident that the only unmarried adult woman who generates a discussion of any length is the one called to testify about her virginity or that of other women; this matters so much that the Mishnah's framers make a special exception to the general rule that women may not testify in person (M. Shebu. 4:1). We shall explore the significance of this and other rules for the personhood of women. But first we must establish the general equivalence of status (in the private domain) between an autonomous woman and an autonomous man.

Equivalence of Autonomous Woman to Autonomous Man

The Mishnah treats as legally autonomous an unmarried daughter who has graduated from the status of pubescent girl (*na'arah*) to that of mature woman (*bogeret*)—an event conventionally assumed to occur at twelve and one-half years and one day.[179] The earlier discussion of the minor daughter opened with the statement that a young girl is controlled by the father until she physically matures, at which time "her father no longer has dominion over her" (M. Nid. 5:7). Legally speaking, the grown woman is emancipated and may do as she pleases in all matters concerning her personal status or private business. The following rule illustrates the importance of the difference in classification between a young girl and her older sister:

A.   An object found by [a man's] minor son or daughter, or by his male or female Canaanite slave, or by his wife—such [objects] belong to him. [*For the minor daughter, cf. M. Ket. 4:1, 4; M. Nid. 5:7.*]

B.   [But] an object found by his grown son or daughter, or by his Hebrew bondman or bondmaid,[180] or by his divorced wife (even though he has not yet handed over her marriage portion)—such [objects] belong to [the finder].

M. B.M. 1:5

Things found by a dependent person belong to the master, whereas things found by an autonomous person belong to the finder. The sages here distinguish *inter alia* between the legal status of the minor child (male or female) and the child who has come of age. A boy under thirteen (M. Nid. 5:6) or girl under twelve and one-half remains within the father's control; a boy over thirteen or girl over twelve and one-half becomes *sui juris*. At this point the father's rights over the child lapse automatically, including his entitlement to anything the child finds.

It is most significant that the law treats the daughter of full age just like the son who has reached majority; the father retains no more rights over the one than over the other. This is one of many instances in which the Mishnah's framers view an emancipated woman exactly like a grown man; indeed, they treat the two equally for all transactions of private law. This equivalence is reflected in the rule that when a man and a mature woman agree to marry, the law grants both of them a twelve-month period of preparation, reckoned from the time that either requests the other to fulfill the promise of marriage.

A. [The sages] grant a virgin [of full age] twelve months from the time the [prospective] husband claims her [*i.e., asks her to carry out her promise to marry him*], to furnish her trousseau;

B. and just as they grant [that period] to the woman, so they grant [a similar period of preparation] to the man [*from the time the woman requests him to carry out his promise*].

C. But [in the case of] a widow, [the period is] thirty days [for both parties]. [*A widow, already owning household effects from her first marriage, requires a shorter period to prepare for a subsequent marriage.*]

M. Ket. 5:2

Here, the sages treat man and woman alike. They accord a woman the same right and demand the same responsibility as they expect of a man. This applies equally to the emancipated daughter and to the divorcée and widow discussed later (in contradistinction to the dependent women discussed in the preceding chapters). Later, we shall discuss the many analogies drawn between the autonomous woman and the autonomous man in their capacity as human beings and as Israelites. For now, we note simply that for purposes of private law the Mishnah's framers treat a woman of full age as equivalent to a man. This fact finds concrete expression in several branches of the law: in the power of an autonomous woman to arrange her own marriage, to engage in litigation, to testify in court (for limited purposes), to swear an oath supporting or rebutting a legal claim, and to make binding religious vows that no one can revoke. The equal responsibility of the woman appears likewise in rules of criminal law that subject her to the same penalties as a man.

Woman's Power to Arrange Her Own Marriage

The most significant legal power of an autonomous woman is that of arranging her own marriage. Here, the sages explicitly contrast her position with that of her minor sister.

A. A man may espouse a woman either by his own act or through his agent.

B. A woman may become espoused either by her own act or through her agent.

C. A man may give his daughter in marriage [to a man of his choice] while she is still a *na'arah* [*i.e. until she reaches the age of twelve and one-half years and one day*] either by his own act or through his agent.

M. Qid. 2:1

The power of a woman of full age (over twelve and one-half years) to arrange her own marriage symbolizes her total legal autonomy in private life. This paradigmatic rule lets her control her most important asset—her sexuality. The decision to marry may be the most important choice a woman makes in her entire life, and the sages credit her with sufficient intelligence to choose for herself. As already noted, not all systems of law permit adult women this degree of freedom; Roman law in mishnaic times kept women under perpetual tutelage regardless of whether they were single, married, divorced or widowed.[181] But the mishnaic system gives control of a woman's personal life only to the man with a legal claim on her biological function.

Here, however, we must enter a caveat. Although recognizing the autonomy of the unmarried adult woman, M. Qid. 2:1 also reveals an important limitation on her powers. For though the linguistic symmetry of the rules at M. Qid. 2:1A and B implies that a woman's power is equivalent to that of a man, the rule at M. Qid. 2:1C, giving a father control over the marriage of his minor daughter, is conspicuously unmatched by any clause giving the *mother* a corresponding right. That clause is lacking because, as we learn elsewhere:

A.   A man can give his daughter in marriage,
B.   but a woman cannot give her daughter in marriage.

M. Soṭ. 3:8

This reminds us of Tosefta's gloss on M. Qid. 2:1:

A.   Just as a man cannot give his [minor] son in marriage, either by his own act or through his agent,
B.   so a woman cannot give her [minor] daughter in marriage, either by her own act or through her agent.

T. Qid. 2:1

The rule of Tosefta, like the first part of the mishnaic unit it glosses, exhibits a superficial symmetry: A father cannot marry off his son, a mother cannot marry off her daughter. But in both cases the symmetry is spurious. The father's inability to give his son in marriage follows from the unstated premise that each male Israelite transacts his own marriage after reaching majority. He cannot be married off by another person, not even by his father. With the daughter, the father has intrinsic power to give her away; but the express reference in M. Qid. 2:1C to the daughter tacitly excludes the son from its scope. The mother cannot marry off her daughter, not because a minor daughter cannot be married off in principle, but simply because the mother's power does not equal that of the father. Hence, if the father dies and the mother purports to give the girl in marriage, the latter can at puberty repudiate the marriage before consummation (M. Yeb. 13:1–2)— which she cannot do when her *father* marries her off. The spurious symmetry of Tosefta's language masks the fact that the mother has less power than the father.

We find a rule similar to M. Soṭ. 3:8 in connection with the Nazirite vow:

A.   A man may devote his [minor] son as a Nazirite;
B.   but a woman may not devote her [minor] son as a Nazirite.

M. Naz. 4:6

Scripture provides no warrant for a father's devoting his minor son as a Nazirite,[182] yet the Mishnah's framers permit it. Paradoxically, they withhold similar power from the mother, despite Scripture's account of Hannah's vow to dedicate to God the son she prays for (1 Sam. 1:11), which could have provided an excellent prooftext to support a mother's power to make her son a Nazirite. But the sages ignore Hannah because they find it inappropriate to grant a woman the power to alter the personal status of her child.

These rules adumbrate the limits of a woman's power. A woman can legally alter her own status, for instance by engaging herself to marry someone, but no woman possesses the power to affect the status of another Israelite.[183] No doubt this fact represents a holdover from the agnatic structure of earlier Israelite society, wherein all power and property resided in males, as reflected in the ancient biblical rules of succession (before the modification recorded at Num. 27:8ff.). A woman's inability to control the life of another Israelite—even her own child—places an important limitation on women's personhood in the mishnaic system.

Woman's Power to Engage in Litigation

The power to litigate is a significant mark of personhood, as it provides an important mechanism for the enforcement of rights. The Mishnah's framers grant women the right to bring or defend a lawsuit: "Women are included in [the law of] damages" (M. B.Q. 1:3). This valuable right enables a woman to sue for damages as well as to resist claims brought against her. A property owner's rights may be worthless unless he or she can bring suit for damages. Here, the sages treat a property-owning woman, for the most part, like a man. But there is one important qualification: though she may bring or defend a suit, she is not generally allowed to testify in person (M. Shebu. 4:1, discussed on p. 120). Male witnesses, of course, may testify on her behalf. As property owner, she possesses enforceable rights; but as a sexual distraction that should stay out of the public forum, she must usually enforce her rights by a male proxy.[184]

The foregoing rules apply to all emancipated women, whether unmarried, divorcées, or widows. The mishnaic examples mostly involve widows and divorcées simply because these women, entitled to collect marriage portions, are the most likely female litigants. Thus, the sages take up the case of a widow or divorcée who sues for her marriage settlement of two hundred *zuz*, asserting that she was a virgin at the time of her marriage. Her divorcing husband (or his heirs, if he has died), dispute this, alleging that she was a widow at the time of marriage, hence entitled only to one hundred *zuz* (M. Ket. 1:2). The Mishnah's framers spell out the standard of proof required to determine who speaks the truth:

A.   [Concerning] a woman who has been widowed or divorced [*and brings suit for her marriage portion*],

B.   [if] she says, "[I was] a virgin [when] thou didst marry me," [*addressing the divorcing husband or "when he married me," addressing her deceased husband's heirs*],

C.   and [the husband] says, "Not so, [thou wast] a widow [when] I married thee" [*or the husband's heirs say, "when he married thee"*],

D.   if there are witnesses that she went forth [from her father's house to her marriage] with hymeneal chants,[185] and with her hair unbound, her k*e*tubbah is two hundred [zuz]. [*It was customary for a virgin's marriage procession to be conducted in this manner, therefore we assume this bride was a virgin as she now claims.*]

E.   R. Yoḥanan b. Baroqa rules [that] the distribution of parched corn likewise [constitutes] proof [*of her claim because this is customary only at the marriage of a virgin*].

M. Ket. 2:1

The woman here appears as plaintiff. Like any plaintiff, she must back up her claim either with eyewitness testimony or some other form of corroboration in accordance with the rule that the burden of proof rests on the claimant (M. B.Q. 3:11). Here, the Mishnah's framers apply normal rules of evidence, treating the woman precisely like a man. Further, we note the significant fact that, in contrast to a woman's strictly limited right to testify (discussed later), the sages take for granted her absolute right as property owner to bring suit to redress a legal grievance—though her success may well turn on the availability of male witnesses (M. Ket. 2:1D and E) to support her claim.

Woman as Legal Witness

This brings us to another important mark of personhood: a woman's intrinsic capacity (despite strict limitations) to testify in court or to swear a bailee's or litigant's oath to support or rebut a claim. Here, the sages acknowledge both a woman's mental competence and the reliance to be placed on her oath or testimony. The sages' assessment of a woman's ability to give a truthful and accurate account reflects their recognition that her mental and moral capacities resemble those of a man.

Women normally cannot testify. The sages do not state this in so many words. To the contrary, the list of intrinsically incompetent witnesses (M. San. 3:3) makes no mention of women.[186] But their general disqualification appears in the rule that "[the law concerning] an oath of testimony (Lev. 5:1ff.) applies to men but not to women" (M. Shebu. 4:1). Not only are women not compellable, they are generally not competent at all, as we deduce from M. San. 3:4, where the list of those who may not testify for or against a near kinsman speaks only of men—taking for granted that women do not testify. However, the Mishnah's framers make exceptions to this rule. Thus, in cases involving virginity, where no independent corroboration exists, the sages let women testify because the matter is peculiarly within their knowledge. Likewise, where a woman is the sole witness to a man's death, she may testify in order to free the man's widow (possibly herself) for remarriage. Again, in some property cases, a woman can be asked to swear that she has not embezzled goods entrusted to her or received payment of money she claims as her due. In accepting a woman's testimony or making her swear an oath, the sages implicitly equate her with a man, for they assume she possesses similar qualities of rational thought and moral choice—two important qualities of personhood. Again, in deciding whether to demand corroboration of a woman's testimony or when to make her swear an oath, the Mishnah's framers use precisely the same criteria they would apply to a man. Equating a woman to a man in these matters manifestly treats her as a person.

Let us begin with the rules that govern women's testimony in virginity suits. We recall that a bridegroom can expect his wife to be a virgin unless she was married before or has lived with captors or gentiles beyond the age of three years (M. Ket. 1:4). If the bride is not intact, the groom may lodge a virginity suit (M. Ket. 1:1) to recover the bride-price of virgins that he paid for her (M. Ket. 1:2). Normally virginity suits lie against the father. But a bride of full age who arranged her own marriage must defend herself against the accusation that she deceived her bridegroom. Here, the sages follow their general principle that a woman may defend a lawsuit (M. B.Q. 1:3). They concede the validity of certain defenses but dispute whether the woman's testimony is acceptable without corroboration.

A. [Concerning a man] who married a woman but did not find in her the tokens of virginity (see Deut. 22:14),

B. [and] she says, "After thou didst betroth me, I was raped, and thy field was flooded" [*to explain her nonvirginal condition at the time of consummation*],

C. but he says, "Not so, but [it happened] before I betrothed thee, and my bargain was a bargain made in error [and hence null],"

D. Rabban Gamaliel and R. Eliezer rule [that] she is credible.

E. But R. Joshua rules [that] we do not rely on her word (lit. not by her mouth do we live!). Rather, [we assume] she lost her virginity before betrothal, and she deceived him—unless she produces corroboration for her statement.

M. Ket. 1:6

A. [If] she says, "I was deflowered by accident" (lit. struck by a stick),

B. but he says, "Not so, but thou wast violated by a man,"

C. Rabban Gamaliel and R. Eliezer rule [that] she is credible.

D. But R. Joshua rules [that] we do not rely on her word. Rather, [we assume] she was violated by a man unless she produces corroboration for her statement.

M. Ket. 1:7

In these cases the Mishnah's framers permit a woman's testimony only because they cannot otherwise get at the truth. But the significant point is that all sages view the woman as intrinsically capable of giving truthful and intelligent testimony. Their willingness to listen to her at all speaks to their perception of her mental processes as comparable to those of a man. Gamaliel and Eliezer accept her testimony because she admits the charge of nonvirginity but offers a plausible excuse. This shifts the burden of proof back to the plaintiff (M. B.Q. 3:11). As he offers no corroboration, she has the last word. On Joshua's view, the self-serving nature of the bride's testimony should lead the court to question her veracity and insist on corroboration rather than accept her words at face value. Either way, the sages invoke the same criteria they would use to assess the credibility of a male. By treating the woman like a man, the Mishnah's framers clearly show that they perceive her as a person.

Similar considerations apply to proving the virginity of mature women who are about to enter a marriage. A woman's eligibility, above all to marry into the priestly caste, was a prime concern of those who framed the Division of Women. Previously married women cannot remarry at all without proof of widowhood or divorce. Further, Scripture forbids a *kohen* to marry a woman who has been violated or divorced (Lev. 21:7, endorsed by M. Ket. 2:9), and a woman's former captive status raises an irrebuttable presumption of rape (M. Ket. 1:4). At issue is the credibility of the woman's testimony on these matters. The sages evaluate her statements differently according to their self-serving, altruistic, or purely gratuitous character.

A.   [Concerning] a woman who said, "I was [once] married, but [now] I am divorced," she is credible,

B.   for the mouth that forbade is the [same] mouth that permitted. [*Her statement that she is now divorced negates her earlier, gratuitous admission that she had been married. As she need not have mentioned her marriage in the first place, we assume she speaks the truth about her subsequent divorce.*]

C.   But if there are [independent] witnesses that she was [at one time] married, and she says, "[True, but] I am [now] divorced," she is not credible [*without corroboration, as, for instance, by producing a writ of divorce. Here, the woman's statement is obviously self-serving because she is rebutting others' testimony that she had been married. Therefore, she must supply extraneous corroboration.*]

D.   [If a woman said], "I was taken captive, but I remain pure [*i.e., I was not raped, hence I am fit to marry a kohen*," as specified in Lev. 21:7*], she is credible,

E.   for the mouth that forbade is the [same] mouth that permitted. [*As at B, she need never have mentioned her former captivity in the first place, so her claim of purity is credible.*]

F.   But if there are [independent] witnesses that she had been kidnapped and she says, "[Nonetheless], I remain pure," she is not credible [*without corroboration, for the same reason as at C*].

G.   But if [such] witnesses [C or F] arrive after she has remarried, this woman does not [have to] go forth. [*Her husband is not required to divorce her on* *the strength of their testimony that she was married or, if her remarriage was to a **kohen**, that she is a former captive.]*

M. Ket. 2:5

A.   [Concerning] two women who were taken captive [together],
B.   if one says, "I was taken captive, yet I remain pure," and the other says "I was taken captive, yet I remain pure," neither of them is credible. *[Since each is an independent witness to the other's captivity, each one's claim of purity is made only in rebuttal and, hence, is self-serving.]*
C.   But when each testifies on the other's behalf, then they are credible. *[If each vouches for the other's continued purity, this is not self-serving, hence, it is credible.]*

M. Ket. 2:6

Once more, the sages judge the woman's credibility as they would assess that of a man. At M. Ket. 2:5A and B and D and E, the woman's statements are not self-serving; to the contrary, they are gratuitous admissions against interest, for she need never have mentioned her former marriage (M. Ket. 2:5B) or her former captivity (M. Ket. 2:5D) in the first place. Hence, the sages give credence to her assertion of present freedom to marry or of untouched virginity, as the case may be. In making this judgment, the sages treat the woman precisely like a man. Rather than attribute her gratuitous admission to pure stupidity, they assume she has enough sense to know she could have kept quiet about her marriage (of which there is no independent evidence) rather than make a false claim of subsequent divorce. In accepting her story, they invoke the same criterion ("the mouth that forbade is the mouth that permitted") normally applied to male witnesses (M. Dem. 6:11). At M. Ket. 2:5C and F, by contrast, independent witnesses to the woman's earlier marriage or former captivity make it impossible for her to conceal this. As her disclaimers are purely self-serving, the sages know that (like any man confronted by adverse testimony) the woman may well be lying about her eligibility. Finally, at M. Ket. 2:6, the women's statements are accepted only if they are testifying on each other's behalf. In that instance the witness has nothing to gain for herself. Her testimony is seen as entirely altruistic, supporting another's claim; hence the sages accept it at face value.[187]

Testimony of a Sole Witness to a Husband's Death

In the uncertain conditions of the ancient world, husbands often disappeared without trace. This situation wreaks havoc for the wife in mishnaic law, which decrees that a putative widow lacking eyewitnesses to her husband's death can never remarry, lest he is still alive. The "grass widow" is called an *ʿagunah* (literally a "chained" or "anchored" woman).[188] The *ʿagunah* suffers great hardship; neither divorced nor clearly widowed, she cannot collect her marriage portion and may become destitute. Her situation is aggravated by the deprivation of a sexual partner. Moreover, her biological function (her prime social value in mishnaic culture) will likely be wasted for the rest of her life—especially unfortunate where the woman is still of childbearing age when the husband disappears (as commonly happens in a society where a girl's first marriage generally takes place at puberty).

The sages are eager to free this woman from the matrimonial bond by any means available within their system. To this end, they relax Scripture's usual requirement of two witnesses (Deut. 19:15) and permit the putative widow to remarry on the strength of testimony from a single witness. Moreover, such testimony may come from anyone, including the woman herself, if she claims to have seen her husband's body. The sages not only enact these rules (M. Yeb. 15:1-2), but in a rare departure from their usual practice they describe at length (M. Yeb. 16:7) the social problem that generates them.

A. [As for] a woman who went together with her husband [to live] overseas, [if there was] peace between him and her, and peace in the world, and she came back [alone] and said, "My husband is dead," she may remarry. [*She will not lie about the death of a beloved husband nor is he likely to disappear without trace in time of peace.*]

B. [If she said], "My husband died [childless]," she may enter levirate union [with the husband's brother].

C. [If there was] peace between him and her but war in the world or [if there was] contention between him and her but peace in the world and she came back [alone] and said, "My husband is dead," she is not credible. [*In the former case the husband may well have disappeared without trace, whereas in the latter she may be lying about the death of a hated husband.*]

D. R. Judah rules that she is never credible unless she comes back weeping and with her garments torn [as a sign of mourning].

E. [But] the sages said to him, "It is all one [whatever her condition]; she may remarry [if the circumstances are as stated at A and B]."

M. Yeb. 15:1

A. The school of Hillel says, "We have heard [such a ruling] only of a woman who came back from the reaping, and [it was] in the same province, and [it was] an actual [not hypothetical] case."

B. The school of Shammai said to them, "It is all one, whether she came from the reaping, or from the olive-picking, or from the grape harvest, or whether she came from one province to another; the sages mentioned the reaping only as a commonplace event."

C. The school of Hillel revised [their view] to teach according to the opinion of the school of Shammai.

M. Yeb. 15:2

These rules are self-explanatory. But they must have been highly controversial, for the sages devote two entire chapters of tractate Y^ebamot to this topic alone, recording many disputes about what testimony is competent to establish widowhood. In a lengthy anecdote they describe the political problems that generated the rule permitting a widow to remarry on the strength of a sole witness' testimony:

A. R. ʿAqiba said, "When I went down to Nehardea [in Babylon] to ordain a leap year, I met Nehemiah of Bet-Deli, and he said to me, 'I have heard that in the Land of Israel no one permits a woman to remarry on the strength of testimony from a single witness, except R. Judah b. Baba.'

B. "And I told him, 'That is so.'

C. "He said to me, 'Tell them in my name—ye know that this province is thrown into confusion by invaders—that I received a tradition from Rabban Gamaliel the Elder that the court may permit a woman to remarry on the strength of testimony from a single witness.'

D. "And when I came and recounted the matter before Rabban Gamaliel [grandson of Rabban Gamaliel the Elder], he rejoiced at my words, saying, 'We have found a colleague to [support] R. Judah b. Baba.'"

E. Rabban Gamaliel thereupon remembered that men had been slain at Tel Arza and Rabban Gamaliel the Elder had permitted their wives to remarry on the strength of testimony from a single witness.

F. And they established the rule that a woman may remarry on the strength of testimony from a single witness [as to what he had heard] from another witness, even from a male slave, a woman, or a female slave.

G. [But] R. Eliezer and R. Joshua rule that one may not permit a woman to remarry on the strength of testimony from a single witness.

H. R. ʿAqiba [adopting an intermediate position] rules, ["I agree with Gamaliel that she may remarry on testimony from a single valid witness] but not on the evidence of [such invalid witnesses as] a woman, or a male or female slave, or near kinsmen."[189]

M. Yeb. 16:7

The sages are deeply divided on this issue. Some object to reliance on a single witness, others to accepting a woman's testimony at all. The result is that the majority establish, over the objections of important dissenters, that a single witness, even one who repeats hearsay from a slave or woman, will permit a widow's remarriage. Whether out of humanitarian concern; or from a desire to legitimate remarriages that, in fact, took place; or perhaps merely to avoid wasting the woman's reproductive potential, a solution was found to a pressing social problem.

The question of a wife's remarriage on technically insufficient proof of her husband's death is a special case of the general problem that arises when a woman's husband has disappeared or refuses to give a divorce when so ordered by the Jewish court. As noted earlier, in a basically polygynous system, this problem affects wives but not husbands; if such a man does remarry in defiance of the rabbinate, his new marriage is halakhically sound and its offspring legitimate. Jewish women, however, suffer to this day through the unwillingness of contemporary orthodox authorities to amend the rules in the only truly effective manner, namely, by evolving mechanisms that would permit a wife to divorce a missing or recalcitrant husband.[190] As discussed earlier (p. 50), Scripture does not explicitly proscribe such a procedure, so the halakhic denial of this method is largely an argument from silence.

From the standpoint of women's personhood in the mishnaic system, the significance of M. Yeb. 15:1 lies in the sages' readiness to give credence to

the uncorroborated testimony of the ʿagunah. In weighing her story according to the facts of her case, the sages view her as an individual, just as they
did in assessing the credibility of the women at M. Ket. 2:5–6. Such rulings
form a striking contrast to the many situations in which the sages treat
women as an undifferentiated group whose members all "look alike"—a
mind-set typical of the male "self" in defining the female "other." To treat
someone as an individual is to perceive him or her as a person. When it suits
the Mishnah's framers, a woman, too, is a person.

Woman's Eligibility to Take an Oath

Allied to a woman's right to litigate or testify is her eligibility to swear
certain kinds of legal oaths. Though women do not normally testify, the
sages distinguish between the biblical oath of testimony discussed earlier,
from which a woman is generally exempt, and the oath of deposit (Lev.
5:21ff.), which the court can require her to take.

> A.   [The law concerning] an oath of deposit applies to men and to women,
>   to unrelated persons and to kinsfolk, to those qualified [to testify] and to
>   those unqualified, to [matters] before a court and to [matters] not before a
>   court.[191]
>
> M. Shebu. 5:1

An oath of deposit may be required of any person to whom goods have
been entrusted in bailment. This includes women as well as others normally
incompetent to testify, whether in general (slaves) or in particular cases
(kinsmen). The sages hold a woman who has charge of another person's
property to the same high standard of integrity as a man. The owner can
require the bailee to swear that he or she has not embezzled or misapplied
the goods. Similarly, anyone having business dealings with another can
require that person to swear an oath that he or she has not misappropriated
the other's property. The mishnaic applications of this rule to women
happen to involve wives, but they would apply a fortiori to unattached
women placed in a similar position.

> A.   [Concerning] a man who sets up his wife as a stallkeeper [to sell his wares]
>   or who has appointed her an administrator [for his property], whenever he
>   wishes, he may require her to swear [an oath that she has not misappro-
>   priated the proceeds.] [*He may require an oath whether or not he brings an
>   actual claim against her, i.e., "whether before a court or not before a court"*
>   (*M. Shebu. 5:1*).]
> B.   R. Eliezer rules [that a husband may require such an oath] even with respect
>   to her spindle and with respect to her dough. [*A man can require his wife to
>   swear that she has not converted to her own use the cloth or baked goods she
>   has made from the raw materials he has furnished her, for the proceeds of
>   her labor belong to her husband* (*M. Ket. 6:1*).]
>
> M. Ket. 9:4

A. The following may be adjured without a claim [being lodged against them]:

B. Partners, and sharecroppers, and trustees, and a wife who transacts business in the house, and a son of the house [*i.e., one of several brothers, who manages property inherited jointly from the father*].

C. If one [of the foregoing] said to [the other], "What dost thou claim of me?" [and the other said], "I wish thee to swear to me [that thou hast not misappropriated my property]," the former is obliged [to swear such an oath].[192]

M. Shebu. 7:8

A woman who handles her husband's goods can be asked to swear that she has not embezzled anything. Why do the sages demand this of one who is normally exempt from such judicial procedures? The answer can only be that a husband who sets up his wife as a stallkeeper or authorizes her to transact business on his behalf makes her his agent—a position normally held by a man.[193] A wife who takes on a degree of responsibility that is usually assigned only to autonomous persons must observe the same ground rules that apply to any agent. So the husband (or any other person doing business with the wife) can require her to take an oath that she has not abused his trust. In a word the framers treat the woman doing a "man's job" as though she were a man.[194]

There are two points of interest here. First, the sages clearly impute to a woman the mental capacity to operate her husband's business, that is, to do a "man's job." Given what we learned earlier of a married woman's status, the discovery that a man may "[set] up his wife as a stallkeeper" (M. Ket. 9:4A) surprises us. Normally a man would sell his wares, from a market stall; the Mishnah's employment of the usual term for "stallkeeper" (*henwanit*) seems to imply that the wife has charge of her husband's stall (*hanut*) in the marketplace.[195] Yet we know the Mishnah's framers normally limit a woman's economic enterprises to such work as baking or weaving, which is carried out in the privacy of the home. The present case, however, contemplates a woman dealing with strangers. Perhaps she sells her wares at home from a stall open to the common courtyard (cf. M. B.B. 2:3), so that the stallkeeper of M. Ket. 9:4 is simply a special case of the "wife who transacts business in the house" mentioned in M. Shebu. 7:8.[196] Either way, the sages obviously credit a woman with the capacity to conduct business and expect her to deal honestly with her husband and her customers.

Second, to make a woman swear that she has not embezzled her husband's property treats her precisely like a man. The husband has appointed his wife as bailee of his goods, so the sages apply their general rule requiring a bailee to swear that any loss or damage occurred without his fault (M. Shebu. 8:1; M. B.M. 7:8). The application of this rule to the wife views her, on the one hand, as prone to the normal human impulse to profit from her situation but, on the other hand, as sufficiently moral to avoid perjury.[197] In judging a woman who operates in a male setting by the same criteria they would apply to a man, the Mishnah's framers treat her as a person.

Vows of an Emancipated Woman

Yet another area in which the Mishnah's framers recognize the autonomy of the grown woman is the law of the religious vow. If a minor girl makes a vow, her father may revoke this at will, but as soon as she comes of age, her father loses that control (M. Ned. 10:2). If still unmarried she becomes autonomous until she decides to marry and subject herself to the husband of her choice. Normally a woman enters the married state within a twelve-month period after betrothal (M. Ket 5:2A; see p. 117). But if the husband fails to bring her into his home when the betrothal period has passed, he at once becomes liable for her maintenance.

> D.[198] If the time [for consummation] has arrived, and [the prospective bride] has not been conducted [to the husband's home] for consummation, she may eat at [the husband's] expense.
>
> M. Ket. 5:2

This rule was obviously designed to encourage a prospective husband to fulfill his promise of marriage; once obligated to maintain the wife, he will most likely move her into his house so that he can benefit from her performance of wifely duties. But if he fails to do so, this raises another question: When he becomes liable for the prospective wife's maintenance, does his authority, including his power to revoke her vows, likewise vest at once?

> A. [In the case of] a grown woman who has waited twelve months [betrothal period] or a widow [who has waited] thirty days [M. Ket. 5:2],
> B. R. Eliezer rules that, since her [prospective] husband becomes liable for her maintenance, he may annul [her vows] [*i.e., vows affecting conjugal relations made after that date but before consummation*].
> C. But sages [in general] rule that the husband may not annul [her vows] until after she enters his domain.
>
> M. Ned. 10:5

The majority here rely on the technical *hayah le'ish* ["to be (i.e., to belong sexually) to a man"] used in the scriptural law of vows (Num. 30:7). On this interpretation, a husband's right to annul his wife's vows accrues only on consummation. Eliezer, however, thinks that a husband's right to annul his wife's vows should vest concurrently with the right to maintenance. Otherwise he may suffer serious inconvenience. Suppose the wife vows to abstain from the produce of a particular vendor, yet the husband can obtain food from no one else (M. Ned. 11:2, discussed in chap. 3). If allowed to stand, the vow will prevent the husband from fulfilling his duty to feed her. Even so, most sages insist that until the woman actually enters her husband's domain, he has no power to revoke her vows even if they affect him adversely. Of course, if her vow involves abstention from intercourse, the law permits him to divorce her with forfeiture of her marriage portion (M. Ket. 7:7). A man's control over a woman is rooted in his claim on her sexuality, and this explains why it does not actually vest until he consummates the marriage.

The point is made even more explicit in another context. In the law of the straying wife, the sages discuss the limits of a husband's right to accuse his wife of infidelity. A man's proprietary right to his wife's sexuality exists only because she is *"under the authority of [a] husband"* (Num. 5:19–20), so a woman's sexual conduct cannot invoke the ordeal unless she was actually betrothed or married to the husband at the time of the liaison of which she stands accused. The sages discuss the implications of the woman's response to the priest's pronouncement of the ritual curse.

A.   To what does she say, "Amen, amen!" [She says] "Amen!" to the curse and "Amen!" to the oath [Num. 5:21].

B.   "Amen! concerning this man" [with respect to whom she stands accused], "Amen concerning any other man";

C.   "Amen, that I have not gone astray while betrothed, or married, or awaiting levirate union, or after consummation [of such a union]";

D.   "Amen, that I have not been defiled; and if I have been defiled, may [all these curses] come upon me."

E.   R. Meir rules [that she says] "Amen that I have not been defiled and that I shall not [in future] defile myself."

M. Soṭ. 2:5

A.   All [the sages] agree that [the husband] may not stipulate with her concerning [what happened] before she was betrothed [to her husband] nor concerning [what happened] after she was divorced [from her husband].

B.   If, after [divorce], she secluded herself [with the man concerning whom she now stands accused] and became defiled, but thereafter [her husband] took her back [i.e., remarried her], [the husband] may not stipulate with her [*concerning what occurred before he took her back*].

C.   This is the general rule: As to any [woman] who has intercourse [with a man] to whom she was not forbidden, [the husband] may not stipulate with her [*with respect to that sexual conduct, which infringed no man's rights*].

M. Soṭ. 2:6

So long as a woman is neither married, nor betrothed, nor shackled to a levir who has not yet released her (M. Soṭ. 2:5C), her sexual conduct is her own business. The Mishnah endorses Scripture's view that a woman on whom no man has a claim can conduct her personal life as she pleases (M. Soṭ. 2:6). This sexual freedom of the autonomous woman in a polygynous society that imposes such strict control on wives bears striking testimony to the sages' understanding of a woman's intrinsic personhood. Only when some man has dominion over her does her sex life cease to be entirely her own affair.

The Divorcée

The earlier discussion of the wife at the point of divorce focused on the mishnaic formalities, which treated her as the husband's sexual property to be unilaterally discarded just as she was unilaterally acquired. In that context the unreleased wife appeared as virtual chattel. In what follows we view the impending divorcée from an entirely different angle—as a woman about to gain freedom from subordination to her husband. Though retrospectively a sexual chattel, prospectively she stands within a hair's-breadth of autonomy and the higher status this brings in its train. On receiving her writ of divorce, a wife becomes *sui juris*: "She acquires her autonomy by a writ of divorce . . ." (M. Qid. 1:1).

The husband's surrender of control produces significant legal results by reactivating the woman's dormant power to make her own decisions in all matters of private law. The same, of course, goes for the widow released by her husband's death. But a divorcée differs from a widow in one important respect: Although a widow's new status arises automatically without ceremony, the divorcing husband must follow complex rules of procedure to release the wife.

The rules we shall now examine reflect the sages' consciousness that a formal ritual is all that stands between the wife's shackled state and her freedom to remarry without impediment. Once preparation of the writ has signaled the husband's intention to release his wife, the Mishnah treats her as autonomous *in potentia*, investing her with legal rights and powers that anticipate the husband's imminent surrender of authority. They grant a prospective divorcée rights of action in connection with her release. She can sometimes complete, advance, or postpone delivery of the *get*—a power that gives her partial control of the moment of her release. She may thus prolong the duration of her marriage and with it her entitlement to certain matrimonial benefits. Conversely, she may expedite matters—for instance, to avoid levirate widowhood if her husband lacks heirs and lies near death.

Besides these *active* powers, the wife also possesses certain *passive* rights, that is, the law requires her husband to act in certain ways so as to secure her entitlements. In particular, a husband may not capriciously modify the divorce formula so as to preclude his divorcée from remarriage to a specified man. In these rules, in contrast to the divorce rules discussed in chapter 3, wherein the husband's unilateral release of his wife treats her as chattel, the powers and rights assigned to a wife on the point of divorce mark her distinctly as a person.

This much said, we cannot assume that the framers of mishnaic divorce law were chiefly concerned to safeguard the rights of the divorcée. Many rules (as we shall see) are designed mainly to clarify the woman's marital status, thus assuring a prospective suitor that the union will not cultically defile him or risk begetting illegitimate children by a woman not validly released from a prior marriage. For instance, the closing words of the divorce formula declare, not that the wife is free to marry any man *of her choice*, but rather that she is "now *permitted to* any man" (*muteret lᵉkol adam*)—emphasizing her *availability* rather than her *right* to remarry. Again, in requiring a husband to prepare a *get* expressly for the wife, the sages are less concerned with women's rights than with the literal implementation of Scripture's injunction, "*and he shall write [a bill of divorce-*

ment] for her [*specifically*]" (Deut. 24:1). Whatever the motivation behind these rules, in effect they treat the wife as individual person rather than anonymous chattel.

The Wife's Active Powers in the Law of Divorce

The use of various formulas permits husband and wife alike to influence the divorce process by controlling the time or place of the wife's receipt of her writ. This power comes into play when husband and wife live in different towns and one or both have appointed an agent to deliver or receive the *get*. Depending on the language employed, either spouse can specify the place at which the wife's release shall take effect.

A.[199] [Concerning] a man who said [to his agent], "Give this *get* to my wife in such-a-place," and [the agent] gave it to her in some other place, [delivery] is invalid. [*Here, the husband has made it a condition of the divorce that delivery take effect in a specified place; as this condition was not met, the divorce is invalid.*]

B. [But if the husband said] "Lo, she is in such-a-place," and [the agent] gave it to her in some other place, [delivery] is valid. [*Here, the place of delivery is not stated in the form of a condition; the husband intends merely to inform the agent of his wife's whereabouts. Hence, the actual place of delivery does not affect its validity; the divorce is complete.*]

C. [As for] a wife who said [to her agent], "Receive my *get* for me in such-a-place," and he received it for her in some other place, [delivery] is invalid. [*Like the husband at A, the wife has made the place of delivery a condition of her receipt of the* get.]

D. But R. Eliezer rules [the delivery] valid. [*In his view, because a man can divorce his wife against her will, she can hardly have power to set conditions as to when and where this shall occur. She must, therefore, be deemed to have intended merely to inform her agent of her husband's present whereabouts, and delivery at some other place adequately completes the divorce.*]

E. [If she said], "Bring me my *get* from such-a-place," and [the agent] brought it to her from some other place," [delivery] is valid. [*Even on the view of the sages at C that the wife can specify the place of delivery, she must be sure to use the correct technical terms. "Receive" (hitqabbel), the term used by the wife at C, sufficed legally to make the place of delivery a condition of the receipt of the* get. *But the term used here, "bring" (habe'), fails to achieve this effect and the wife is deemed indifferent to the actual place of delivery. However, the informal language suffices to validate delivery when the writ reaches her hand.*]

M. Git. 6:3

A. [If the wife of a *kohen* said to her agent] "Bring (*habe'*) me my *get* [that is, using informal language], she may eat of *t^erumah* ["heave-offering", priestly rations donated by lower-caste Israelites] until the *get* reaches her hand. [*Her failure to use formal terminology means that her agent's taking the writ from the husband or his agent does not constitute delivery to the*

*wife. Thus her marriage, and with it her entitlement to eat t^erumah,
continue in effect until the writ reaches her hand.*]

B. [If she said] "Receive my *get* for me," she is at once forbidden to eat *t^erumah*
   [*because the formal terminology makes delivery to her agent equivalent to
   delivery to herself*].

C. [If she said] "Receive my *get* for me at such-a-place," she may eat *t^erumah*
   until the *get* reaches [her agent at] the specified place.

D. But R. Eliezer precludes her at once [*consistently with his view that a wife
   cannot set conditions about the time or place of receipt*].

M. Giṭ. 6:4

The sages (Eliezer dissenting) permit husband (M. Giṭ. 6:3A) and wife
(M. Giṭ. 6:3C) alike to stipulate the place of the writ's delivery. The significant point is that the rules assign equal potency to the words of either
spouse. Even though we know the husband retains ultimate control
through his power to convert the wife's agent-for-receipt into his own
agent-for-delivery (M. Giṭ. 6:1C, discussed on p. 49), his forbearance from so
doing gives the wife's formula (M. Giṭ. 6:3C) equal validity with his own
(M. Giṭ. 6:3A). Here, then, the sages treat a woman just like a man in letting
her words produce a particular legal effect. Conversely, nonformulaic language by either party fails to make the place of delivery or receipt a necessary
condition; if the agent of either spouse executes his commission in some
other place, the divorce takes effect just the same. However, the wife's
informal request ("bring me" instead of "receive for me"), although not
making the place of receipt a condition of the transaction, does suffice to
achieve a valid delivery. The sages, intent on releasing the wife even if she
does not know the technical formula, accept her informal words as a valid
commission to her agent. Motivated by their desire to avoid the complications that can ensue when a wife mistakenly thinks she is properly divorced
(M. Giṭ. 8:5; see p. 65), their willingness to implement her intention despite its legally inelegant expression invests the woman with significant
power.

An obvious objection springs to mind. Because delivery of a writ of divorce
marks the moment at which a husband surrenders his claims on the wife, the
matter clearly involves his ownership of her sexuality. Given my postulation
of the sexuality factor, how can the sages permit a wife *any* control over this
moment? Indeed, when discussing a husband's power to retain ultimate
control by turning the wife's agent into his own and thus subverting her
wishes (M. Giṭ. 6:1), I claimed this illustrated the husband's inviolate right to
decide whether and when to surrender his claim on his wife's sexuality. How
is that case distinguishable from those at hand? The answer is clear. In the
earlier case the husband, by subverting the wife's agent, gave concrete expression to his desire to retain control, countermanding his earlier plan to release
her. Here, by contrast, the husband has expressed no change of mind. His
dispatch of the *get* sufficiently demonstrates his willingness to release the wife.
So long as he does not gainsay that intention, he places his wife in a position
very like that of the levirate widow whose levir has rejected her. Both Scripture

and Mishnah treat that woman as freed *in potentia*, thus enabling her to take an active part in the actual rite of release. Here, likewise, the husband's expressed intention to release the wife achieves a similar effect even before the formal steps are complete.[200] Thus it is the husband, not the sages, who at his option puts the wife in a position to control the moment of release. At the same time everyone knows that if the wife should remarry before actual receipt of the *geṭ*, the sages would inflict enormous penalties. Here is an unresolved paradox that serves to point up the persistent anomaly of woman's hybrid status in the mishnaic system.

Eliezer's minority view (6:3D and 6:4D) is of some interest. Because he regards the wife's attempt to control the time or place of divorce as totally lacking in effect, the husband need not even bother to countermand her. For Eliezer, a wife's power to set conditions conflicts with the rule that the husband can divorce her willy-nilly (M. Yeb. 14:1). If she has no say in *whether* he will release her, *a fortiori* she cannot control *where* or *when* this shall take place. The sages' refusal to see things Eliezer's way assigns the prospective divorcée more personhood, making her virtually equal to her husband in personal status and legal power as soon as, by executing the writ, he has signaled his intention to release her.

Furthermore, the wife's limited control over the moment of divorce has some practical value. The priest's wife at M. Giṭ. 6:4, who sends her agent to pick up the *geṭ* from her husband in a distant town, can extend the duration of her marriage, and with it her valuable entitlement to eat priestly rations, by taking care to use informal language, so that delivery to her agent will not constitute receipt by her. Conversely, if the divorcing husband plans to send the *geṭ* from a distant place, the wife can expedite her release by sending her agent to "receive" the *geṭ* rather than waiting for the husband's agent to reach her. This option can have real value if she has already selected a new marriage partner, or if her childless husband lies at death's door and could leave her in the status of levirate widow at any moment. This power to control her own life, however limited in scope, significantly transcends a wife's normal rights; the prospective divorcée is suddenly more of a legal person than she was throughout her years of marriage.

The Wife's Passive Rights in the Law of Divorce

Though unable to resist the husband's divorcing her at will, the prospective divorcée benefits from certain procedures that her husband must legally observe. These include, first and foremost, his duty to prepare a writ expressly for her; he may not simply take a document originally prepared for another woman and substitute his wife's name.

A. Every *geṭ* that is not written [expressly] for a designated woman is invalid. How so?

B. If [a man] was passing through the marketplace and heard the voice of scribes calling out, "Such-a-man is divorcing such-a-woman of such-a-place," and [the man] said, "That is my name and my wife's name," [and he acquired the document with the intention of using it to divorce his wife], it is invalid [as a legal instrument] wherewith to divorce [her].

C.   Furthermore, if he wrote [a *get*] wherewith to divorce his wife [and then reconsidered] and a fellow townsman found him and said to him, "My name is the same as thine, and my wife's name the same as thy wife's," [the prepared document] is invalid [as a legal instrument] wherewith to divorce [the other man's wife].

D.   Furthermore, if [a man] has two wives whose names are identical, and he wrote [a *get*] wherewith to divorce the elder, he may not divorce the younger therewith.

E.   Furthermore, if he said to the scrivener, "Write [it] so that I may divorce whomsoever I may wish," [the document] is invalid to divorce [any woman at all] therewith.

M. Giṭ. 3:1

These provisions are designed to implement the words of Scripture, "*and he shall write a bill of divorcement* for her" (*wᵉkatab lah*, Deut. 24:1). The sages took the phrase to mean that the husband must prepare the *get* expressly for the wife he plans to divorce. This rule, by forcing him to contemplate her as an individual, may even induce a change of heart in a hasty husband. While not claiming that the framers of this rule consciously desired to help the wife, we note this serendipitous side effect of their interpretation of Scripture.

Insistence on the letter of the law also means that release is not complete until the *get* reaches the wife. Scripture requires that "*he shall give* [*the writ of divorce*] into her hand" (*wᵉnatan bᵉyadah*, Deut. 24:1). When the husband personally delivers the *get*, no problem arises; but if he employs an agent, complications may ensue. As the divorce will not be complete until the *get* reaches the wife, it follows that so long as the agent retains the document, the husband retains the right to change his mind. But if he does so, the wife needs to know about this, lest she mistakenly contract another marriage. So the sages insist that the husband either intercept the agent or inform his wife before the agent reaches her. They even record an amendment enacted to frustrate the designs of husbands who ignore the rules.

A.   [Concerning] one who sent a *get* to his wife but [subsequently] caught up with the agent, or sent after him a [second] agent, and [the husband or the second agent] said to him, "The *get* that I gave you is void," this [*get*] is void [*and the agent must not deliver it*].

B.   If [the husband] reached his wife first, or if he sent to her a [second] agent [who arrived before the first], and [the husband or the second agent] said to her, "The *get* that I have sent you is void," this [*get*] is void. *The wife is thus informed that the document in the hands of the first agent will not have the legal effect of releasing her.*]

C.   But if [the husband or second agent arrived] after the *get* had [already] reached her hand, [the husband] can no longer render it void.

M. Giṭ. 4:1

A.   Originally, [husbands] used to convene a court [of three judges] in another place [*i.e., without the knowledge of the wife or of the husband's agent who was carrying the* get], and declare [the *get*] void.

B.   But Rabban Gamaliel the Elder amended [the law] to the effect that they must not do so, for the welfare of society (*mip*ᵉ*nei tiqqun ha*ᶜ*olam*). [*The law was amended to obviate confusion about the status of a wife who receives a* get *from an agent without knowing that her husband has mean-while exercised his right of retraction.*]

C.   Originally, a man might change his name, or his wife's name, or the name of his town or her town [*for reasons not necessarily related to the divorce and then use the new names in the* get, *thus generating confusion as to the identity of the parties*].

D.   But Rabban Gamaliel the Elder amended [the law] to the effect that [the husband or scribe] must write, "Such-a-man"—[here listing] every name he had used—or "such-a-woman"—[here listing] every name she had used—for the welfare of society. [*This rule eliminates the possibility of confusion as to precisely which husband is divorcing which wife, and it guarantees that the* get *cannot later be nullified on a technicality.*]

M. Giṭ. 4:2

These provisions flow from the sages' intense preoccupation with the problem of women's marital status. Their desire for certainty explains both the basic rule (M. Giṭ. 4:1) and the special amendment (M. Giṭ. 4:2). The primary goal of avoiding illicit remarriage and consequent illegitimate births is inherent in the statement that Gamaliel acted "for the welfare of society." The legislation, though not chiefly concerned with the welfare of a prospective divorcée, still gives her a valuable personal right. By negating the husband's power of arbitrary retraction, it ensures the wife's freedom to remarry without fear that her husband may then claim to have revoked her get before it reached her. The rule at M. Giṭ. 4:2D provides added assurance; no one can later allege that she is not the wife named in the get (hence not free to remarry).[201]

Release of a Woman Morally Entitled to Divorce

The fundamental rule of mishnaic divorce law is that "a woman may be divorced with or without her consent, but a man divorces only with his own consent" (M. Yeb. 14:1). But the Mishnah's framers seem to have had second thoughts on the desirability of the husband's absolute control, for they modify their own assertion that divorce depends solely on the will of the husband by ruling, on the one hand, that the court can compel the husband to issue a get in an appropriate case and, on the other hand, that a woman may legally induce her husband to divorce her by agreeing to forgo the return of her marriage portion. Both rules improve the status of a prospective divorcée by making it easier for her to obtain her freedom from an unfortunate marriage.

A.   A *get* [whose delivery is] compelled by [a court of] Israelites is valid,
B.   but [a *get* whose delivery is compelled] by [a court of] gentiles is invalid.
C.   Yet [if it is compelled] by gentiles beating [the husband] and telling him, "Do as the Israelite court orders thee," it is valid.

M. Giṭ. 9:8

A.   [If a husband says to his wife,] "This is thy *get* on condition that thou give me two hundred *zuz*," this woman is [validly] divorced provided she gives [the agreed sum to her husband]. [*Two hundred zuz is the standard sum stipulated in the marriage settlement that is to be paid to a faultless wife on divorce. Thus a stipulation that a wife pay this sum in consideration of the husband's releasing her is equivalent to her forgoing her marriage portion.*]
B.   [But if the husband said,] ". . . on condition that thou give me [the money] within thirty days from now," then if she gives it to him within thirty days, she is [validly] divorced; but if not, then she is not divorced.

M. Giṭ. 7:5

In these cases the wife's right to release may not have been the sages' primary concern;[202] but in practice these rules surely improve her position. Certainly the theoretical assumptions of M. Yeb. 14:1 are significantly modified by rules designed to compel the husband to deliver a *get* in specified cases. In M. Giṭ. 9:8 the court will force the delivery of a *get* when it sees fit, even enlisting the aid of gentile authorities to coerce a reluctant husband. According to law, the husband must deliver the *get* of his own free will. But in the case of a husband who resists the court's order, the sages expressly declared that "we twist his arm until he says, 'I will'" (M. ʿArak. 5:6). Specified cases include those discussed in chapter 3, wherein the sages insist on the divorce of a wife whose husband, by forswearing intercourse with her, defeats the primary purpose of marriage and wastes the woman's reproductive function. It might be claimed that a husband's abjuring sexual relations with his wife places him in a position analogous to the man who has decided to divorce his wife or release his levirate widow. Just as those women gain virtual autonomy on the strength of those decisions, so here the court asserts a wife's right to release for the selfsame reason. Thus any woman whose husband chooses to forgo his right to her sexuality is morally and legally entitled to release, and the court will go so far as to solicit the aid of gentiles to achieve this.[203]

The rule of M. Giṭ. 7:5 that lets a husband divorce his wife without returning her marriage portion—provided she agrees to this—holds particular interest. In effect, it permits a woman to buy back her freedom. Because she wants to deprive her husband of the very thing for which he paid bride-price, namely, the exclusive right to her sexuality, it is only fair that she return the money. So once he has divorced her and handed over her portion, she is morally bound to return it to him at once. At M. Giṭ. 7:5B, the sages (aware that cheating is not confined to males) hedge their bets by providing that if she fails to hand over the money by the specified time, the divorce will be retrospectively invalidated. Although M. Giṭ. 7:5A does not give the wife equal divorce rights with the husband (as he can always refuse her request for release), it does improve her position by permitting her to take the initiative. Here, we have the reverse of the situation of M. Giṭ. 9:8. That rule contemplates *inter alia* a man who has forsworn his right to use the wife's sexuality and ought morally to let her go, whereas in M. Giṭ. 7:5 it is the wife who asks the husband to give up that claim and ought, therefore, to give back the bride-price.[204] But the two cases have this much in common: Once it is clear that the parties' sexual relationship is coming to an end, the prospective divorcée appears to the sages as potentially autonomous. Either the husband's active desire to end the sexual relationship or his willingness to release the wife for a financial consideration invests her with a moral right to freedom that she lacks so long as he wishes to continue the relationship. These rules mitigate the rigors of a system that in theory lets men acquire and dispose of wives like chattel.

The Total Autonomy of the Divorcée

The best proof of the prospective divorcée's impending autonomy appears in the rule that the man who divorces her must free her completely, with no strings attached. The sages forbid the husband to restrict his divorcée's choice of future husband. She may marry whomsoever she pleases (within the limits of caste restrictions and other prohibited unions).

A.   [Concerning] one who divorces his wife and says to her, "Lo, thou art permitted to every man except so-and-so,"

B.   R. Eliezer permits [this, and the *geṭ* remains valid].

C.   But sages [in general] forbid [it, and it invalidates the *geṭ*].

D.   So what should [the husband] do [to rectify the situation when he has delivered the *geṭ* in this manner]? He should retrieve it from her and give it to her again, saying to her, "Lo, thou art permitted to any man."

E.   However, if he wrote [the restriction mentioned at A] within [the document] itself even though he went back and erased it, [the *geṭ*] remains invalid [*and he must prepare a new writ without the restriction*].

                                             M. Giṭ. 9:1

A.   [If the husband said,] "Lo, thou art permitted to any man except my father and thy father, my brother and thy brother, a slave or a gentile"—or to any one to whom she cannot legally become espoused—[the *geṭ*] remains valid. [*The husband's stated restrictions are redundant because the general law in any case forbids those marriages.*]

B.   [But if he said,] "Lo, thou art permitted to any man except a high priest"— she being a widow [when he married her]; or "an ordinary priest"—she being a divorcée or released levirate widow [when he married her]; or "an Israelite"—she being a *mamzeret* or *neʿtinah*; or a *mamzer* or *natin*"—she being an Israelite's daughter; or anyone to whom she can validly be married even though [her doing so would be] an infraction [of caste guidelines], in any of these cases [the *geṭ*] is invalid. [*The restrictions listed at B, unlike those at A, involve marriages that are not absolutely forbidden. Though technical violations of the caste system, and forbidden* **ab** initio *they are treated* **ex** post facto *as valid. So here the husband's attempted restrictions are not redundant and will invalidate the divorce.*]

M. Giṭ. 9:2

A. The substance of a *geṭ* is "Lo, thou art permitted to any man." R. Judah rules [that the *geṭ* should state, in Aramaic] "and let this be to thee from me a bill of divorce and a deed of dismissal and a writ of release, so that thou mayest espouse thyself to anyone thou wilt."

B. [This is similar to] the substance of a writ of emancipation [for a female slave], "Thou are a free woman, thou art *sui juris.*"

M. Giṭ. 9:3

Once the wife is released from her husband's authority, he loses his power to control her life. Above all, he cannot restrict her choice of future marriage partners within the limits of the law (M. Giṭ. 9:1-2). The very essence of a writ of divorce is that the husband has relinquished his claim on his wife's sexuality; so far as he is concerned, any man can have her (M. Giṭ. 9:3A) once she has waited out the three-month period required lest she be carrying his child at the time of divorce (M. Yeb. 4:10).[205] M. Giṭ. 9:3B makes the point even more explicit by analogy: A man who emancipates a female slave must state expressly that she is now *sui juris*, which means she can do as she pleases. This analogy underscores the fact that a released wife cannot be more restricted than a freedwoman.

Given their horror of illicit unions, the Mishnah's framers wish to make it crystal clear that the divorcée, no longer bound to her husband, is free to marry any suitor she chooses. Sages claim (M. Soṭ. 5:1) that a woman divorced for adultery is prohibited to her paramour, but this restriction, being of rabbinic and not biblical origin, has never been strictly enforced. The rule denying the husband's power to limit her right of remarriage highlights the effect of divorce on a woman's level of personhood. The *geṭ* restores her autonomy *precisely because of the operation of the sexuality factor*: The husband has relinquished his sexual control. She can thus choose another man without hindrance. Moreover, a divorcée's level of personhood becomes higher than before. Subject first to her father's authority and then to her husband's, she now (probably for the first time) controls her own private life. She has attained the highest level of legal personhood available to women in the mishnaic system.

The Widow

Like the divorcée, the widow is autonomous, falling under no man's jurisdiction. So we expect her to have power to conduct her personal affairs freely within the limits of the law; and this is precisely what we find. The sages permit a widow to execute her own business transactions, above all in the purchase and sale of property. This power can have great value because a widow may well possess considerable wealth—not to mention the intangible power that wealth tends to generate.[206] The husband's death entitles the widow to collect all the property he held in trust for her, including the bride-price stated in her marriage settlement plus whatever property she brought to the marriage as dowry.

The Widow's Rights Against Heirs of a Deceased Husband

The Mishnah's framers, taking for granted a widow's capacity to buy and sell property, realize that this power is useless unless she can gain prompt access to her marriage portion on her husband's death. So they make rules to protect a widow's property rights against her husband's heirs. A newly bereaved widow is entitled to the return of the property (bride-price and dowry) originally entrusted to her husband. Further, she can choose when to collect her marriage portion; she may do so at once or defer her claim for as long as she likes. If she defers her claim, she continues to be maintained out of her husband's estate (M. Ket. 4:12, discussed in chap. 3). In return she must give the heirs whatever she earns if she continues working while they maintain her.

A. A widow is [to be] maintained from her husband's estate (lit. the property of the orphans) and [the proceeds of] her labor belong to them [*in return for maintaining her, just as with husband and wife (M. Ket. 6:1; see p. 87)*].

B. But [unlike a husband], they are not responsible for [the cost of] her burial; her [own] heirs, who inherit her k^e*tubbah*, are responsible for her burial. [*I.e., only her own children, not those of her husband by other wives, must pay for her burial.*]

M. Ket. 11:1

A. A widow, whether [her husband died] during the betrothal period or after consummation, may sell [her husband's property that is security for her k^e*tubbah*] without [permission of] the court. [*I.e., she may forthwith sell such property for her maintenance if her husband's heirs neglect to maintain her.*]

B. R. Simeon rules [that if widowed] after consummation, she may sell [said property] without [permission of] the court; [but if widowed] during betrothal, she may sell only with [permission of] the court—

C. for [a woman widowed during betrothal] has no right to maintenance [from the betrothed husband's estate]; and a woman who has no right to maintenance may not sell [her deceased husband's property] without [permission of] the court. [*As she has no right to maintenance, she should simply claim her k^etubbah from the heirs at once.*].

M. Ket. 11:2

A. If [a widow] has sold [her husband's property that is subject to a lien for] her k^e*tubbah* property, or part of it; or if she has pledged her k^e*tubbah* property, or part of it; or if she has given to another person her k^e*tubbah* property, or part of it [*in each case, to cover the cost of maintenance, when her husband's heirs have refused to maintain her after her husband's death*],

B.   [in each case] she may sell the remainder only with [permission of] the court. [*Having provided for her maintenance, she must now claim the rest of the k*ᵉ*tubbah or its increments in the normal way. This is the view of Simeon (continued from M. Ket. 11:2B.)*]

C.   But sages [in general] rule [that] she may sell [portions of the property], four or five times [if need be].

D.   And she may sell it for maintenance without [permission of] the court if she declares in writing, "I have sold it for maintenance."

E.   But a divorcée may sell only with [permission of] the court. [*A divorcée is not entitled to maintenance but only to her k*ᵉ*tubbah, so if her husband has not given her her k*ᵉ*tubbah, she must go to court in order to claim it (M. Ket. 11:2C.)*]

                                                                    M. Ket. 11:3

The Mishnah's framers attribute to the widow legal rights, moral obligations, and human intelligence like those of an Israelite man. They take for
granted her intrinsic power to transact business and handle property. More
strikingly, they even empower the widow to sell property not strictly her
own; if her husband's heirs fail to maintain her, she may sell their inheritance, on which she has a lien for the payment of her marriage portion (M.
Ket. 8:8). The sages wish to ensure that the widow receives her due from
reluctant heirs. (These may well include co-wives' sons who resent this
woman's indefinite entitlement to maintenance at their expense.)

At the same time the sages will not let the widow abuse her power by
selling more of the deceased's property than is needed for her maintenance
in a given period. They take care to balance her rights against those of
her husband's heirs. What is equitable in one case may be unfair in others.
In general, the widow can expect the heirs to maintain her only if she agrees
to remain in the matrimonial home where they can conveniently support
her.

A.   [Concerning] a widow who said, "I do not wish to move from my husband's house,"

B.   the heirs have no power to say to her, "Go to thy father's house, and we shall maintain thee [there.]"

C.   Rather, they must maintain her in her husband's house and give her a dwelling befitting her station.

D.   [If] she said, "I do not wish to move from my father's house" [*where she has returned following her husband's death*],

E.   the heirs have power to say to her, "If thou [remain] with us, thou shalt have maintenance, and if not, thou shalt not have maintenance." [*She cannot have it both ways: If she chooses maintenance instead of claiming her marriage portion, she must remain in the husband's household; if she prefers to go back to her father's house or even to live alone, she cannot expect maintenance from the heirs but instead should claim her marriage portion at once.*]

F.   But if she pleaded thus because she was a young girl and they were youths [*i.e., the youthful heirs are her husband's sons by a previous wife and it is unseemly for them to live with their father's young widow, lest they be tempted to violate the prohibition of relations with their father's wife (Lev. 18:8)*], they must maintain her, yet she [may reside] in her father's house.

M. Ket. 12:3

Like the preceding rules, this unit maintains an equitable balance between the widow's rights and those of her husband's heirs. In ensuring that the widow gets no less—but also no more—than her due, the sages treat her just as they would a man. They enforce her rights against her late husband's estate while guarding against her natural human propensity to exploit her situation at the heirs' expense. In sum, they treat her as a person.

The Widow's Compellability to Swear an Oath

The Mishnah's framers sometimes require a widow to swear an oath when claiming property due to her. If she claims she has received only part of the marriage portion that accrued to her on her husband's death—or none at all—the sages rule that before handing over the balance, the husband's heirs may require the widow to swear to the truth of her claim. If she says she has received nothing, they may permit her to take a religious vow in private rather than swear a legal oath in public.

A. [Concerning] a woman who impairs her marriage portion [*i.e., who claims to have received some part but not the whole of what is due to her (M. Ket. 9:8)*], she shall not be paid [the balance] except on [her] oath [that she has not received the full amount].

B. [If] one witness testified concerning [the marriage portion] that it had been paid [to her], she shall not be paid except on [her] oath [that she has not received it]. [*The testimony of a single witness would not suffice to controvert her testimony; but it does invoke the requirement that she swear an oath in rebuttal (M. Shebu. 7:1, 7:4).*]

C. [If a widow claims her marriage portion] from her husband's estate (lit. the property of the orphans) or from property subject to [her] lien [*that her husband had sold to purchasers even though it was security for her marriage portion*] or [if she is to be paid] not in the presence of [the present holder of the property]; she shall not be paid except on [her] oath [that she has not received her marriage portion].

M. Ket. 9:7

A. A widow may not be paid [her marriage portion] from her husband's estate (lit. the property of the orphans) except on [her] oath [that she has not yet received her due].

B. But when they [*i.e., the court*] refrained from making her swear an oath, Rabban Gamaliel the Elder amended the law, so that she should [merely] swear a religious vow to the heirs (lit. orphans) howsoever they wish, and [thereafter] she may collect her marriage portion. [*When the court abolished the widow's oath to obviate the necessity of a court appearance, Gamaliel substituted the religious vow to prevent the widow from taking advantage of her husband's heirs by falsely claiming she has not received her marriage portion.*]

M. Giṭ. 4:3

In these cases the Mishnah's framers treat the widow very like a man in similar circumstances. The testimony of a single adverse witness (M. Ket. 9:7B) although not sufficient to rebut her claim, does invoke the requirement of an oath to support it, in accordance with normal court procedure (M. Shebu. 7:1, 7:4).[207] The sages know that a woman, like a man, is bound by Scripture's injunction that the Israelite keep his word (Num. 30:3); and they take for granted that the widow understands the nature of an oath and will not perjure herself (M. Ket 9:7). In other words they perceive her as possessing both intelligence and morality. Gamaliel (M. Giṭ 4:3B) likewise assumes the widow will take seriously the religious vow substituted for the oath.

What motivates the sages to treat the women in these cases like men? The common denominator among them is twofold. First, these women have unrestricted control of property, an important power normally held by men. Second, the widow (like the emancipated daughter and the divorcée) enjoys autonomy, another "male" attribute. Hence the sages' willingness to subject these women to the oath, a procedure normally imposed only on men. The sages' recognition of a woman's intellectual and moral capacity to perform like a man (when they find this appropriate or expedient) once more treats her as a person.

The Vows of a Widow or Divorcée

The vow of a widow or divorcée presents special problems for the Mishnah's framers. Such women being *sui juris,* Scripture insists that nobody can countermand their vows (Num. 30:10). The sages discuss the widow or divorcée who makes a vow intended to take effect at a later date. If she remarries between the date of the vow and the date of its operation, can her new husband use his authority to forestall the operation of the vow by countermanding it? The sages then consider the converse case of a wife who makes a vow intended to take effect later and whose husband revokes her vow and then divorces her before it takes effect: Does the vow remain revoked?

A. *"But the vow of a widow or divorcée . . . shall stand against her"* (Num. 30:10). How so?

B. [If a widow or divorcée] said, "I shall become a Nazirite after thirty days!" even though she remarries within [those] thirty days, [her husband cannot annul [this vow] *because she made it before coming under his control*].

C. [But if a woman] vowed [such a vow] while she was in the domain of a husband, he can annul [it] for her. How so?

D. [If] she said, "I shall become a Nazirite after thirty days!" [and the husband annulled this vow], even if she becomes widowed or divorced within [those] thirty days, this [vow] remains annulled [*because she was under his control when she made it*].

E. [If] she vowed on a certain day, was divorced on the same day [before her husband had annulled the vow], and [her husband] took her back on the same day, he cannot annul [it]. [*This is because her intervening period of autonomy destroys his right to do so*].

F.   This is the general principle: [Concerning] any woman who acquired her autonomy [even] for a single moment, no one [who later acquires her] can annul [vows made before she comes under his authority].

M. Ned. 11:9

A man generally can annul his wife's Nazirite vow because it may impair conjugal relations (M. Naz. 4:1ff., app. 4).[208] But here we have a woman who occupies one status when she makes that vow and another when it takes effect. Which point in time determines the outcome? The sages settle for the time she made the vow. The new husband at M. Ned. 11:9B cannot annul a Nazirite vow made during the widow's period of independence, even though it takes effect only after marriage, because she was not subject to him when she vowed. By contrast, the husband at C and D can effectively revoke his wife's Nazirite vow made during marriage; and it will not revive if he dies or divorces her before the operative date of the vow because his revocation has wiped it out completely. Most interesting is the hypothetical case at M. Ned. 11:9E that illustrates the effect of autonomy on the woman's personhood. Even a short period of independence suffices to break the chain of control. The instant the wife becomes a widow (or divorcée), the husband no longer owns the right to her sexuality and hence can no longer annul her vows made during their first marriage, even after he takes her back.

Perhaps significant here is the fact that the Nazirite vow is usually limited to a short period (often thirty days). The sages are willing to tolerate temporary inconvenience to the husband who marries a woman subject to such a vow. In any case the incommoded husband has a last resort if his wife has, in fact, devoted herself for an unlimited period. He can simply avail himself of the rule that one who marries a woman who is subject to vows that impair the conjugal relationship may divorce her with forfeiture of marriage portion (M. Ket. 7:7; see p. 85).

Summary

The legal status of autonomous women is poles apart from that of their dependent sisters. In contrast to a minor daughter, one who attains full age while still unmarried becomes independent for all purposes of private law. Her right to choose her own spouse is matched by her power to contract her own marriage. She may engage in lititgation, transact business personally or through agents, and (sometimes) testify in her own behalf—powers that reflect the sages' recognition of her capacity to make intellectual judgments and moral choices. Even the sages' criteria for assessing her crdibility show that they perceive her thought processes as similar to those of a man. The intrinsic equality of men and women in matters of private law is further borne out by the legal duties imposed on a woman who performs what the sages regard as a "man's job." Thus a female bailee of goods can be made to swear an oath concerning her proper care and disposition of the bailor's property, just as a male bailee would have to do in similar circumstances.

These remarks apply equally to all emancipated women, whether single, divorced, or widowed. But special rules governing divorcées serve to reinforce the point. For instance, though the unilateral formalities of divorce procedure treat divorcées as chattel, the substance of the law treats the prospective divorcée as autonomous in principle. Her autonomy starts to take effect even before the writ is delivered, giving the divorcée some control over the timing of her release. Rules preserving a divorcée's unconditional freedom to remarry emphasize that her husband has yielded his power to control her sexual function. A husband's option to release his wife if she forgoes her marriage portion gives the wife a chance to bargain amicably with her husband for her freedom.

Finally, the case of the widow shows the considerable economic clout attainable by the autonomous woman. She can remain in the matrimonial home as long as she likes, forcing her husband's heirs to maintain her indefinitely. She can even attach the property of the heirs if needed for her support.

The widow's high legal status, of course, may not be accompanied by high socioeconomic status. A woman's autonomy may sometimes prove illusory in the mishnaic culture. Many emancipated women, especially widows or divorcées with small marriage settlements, may not be economically as well off as they were during marriage. The legal freedom to do as she pleases may be of little benefit to a woman whose life options are restricted for economic or other reasons. There is some evidence that such a woman, though legally emancipated, might be financially forced to return to her father's house (assuming he will have her). M. Ket 4:8, for instance, contemplates a priest's daughter who returns home after divorce. Nonetheless, for a wealthy urban widow or divorcée autonomy may well improve her position, since it increases her freedom to operate in the world of commerce without restraints imposed by a husband possibly possessing less business acumen. In early medieval Islam, where both Jewish and Arab women's status was governed by laws very similar to those of the Mishnah, there are documented cases of wealthy widows who were successful businesswomen. The widow Khadija, first wife of the Prophet Muḥammad, springs to mind, as does the widow Wuḥsha, beautifully sketched for us in Goitein's monumental study of documents from the Cairo Geniza.[209] Thus, we cannot make blanket judgments about the effect of legal autonomy on the lives of autonomous women in the mishnaic system, even assuming (as we have done in this study), that the rules of the system reflect some kind of reality.

The common denominator of autonomous women—and the significant difference between them and their dependent counterparts—lies in the now-familiar sexuality factor. Autonomous women control their own biological function; this *and only this* accounts for the willingness of the Mishnah's framers to let them go their own way. The power to make their own choices in virtually all aspects of their personal lives clearly gives autonomous women a higher status than dependent women in the private sphere. Things are far otherwise, however, when we turn our attention to the position of women in the public domain.

6

WOMAN AND
THE PUBLIC DOMAIN

Given the patriarchal background of the Mishnah, many of the women discussed in the previous chapter enjoyed a surprising degree of personhood. Indeed, an autonomous woman's legal entitlements and obligations in matters of personal status and private commerce scarcely differed, in theory, from those of a man. Yet even autonomous women (much less dependent woman) never attain total equality with men because law and custom conspire to exclude women in general from the public domain of mishnaic culture.

Already in the private domain the cards are stacked against any claim of total equality of the sexes. The sages make this clear in discussing the respect that children must show parents. Most scriptural references to parents mention the father first; but in one case, the mother precedes the father. Here is how the sages resolve the dilemma:

A.   The father precedes the mother everywhere [that Scripture mentions them]. [*See Gen. 2:24, 28:7; Exod. 20:12, 21:15 and 17; Lev. 16:32, 18:7 and 9, 19:3, 20:9 and 17, 21:2 and 11; Num. 6:7; Deut. 5:16, 21:13 and 18–19, 22:15, 27:16 and 22, 33:9. "Everywhere" is a generalization. There are two exceptions, the more significant being noted at C.*][210]

B.   One might conclude that [this is because] the honor due to the father exceeds the honor due to the mother.

C.   Yet Scripture says, "*You shall each revere his mother and his father*" (Lev. 19:3).

D.   This verse [*weighed against the citations listed at A, in particular against Exod. 20:12, "Honor your father and your mother"*], teaches that the two of them are equivalent [*thus refuting the suggestion at B*].

145

E.   But the sages have ruled that the father precedes the mother in every case
      because both [the child] and his mother are bound to honor the father.

                                                                    M. Ker. 6:9

The sages solve the problem quite arbitrarily by their ruling at M. Ker.
6:9E. They simply retreat from the problem inherent in the placing of the
mother before the father in Lev. 19:3. Their patriarchal system holds it
axiomatic that the free adult Israelite male—the mishnaic yardstick of legal
and social status—takes precedence over his wife; moreover, Scripture has
decreed that *"he shall rule over [her]"* (Gen. 3:16). Hence, even from the
standpoint of their children, who should theoretically weigh Exod. 20:12
against Lev. 19:3 and treat father and mother with equal honor and respect,
in the last analysis the *paterfamilias* takes precedence.

The Intrinsic Superiority of the Male

If the male reigns supreme in the private sphere, this is even clearer in the
public domain of Israelite life. Here, we find a yawning gulf between the
sexes. Even the highest-ranking woman runs into a roadblock that severely
restricts her life options: She is not allowed to participate in the public
culture of the Israelite community. The mishnaic system denies women
access to precisely those aspects of Israelite culture—in the world outside the
home—that constitute the life of mind and spirit, and it likewise excludes
them from leadership roles in communal life.[211]

Many religions of antiquity, organized by men, excluded women from
participation in public religious rites except perhaps as cultic prostitutes on
the one hand or vestal virgins on the other.[212] But such women were
obviously exceptional in their deviation from the gender norm for women
in patriarchy. The vast majority, playing domestic roles and fulfilling their
biological destiny, could not aspire to positions of authority in religious
affairs.[213] Here mishnaic Judaism was no exception. But the framers of the
Mishnah went further: They barred *all* women, whatever their domestic
situation and regardless of dependent or autonomous status, from participating in public religious exercises.

In seeking the reasons, our starting point, as always, is Scripture. The
sages' disqualification of women from performing sacrificial rites and other
forms of public worship relies in part on scriptural precedent. First and
foremost, the cult of the Sanctuary described in the Priestly Code of Leviticus and Numbers is the exclusive preserve of *males*. All men of the priestly
caste (descendents of Aaron) are eligible—indeed required—to perform sacrificial and other rites; but Scripture assigns no such role to *women* of
priestly descent.

In regulating women's relationship to the cult, the sages seem to have
deduced from the biblical paradigm that the actual execution (as opposed to
the offering) of sacrifice is the preserve of men. In specifying the religious
duties of lay Israelites, Scripture already makes a similar distinction. A man

who brings offerings to the priest explicitly comes *"before the LORD"*; a woman, by contrast, does not.[214] This distinction emerges from a subtle difference in the regulations for the cleansing of men and women who suffer a genital flux (Lev. 15). The man in this plight must take the cleansing sacrifice and *"come before the LORD (YHWH) at the entrance of the Tent of Meeting and give them to the priest"* (Lev. 15:14). The woman in the parallel case must take her offerings and *"bring them to the priest at the entrance of the Tent of Meeting"* (Lev. 15:29). Here, the text says nothing of coming before Yahweh. Although Scripture specifies no difference in the physical location at which men and women respectively deliver their offerings, the deliberate omission of the phrase *"before YHWH"* in otherwise identical descriptions must have some significance. This assumption is reinforced by the text's requirement that the man immerse himself before going to the Tent of Meeting (Lev. 15:13), whereas no such cleansing ritual is specified for the woman in the like case—presumably because, unlike the man, she will not *"come before YHWH."*[215] This denial of a woman's capacity to approach YHWH in the same way as a man symbolizes Scripture's view that women inherently fail to qualify for participation in cultic rites.

The Mishnah's framers draw the obvious conclusion: God excludes women from cultic rites because these are the province of men. Hence they interpret two other cultic rituals—the rite of the first fruits (Deut. 26:1-11) and the donation to the Sanctuary (Exod. 30:13)—as beyond the domain of women, thereby endorsing Scripture's view of women as probably ineligible and certainly exempt from the performance of cultic rites. But the sages go far beyond Scripture in excusing women from many religious practices not directly connected with Sanctuary or Temple. These exemptions cover most practices of the rabbinic Judaism that replaced the sacrificial cult after the destruction of the Temple in 70 C.E. Women are excused from such devotions as twice-daily recitation of *Sh^ema^c* (Deut. 6:4-9, 11:13-21; Num. 15:37-41), use of phylacteries during prayer (mandated by Deut. 6:8), active participation in public worship (especially in leadership roles), and most important of all, participation in communal study of sacred texts.

Why did the Mishnah's framers go beyond Scripture in banning women outright (or exempting them in theory and discouraging them in practice) from activities that enrich the Israelite's intellectual life and symbolize the spiritual commitment of the Jew to his cultural heritage? The mere framing of this question would have perplexed the sages, whose mind-set about the cultural image, social role, and legal status of women naturally reflected the patriarchal nature of their society. For us, however, the question—and the answer—are crucial.

Although the sages do not tell us exactly what they think about women and the cult, close scrutiny of the exemptions and exclusions reveals their underlying rationale. Four themes come into play: first, a legal presumption that men, as heads of households, perform cultic precepts on behalf of wives, children, slaves, and all within their jurisdiction; second, a tacit assumption that women are properly confined to the private, domestic sphere; third, a rationalization that women, exempted by the sages, cannot conduct communal rites on behalf of those obligated to perform them; and fourth, an atavistic fear of women as sexually disturbing and dangerously contaminating creatures who must be barred from the public domain lest their presence distract men from intellectual and spiritual pursuits.

Women's Subordinate Status and Exclusion from the Cult

Some exclusions of women from cultic and religious practices directly reflect women's subordinate legal status. Thus, religious duties that devolve upon the *paterfamilias* as head of household cannot be performed by a woman because she cannot occupy that position. Slaughter and consumption of the paschal lamb is one household observance in which women participate only as dependants of their menfolk.

> A. A woman [living] in her husband's house, if her husband has slaughtered [the paschal offering] on her behalf and her father has [also] slaughtered it on her behalf [*perhaps forgetting that his daughter will be married off before the festival*], shall eat of [the sacrifice of] her husband [*because her marriage transfers her from the domain of her father to that of her husband*].
>
> B. [But] if she went to observe the first [Passover] festival [after her marriage] in her father's house and both her father and her husband had slaughtered [the paschal sacrifice] on her behalf, she may eat of whichever she chooses.
>
> M. Pes. 8:1

> A. One may not slaughter the paschal sacrifice on account of a [single] individual. So holds R. Judah. [*A single individual cannot consume the entire sacrifice; hence some meat would be left over, in violation of Exod. 12:10.*]
>
> B. But R. Yose permits [this].
>
> C. Even [for] a fellowship of one hundred [people], [one may not slaughter the sacrifice] if they are unable to eat [as much as] an olive's bulk [per person]. [*Consumption of less than this amount does not fulfill the religious obligation and the sacrifice will be invalidated*].
>
> D. And one may not constitute a fellowship group (*ḥaburah*) of women, slaves, and/or minors. [*Such a gathering, lacking a free adult male leader, cannot qualify as a fellowship group.*]
>
> M. Pes. 8:7

Because the paschal lamb must be slaughtered by the head of the household (Exod. 12:3), women cannot offer it in their own right. Even widows, divorcées or emancipated women living alone do not qualify as heads of households in the mishnaic scheme. Moreover, following Judah (M. Pes. 8:7A), one may not sacrifice the lamb on behalf of a single woman alone. Even on the view of R. Yose (whose opinions later became halakhic rules), it is not clear that an autonomous woman living alone could (at least *ab initio*) slaughter the sacrifice for herself.[216] Most women are presumed to be members of a man's household—that of their father or husband. Moreover, though Scripture permits—indeed prescribes—the banding together of small households (Exod. 12:4), the mishnaic rule would apparently preclude autonomous women from combining in a fellowship group (*ḥaburah*) to celebrate the Passover rite (M. Pes. 8:7D).[217] Though a combination of households may function as a fellowship group, an assembly composed of women is unacceptable.[218] The mishnaic rules effectively prevent autonomous women from sacrificing the paschal lamb in their own right.[219]

Women are likewise excluded from the rite of the first fruits—the annual offering that symbolizes God's gift of the Promised Land to Israel:

A.[220] Guardians [of an orphan's land], and agents, and slaves, and women, and persons of doubtful gender, and androgynes, may bring [the first fruits] [*to the priest, as set forth in Deut. 26:1–11*].

B. But they may not recite [the prescribed declaration].

C. [This is] because they cannot [legally] declare [Deut. 26:10], "*The first fruits of the soil which you, O LORD, have given me.*"

M. Bik. 1:5

God gave the Land of Canaan as a heritage to the Children of Israel (Deut. 26:1). But women possessed no right of inheritance at the time (before the enactment of the rule in Num. 27:8), so women landowners in mishnaic times could not claim that "the soil" was originally given *to them*. Hence, women are classified with other ineligibles. Though all may bring first fruits from land that they now own or farm,[221] those listed here cannot recite the cultic formula that legitimates and reinforces Israel's claim to the Land.[222] Guardians and agents, although capable of holding land, do not own the land of their principals; other categories lack intrinsic capacity to make the declaration because none can claim to have inherited the Land. Slaves have no share in the Land (M. M.S. 5:14). Persons of doubtful gender may be women and androgynes by definition are part women, hence unable to recite the declaration. Women, like slaves and individuals of indeterminate sex, are not full persons in the mishnaic scheme, but only part of a man's household; this excludes them from ownership of land and, more important, from active participation in the cult.

Again, Scripture requires all Israelites counted in the census to give an annual donation for the upkeep of the Sanctuary. But not every Israelite gets counted in the census.

A. From whom did [the Temple priests] exact pledges [*of the half shekel prescribed in Exod. 30:13ff. to be donated annually to the Sanctuary*]? From Levites, Israelites, proselytes, and freed slaves;

B. But not from women or slaves or minors. [*Because these were not included in the census (Num. 1:2), they cannot be* required *to donate—though if they do so voluntarily, this is accepted (M. Sheq. 1:5).*]

M. Sheq. 1:3

In common with other "second-class citizens," women are exempt from donating to the Sanctuary. Though Israelite-born, they rank, here, below proselytes and freedmen—non-Israelites by birth who later acquire that status. Herein lies a paradox: Although slaves and minors are not full persons in the private domain, an autonomous woman certainly is. But the annual donation to the Sanctuary, a public-domain activity, falls squarely on those counted in the biblical census, which included only free males over twenty (Num. 1:2).²²³ When it comes to cultic obligations, women simply do not count as full members of the community. Minors, slaves, and even foreigners (proselytes) can outgrow or otherwise overcome their respective handicaps and qualify as full Israelites; a woman never can.

Confinement of Women to the Domestic Sphere

All Israelites must in principle observe the precepts of Scripture. Yet for Israelite *women* the sages create exceptions unknown to Scripture. They explicitly hold women exempt from performing "every positive precept" whose obligation accrues at a specified time.²²⁴ Yet women are bound equally with men to observe all other positive duties and all negative precepts.

A. [With respect to] every scriptural duty owed to sons by parents [*such as circumcision or redeeming the firstborn*], men are obligated but women are exempt. [*Such duties devolve on the father but not on the mother.*]

B. But [with respect to] every scriptural duty owed to parents by sons [*such as the commandment to "honor" and "revere" the father and mother*], both men and women are [equally] obligated. [*A duty owed to the parents devolves on sons and daughters alike.*]

C. [With respect to] every positive precept that accrues at a specified time [*such as reciting the Shᵉmaᶜ, binding tᵉfillin, hearing the shofar, or dwelling in the sukkah*], men are obligated but women are exempt. [*Though the sages give no reason, later interpretations (e.g., the fourteenth-century Sefer Abudarham) suggest that the rule stems from a fear that such observances may interfere with a woman's domestic chores.*]

D. But [with respect to] every positive precept that does not accrue at a specified time [*such as reciting the Tᵉfillah, or giving charity*] both men and women are equally obligated. [*A woman can and must carry out such precepts when her other duties permit.*]

E. And [with respect to] every negative precept, whether or not it accrues at a specified time, both men and women are equally obligated [*because observance of a prohibition merely requires abstention, which is not time-consuming*]

F. except for [the prohibitions] against marring [the corners of the beard], rounding [the corners of the head], and contracting cultic impurity by [touching] dead bodies. [*Rules concerning the correct mode of cutting the hair and beard (Lev. 19:27) do not apply to women; and the law forbidding members of the priestly caste to contaminate themselves by contact with corpses (Lev. 21:1) does not apply to women of that caste as they are excluded from performing priestly rites, hence need not maintain cultic purity at all times.*]

M. Qid. 1:7

A. [The rites of] laying on of hands [on a beast's head prior to slaughter (Lev. 1:4)], waving [peace offering (Lev. 7:30)], bringing near [the meal offering (Lev. 6:7)], taking the handful and burning it (Lev. 2:2), burning the incense, wringing the necks [of bird offerings (Lev. 1:15)], sprinkling [the sacrificial blood], and receiving [the blood] apply *by custom* to men but not to women (emphasis added)

B. except for the meal offering of the suspected adulteress (Num. 5:18; M. Soṭ. 3:1) and the female Nazirite (Num. 6:2; M. Naz. 6:9), which they [personally] must wave.

M. Qid. 1:8

These rules give us crucial information about the personhood of Israelite women. In endorsing women's obligation to perform most of Scripture's precepts (M. Qid. 1:7D through E), especially those governing relations between man and man, the Mishnah's framers clearly recognize women as persons. But in excluding women (for no stated reason and by appeal to "custom," M. Qid. 1:8A) from most cultic duties owed by man to God, they reduce a woman's status below that of a man, for they deprive her, arbitrarily and without scriptural warrant, of important religious privileges. M. Qid. 1:8 proscribes women from most cultic acts associated with the laws of sacrifice set forth in the Priestly Code. Even where such duties devolve on Israelites in general (and not on the priestly caste alone), actual performance is restricted to males. The sages, interpreting scriptural provisions that do not explicitly bar women, nonetheless preclude their participation in sacrifice—the most prestigious rite of the Israelite cult—except in the two cases Scripture expressly requires.[225] They thereby endorse the implication of Lev. 15:29 that a woman does not come *"before the LORD."*

Again, at M. Qid. 1:7C, the Mishnah's framers give no reason for exempting women from precepts that must be performed at a specified time.[226] This omission forces us to speculate, without guidance from the text, on the sages' rationale. One logical explanation suggests itself: They wish to release women from religious obligations that might interfere with domestic duties. But if so, we must draw a conclusion about the woman's social role. Her value as enabler (the *"fitting helper"* of Gen. 2:18) in freeing her man from domestic chores that might impede his own performance of Scripture's precepts overrides any personal desire she may have for more active involvement in the cult. Women's duty—first, last, and always—is to take care of the physical needs of husband, home, and children so that men may pursue unhampered the more intellectually and spiritually rewarding cultic and religious duties of the Israelite.[227]

Another factor may come into play. The wife's assigned tasks of spinning and weaving (M. Ket. 5:5) represent an important economic function. If she drops her work three times a day to run to synagogue, her output will surely suffer; and her husband has a personal stake in this because the law assigns him the proceeds of her labor (M. Ket. 6:1).[228] Israelite men profit by exempting their women from cultic obligations and confining them to the private, physical domain of domestic activity; so it makes sense to discourage women from seeking time-consuming intellectual satisfactions like participation in communal prayer and study of sacred texts, which constitute the life of mind and spirit in mishnaic culture. Granted, mere *exemption* rather than outright *exclusion* of women acknowledges their Israelite personhood; they may, of course, waive their exemption. But the exemption still makes women into second-class citizens along with slaves and minors who are likewise excused from full observance of the commandments.

At the same time women's obligation to observe negative precepts (the thou-shalt-nots) (M. Qid. 1:7E) stamps them as responsible Israelites. Violations incur the same punishment for women as for men—both, for instance, must be stoned for bestiality (M. San. 7:4) or scourged for illicit intercourse (M. Ker. 2:4). This equal liability symbolizes women's equal responsibility to accept the yoke of God's commandments. Abstention from prohibited acts, of course, does not impede a woman's domestic duties in any way. Nor do positive precepts about human relations (like giving charity), so here too women receive no exemption. But when it comes to religious precepts that express the relationship between man and God, the case is very different. Most cultic obligations must be performed at specified times; hence exempting women from these precepts discourages them precisely from entering *the public domain of religious practice.*

The application of women's exemption involves some rather fine distinctions. If a religious duty accrues at a precise hour of the day or within rather narrow limits, a woman is exempt; if not, she is bound. If the act must be performed at a specific time of year, she is exempt even when its duration is sufficiently lengthy for her to manage part performance (like dwelling in the Sukkah).

A. Women and slaves and minors are exempt from reciting the *Sh^ema^c* and from wearing *t^efillin* ("phylacteries") [*because both observances must be performed at specified times of day; performance outside the time limits does not count*].

B. But they are obligated to [recite] the *T^efillah* [*basic devotional prayer that forms the core of all Jewish worship*], and to [affix] the *m^ezuzzah* [*amulet containing certain Scriptures, required by Deut. 6:9 to be affixed to the door of a Jewish house*], and to [recite] the grace after meals. [*These rites need not be performed at a specific time; the time for reciting the* **T^efillah** *is flexible, grace need not be recited immediately following the meal, and a* **m^ezuzzah** *may be affixed when convenient*].

M. Ber. 3:3

A. Women, slaves, and minors are exempt from the [law of dwelling in a] *sukkah* [Lev. 23:42] [*because this precept must be performed at a specific time—the Feast of Booths, from the fifteenth to twenty-first days of the seventh month*].

B. But a minor boy who no longer needs [to remain constantly with] his mother is obligated to [observe the law of] the *sukkah* [*because Scripture decrees that* "all who are homeborn in Israel shall dwell in booths" (*Lev. 23:42*)].

C. It happened that the daughter-in-law of Shammai the Elder gave birth [during the festival], and he broke off some of the roof plaster [of the house] and made a *sukkah*-roofing over the bed for the sake of the infant boy.

M. Suk. 2:8

Rigid adherence to formal criteria produces absurd results. For instance, the time limits for reciting the *Sh^ema^c* (a relatively short prayer) are rather narrowly defined (M. Ber. 1:1-2), whereas the opportunity to recite the *T^efillah* (a relatively long prayer) covers a longer period (M. Ber. 4:1). Hence the woman, exempted from the first, less time-consuming recitation (M. Ber. 3:3A), remains bound to perform the second, more time-consuming one (M. Ber. 3:3B). If the sages wished primarily to discourage women from interrupting their domestic duties, this makes no sense at all. But whatever the motive, any rule that exempts women from a religious duty incumbent on men *ipso facto* diminishes women's status. Obligations, like privileges, are marks of personhood; and Judaism in any case regards subjection to onerous religious duties as a great privilege.[229]

In the same vein, Scripture ordains that on the Feast of Booths (*Sukkot*) *"all who are homeborn in Israel shall dwell in booths"* (Lev. 23:42). This includes even a newborn—if it is male. Yet women are excused because this precept accrues at a specified time. It would be hard to find a more graphic illustration of the superiority of the male than to insist that from the moment of birth he incurs more religious duties (hence more privileges) than his own mother, a grown woman. This rule reflects the boy's greater potential; the passage of time will eventually turn him—but never his mother—into a full person in the mishnaic system.

Women's Incapacity to Fulfill Others' Religious Obligations

Though not immediately apparent, a principal effect of the rules just described is the total exclusion of women from positions of communal religious leadership. How does a mere *exemption* produce this far-reaching result? Simple—by an exercise in legal sophistry. A person bound to perform a particular precept can absolve others similarly bound by performing it on his own behalf and theirs. Thus, one who must recite specified prayers may fulfill the duty of other obligated persons by leading a communal prayer service as agent of the congregation (*sh^eliah-ṣibbur*). But the sages impose an important limitation: *Only* someone who is actually *required* to recite the prayers can absolve others by reciting on their behalf. As women are expressly excused from attending prayer services, it follows that women lack the power to lead the congregation in prayer.

A. A deaf-mute, an imbecile, and a minor cannot [by public performance of a religious precept] absolve members of the congregation from their duty [to perform it]. [*Such individuals cannot form a valid intention, hence can perform neither on their own account nor on behalf of others.*]

B.   This is the general rule: Whoever is not obligated with respect to a precept, cannot [by public performance of that precept] absolve members of the congregation from their duty [to perform it].

                                                                    M. R.H. 3:8

Though not mentioned at M. R.H. 3:8A, women are included by implication at M. R.H. 3:8B. Herein lies a paradox. Their omission at M. R.H. 3:8A indicates that the sages by no means include women among those who cannot form the mental intention needed for valid performance. To the contrary, the Mishnah concedes elsewhere (M. B.M. 7:6) that a woman has the required intelligence (*da'at*). But if the precept is one from which a woman is excused, then even though she can validly perform the precept for *herself* by voluntarily forgoing her exemption, she lacks the capacity to fulfill the obligation of *others*.

A.   [As for one] for whom a slave, a woman, or a minor recites [the *Hallel* liturgy] [*because he is illiterate and cannot recite Psalms without help*], he must repeat after them what they say—and let it be a curse to him [that he cannot perform this rite by himself]! [*A woman is not bound to recite* **Hallel**, *so she cannot fulfill that obligation on behalf of someone who is so bound. Hence, the illiterate man must repeat each word after her.*]
B.   [But] if a male of full age recited the words on behalf of [the illiterate], he need [only] respond after him, "*Hall*ᵉ*luyah!*" [*The helper, being a male of full age, is bound to recite* **Hallel** *for himself. Hence, his recitation validly fulfills the obligation of the illiterate, who need not repeat the actual words but can adopt them by making the appropriate response.*]

                                                                    M. Suk. 3:10

Such rules diminish the personhood of women by denying the value of their performance of religious rites viewed as the responsibility of the male. Curiously, the sages hold performance of a *required* duty to have more value and merit than a *voluntary* act of supererogation. Those who are not legal persons (such as slaves) or not full persons (such as minors) are either excluded or exempted from active participation in Israelite rites. But the exemption of women along with slaves and minor boys is an anomaly. The slave lacks full personhood because of his unfree status; the minor cannot validly perform religious precepts because he lacks the requisite mental capacity. The woman's case, however, is quite different. Her ability to carry out commandments is not limited by youth, unfree status, or mental incapacity; nor do the sages exempt her from *all* religious duties, but only from *some*. We must therefore inquire into their true purpose.

Though the Mishnah gives no reason for women's exemption, the likeliest explanation lies in the pervasive androcentrism of the sages. Viewing woman primarily as man's enabler, they wish to avoid situations that may impede that function—above all, to prevent women from exercising a possible preference for some alternative role. To this end they first *exempt* women from precepts whose performance might interfere with domestic duties, and then—in a classic catch-22—argue that women cannot lead others in the performance of precepts *from which they are exempt*. In this way they kill two birds with one stone; they encourage women's private domestic role by the very move that denies the value of their participation in public religious exercises and keeps them from aspiring to communal leadership.

Yet the sages' claim that they are exempting women from time-contingent positive precepts (M. Qid. 1:7) does not match the facts.[230] Whenever it suits them, they revoke that exemption and explicitly require women to perform such precepts (or conversely exempt or exclude women from precepts they must otherwise perform). Thus women must eat unleavened bread on Passover, though this precept is time-contingent, whereas the study of Torah, in no way time-contingent, is barred to them. Moreover, in situations that matter most to men, women's performance is encouraged by threatening them with death in childbirth for failure to carry out the rites in question.

A. For three transgressions women die in childbirth:
B. for carelessness with respect to [the laws of] the menstruant [Lev. 15:19ff., 18:19, 20:18] [*rules concerned with avoiding cultic contamination*],
C. and with respect to [the law of separating] *ḥallah* [*dough offering taken from a batch of dough before baking it (Num. 15:20)*],
D. and with respect to the lighting of the [Sabbath] lamp [*an obligation established by the sages (M. Shab. 2:1) not found in Scripture*].

M. Shab. 2:6

Why do the Mishnah's framers single out precisely these three violations for the threat of such dire punishment, for which there is no scriptural warrant? The answer is not far to seek. The three cultic duties listed here, like other biblical precepts, are primarily incumbent on *men*, but they happen to be *the three rites most often delegated to women*. Responsibility for observing complex laws of menstruation (discussed later) necessarily devolves on the wife, who alone can know the precise state of her cycle. So her husband must rely on her judgment to avoid contamination by menstrual blood. The separation of dough offering (Num. 15:17–21), likewise incumbent on Israelite males, is delegated to wives because they normally bake the bread (M. Ket. 5:5). The duty of lighting the household lamp before the Sabbath begins falls to a wife whose husband, after ordering that the lamp be lit (M. Shab. 2:7), has gone off to synagogue for sabbath inaugural prayers. When he returns, night will have fallen, and if the wife has carelessly forgotten the lamp, the inconvenience of sitting in the dark may tempt some household member to transgress the Sabbath by kindling a light (in violation of Exod. 35:3). A *wife*'s neglect of these religious duties makes her *husband* a transgressor. As all three duties are technically time-contingent precepts[231]—hence not strictly incumbent on women—the sages encourage wives to observe them by threatening the worst punishment they can imagine. This departure from their own regulation illustrates *par excellence* their perception of the wife as enabler; she must fulfill these commandments not on her own account, but as her husband's agent; and the sole motivation is to prevent her husband from falling into transgression. True, some other time-contingent precepts are binding on women,[232] but the three mentioned in M. Shab. 2:6 clearly receive special treatment because their omission inculpates the husband.

Women's Sexuality and Public Decorum

A close look at the list of women's actual obligations confirms the view that the time-contingent feature is not the true criterion for women's exemption from religious duties.[233] Behind the desire to promote woman's domestic role lurks another motivation. The exempting of women from cultic or religious practices rests on the sages' tacit belief that women should stay out of Israelite communal life. Although they never explicitly give this reason, nothing else adequately explains the following rule, which excludes certain classes from joining in a quorum for communal recitation of grace after meals. *Inter alia*, a woman, though explicitly *required* to say grace, may not form part of a public quorum for a grace offered in common.

> A.   Three [people] who have eaten together, are obligated to summon [each other] [*to say grace in common by commencing with the invocation, "Gentlemen, let us say grace!"*][234]
>
> M. Ber. 7:1

> A.   [As for] women, slaves, and minors, one does not summon them [*to join in the quorum for communal grace*].[235]
>
> M. Ber. 7:2

Women, slaves, and minors certainly must thank God for their food (M. Ber. 3:3B; see p. 152). Yet they may not form part of a quorum for reciting *communal* grace. This puzzling discrepancy needs careful analysis, for the listing of women with the other two categories obscures an important difference in the sages' reasoning with respect to women as contrasted with the other two groups. Slaves (i.e., gentile slaves as opposed to Israelite bondmen) and minors are excluded because they are in general not bound to observe the precepts of Jewish law. The sages mention them here only to make clear that the special provision at M. Ber. 3:3, which requires slaves and minors to recite grace for themselves, does not endow them with legal capacity to participate in communal rites. The case of women, however, is quite different. Where slaves and minors need not observe precepts *except when explicitly required*, women as free adult Israelites must observe them *except when specifically exempted or excluded*. So the exclusion of women from communal recitation of grace reflects a deliberate decision by the sages to bar women from joining in public rites. The sages give no reason for the rule, nor is there any scriptural warrant for it. But the reference to "three or more who have eaten together" seems to mean three adult Israelite males (probably from different households) eating together in a *ḥaburah* (commensal fellowship group). Hence the meal in question qualifies as a communal repast. The rule at M. Ber. 7:2 either assumes or necessarily implies that women do not join together with men for purposes of *communal worship*[236] even when the benediction itself is incumbent on women.[237]

Women's exclusion from cultic activity in the public domain appears also in Mishnah's interpretation of the biblical requirement that Israelites make pilgrimage to Jerusalem three times a year. Here, the sages stand on firmer ground. For the exemption of women fits the rule about positive precepts accruing at a set time as well as Scripture's implicit exemption of women from this duty.

> A. All [Israelites] are obligated to appear [before YHWH] [*on the three pilgrim festivals* (haggim), *namely, Passover* (Pesah), *Weeks* (Shavuot), *and Booths* (Sukkot) *as required by Exod. 23:17 and Deut. 16:16*]
>
> B. except a deaf-mute, an imbecile, and a minor, and a person of doubtful gender, and an androgyne, and women, and slaves that have not been freed, and one who is lame, or blind, or sick, or aged [*hence physically unable to travel*], and anyone who cannot walk on his feet [*because Scripture, in designating these three "foot festivals" (a pun on r^egalim, Exod. 23:14) requires celebrants to walk from Jerusalem up to the Temple*].

> M. Hag. 1:1

Scripture explicitly ordains that *"three times a year all your* males *shall appear before the Sovereign, the LORD (YHWH)"* (Exod. 23:17, emphasis added). The Mishnah's framers infer that this rule exempts women although not totally barring them. Cultic celebrations of primary importance, communally held in the public domain, thus become rites in which women do not participate.[238] This particular rite involves the cult of a Temple no longer standing in mishnaic times. But we can easily see how Scripture's exemption of women from pilgrimage might be held by analogy to exempt them from the congregational synagogue worship that came to replace the Temple service. Once more, the woman is discouraged from coming *"before YHWH."*

This brings us to the question of women's eligibility to perform the rite that constitutes the central feature of synagogue worship: reading from the Torah scroll before the assembled congregation. The Mishnah's comment on eligibility for this task includes minors and excludes "anyone dressed in rags" (M. Meg. 4:6), but it fails to mention women either way. However, one rule on a related topic seems to assume the intrinsic fitness of women for this role— especially when taken in conjunction with two tannaitic statements on the subject of Torah reading. Let us first examine the mishnaic rule.

> A. All are eligible to read [publicly] the Scroll of Esther [on the feast of *Purim*],
> B. except a deaf-mute, an imbecile, or a minor.
> C. R. Judah holds a minor eligible.

> M. Meg. 2:4

Although the rule speaks only of the Book of Esther (and not the Torah), the statement that all are eligible except the three categories that lack sufficient understanding would logically include women among those who may read.[239] Hence, though the Mishnah nowhere mentions women's eligibility or ineligibility to read publicly from the Torah scroll, the sages seem to have thought women qualified in principle. This argument from silence is strengthened by two rules—one from Tosefta and the other found in a tannaitic statement (*baraita*) cited in the Babylonian Talmud.

A. [240]And all may be included in the quorum of seven [called to read from the Torah at Sabbath worship], even a woman or a minor.
B. [But] one does not bring a woman to read [the Torah] in public.

T. Meg. 3:11

A. All may be included in the quorum of seven, even a minor or a woman;
B. but the sages ruled that a woman should not read from the Torah because of the dignity of the congregation (*mip^enei k^ebod ha-ṣibbur*). [*The Talmud offers no explanation of this phrase.*]

B. Meg. 23a

Although some sages of mishnaic times clearly thought women eligible to read publicly from the Torah, others apparently chose to exclude women for some reason connected with the public setting and involving "the dignity of the congregation." Perhaps the sensibilities of male congregants would be affronted by the need to resort to a woman's services (implying that no man present possessed the requisite skill)[241] or possibly some sages feared that sexual distraction generated by the presence of women might disrupt the public devotions. This last consideration does seem to have motivated segregation of women at one annual Temple rite. Generally women gathered in a special place called the Court of Women. Despite its name, this area was not strictly segregated, as men had to pass through it to reach the Court of Israelites. But the Mishnah speaks of a balcony specially constructed to separate the sexes at the festival of water libation during the Feast of Booths.

A. At the close of the first day of the Feast (*Sukkot*), they would go down to the Court of Women, where they had instituted a great improvement (*tiqqun*). [*This "improvement" was taken to denote the construction of a women's balcony to discourage the unusual levity and license that attended this celebration. (See B. Suk. 51b–52a).*]

M. Suk. 5:2

The balcony that constituted the "improvement" is described as follows:

A.[242] At first, [the Court of Women] was bare [of structures];
B. but [later] they surrounded it with a balcony, so the women could look on from above, and the men from below,
C. so that [the sexes] would not be intermingled.

M. Mid. 2:5

The Mishnah's recording of these quasi-historical details of Temple practice presumably reflects the sages' concern about the intermingling of the sexes when frivolity was the order of the day. Although the festival of water-drawing (probably a relic of ancient pagan orgies) was more conducive to license than most celebrations, some sages seem to have worried that women might disturb men's devotions on less convivial occasions. This suggests a general concern with the presence of women in the public domain. Certainly the sages evince a desire to restrain women from active participation in communal religious functions; and following the destruction of the Temple and the cessation of sacrifice, Torah reading at synagogue worship became the chief religious exercise in the public domain.

Whatever the motivation, one thing is abundantly clear: The exclusion of women from precisely those aspects of mishnaic culture that nurture the life of mind and spirit inevitably reduced the quality of women's life and personhood. I do not claim that the Mishnah's framers specifically intended that result; their androcentric mind-set probably never perceived the pernicious effect of this deprivation on women's lives. But it was ancillary to their major concerns—the maintenance of patriarchal control and the preservation of public decorum. In that context, barring women from communal affairs makes perfect sense; among other things, it reduces the chance of their harassment by strangers who may view them as sex objects, thus obviating a potential source of trouble. At the same time the sages' lack of concern for the deleterious effect of such restrictions on the lives of women bears out my earlier contention that woman as sex object becomes chattel rather than person and her "civil rights" are suspended and held in abeyance.

Women's Sexual Morality: The Sages' View

The exclusion of dependent and autonomous women alike from communal religious exercises suggests that still other considerations enter into the sages' calculations; and it is easy to discern what these are. The Mishnah's framers insist that women are prone to moral laxity and cannot be trusted to behave themselves if left alone with strange men. The sages' rules on sexual propriety express, on their face, equal concern for moral lapses of both sexes. But, in fact (as the Tosefta makes clear), they ascribe a weaker sense of morality to women.

A. A man may not remain alone with two women, but a woman may remain alone with two men.

B. R. Simeon rules that even one man may remain alone with two women provided his wife is with him [*i.e., is one of the two women*]; and he may even sleep with them [in one room] at an inn as his wife guards him [from the other woman].

C. A man may remain alone with his mother or with his daughter and may [even] sleep with them in bodily contact.

D. but if [all the parties involved] are physically mature, the female must sleep in her clothes and the male must sleep in his clothes.

M. Qid. 4:12

A.   An unmarried man may not teach schoolchildren nor may a woman teach schoolchildren. [*When parents collect their children a male teacher may find himself alone with a mother and child or a female teacher may find herself alone with a child and its father. In either case the child's presence will not suffice to discourage the woman from fornicating with the man (so B. Qid. 82a).*]

B.   R. Eliezer rules that even [a married man] who has no wife [with him] may not teach schoolchildren.

M. Qid. 4:13

A.   R. Judah rules that an unmarried man should not herd cattle [*for fear of bestiality*] nor should two unmarried men sleep under a single cover [*for fear of sodomy*].

B.   But the sages [in general] permit it.[243]

C.   Whoever has business with women should not remain alone with women;

D.   and a man should not teach his son a craft [that is practiced] around women.[244]

M. Qid. 4:14

These rules must be read together with Tosefta's gloss explaining why one woman may remain with two men but not two women with one man.

A.   A woman may remain alone with two men. (M. Qid. 4:12A) [*because she will be ashamed to act lewdly with one in the presence of the other*].

B.   [She may remain with two men] even if both are Samaritans, even if both are slaves, even if one is a Samaritan and one a slave. [*Sages assume that Samaritans and slaves will not violate in each other's presence the caste taboo on sexual relations with an Israelite woman.*][245]

C.   [A woman may remain alone with two men] except [where one is] a minor.

D.   For [a woman] is not ashamed to have intercourse in [a minor's] presence [*as opposed to the presence of an adult male onlooker*].

T. Qid. 5:9

The sages pin most of the blame for sexual lapses on women. The rule permitting one woman to remain alone with two men but not one man with two women (M. Qid. 4:12A) assumes that two men will act responsibly in each other's presence rather than take advantage of a woman and that the presence of two will deter the woman from seducing either, as might otherwise happen (T. Qid. 5:9C and D). Conversely, the rule forbidding one man to remain with two women rests on the belief that neither woman's presence will discourage the other unless one of them happens to be the man's wife (M. Qid. 4:12B). The sages' androcentric perspective blames the dangers of private encounters between the sexes on women's moral laxity rather than on men's greater susceptibility to arousal.

The tendency to blame women for men's inability to control their sexual urges is, of course, not unique to the Mishnah, being found in varying degrees in all patriarchal cultures. In the words of one scholar of comparative religion:

One might even venture the generalisation that the more a male culture is (consciously or subconsciously) obsessed by its dubiously controlled sexual desires, the more it is obsessed a) with the notion of the irredeemably libidinous nature of woman, and/or b) with the need to guard the virginal purity of [its] womenfolk. One does not have to be a psychoanalytic expert in the mechanism of projection in order to guess that the naturally pure men are the obvious and appropriate guardians of female purity.[246]

Earlier I mentioned women's exclusion from the most prestigious occupation: study of Torah. The sages never envisaged the possibility of men and women studying *together*. But some go beyond this, questioning whether women should study Torah *at all*, given the laxity of their morals:

A. Ben ʿAzzai says: A man is obligated to teach his daughter the law (*torah*) so that if she has to drink [*the draught of the ordeal discussed in chap. 3*], she may know that the merit [acquired by good deeds, etc.] holds her punishment in abeyance [*though not commuting it altogether*].

B. R. Eliezer says: If anyone teaches his daughter the law (*torah*), it is as though he taught her lasciviousness.[247]

C. R. Joshua says: A woman prefers one *qab* [measure of food or drink] with lasciviousness to nine *qabs* with abstinence.

M. Soṭ 3:4

What Ben ʿAzzai and Eliezer mean by their reference to "the law" (*torah*) is not entirely clear. In context their comments almost certainly refer only to the law of the ordeal, which Scripture calls *torat ha-qᵉnaʾot* ("the law of jealousy"). "*Torah*" in the Mishnah generally has the limited connotation of a specific law or set of rules, as here, rather than denoting "the Torah" in the general sense that talmudic Hebrew later assigns to the term. If the meaning here is specific, both comments make sense. Eliezer in particular fears that a knowledgeable woman may gamble on the chance that her good deeds will outweigh her occasional lapses. This limited interpretation of *torah* would harmonize M. Soṭ 3:4 with another rule in which the sages allude to the religious duty of teaching sons *and daughters* Scripture (*miqra'*).

A. [If a man is precluded by vow from taking any benefit from his fellow], [his fellow] may [nonetheless] . . . teach him scriptural exegesis (*midrash*), legal rules (*halakot*), and homiletics (*aggadot*),

B. but he should not teach him Scripture (*miqra'*). [*The teaching of Scripture, as opposed to the transmission of oral traditions, is usually compensated; and if the teacher declines payment, he will confer a financial benefit on the man who has sworn not to receive such benefits from him. (So B. Ned. 37a).*]

C. However, [his fellow] may teach [the first man's] sons and daughters Scripture (*miqra'*). [*A man may always carry out a religious duty on behalf of another, and the father does have a duty to teach his sons and daughters Scripture.*]

M. Ned. 4:3

The rules assume (at M. Ned 4:3C) that the teaching of Scripture to daughters as well as sons is a religious duty. Moreover, the normal mishnaic

term for Scripture, as used here, is not *torah* but *miqra'*. So, again, Ben
ʿAzzai and Eliezer (M. Soṭ 3:4A and B) should be narrowly construed to mean
by *torah* only the law of the ordeal. But their social commentary reveals the
extent of male ambivalence toward women. Is a woman required (or even
permitted) to study Torah? Ben ʿAzzai (the devil's advocate of the Mishnah)
says yes. But Eliezer (the Mishnah's resident male chauvinist) fears that the
more a woman knows, the more liberated she may become—above all, in her
sexual conduct. Joshua (M. Soṭ 3:4C) in the same vein claims that women
value sexual indulgence more than wealth; a wife prefers a husband who
earns less but stays home more.[248]

These statements convey the general impression that the sages think it
socially undesirable, if not actually prohibited, to teach women the sacred
texts. Certainly they would not countenance men and women studying
together. As Israelites, women theoretically must study Torah (since this is
not a time-contingent precept). Yet the assumption that women as a gender
should not engage in study leads first to their exemption and then, inexora-
bly, to their exclusion.[249] This apparently results from the insight that too
much education may liberate a woman's body as well as her mind. Another
catch-22 surfaces here; having first blamed women for lax morality (the flip
side of male fear of female sexuality?), the sages then use this canard to
justify confining women to the domestic sphere and excluding them from
the cultural public domain.[250] The inequity of obligating women to the
negative precepts while granting them fewer religious privileges than men
seems to have escaped the Mishnah's framers.

Woman as Cultic Contaminant: The Menstrual Taboo

One facet of women's sexuality that bears on the exclusion of women from
communal religious activities is the phenomenon of menstruation. No
Mishnaic rule forbids menstruants to set foot in the public domain (whether
street or synagogue); Scripture's only reference (Lev. 12:4) merely prohibits
menstruants from entering the Temple presincts. The framers' deep-seated
fear of cultic pollution has led many to suppose, erroneously, that menstruants are barred by analogy from the synagogue. Clearly menstruation played
a psychological role (in the minds of men and women alike) in keeping
women out of the public domain and reinforcing their inability to function
as religious leaders.

Scripture (Lev. 15) lists blood among several genital discharges that
render the sufferer (male or female) cultically unclean (*tame'*).[251] That
impurity in turn contaminates objects and people touched by the unclean
person. The Mishnah's framers develop this taboo into a complex system of
rules for avoiding intercourse during and after the period.[252] A woman must
make frequent self-examinations and avoid sexual relations until the flow
has ceased and she has undergone purification by ritual immersion. Scripture forbids intercourse with a menstruant on pain of divine punishment for
both partners (Lev. 18:19, 20:18). The Mishnah devotes a whole tractate to

practical problems generated by women with menstrual and nonmenstrual discharges.[253] For convenience, I here use the term "menstruant" (*niddah*), from the root *n-d-h*, "banned, shunned, ostracized," to denote a woman suffering a flow of vaginal blood from whatever cause.

The sages' interest in menstruation stems entirely from their concern with the cultic purity of *men*. In the mishnaic system, Israelite men must keep themselves in a state of fitness to engage in cultic or religious practices. In the broadest sense cultic practice includes meals taken at home, where ablutions are performed and blessings recited over the food in imitation of the sacrificial rites of the lost Temple. The requirement of cultic purity falls alike on the hypothetical priest sacrificing in the nonexistent Temple and on the humble Israelite eating his bread in compliance with mishnaic sanctity. Cultically unclean objects must be rigorously avoided, for the pollution they impart precludes a man from engaging in cultic activity until, like the menstruant herself, he undergoes ritual purification.

How does the problem of menstruation relate to the personhood of women? As explained, Israelite men must avoid sexual relations with women during the menses. But procedures for calculating that period (which includes seven days following the cessation of flow) rely heavily on the menstruant, who alone knows the stages of her cycle. This creates a curious paradox: The sages contemplate a woman both as an *object* that generates pollution and as a *person* who must actively avoid transmitting her impurity to vulnerable men.[254]

The view of the menstruant as object is inherent in the location of tractate *Niddah*, placed by the Mishnah's redactors in the Division of Purities, which deals mainly with things that transmit or absorb cultic pollution. Why was a topic so intimately connected with women not placed in the Division of Women? The answer is simple: menstruation in itself has no bearing on the topic of women's personal status but only on that of cultic purity. The menstruant is the subject of a cultic taboo that places her off limits to all Israelite men. The language of M. Nid. 2:3 makes this clear: "If [a woman] observes a bloodstain [on her skin or clothing], she has contaminated the man who [most recently] had intercourse with her." Here, the deliberate choice of the Hebrew term *boʿalah* ("one who lays her") as opposed to *baʿalah* ("her husband") contemplates the woman's sex partner as not necessarily the legal owner of her biological function. Ownership is irrelevant in the context of pollution, for the sages' concern here involves not the *social* legitimacy of the sexual act, but simply the Israelite male's avoidance of *cultic* contamination. In that context the menstruant is simply a polluting object.

At the same time the rules demonstrate a view of woman as a person. In requiring her to examine herself regularly and to keep an accurate record of her cycle, the sages assume that she can and will follow complex procedures to determine precisely when her period begins and ends. Her husband may rely on this even when he has been away on a journey and she could have counted her days less carefully during his absence.

A. All women are in a presumptive state of cultic purity for their husbands [*unless they tell their husbands otherwise*].

B. [Even] husbands who come [home] from a journey [may assume that] their wives are in a presumptive state of purity for them. [*The traveling husband may assume that despite his absence, his wife continues to examine herself and will thus know what is needful when the husband returns.*][255]

M. Nid 2:4

To entrust such matters to the wife is to rely on her intelligence and morality. Furthermore, the sages invest the woman with power to achieve legal effects in that her self-representation as cultically clean suffices to permit the resumption of intercourse.

Besides relying on the woman to keep an accurate count of days, the sages assume she can make accurate judgments about the provenance of bloodstains.

A. She who sees a stain upon her flesh in line with the pudenda is [cultically] unclean; but [if] not in line with the pudenda, she is clean [*because the degree of proximity to the source of menstrual flow determines the likelihood that this has caused the stain*].

B. [If it was] on her heel or the tip of her big toe, she is unclean [*because her heel or toe may well receive a menstrual stain while the woman is in a crouching position*].

C. [If it was] on the inner side of her thigh or her toes, she is unclean; [if it was] on the outer side, she is clean; and [if it was] on her hips on either side, she is clean [*because menstrual blood is highly unlikely to reach those areas*].

D. If she saw [a bloodstain] on her shift, [if it is] below her belt, she is unclean, and [if it is] above her belt, she is clean.

E. If she saw [it] on the sleeve of her shift, if [that part of the shift] could reach close to the pudenda, she is unclean; but if not, she is clean.

F. If she had taken [the shift] off or put it on at night [*i.e., in the dark*], then no matter where the stain is found on it, she is unclean; for [the shift] may have moved around [*through her reversing it in the dark*].

G. So, too, with a cloak (*pallium*) [*a large square garment that can be worn several ways and thus may inadvertently be turned around*].

M. Nid. 8:1

A. Moreover [*referring back to M. Nid. 8:1*], she may attribute [the stain] to any cause to which she can [plausibly] attribute it.

B. If she had slaughtered a beast, a wild animal, or a bird [while wearing the garment, she may pin it on that]; if she had been handling [anything involving] bloodstains or sitting beside people who were handling such things [she may pin it on that]; or if she had killed a louse, she may ascribe [the stain] to that.

C. Up to what size can she ascribe it [to a louse] [*because a squashed louse can hardly produce much blood*]? R. Hanina b. Antigonus rules: Up to the size of a split pea; and even if she has not killed [a louse, she may attribute it to a louse].

D. Moreover, she may attribute [the stain] to her son or her husband [*if either has a running sore or wound—in which case it is not regarded as a menstrual stain*].

E.   If she has an internal wound, which can be opened by scratching so as to exude blood, lo, she may attribute [the stain] to this [*and not to menstruation*].

M. Nid. 8:2

These complex rules call for meticulous judgments on the provenance of bloodstains. To permit a woman to make such judgments is to recognize her intelligence, responsibility, and personhood.

Inherent in the law of the menstruant is the same anomaly we have seen before. Despite the sages' general insistence on clear-cut categories, their rules, here, treat the menstruant as object and person at once. On the one hand, she is a source of pollution. Cultic pollution disqualifies those who engage in cultic practices, namely, men. Scripture applies the rules of contamination to "*anyone, male or female, who has a discharge, and* also the man who lies with a cultically unclean woman" (Lev. 15:33, emphasis added). A woman who has intercourse with a cultically unclean man is not mentioned because the only pollution that matters is contamination of male by female. Mishnah, following Scripture, worries about women's cultic purity only as it affects their male contacts. The woman is a polluting *object*, the man is a *person*. Wives must maintain the rules of cultic purity "*for their husbands*" (M. Nid. 2:4A). On the other hand, this same contaminating object possesses legal responsibilities assignable only to persons. The sages rely on the woman to examine herself properly, keep track of her cycle, and deal honestly with her husband in this critical matter. Otherwise a man could never be sure of his own state of purity nor engage in conjugal relations without risking divine punishment. The very circumstance that makes a woman a polluting object forces the system to rely on her personal sense of responsibility to protect men from sin.

Public Man, Private Woman: Sexuality as the Key

The mishnaic exemption of women from cultic or religious duties employs many different rationales. Sometimes it rests on a woman's subordinate status as a dependent of her husband or father. At other times sages treat a wife's duty to her husband as taking precedence over her duty to God. Indeed, they perceive her relationship to her husband as analogous to her husband's relationship to God—a view for which abundant evidence appears in Jewish, Christian, and Muslim religious literature. As for the life of synagogue and study house, the Mishnah's framers either deliberately bar women or simply assume their ineligibility.

What is the common denominator of these mishnaic judgments? All seem to hinge on the woman's sexuality. Clues scattered about the Mishnah suggest that the true explanation for women's exclusion from public affairs lies precisely where our analysis leads us to expect it—in her sexual and biological function. To begin with, a woman's reproductive function kept her physically at home much of the time. Further, it constituted her main value to mishnaic society; and the law of comparative advantage precluded wasting this precious asset by letting women choose an alternative life-style.[256] Hence (in contrast to surrounding cultures) the mishnaic system found no place for vestal virgins who, having forsworn their biological destiny, produce no offspring at all, or for cultic prostitutes whose offspring are of doubtful paternity. The closing of those doors left women with no public religious role.

If a woman's reproductive function confined her to the domestic scene, it was her sexuality *per se* that kept her out of the public domain. Here, three male fears coalesce. First, the presence of women is a sexual distraction to men struggling to engage in the life of mind and spirit. Second, the status of dependent women as the sexual property of particular men militates against their appearing in public, where strangers may pay them illicit attention. Third, the taboo of the menstruant as cultic contaminant makes it danger-ous to allow any woman (dependent or autonomous) to rub shoulders with men in synagogue or study house even though no actual law forbids a woman's presence there. These fears conspire to produce the result we actually find: Man is a public creature, woman a private one. This with-holding of women's rights in the public domain in response to the sexual threat posed to men at large neatly matches the sages' suspension of a woman's private rights in situations sexually threatening to individual men—a parallel surely not lost on the symmetry-conscious men who made these rules. In the end women play no part in the rituals of synagogue or study house, the most prestigious communal activities of mishnaic culture. Denied access to the life of mind and spirit, a woman's physicality becomes even more pronounced, and her confinement to hearth and home a self-perpetuating social fact.

This reduction of woman's personhood generates a view of women as intrinsically less worthy than men, which—shockingly, to the modern mind—informs mishnaic priorities for safeguarding the life, the property, or the sexual integrity of men and women, respectively. In almost every case the man comes first.

A. A man precedes a woman [if one must choose which is] to be saved alive,
B. or [if one must choose which is] to be compensated for a loss.
C. But a woman precedes a man [if one must choose which is] to be clothed [by a sole available garment]
D. or [if one must choose which is] to be ransomed from captivity.
E. However, when both [a male and a female captive] are exposed to sexual abuse [by male captors], [the ransom of] the man takes precedence over the woman.

M. Hor. 3:7

How can we make sense of these rules? The sages offer no explanation, nor do we find one in the commentaries of the Palestinian or Babylonian Tal-muds (except for the ruling at M. Hor. 3:7E, which I shall presently discuss). The rules at M. Hor. 3:7C and D seem self-evident to ancients and moderns alike. In Western culture public nudity is thought more embarrassing for women; and the sages take for granted (as we saw earlier) that a captive woman is always at risk of rape. Further, the priority of reimbursing a man's economic loss before that of a woman is justified by the likelihood that the man has a family to support. But what of the rulings at M. Hor. 3:7A and E? Why should the killing or rape of a woman be more tolerable than the killing or rape of a man? Here, Maimonides explains the mind-set of the sages:

> You [the reader] already know that all the precepts [of Scripture] are incumbent on males, while females are bound only to perform some of them . . . so [the man at M. Hor. 3:7A] is more sanctified than [the woman]; therefore his life takes precedence [over hers]. And the sages ruled that "when both [a man and a woman] are exposed to sexual abuse," that is, when both are in captivity and may be forced to have intercourse [with male captors], one must rescue the man before the woman, because it is not a man's way [to have intercourse with males], so they are demanding of him something against his nature.[257]

Maimonides' interpretation of M. Hor. 3:7 substantially adopts the explanation given by Palestinian rabbis (Y. Hor. 18b). To his credit he presents only the first part of their statement, namely, that intercourse with males is contrary to a man's nature, and he glosses over their assertion that intercourse with males (even forced, as here) is "natural for a woman." Although the modern mind finds rape of a female just as reprehensible and traumatic as rape of a male, the sages' view of women as sex objects justifies their ruling here.

Still more disturbing to the modern mind is the ruling that values a man's *life* higher than that of a woman. If Maimonides interprets the Mishnah correctly, woman is the victim of a double discrimination. First, the sages exempt her from the performance of time-contingent precepts, then they claim that, being subject to fewer religious obligations, she is less sanctified than a man and her life correspondingly less valuable. By their own logic the sages are quite right; it is true that their exclusion of the Israelite woman from the life of mind and spirit has made her life qualitatively poorer, hence objectively worth less than that of a man.

In conclusion we note the psychological reinforcement of the woman's lesser personhood by the term routinely used to identify her. The standard mishnaic expression *bat yisra'el* ("daughter of an Israelite") demeans the woman. Although a male Israelite is always called simply *yisra'el* ("Israelite"), never *ben yisra'el* ("son of an Israelite"),[258] mishnaic Hebrew knows no semantically equivalent form of *yisra'el* to denote an Israelite woman. Instead of using a parallel expression for female Israelite (such as *yisra'elah* or *yisra'elit*),[259] the Mishnah's framers always refer to her as "daughter," a clearly belittling term when applied to an adult woman.[260] This effectively denies her the dignity of being an Israelite in her own right; even as an adult, society continues to define her ethnicity and her personal status solely by reference to men. Even an autonomous woman, free of the legal constraints imposed by being this man's daughter or that man's wife, remains first, last, and always "an Israelite's daughter." She can never aspire to full personhood in the sight of God or man.

7

THE ANOMALY OF
WOMAN IN THE MISHNAH

The law of women's status forms one well-defined part of a larger system of jurisprudence, the totality of mishnaic law. So in analyzing the rules that govern women, we need to consider how well the law of women, in form and in substance, meshes with the mishnaic system as a whole. How far do the sages succeed in integrating women into their blueprint for the ideal Israelite way? And how well does their treatment of women fit the general method of the Mishnah? To set these questions in context, we shall briefly review our major findings and their significance.

Dependency, Autonomy, and Sexuality

In the Mishnah a woman's personal status varied with the sexuality factor, that is, her level of personhood depended on who owned her reproductive function. If some man had a legal claim on that function, the woman was legally dependent on, and subject to, that man; if not, she was legally autonomous and subordinate to none. Within this primary classification into dependent and autonomous women, we found a further division of these two categories into three subgroups consisting of matched pairs. Minor daughters, wives, and levirate widows were dependent on the men who owned their biological function (fathers, husbands, or levirs); their autonomous counterparts—adult daughters, divorcées and regular widows—were independent because no man had a claim on their sexuality, some event having severed or avoided their bond to the man in question. These relationships may be set out schematically.

168

This taxonomy accounts for the Mishnah's treatment of women in the domain of private law. The sages explicitly distinguished the minor daughter from her grown sister by contrasting the father's dominion over the one with his lack of jurisdiction over the other. They distinguished the dependence of the "acquired" wife from the autonomy of the widow or divorcée who "acquired herself" by the termination of marriage. The levirate widow differed from the normal widow in much the same way, being acquired automatically by her deceased husband's brother unless released either by his choice or by the Mishnah's complex rules of exemption.

The sages' taxonomy of women and the consequences flowing therefrom rested on the "analogical-contrastive" mode of exegesis that pervades the Mishnah throughout.[261] Neusner has described the process of mishnaic logic thus:

> [In deriving rules from Scripture, the mishnaic sages employ either analogy or contrast.] That is, something (1) either is like or (2) unlike something else. If (1) it is like that other thing, it follows its rule. If (2) it is unlike that other thing, it follows the exact opposite of its rule. If, again, Scripture states a rule and its condition, then the presence of the opposite *condition* will generate the opposite of the stated *rule*.[262]

Neusner's formulation may be restated as follows: If category X possesses attributes a, b, . . . n, things placed in that category must by definition exhibit those features, whereas things placed in category *not-X* must lack them. Furthermore, mishnaic polarity assumes that items defined as *not-X* will not only lack the features of X but will actually possess diametrically opposed attributes. This mode of thought generates binary distinctions between dependent women and their autonomous counterparts. Thus, because Scripture explicitly states that men control the vows of their minor daughters and wives (symbolizing their legal authority over these women), it follows logically that the women's opposite numbers (grown daughters and ex-wives) are exempt from that control. Likewise, because Scripture gives men sexual rights over the widows of their brothers who die without male issue, no such right can exist when the deceased brother has left an heir nor *a fortiori* over the widows of strangers. These arguments, of course, are clinched by Scripture's explicit rulings that a man may not (ordinarily)

The Mishnaic Taxonomy of Women

Owner of Biological Function	Dependent Woman	Autonomous Woman	Owner of Biological Function
Father	Minor Daughter	Adult Daughter	Herself
Husband	Wife	Divorcée	Herself
Levir	Levirate Widow	Widow	Herself

marry his brother's widow and that no man can annul the vows of a widow or divorcée; but in any case the sages' Hellenistic logic would have led them to the same conclusions.

This logic of analogy and contrast generated important practical distinctions and produced substantial variation in the personhood of dependent and autonomous women as expressed in their legal entitlements and obligations. Thus a minor daughter could not reject the husband her father selected, yet her older sister could arrange her own marriage. A wife could not sell her own property without her husband's consent, but a divorcée could force a court sale of her ex-husband's property to realize her marriage portion. A widow enjoyed even greater powers: not only did she totally control the disposition of her own property, but her automatic lien for maintenance let her sell part of her late husband's estate without seeking judicial approval. And whereas a levirate widow had to marry her brother-in-law unless he released her, a normal widow could marry the suitor of her choice. In legal theory, at least, an autonomous woman in the mishnaic system, with more entitlements and fewer obligations than her dependent sister, enjoyed a higher level of personhood. Whether in practice this elevated legal status was matched by an advantaged socioeconomic position is quite another matter. We cannot make conclusive judgments, based on legal rules alone, about attendant social realities. The very event that legally emancipated the widow might at the same time reduce her economic position, unless her marriage settlement was very large, in which case she could enjoy high social prestige in the private domain.

Woman as Chattel

Yet the difference between autonomy and dependency did not tell the whole story. In particular it did not explain the wide variation in the Mishnah's treatment of *dependent* women. Although autonomous women retained consistently high personhood in all matters of private law, a dependent woman's status varied enormously with context. In situations unaffected by her sexuality, the dependent woman, like her autonomous sister, always remained a person; but in cases affecting a man's ownership of a woman's biological function, the law ignored her personhood and treated her as his chattel.

The sages' perception of a wife's sexuality as her husband's property explained why marriage and divorce took the form of unilateral transactions in which the man acquired or discarded his exclusive legal claim on the woman's sexual function. Once married, if a woman's conduct challenged or threatened his exclusive claim on her, the paramount goal of asserting or enforcing the man's sexual rights overrode the woman's normal rights of personhood. So a husband could revoke his wife's vows inimical to conjugal relations, could put her to the ordeal without due process, and in divorce could control the time of her release by converting her agent-for-receipt of the writ into his own agent-for-delivery. The minor daughter, likewise, was a mere chattel whose market value, based on her sexual potential, belonged to her father and was called bride-price, and the levirate widow was inherited by her late husband's heirs to exploit her reproductive function. In sum, the rules of marriage and divorce consistently demonstrated that women in the mishnaic system, though clearly perceived as persons in all other private contexts, would arbitrarily be treated as chattel *whenever this was necessary to establish or enforce the sexual rights of the man solely entitled to benefit from a woman's biological function.*

Our conclusion that the framers of the Mishnah treated women like chattels *if* they were legally dependent *and* the matter concerned their biological function was reinforced by a subsidiary finding about the effect of uncertainty. Doubt about ownership of a woman's sexuality produced a knee-jerk response in which the sages reduced such women to mere objects deprived of personal rights. Thus, a woman who engaged herself to marry two different men, in circumstances where it was unclear which contract came first, lost her normal right to choose her spouse and became an object over which men haggled. In fact, the sages treated her exactly like the minor daughter promised by her father to two different men—thus reducing the grown woman to the same chattel status as the young girl. A husband who used ambiguous language in a writ of divorce condemned his wife to a limbo that treated her as divorced-and-not-divorced: she lost her conjugal rights at once, yet could not remarry while he remained alive. But the most striking loss of status accrued to the woman who, thinking herself widowed, divorced, or exempt from the levirate, mistakenly entered a second marriage while still tied to husband or levir. When it turned out that the first marriage remained in force (the missing husband resurfaced, or a technicality invalidated the divorce, or the widow's exemption from the levirate proved nugatory), she was punished out of all proportion to her offense. The sages deprived her of valuable economic and other benefits, not only those pertaining to the illicit union (as we might reasonably expect), but also those arising from the earlier, legitimate marriage or levirate bond.

This confiscation of rights and negation of the woman's personhood strikes us as doubly unfair because the ambiguity stemmed from her innocent mistake or was traceable to the negligence of some man who, by contrast, incurred no penalty. But fairness turned out to be irrelevant because here the woman was viewed not as a *person* to be punished for wrongful behavior, but simply as a misplaced *object* to be arbitrarily restored to an appropriate category at whatever personal cost. To the sages the best way to deal with a woman who looked like the wife of two men at once was to defuse the situation by making her the wife of neither—this meant confiscating her rights in both marriages. This case illustrates the pervasive mishnaic concern with order as well as the reverse of that coin: the fear of chaos generated by the displacement of objects from their proper place. To ward off that chaos the sages dealt with the misplaced woman in a manner normally reserved for chattels.

Woman as Person

The findings just discussed largely support feminist assertions that patriarchal cultures treat women like chattel.[263] But these cases do not tell the whole story. An equally significant corollary was likewise proved: Unless male ownership of a woman's sexuality was threatened, mishnaic law consistently and unequivocally treated the woman as a person. Take the paradigmatic case of the wife. The sages granted her substantial personal rights, including a guaranteed standard of living, the right to conjugal visitation, the return of her marriage portion on widowhood or divorce, freedom to eat and wear what she chose and to visit parents and neighbors from time to time, even the right to have the court try to compel her husband to divorce her if he became unbearably repulsive. Beyond these basic rights the wife enjoyed significant power to make personal decisions (including vows that temporarily renounced intercourse, if her husband acquiesced), to engage in litigation for damages, to sell her property or stop her husband from selling it, and many other legal powers.

Besides these valuable entitlements, mishnaic law invested the wife with many obligations indicative of personhood: domestic and economic duties appropriate to her station, observance of Mosaic law and Jewish custom, and the duty to disclose any possible impediments to conjugal relations with a prospective husband. Statutory limitation of her work-load (which, like her guaranteed maintenance, clearly distinguished the wife from a slave) was yet another mark of personhood. The matrimonial relationship appeared as a reciprocal nexus of entitlements and obligations; the husband maintained the wife in return for her performance of household chores and both spouses possessed mutual rights and duties in their general conduct toward each other. Parties to such a reciprocal relationship, even if not of equal status, are by definition legal persons.

The Autonomous Woman

If the mishnaic wife appeared as a person, this was even truer of the autonomous woman. Her independent status stemmed from a crucial circumstance: the absence of male ownership of her biological function. This fact permitted her to make her own marriage arrangements or, in theory, to eschew marriage altogether. Legally she could even choose a life of prostitution—a fact glossed over by the Mishnah's virtual silence on this topic, though the sages surely would not have approved. The point is that the autonomous woman legally controlled her private life, including her sexual choices, and exercised unfettered power to dispose of her property. The freedom of such women from patriarchal control distinguished mishnaic law from other contemporary systems, like Roman law, in which femaleness *per se* kept almost all women under perpetual male tutelage.

Why did the sages accord women all these entitlements and obligations? The evidence suggests, first, that despite their predilection for polarities, they understood perfectly well that women resembled men in significant respects, above all in their general intelligence and morality. This unstated premise explains the endorsement of women's competence to testify on certain matters, to bring or defend damage suits in contract or tort, to buy and sell property, and to conduct financial affairs without male supervision. It accounts for a wife's capacity to act as her husband's agent, to make decisions (within limits) about her personal life-style, and to enter into the reciprocal nexus of rights and duties that marks the matrimonial relationship. Finally, the sages' insistence that a woman who violated Jewish law should incur the same punishment as a man shows that they viewed her as a responsible Israelite. To conclude, the Mishnah's framers regarded women basically as persons *who could, however, be treated as chattels for the strictly limited purpose of protecting a man's legal claim on their biological function.* The inherent anomaly was not lost on the sages; though, as we shall see, their options for dealing with it were limited by the logic of their system.

Private and Public Domain

Dependency/autonomy was not the only dichotomy that affected the status of women in mishnaic law. Equally important was the polarity of private and public domain. Behind the many rules designed to keep women out of the public arena lay two distinct rationales—one positive, one negative. On the one hand, woman's place is in the home, on the other, women should stay out of public view. The latter motive (and not their supposed lesser intelligence) accounts, for instance, for the general exclusion of women as courtroom witnesses. Women's testimony on virginity or on a husband's death was admitted only when the exigencies of the case outweighed the strictures against a woman's public appearance. As for other excursions from the home, a wife could go to visit parents or neighbors on occasion, but the sages threatened her with divorce and forfeiture of marriage settlement if she flaunted herself in public or spoke with strange men.

Confining *dependent* women to the home protected their sexuality (hence, their husbands' honor) from abuse. But if that were the sole criterion, the sages would not have minded the presence of *autonomous* women in the public domain; so their refusal to permit this implies some additional motive. Transcending the need to protect wives and daughters, they exempted (and ultimately excluded) dependent and autonomous women alike from taking an active part in communal enterprises. By disqualifying *all* women from participation in the most meaningful intellectual and spiritual aspects of Israelite culture, the sages effectively prevented them from attaining the full personhood of the free adult Israelite male. The chief effect of the rule exempting women from observance of religious precepts that accrued at a set time was to relieve them of the duty of public worship, which would otherwise devolve on them as Israelites. Likewise, the sages' insistence that women could not lead the congregation in prayer, study sacred texts, or serve as schoolteachers, kept women out of the public domain. The same result ultimately followed from the fear that contact with menstruants would generate cultic pollution and from the outlawing of female fellowship groups that might, like male fellowships, seek to assemble in the public domain to pursue the life of the mind.

These rules clearly betoken more than a desire to protect women who belong to particular men. They exclude women as a gender from pursuits that not only might lead to the neglect of "women's work," but—far worse—could also interfere with "men's business." Clearly, male fears of female sexuality, expressed in the menstrual taboo and in the banning of sexual temptation from synagogue and study house, lay at the root of measures excluding women from the public domain. The sages tried to camouflage this with rationalizations blaming women for the distraction of men.[264] But their portrayal of men as possessing more self-control and self-respect (e.g., in the rule permitting a woman to remain in the company of two men while forbidding one man to remain with two women) hardly convinces us. The sages could imagine no public role for women but that of harlot; yet (as noted) the Mishnah barely alludes to prostitution, finding the subject beneath its contempt and largely irrelevant to its concerns.[265]

The Mishnah's image of women is sharply defined. Whether or not the sexual property of particular men, they belonged in the material world of domesticity and private commercial transactions. The spiritual world of ideas was the preserve of men—to be guarded at all costs from female intrusion. In the result, denial of women's access to the culture of synagogue and study house substantially diminished their personhood.

Yet once the Mishnah's framers had taken steps to restrain women from challenging men's ownership of their sexuality or men's monopoly on the life of the mind, they invested women with a measure of personhood we hardly expected in a patriarchal culture. By holding women to the same standards of observance in the violation of scriptural or mishnaic prohibitions, and by assigning them many rights, powers, and duties corresponding to those of men, the sages acknowledged women's intrinsic moral and intellectual equality with men.

Here we must enter a caveat. Whatever her theoretical position, the actual life of a woman in mishnaic society (if that culture was a real phenomenon and not just a hypothetical construct)[266] was very restricted in practice. Because a father could force his young daughter into marriage and a wife's routine was circumscribed by household duties, very few women can have broken out of the domestic mould or escaped male control of their lives. Widowhood or divorce might release a woman from legal dependence on a man; at the same time it could also turn her into a marginal member of Israelite society with no clearly defined domestic or public role and cast her into a lower economic status unless her marriage portion was substantial. She might, of course, support herself as a merchant or artisan; but for many women, the only sensible course might be to remarry and surrender their autonomy in return for economic security. After all, how valuable was an autonomy that did not give a woman access to the public cultural activities in a society where men reserved for themselves the intellectual enterprises that raise humanity above the lower orders of creation?

Woman as Anomaly

In the introduction we discussed a mythical beast called the *koy*. This creature was a metaphor for hybridism, a status repugnant to the Mishnah's framers. Actually, mixtures were abhorred by the biblical Israelites centuries before the framers of the Mishnah focused on them. One need only point to the "abominations of Leviticus" (to borrow Mary Douglas's felicitous phrase),[267] which include creatures not readily classifiable as fish, flesh, or fowl (Lev. 11; Deut. 14), linsey-woolsey cloth combining yarn from animal and vegetable sources, diverse seeds sown together in a field, and offspring produced by mating different species of cattle (Lev. 19:19). The Israelite aversion to hybrids may (following a recent suggestion by Shaye Cohen)[268] partly account for Ezra's ban on miscegenation between Israelites as the in-group and gentiles as the out-group and even (following an incisive insight of Jean Soler)[269] for the Jews' rejection of the divinity of Jesus, who, as god-man, represented the ultimate in unacceptable hybrids.

What has all this to do with the anomaly of woman in the Mishnah? It turns out that the problem of the hybrid sheds much light on women's ontological status in the mishnaic taxonomy—in particular on their legal status and level of personhood. As we have seen, the sages chose to perceive woman sometimes as *person* and sometimes as *chattel*, depending on context, and to treat her accordingly. This is a chicken-egg problem in which the sages' response may bear two possible interpretations. At first sight the rejection of hybrids makes it impossible in principle to locate women consistently in a system where they occupy, both literally and figuratively, a no-man's-land. The mishnaic woman stands on middle ground between two clearly defined polarities of chattel, on the one hand, and person, on the other. Viewed as human being, woman is *like* a man, hence a person (though not necessarily a man's equal).[270] Viewed as female, however, she is *unlike* the male, hence, by the sages' logic, not a total person. Feminist theoreticians, following Simone de Beauvoir, have pointed out that the same dichotomy appears in the Aristotelian characterization of the male as the absolute type of humankind, whereas the woman becomes an aberration, an anomaly, an Other.[271] In the mishnaic system this ambivalence sometimes reduced woman from the status of person to the status of chattel; and in one highly important context, the life of the mind, her otherness resulted in her exclusion from men's world altogether.

On second thoughts, however, we could argue that the sages were not the slaves of their system but its masters. If so, we must conclude that they applied the logic of the *koy* to the woman not because they had to but because it suited them. Though aware that she was not a *biological* hybrid, they clearly considered her a *logical* anomaly.[272] Their solution was to handle her exactly like the *koy*. Following the model of M. Bik. 2:8, the sages sometimes viewed woman as person and sometimes as chattel; in some cases they treated her as both at once; and in one context—the public domain—they treated her as neither, that is, they simply excluded her, thus obviating the need to consider her at all.

Of all the features of the laws governing dependent women, one in particular underscored the woman's anomalous position. This was the case of doubt concerning her marital status when she had remarried on the strength of a writ of divorce later invalidated for technical error or when her husband resurfaced after her remarriage in reliance on witnesses' reports of his death. These women incurred dire penalties, including the loss of their matrimonial property rights, both in the genuine first marriage and in the spurious second one (M. Git. 8:5; M. Yeb. 10:1). But why did the sages penalize so harshly a poor woman whose only crime was an innocent mistake?

The answer lies in the Mishnah's abhorrence of ambiguity. Ambiguity is functionally similar to anomaly because ambiguous objects, like anomalies in general, defy classification.[273] The putative widow or divorcée looks like the wife of two men at once; like the *koy*, she cannot be definitively classified. The sages rectified this intolerable situation by the drastic solution of reducing the woman to the status of nobody's wife at all. But this expedient involved an arbitrary suspension of her rights of personhood. From being a *person* with clearly assigned rights, she suddenly became a tarnished *chattel*, discarded by both "owners" alike. At the root of this treatment lay the fact that, no matter how innocently, *a woman whose sexual function belonged to one man had allowed another to make use of it.*

The same emphasis on woman's hybrid character appears in the Mishnah's portrayal of the suspected adulteress as chattel and person at once. Following the biblical law of jealousy (Num. 5:11–31), the wife could be put to the *ordeal* on the basis of mere suspicion (tractate *Sotah*). But a husband who chose to *divorce* her without proof faces an interesting legal dilemma. On the one hand, a man can unilaterally discard his wife at any time even without cause (M. Git. 9:10).[274] On the other hand, a woman divorced without proof of fault is entitled to collect her marriage portion (M. Ket. 4:7), for she cannot be deprived of property without due process. As sex object, she is *chattel*, but as property owner, she is *person*. Thus the context of the ordeal treats a woman as chattel and person at once. But this dualism flies in the face of mishnaic taxonomy. The sages, intolerant of inconsistency, harmonized matters by refusing to permit the ordeal unless the husband had previously warned his wife before witnesses (M. Sot. 1:1). Then, if she secluded herself with the suspected lover even without proof of adultery, her husband could use those witnesses to forfeit her marriage settlement on divorce.[275]

A similar duality in the wife's status appears in the general law of divorce. On the one hand, mishnaic law permits a man to divorce his wife at any time for no reason (M. Git. 9:10), but she cannot divorce him even for cause (M. Yeb. 14:1); on the other hand, the sages list many grounds that morally entitle a wife to petition for divorce (M. Giṭ. 7:1–5, 7:10). These include various forms of cruelty, like depriving her of her favorite foods or jewels or precluding her from leaving home to visit her parents. Such an abused wife, as *person*, was morally entitled to a divorce; but as *chattel*, she could not divorce her husband and must rely on the good offices of the court to coerce him to release her (M. Giṭ. 9:8).[276] Here again the sages treat the woman as chattel and person at once, contrary to their own canons of taxonomy whereby an object cannot be both X and not-X at one and the same time.

Further examples abound. In another divorce scenario, M. Giṭ. 6:1 empowers a wife to send an agent to her husband to receive her writ of divorce. The power to appoint agents is clearly a right of personhood. Yet because receipt of the writ released the wife at once, the sages insisted that the ultimate determination of that moment rest with the husband. If he declined to relinquish sexual control of his wife by handing the writ to her agent, the husband could countermand the latter's commission, transforming him from wife's agent-for-receipt into husband's agent-for-delivery, and thus delay the wife's release until the agent returned and actually handed her the writ. Once more we see the wife in a context where her rights as *person*, conflicting with her status as the husband's sexual *chattel*, are defeated by the sexuality factor.

Equally interesting is the case of the levirate widow for whom the process runs in reverse. Inherited by her levir on her husband's death without heirs, she is his sexual *chattel*. But if the levir rejects her, she at once becomes her own *person*—so much so that the levir's mere declaration of rejection lets the woman assume the active part in the ritual of release. It is she who removes the man's shoe, spits at him, and verbally expresses society's condemnation of the man who has shirked his levirate duty (Deut. 25:9; M. Yeb. 12:6). Again, we see the anomaly of woman as chattel and person in a single context.

In all these cases the sages' treatment of women, seen through the bifocal lens of mishnaic logic, poses problems because of the sages' recognition that women do not fit consistently into a single clear category. The sages (as we have seen) classify things chiefly by a process of analogy and contrast. The mere establishment of category X conjures up the idea of not-X. Lévi-Strauss and Turner have shown how this penchant for binary distinctions is reflected in the structure of human societies.[277] The self-identification of an in-group ("us") automatically places all others in an out-group ("them"). In addition individual egocentrism and group ethnocentrism insist on the superiority of the dominant group, at best according equality to those perceived as "like" the members of that group and downgrading those thought to be "different." Familiar in-groups and out-groups include Greek and barbarian, Jew and gentile, white and black, anti-Semite and Jew.[278] Likewise in patriarchy, notions of superiority and subordination inform the rules that men as the in-group make for the governance of women as the out-group.

How does this polarization of "us" and "them" manifest itself in the mishnaic treatment of women? First, the mere fact that the Mishnah is the creation of men makes "male" the norm and "female" the deviant anomaly.[279] Second, in practice, woman disrupts the Israelite male's ordered world, both as a source of contamination and by distracting his concentration on intellectual and spiritual concerns. Hence his need to control her; man must become not just the Self but the *superior* Self, whereas woman becomes not merely the Other but the *subordinate* Other. As Douglas noted, systems in which women contaminate men, but not vice versa, reflect a society based on hierarchy as opposed to symmetry.[280] Here, though they never make this explicit, the Mishnah's framers clearly derive tacit support from the divine fiat, *"he shall rule over thee"* (Gen. 3:16) in the creation myth.

But the status of women in the Mishnah is far more subtle and complex. Beyond women's anomalous character, the logic of mishnaic taxonomy presents additional problems for the sages—and for a very simple reason. *Their bipolar logic does not work in practice because their theoretical system does not match reality.* The sages, after all, were real people living in a real world (even though parts of their system depict an imagined one). They could hardly blind themselves to the actual responses of people to real-life situations. In particular they could not help noticing that women often behaved just like men in similar circumstances. But if so, women could not always be treated as Other, for they sometimes acted like Self.

Because empirical observation made it impossible always to treat woman as Other, the sages settled for a pragmatic compromise. Depending on context, they sometimes identified women with Self and treated them as persons; at other times they viewed women as Other and treated them as chattels. This oscillation between two poles, arising from woman's ambiguous ontological character, makes her the outstanding anomaly of the Mishnah.[281] For though the framers could not fit her consistently into either of the polar categories *chattel* or *person*, they declined to create a third, intermediate category to contain her.[282] Here, we recall once more the case of the *koy*. The sages' reluctance to recognize a hybrid (stemming from their dislike of the excluded middle) forced them to place the *koy* sometimes in one and sometimes in the other of two polar categories, sometimes in neither, and sometimes in both at once.

This illustrates the Mishnah's addiction to "the Greek penchant for combining symmetry with alternatives."[283] I suggest that it was precisely this Hellenistic logic of dichotomies that generated the mishnaic system of taxonomy. In Greek as in mishnaic thought, not only must all phenomena in principle be classified as X or *not-X*, they must also by virtue of inclusion in, or exclusion from, category X possess either the attributes of X or the diametrically opposed qualities, as the case may be. Between X and *not-X* there can be no middle ground whose blurred boundaries encompass monstrosities that look like X and *not-X* at once. Such hybrids evoked in the Mishnah's framers a fascinated repugnance; certainly they expended much intellectual energy on the consideration of mixtures. Their paradigm, the *koy*, like its counterpart, the Greek *tragelaphos*,[284] is a mythical beast, which can neither exist logically nor subsist biologically. Just as the sterility of the mule registers nature's disapproval of crossing a horse with an ass, nature's disapproval is echoed in fears that led many cultures to erect taboos around composite monsters.

The sages responded to woman much as they reacted to the *koy*, which they broke down into its component parts, assimilating it sometimes to wild beasts and sometimes to domestic animals. When woman's resemblance to man struck them as significant, they placed her in category X, that of person. When what mattered was her difference from man, they relegated her to category *not-X* and treated her as a nonperson. But what exactly did the sages regard as significant resemblances and differences between men and women?

The principal sign of a woman's difference from a man obviously lay in her sexuality. So when this aspect mattered most, the Mishnah's framers treated her as Other—not-quite-human, hence reducible to chattel in that context. But so long as her sexuality was irrelevant, the sages freely acknowledged her resemblance to man and treated her as a person. This fluctuating perception of woman fully explains why rules protecting men's ownership of sexuality treated woman as chattel, whereas rules governing other matters, like her rights as property owner or her entitlement to maintenance and fair treatment, contemplated her as person. It also accounts for rules keeping dependent women out of the public domain, where they might suffer—or even invite—illicit sexual contacts.

But (as we have seen) the law went further, forbidding both dependent and autonomous women to join with men in public expressions of religious devotion. That ban clearly did not stem simply from a view of specific women as particular men's property to be kept in seclusion. Rather, I conclude that it was above all the sense of women's Otherness, rooted in gender difference and aggravated by the menstrual taboo and the fear of sexual distraction, that made women unfit to be men's companions or partners in cultural creation as opposed to natural procreation.

This ambivalence toward women, perceived as somehow like men yet somehow different, is by no means unique to the Mishnah. The same conflict—between, on the one hand, the Hellenistic perception of female inferiority and, on the other, Scripture's assertion that man and woman alike reflect God's image (Gen. 1:27)—troubled the patristic writers no less than the Mishnah's framers. Augustine in particular found himself unable to reconcile Gen. 1:27 with 1 Cor. 11:7, in which Paul (adopting the Aristotelian view of soul and intellect as masculine attributes) asserts that only man and not woman is created in God's image. Augustine believed that insofar as woman is *homo*, she must reflect the image of God in her rational soul. But insofar as she is *femina*, she does not reflect this image. Hence woman, in contrast to man, presents a dualism that, like that of the *tragelaphos*, can never be satisfactorily resolved.[285] In my view an analogous conflict largely accounts for the sages' ambivalence toward women's person-hood and their consequent inability to place women always in a single clear cut category. Combined with their abhorrence of hybrid classifications, this conflict between male insistence on female otherness and a more sophisti-cated real-life perception of women's obvious human qualities, made woman the great anomaly of the Mishnah.

The Substance of Sanctity

Turning now to the substantive aspect, how well did the sages' treatment of women integrate with the mishnaic worldview as a whole? Earlier, I sug-gested that the Mishnah constitutes a blueprint for the sanctified life God demands of "a kingdom of priests and a holy nation." Each of the Mish-nah's six divisions deals in some way with the sanctification of Israelite life.[286] In four of these divisions, the very subject matter makes this clear. Agriculture and Appointed Times are concerned with sacred space (the Holy Land) and sacred time (the holy days ordained in Scripture). Hallowed Things and Cultic Purity treat of matters pertaining to the Temple cult and the avoidance of pollution that disqualifies men from performing sacred rites. The remaining divisions, Women and Damages, deal with topics in which the element of sanctity is not necessarily inherent but, nonetheless, appears in the conduct of family relationships and the context of social contacts at large.

In the mishnaic law of women, the importance of sanctity emerges from the terminology of holiness that pervades the division. The central rite in the three-part marriage procedure, espousal, is called *qiddushin* (lit. act of sanctification). By performing that ceremony, the man who espouses (*meqaddesh*) a wife declares her to be reserved or consecrated (*mequddeshet*) for his exclusive sexual use. The procedure consciously uses the terminol-ogy of holiness. Moreover, these rules rest on the belief that intercourse with a forbidden woman—one consecrated to another man's use—is a prime cause of pollution. That defilement destroys a man's sanctity (*qedushah*) and purity (*taharah*) and disqualifies him from participating in the sacred rites of the cult.[287] Thus the entire corpus of rules governing men's contacts and relationships with women exhibits the same concern with sanctity that pervades the Mishnah as a whole.

From a substantive perspective, the sages did a farily good job of inte-grating women into their androcentric system of holiness. Even from the formal standpoint, we find a certain consistency in their analogous treat-ment of the woman and the *koy*, both cases illustrating the mishnaic solution to the problem of the hybrid. But at the same time it must be said that the sages' constant vacillation between two poles and their ultimate inability to treat woman exclusively as chattel or as person reflects a built-in problem of inconsistency. After all, given the utopian character of other sections of the Mishnah, they could have chosen to devise a set of rules that treated women always as one or always as the other. Or, sitting in their

Grove of Yavneh, they could even have created a utopia that abolished invidious gender-based distinctions, like Plato in his Grove of Academe or Paul in his vision of the Kingdom of Christ in Gal. 3:28. The sages' failure to do either of these things reflects, on the one hand, their hesitancy to dehumanize woman completely and, on the other, their reluctance to place her on terms of equality with men in the realm of sexual entitlement and cultural endeavor. Perhaps the framers of the Mishnah were as much the prisoners of their androcentric world as were the women they controlled; but their inability to resolve the problem made woman the outstanding anomaly of the Mishnah.

8

THE MISHNAIC WOMAN
AND FEMINIST THEORY

The raising of women's consciousness in the past two decades has generated both secular and religious feminism in the Western world. Jewish, Christian, and Muslim feminists share a strong interest in understanding the relationship between patriarchy and religion; but the focus of discussion varies in response to different doctrinal and practical problems in the three traditions. After reviewing some of the more important differences, we shall discuss some recent Jewish feminist scholarship that has particular relevance to the present study.

Though feminists in all three traditions have struggled with both doctrinal and practical issues, Christian feminists have tended to stress matters of theology. There are two reasons for this. First, Christianity is predominantly a religion of dogma and doctrine, placing less emphasis on religious law than does Judaism or Islam. The New Testament contains a number of statements (mainly in the Pauline corpus) that present a more explicit interpretation of God's will for women than we find in the Old Testament.[288] Many of Paul's strictures expressly define the subordinate status of women, both in relation to their husbands (i.e., in the private domain of the home) and with respect to woman's place in church (i.e., in the public domain of religion), whereas the Old Testament and the Qur'an convey the position of women in the public domain mainly by implication. Second, the rites of Christianity (as opposed to its ethical principles) do not claim to govern all aspects of human life, which is figuratively divided into the realm of God and the realm of Caesar. Even for Christians whose lives are largely informed by their religious beliefs, the primary sanctions for enforcement of socially desired conduct are those imposed by the civil law of the sovereign state; and in the modern West, civil law is slowly but surely proceeding to bring women to a status of equality with men.

Even where concrete problems look alike for Jewish and Christian women (e.g., with respect to religious ordination), abstract rationales differ. Catholic women cannot become priests precisely because Jesus Christ, the role model for priests, was incarnate in the form of a man. This is an overt theological disqualification. Orthodox Jewish women, by contrast, cannot become rabbis, not because women are not made in God's image, but because rabbinic ordination is perceived by Orthodox Jews as a male cultural enterprise. The problem of women's exclusion from the rabbinate is more rooted in sociology than in theology, which explains why it has been successfully resolved in the Reform, Reconstructionist, and Conservative rites of Judaism[289] and why even Orthodox feminists have begun to argue that no halakhic principle actually precludes the ordination of women.

As for Muslim women, their religious problems (though likewise chiefly sociological), differ from those of Jewish women because, though Jewish and Islamic law alike claim to govern all spheres of human life, Jewish women live mainly in cultures where adherence to religious law is largely a matter of individual choice, whereas for most Muslim women compliance is socially imposed if not legally required. Even where the problems of Jewish and Muslim women theoretically coincide (e.g., in marriage and divorce law), the practical problems are not the same. The Jewish woman cannot obtain a divorce the husband refuses to grant; the Muslim woman cannot avoid being divorced against her will. For these and other reasons, the social and religious agendas of feminists in the three monotheistic traditions diverge more than they converge.

Jewish Feminism

Jewish feminists—coming from a tradition in which religion and law are virtually inseparable and in which practice takes on greater prominence than doctrine—have tended to concern themselves mainly with improving Jewish women's position in religious law (i.e., their halakhic status in both private and public domains). Because very little radical surgery has been performed on the laws governing women during the two millennia since these were first articulated in the Mishnah, halakhic rules today remain basically unchanged from those discussed in this book (with only two important exceptions: the ban on polygyny and the prohibition of divorcing a faultless wife against her will).

Scholarship on this topic is too extensive to review here.[290] But some recent work that combines respect for Jewish tradition with awareness of its limitations has particular relevance to the present study. The best discussions come from scholars who are sympathetic to the tradition but eschew Orthodox apologetics, responding to feminist concerns while rejecting the polemics of extremism.

Is the Right Question Sociological?

A good exposition of the sociopsychological dimensions of the problem comes from the pen of Cynthia Ozick. In a series of reflections entitled "Notes Toward Finding the Right Question," Ozick maintains that the "right question" is not theological but sociological because, in contrast to Christianity, Judaism has very little theology.

> Concerning the nature of God, we are enjoined to be agnostic and not to speculate. "You will see My back, but my face you will not see." And when Moses asks God about the nature of divinity, the reply is only: "I am that I am." In Deuteronomy we encounter a God who asserts that the mysteries of the universe belong to God, and that *it is our human business only to be decent to one another*, steering clear of what we have not the capacity to fathom.[291]

For Ozick, the sociological *status* of the Jewish woman in Halakhah (rather than her theological *image*, which preoccupies Christian feminists dealing with the role of Eve in the doctrine of the Fall) is what matters most. Noting the paternalistic tendency of rabbinism expressed in the traditional definition of the Jewish woman as *bat yisra'el* (Jewish daughter) she complains:

> My own synagogue is the only place in the world where I, a middle-aged Jewish adult, am defined exclusively by my being the female child of my parents. . . .
> To exempt is to exclude.
> To exclude is to debar.
> To debar is to demote.
> To demote is to demean.[292]

As Ozick cogently observes, the rationale for barring women from reading the Torah in public (*kᵉvod ha-ṣibbur*, the honor of the community or dignity of the congregation) illuminates the fact that in Judaism the status of women is a social, not a sacral question. As such, that status is not divinely fixed, hence it is amenable to what Ozick calls "repair." (Here she may mean either *taqqanah*, the technical term for a halakhic amendment, or *tiqqun*, the theological term for "repair of the world," a prominent feature of Jewish messianism.) Yet paradoxically, Ozick's ultimate prescription for repair is quasi-theological—it requires the incorporation of a "missing" Commandment: *"Thou shalt not lessen the humanity of women."* To that extent, even for Ozick, sociological repair of Jewish women's lives depends on a theologizing *midrash*.

Most women who value Jewish tradition would agree with Ozick that the problem is one of sociology. Two recent works sharing this viewpoint are those of Blu Greenberg (1981) and Rachel Biale (1984). Greenberg, a scrupulously observant Jew, steers a middle course between apologetic and polemic:

> Though the truth is painful for those of us who live by Halakhah, honesty bids us acknowledge that Jewish women, particularly in the more traditional community, face inequality in the synagogue and participation in prayer, in halakhic education, in the religious courts, and in areas of communal leadership.[293]

Greenberg advocates improving Jewish women's status by continued reinterpretation of Halakhah in the spirit of the ongoing process of balancing tradition and change that has characterized Jewish law down the centuries. But she overlooks the extent to which the improvements she documents have occurred in response to extraneous influences from dominant surrounding cultures, notably Christendom and Islam.[294] That fact should remind us that there has always been a halakhic warrant for attending to changes in the social attitudes and practices of the dominant culture and tailoring the Halakhah for a judicious fit. The maxim *dina d*ᵉ*-malkhuta dina* ("the law of the land is the law [for its Jewish inhabitants also]") (B. B.Q. 113b, attributed to the third-century Babylonian scholar Samuel), might well justify a *taqqanah* to conform to twentieth-century Western notions about women's rights.

On the disqualification of women in the public domain, Greenberg cogently argues that the principal basis, namely their exemption from time-contingent precepts, could be reformulated in terms of *function* rather than *gender*: It should cover only those women whose domestic situation at a particular time warrants the benefit of the exemption. Other women could be deemed obligated like men, hence equally eligible for active participation in synagogue and seminary. Indeed, Greenberg goes further, proposing in the service of egalitarianism that the adjustment of women's exemptions could be an intermediate step leading ultimately to exemption by function *for men and women alike*. This would certainly comport with the growing practice in young Orthodox families, where it is now commonplace for fathers to help mothers with domestic chores—especially with the nurture of the frequently numerous offspring. Greenberg's proposals make good sense. Exemption from the duty of communal prayer with the *minyan* would obviate the need for the young father's abrupt flight to synagogue each morning just as the children are waking and tend to be most demanding; the same of course applies to evening prayers, which, held at dusk, frequently coincide with the busiest hour of child care. Or perhaps parents could take turns going to pray with the *minyan*. Clearly, these ideas have great merit. But it is one thing to claim that such reforms are theoretically feasible within the spirit of Halakhah and quite another to persuade those who call the halakhic shots to respond in practice to Greenberg's suggestions.

Rachel Biale has rightly pinpointed women's powerlessness to decide Halakhah as the nub of the problem. Complementing Greenberg's discussion with detailed historical source material for many halakhic rulings, she adopts a similarly nonpolemical yet nonapologetic stance. Biale's panacea is more specific than Greenberg's. Rather than rely on the slowly changing attitudes of Orthodox men (who prefer to wait for the Messiah to come and repair the world), Biale firmly insists that "new authorities must emerge" to transform the Halakhah. These authorities could include women; but, she says, this cannot happen until traditional Jewish women make it their business to become thoroughly versed in Halakhah so that they can contend with male halakhists on equal ground:

Certainly the ordination of women rabbis is a step in this direction. But authority in the Jewish tradition comes less from formal titles than from learning.
Jewish women of all religious persuasions and commitments must become
learned in the Halakhah, even if they do not actually live by it, for it is the
framework and vocabulary of Jewish life. The first and most important step in
the dialectical revolution of preserving and changing is *talmud torah*: the serious
study of the Halakhah. Only those who explore the historical roots of the
Halakhah and master its logic may become part of its future growth.[295]

Is the Right Question Theological?

In contrast to Biale and Greenberg, who (like Ozick) stress the sociological
character of the system they seek to modify, other Jewish feminists (especially those who adhere to the less rigorous Conservative or Reform traditions, hence do not personally have to contend with exclusion from synagogue leadership and seminary learning) maintain that in Judaism no less
than Christianity the question of women's status is at heart a problem of
theology. Thus in a direct response to Ozick's reflections, Judith Plaskow
claims that the "right" question, at least in theory, remains theological
because at the level of "fundamental presuppositions" of the halakhic
system, it is the notion of the otherness of women, not simply *vis-à-vis*
men but with respect to *the male patriarchal image of God*, that ultimately legitimates women's subordinate status.[296] Invoking Clifford
Geertz's classic essay on "Religion as a Cultural System,"[297] Plaskow points
out that religious symbols express the way in which a society constructs and
explains its world. The male-God idiom of the Hebrew Bible functions both
as a *model of* God and as a *model for* the ethos of a community that strives
for *imitatio Dei*. That is to say, it justifies the reservation of power and
authority to men who, as patriarchal males, conform most closely to the
image of God.

I do not think this makes the question theological. It is no accident that
Geertz himself, on whom Plaskow draws, is no theologian but an anthropologist. His model of religion is a sociological one, contemplating a
society that, in Durkheimian terms, makes God in its own image. In the last
analysis the distinction between theological and sociological questions is
not as clear-cut as either Plaskow or Ozick would have us believe. Plaskow is
right, however, about the reciprocal nature of the process. The norm of
maleness automatically makes the female into the anomalous Other and
compels her, by her very otherness, to play the liminal, antistructural role
described by Victor Turner[298] and adumbrated, for women in Judaism, by
Jacob Neusner.[299] This reinforces and legitimates the social structure
thrown into relief by woman's opposition to those in authority.

Another scholar who has addressed both the theological and sociopsychological aspects of women's place in Judaism is Ellen Umansky. Writing
on "(Re)imaging the Divine," she describes the frustrations of many religious (not necessarily Orthodox) women with the man-made liturgy, as they

comb the prayerbook in vain for a vocabulary that meaningfully expresses the Jewish woman's relationship with the God of Israel:

> How much longer can I turn to the God of Our Fathers without screaming: "I thought the covenant was made with our mothers too!" The image that dances before me of a male god who blesses *His* sons, those human beings (our fathers) who were truly created in *His* image. . . . I'm not rejecting God as Father, Lord or King, but unless *She* is also Mother of Creation, Mistress of Heaven and Queen of the Universe, it is impossible for me to feel that I too have been created in the image of the Divine. . . . Similarly, as long as God is only the God of our fathers and not our mothers, men will be perceived as having (and will perceive themselves as having) both a closer relationship with God and a higher religious status.[300]

These brief extracts cannot capture the balanced sensitivity of Umansky's reflections, which afford a refreshing contrast to the shrill tones of earlier radical rejections of the andromorphic Hebrew prayerbook. Though sharing the widespread desire of Jewish feminists for changes in the liturgy, Umansky calls for something beyond mere recourse to feminized God-images and feminine pronouns writ large. If men and women alike are created in God's image, then God is neither exclusively male nor exclusively female but must encompass images of both. "Women's prayerbooks" are not the answer.

Umansky pinpoints the twin problems of image and status. On the one hand, she asks, how can the existing metaphors let women subjectively *feel* themselves made in God's image (as opposed to *knowing* this intellectually)? On the other, how can women's objective status in Judaism be improved, so long as the same God-language that discourages women reinforces "the notion that social, political and religious power resides with men"? This last point is neatly illustrated in Umansky's monograph on the life and work of Lily Montagu, scion of Anglo-Jewry and founder of Liberal Judaism. While researching materials for the book, Umansky repeatedly found that Lily Montagu's contributions to the Liberal Jewish movement in England "had either been glossed over or ignored. . . . As one historian, not atypically asked me, 'If she's so important, why don't we know about her? Why hasn't anyone written about Lily Montagu before?' "[301]

The answer, to feminists, is self-evident. It is the same answer given by Elisabeth Schüssler Fiorenza in her excellent work on feminist theological reconstruction of Christian origins, which takes as its paradigm the woman rebuked for anointing Jesus with a jar of costly perfume. Despite Jesus' defense of her action and his promise that *"wherever the gospel is preached in the whole world, what she has done will be told in memory of her"* (Mark 14:9), we do not even know this woman's name.[302] The Gospel writer simply did not see fit to record so unimportant a detail. This anonymous woman forms the paradigm for all women who seek to function in the public domain of patriarchal religion. Despite the many people (including the present writer) who were privileged to hear her preach during her lifetime, Lily Montagu, after her death, "wasn't there" until Umansky resurrected her. The mishnaic doctrine that women do not appear in the public domain still takes its toll. The right question, in the end, is sociological.

Feminist Theory and the Mishnaic Woman

In conclusion let us briefly consider the relevance of current feminist scholarship to the findings of this study, and the implications of this study for feminist scholarship, in the light of some general feminist explanations of women's subordinate status in patriarchal cultures.

In a recent essay on the status of women in rabbinic Judaism,[303] Judith Baskin surveys the evolution of Jewish women's status during the period of formative Judaism, that is, during the creation of the Mishnah and of the two Talmuds (Palestinian and Babylonian) that built upon the Mishnah during the second to sixth centuries. She rightly points out that the logical basis of rabbinic thought may be illuminated by viewing it in the context of the underlying logic of other social systems:

> By viewing rabbinic Judaism as a cultural system, and by examining the ways in which rabbinic structures correspond to ordering patterns found in societies throughout the world, rabbinic separation [of women] can be seen in a sharper light.[304]

Baskin examines the status of women in rabbinic Judaism in the light of conceptual categories proposed by feminist theoreticians to interpret anthropological data on the condition of women in various cultures. Though she chooses not to treat the Mishnah as a separate system from the talmudic Judaism that later appropriated it, much of her discussion applies to the mishnaic system in and of itself. Baskin discusses two feminist scholars whose work is especially relevant here. She begins with Michelle Zimbalist Rosaldo's distinction between "domestic" and "public" spheres of human activity. This seems applicable to Jewish women in the centuries of formative Judaism, when they were excluded from participation in communal endeavors. As Rosaldo sees it, this separation of domains arises initially from a universal biological phenomenon:

> It will be seen that an opposition between "domestic" and "public" provides the basis of a structural framework necessary to identify and explore the place of male and female in psychological, cultural, social, and economic aspects of human life. . . . Women become absorbed primarily in domestic activities because of their role as mothers. . . . This orientation is contrasted to the extra-domestic, political, and military spheres primarily associated with men. Put quite simply, men have no single commitment as enduring, time-consuming, and emotionally compelling—as close to seeming necessary and natural—as the relation of a woman to her infant child; and so men are free to form those broader associations that we call "society," universalistic systems of order, meaning, and commitment. . . . I suggest that the opposition between *domestic* and *public*

orientations (an opposition that must, in part, derive from the nurturant capacities of women) provides the necessary framework for an examination of male and female roles in any society.[305]

Although Baskin correctly perceives the relevance of Rosaldo's analysis to the treatment of women in rabbinic Judaism, she does not question Rosaldo's equation of "private" with "domestic." But these two terms are not, in fact, synonymous. For instance, a contract of sale, though not domestic, is not a public activity, but a transaction between private parties. The mere fact that law or custom may require attestation of the contract before witnesses or even an entry in a register kept in the public domain does not turn a private transaction into a public one. So Rosaldo's domestic/ public dichotomy obscures the fact that women in the mishnaic system could legally conduct such extradomestic activities as commercial transactions and legal claims and yet remain excluded from the public domain because the implementation of such powers does not constitute performance of a public act. For example, the legal documents of a woman called Babata, found in the Cave of Letters of Bar Kokhba, do not necessarily support a claim that other forms of Judaic culture contemporaneous with mishnaic and talmudic Judaism gave women significant roles in the *public* arena that were denied to women in the mishnaic system.[306] As we have seen, the Mishnah, in common with the other Jewish cultures mentioned by Baskin, does permit women to conduct *private* litigation and financial business, but this does not accord them a place in the *public* domain.

In mishnaic society, the public sphere of cultural activity connotes a *communal* enterprise of some kind, whether political, religious, or otherwise. Important in this context is Bernadette Brooten's interesting study (cited by Baskin) of synagogue and tombstone inscriptions in the Greco-Roman world.[307] Brooten's interpretation of first- through sixth-century Greek and Latin inscriptions in various locations in the Mediterranean world of late antiquity strongly indicates that Jewish cultures outside rabbinic Judaism allowed women to be "active in the public sphere of Jewish society."[308] Brooten thinks it probable that a woman's designation (on a plaque commemorating her generous donation to a synagogue) as "head of the synagogue," "leader," "elder," "mother of the synagogue," or even "priestess" signifies that the woman herself actually functioned in that communal capacity, and these titles were not just honorific expressions of gratitude or even feminine grammatical forms of masculine counterparts, identifying the donor as the *wife* or *widow* of a man who functioned in the stated capacity.[309] A more recent note by Ross Kraemer on an inscription not discussed by Brooten lends support to the latter's case that women may have functioned as synagogue elders in the Greco-Roman world; the inscription in question describes a wife as an "elder" while assigning a different title to her husband.[310]

Whether Brooten's fascinating hypothesis is correct or not, Rosaldo's taxonomy of *domestic* versus *public*, though useful as starting point, still does not fully account for the status of women in the mishnaic system. Her analysis falls short for another reason. The fact that *most* women in traditional societies spend much of their life in child nurturing neither justifies nor, more important, explains the exclusion from the public domain of *all* women, including those not burdened by time-consuming domestic chores and not legally controlled by men. Yet, as we know, the mishnaic system bars autonomous women as much as dependent ones from active participation in communal worship and study of sacred texts—thus precluding women from attaining positions of public eminence, such as judge or rabbi, that depend on mastery of sacred lore. So we must look beyond Rosaldo's categories for further theoretical insights into the exclusion of autonomous women from the public sphere of mishnaic society. In other words a more complex male perception of women's capacities and limitations may disqualify women from public life in those societies that have traditionally excluded them.

Baskin next turns to the work of Sherry Ortner, who focuses on a different dichotomy, that of "nature" versus "culture":

> [E]very culture implicitly recognizes and asserts a distinction between the operation of nature [understood as biological needs and processes] and the operation of culture (human consciousness and its products); and further, that the distinctiveness of culture rests precisely on the fact that it can under most circumstances transcend natural conditions and turn them to its purposes. Thus culture (i.e. every culture) at some level of awareness asserts itself to be not only distinct from but superior to nature, and that sense of distinctiveness and superiority rests precisely on the ability to transform—to "socialize" and "culturalize"—nature.[311]

As culture is that unique human enterprise that humankind adds to nature, these two realms of activity are not accorded equal worth, culture being perceived as of a higher order than nature. Furthermore, as women's greater bodily involvement with natural functions gives rise to a perception that they are "closer to nature than men,"[312] the dialectics of analogical-contrastive reasoning lead to the conclusion that nature (intrafamilial relationships) is the domain of women, whereas culture (interfamilial relationships) is the domain of men. This, in turn, accounts for what Ortner calls the "universal devaluation of women."[313] The pancultural phenomenon of female inferiority, says Ortner, is evidenced in any particular culture by one or more of the following three kinds of data:

> (1) elements of cultural ideology and informants' statements that *explicitly* devalue women, according them, their roles, their tasks, their products, and their social milieux less prestige than are accorded men and the male correlates; (2) symbolic devices, such as the attribution of defilement, which may be interpreted as *implicitly* making a statement of inferior valuation; and (3) social-structural arrangements that exclude women from participation in or contact with some realm in which *the highest powers of the society* are felt to reside.[314]

Examples of all three phenomena in Ortner's list appear in mishnaic law. The sages' cultural ideology devalues women by making rules that explicitly or implicitly reflect their view of women's inferior value or that treat women as the property of men; the symbolic attribution of defilement appears most clearly in the laws of the menstruant; and social-structural arrangements are embodied in rules that exclude women from participation in the intellectual and spiritual life of the community, in which the highest powers of mishnaic society are certainly felt to reside. Mishnaic law thus meets all three of Ortner's criteria for a system that downgrades women with respect to men.

Ortner's theoretical framework matches my findings better than Rosaldo's. But it fails to satisfy completely for two reasons. First (as Ortner herself concedes), the nature/culture dichotomy is not absolute. The best formulation she can attain is that women are perceived as closer to nature than men; she cannot claim that women perform no cultural functions at all. Certainly such a claim would not fit the Mishnah, which grants women many legal powers barely distinguishable from those of men and whose exercise is clearly a cultural activity.

Ortner's theory has been criticized for its lack of rigor on this point—for instance by Carole MacCormack and Marilyn Strathern, who point out that Ortner "retreats from the extreme position by acknowledging women's role in mediating between nature and culture."[315] Moreover, the nonexistence in real life of an absolute nature/culture dichotomy between the spheres of female and male activities was already noted by Lévi-Strauss, who states that in primitive societies the role of women is that of mediator between nature and culture, the "system of women" being a "middle term between the system of (natural) living creatures and the system of (manufactured) objects."[316] What actually happens, says MacCormack, is a process in which women mediate between nature and culture by performing the task of socializing children to the roles that they will later play in society. Thus, Ortner's nature/culture dichotomy, like Rosaldo's domestic/public dichotomy, fails to offer a complete description of the status of women in any given society.

Other feminist theoreticians have proposed a purely economic basis for women's place in society. Several have offered specifically Marxist interpretations. Thus Catherine MacKinnon, comparing men's exploitation of women to the exploitation of workers by capitalists, asserts categorically:

> Sexuality is to feminism what work is to marxism: that which is most one's own, yet most taken away . . . As the organized expropriation of the work of some for the benefit of others defines a class—workers—the organized expropriation of the sexuality of some for the use of others defines the sex, woman.[317]

This formulation obviously contains more than a kernel of truth. My findings show that the framers of the Mishnah certainly appropriated the sexuality of women for men's exploitation. But the explanation is too simplistic in its generality; it fails to recognize, let alone explain, the fact that some systems do not exploit the sexuality of *all* women indiscriminately. In particular mishnaic law, by granting autonomous women control of their own sexual function, confounds MacKinnon's interpretation.

One critique of the Marxist analysis comes from Annette Kuhn and Anne-Marie Wolpe, who argue as follows:

> [I]n the marriage relationship the wife does not exchange her labour power for a wage. The domestic labour she performs is unpaid. The relations of domestic labour are thus crucially different from the relations of capitalist production, and they place the wife in a position of subordination *vis-à-vis* the husband, who through the marriage contract becomes in effect the controller of her labour power . . . Although, then, domestic labour is both socially useful labour and beneficial to capital, it is performed within an arena of social relations in which these economic relations are displaced onto and take the appearance of personal relations between two individuals.[318]

Kuhn's analysis, though plausible, takes for granted that within marriage the husband appropriates the wife's labor without having to pay for it. However, this assumption overlooks the fact that patriarchal systems generally require the husband to maintain the wife. As the Mishnah testifies, that rule can turn what might otherwise be a purely exploitative arrangement into a reciprocal nexus of rights and duties that upgrades rather than downplays the personhood of the wife.

More important is the main thrust of Kuhn's analysis, which, claiming that patriarchal culture "unites property and psychic relations" between men and women, seeks to combine economic and psychoanalytic theory.[319] This approach responds to de Beauvoir's assertion that neither economics nor psychology alone can suffice to explain the subordination of women. She had rejected Engels's notion that the exploitation of women follows specifically from the institution of private property, just as she had rejected a purely Freudian interpretation of women's subordinate status. Rather, she sought existentialist explanations rooted in "the total perespective of man's existence."[320] In the framework of that total perspective, man perceives woman primarily as the Other.

De Beauvoir and the Concept of the Other

To my mind the most useful theoretical approach is one that develops de Beauvoir's emphasis on the factor of otherness. She puts matters thus:

> Now, what peculiarly signalizes the situation of woman is that she—a free and autonomous being like all human creatures—nevertheless finds herself living in a world where men compel her to assume the status of the Other.[321]

Given the binary propensity of human thought, it is not surprising that man should perceive woman as the Other. As we have seen, the framers of Mishnah certainly regarded her thus. Yet we also saw that this perception justified treating women differently from men *only in highly circumscribed situations*. So we must seek the root cause of female otherness in some specific factor that adequately explains this variable treatment of women. Obviously the perception of otherness must lie in some perceived difference between men and women. Now, from the standpoint of the male, the most obvious difference between men and women appears in a woman's anatomical form and biological function. That is to say, woman is most other when it comes to her sexuality, which, for obvious reasons, is the very aspect of woman that matters most to men. Even so, the mere physical otherness of the female might not suffice to exclude women from the public domain, were it not accompanied by male interpretation of female difference as a kind of imperfection or incompleteness that disqualifies women for intellectual pursuits. And, as it turns out, there is good reason to suppose that this notion of woman's incompleteness was familiar to the Mishnah's framers.

The conception of woman as an incomplete creature (specifically an imperfect man) was widespread in Greek culture. This Aristotelian view of women's biological nature[322] prevailed throughout the Hellenistic world well before the mishnaic period.[323] The first-century exponent of Hellenistic-Judaic thought, Philo of Alexandria, repeatedly describes the female as physically, intellectually, and morally inferior to the male.[324] Philo's denigration of women seems to have been shaped at least as much by his Hellenistic background as by his interpretation of Jewish Scripture.[325] Indeed, the notion of female incompleteness appears in all Western systems influenced by Greek philosophy. We find clear evidence of it in the Mishnah; the sages, endorsing Scripture's denial of women's right to appear *"before YHWH,"* explicitly classified women with other imperfect beings—such as blemished members of the priesthood, deaf-mutes, imbeciles, minors, androgynes, slaves, the lame, the blind, the sick, and the aged—who were likewise disqualified. The notion of female imperfection or incompleteness, then, may lie at the root of female otherness as perceived by the mishnaic male.

But this emphasis on male *perception* of female otherness skirts one very important question. Is that otherness the purely *subjective* result of cultural conditioning or has it some *objective* basis in demonstrable and immutable facts? The first position is that of de Beauvoir, who believes that men's compelling women to assume the status of the Other is a cultural process. The second possibility was raised by E. E. Evans-Pritchard's insistence, in an early response to *The Second Sex*, that de Beauvoir's claim is merely "a reification that explains nothing—certainly not so universal a feature of social life as the leading role men play in it."[326] Evans-Pritchard implies that women's subordination may, in fact, be more a matter of nature than of culture. The question whether woman's otherness and resultant subordination by males is wholly imposed from without or is partly instrinsic to her nature and inherent in her social role (assigned by God or nature) obviously cannot be ignored and has been exhaustively discussed by Rosaldo and Lamphere and by Ortner.[327] But the results of the present study suggest that it is primarily man's economic and psychological stake in controlling woman's biological function (rather than some abstract perception that she epitomizes Nature as opposed to Culture) that lies at the root of the subordination of women in patriarchy.[328] We found abundant evidence that woman in the mishnaic system was most subordinated at precisely those points where some man had a legal interest in the use she made of her sexual and reproductive functions. Above and beyond that, she was legally man's virtual equal in the private domain. As for her exclusion from the public domain, this was less a matter of inferiority than of what I shall here call the men's-club syndrome.

The men's-club hypothesis was developed at length by Mary O'Brien,[329] who claims that the separation of the private and individual realm from the public and political realm of society results from oppositions inherent in the dialectics of human reproduction. In that process men, once they have deposited their seed, become alienated, separated from the world of repro- duction and nurture that forms the principal focus of the private domain and the primary concern of women. In response, claims O'Brien, men go out and create their own "second nature," the sociopolitical world in the public domain to compensate for their loss of—indeed, perceived rejection from—their natural function in the private domain. In other words it is not that men *commence* by excluding women from the public domain. Rather, what happens is that men, by nature deprived of continuous involvement in the creative natural process of reproduction, feel the need to generate substi- tute forms of production to satisfy their creative urge. Hence they turn to cultural production instead—in particular to the creation of intellectual and spiritual culture.

O'Brien's analysis is especially interesting for the light it sheds on one important problem not solved by a purely economic analysis of women's status. Economic motivations cannot adequately explain why the sages of the Mishnah exclude *autonomous* as well as *dependent* women from the public domain, for the Israelite male has no legal or economic stake that would justify confining autonomous women to the private sphere. To the contrary, the mishnaic taxonomy of women would seem to militate in favor of admitting autonomous women to the public domain. But O'Brien's analysis readily accounts for their exclusion. Her postulation of men's psychic need to forge a domain of production and creativity specific to themselves goes far to explain the interdiction of women as a class and not merely of those engaged (actually, like wives, or potentially, like minor daughters and levirate widows) in the natural enterprise of procreation and nurture.

If O'Brien is right, we should expect the true motivation for women's exclusion to operate only at the level of the Freudian unconscious; and, indeed, the data of the Mishnah seem to bear out that prediction. For the overt consciousness of its male creators generates only some obvious ra- tionalizations about avoiding cultic contamination by menstruants or dis- ruption caused by women's supposedly uncontrolled sexuality. These fears then justify barring women from the world of ideas and the life of the mind. Yet the underlying motive may well be, as O'Brien claims, the urge to define a domain of cultural production (in the case of the Mishnah, predominantly intellectual and spiritual creation) that will be the preserve of "men only."

Beyond these considerations, however, lies another question that is addressed neither by the economic theories of MacKinnon, Kuhn, and others
nor by O'Brien's compensatory theory of the men's club. None of these
explanations accounts for every rule governing women's status in mishnaic
law. Economic theories postulate male exploitation of women as the principal motivation for their suppression and subordination. But if so, one
would expect to find patriarchal systems subjecting *all* women, not just
some women, to male domination throughout the private domain; yet we
do not find this in the Mishnah. It is obviously true, as Kuhn suggests, that
rules of customary law or terms of a marriage contract may stipulate that the
wife shall perform certain household and other economic tasks for the
husband. We recall the mishnaic requirement that the wife work at specified
household chores and produce a prescribed amount of yarn or cloth besides
and that the proceeds of surplus production not needed for domestic consumption accrue to the husband.[330] But this does not necessarily constitute
exploitation of the wife, particularly when the rules also require a husband
to maintain his wife at, or above, a specified minimum level and (still more
significant) set strict upper limits to her work norm. On the whole, calculated economic exploitation of women can hardly be said to play a major
role in a system that exhibits such features. A woman's economic contribution seems, rather, to have constituted legal consideration for a reciprocal
bargain whereby the husband provided maintenance in return for the wife's
limited domestic and economic services.

As for Israelite evaluations of women's work, we may note in passing
one ingenious non-Marxist interpretation. Carole Meyers confirms the levitical assessment of a grown woman's worth at precisely three-fifths that of a
man (Lev. 27:2–4) by means of a statistical computation. Her calculations
suggest that this represented a fair valuation of women in early Iron Age
Israel based on their average percentage contribution to the work-product of
a typical family.[331] While not qualified to judge the statistical merits of
Meyers' analysis, I record it as an interesting exploration of congruence
between social scientific theory and the socioeconomic rules of an ancient
culture.

Returning to the problem of women's subordination in patriarchal
cultures, we see that in the mishnaic system even dependent women, such as
wives, were not the victims of unbridled exploitation. But there remains an
even more basic question—not solved by O'Brien's analysis—that, indeed,
seems to contradict Marxist economic arguments also. It is this: We still lack
an adequate explanation for the initial exemption of *any women at all*—
especially those *of three entire classes*—from men's legal and economic
control. Why does the mishnaic system grant autonomy to single women,
widows, and divorcées? After all, many such women are still young enough
to produce offspring; and even those past childbearing age normally retain
some economic value through their spinning, weaving, and other skills.
Why, then, would any patriarchal system permit such women legal independence? It would have been a simple matter to return these women to

their fathers' or brothers' authority, thus keeping them under perpetual male tutelage as was done in contemporary Roman law. So we must look beyond both O'Brien's discussion and the various feminist economic theories for some other explanation—some reason so compelling that the Mishnah's framers were unable to resist it despite its possible economic detriment to the Israelite male.

An important clue to this mystery may lie in the fact (discussed in chap. 1) that the sages of the Mishnah considered themselves bound in principle by the authority of Scripture. Sometimes, when it suited them and the text left room for maneuver, they might circumvent the rules or interpret them in conformity with their requirements; but we have seen that where Scripture speaks explicitly, Mishnah cannot presume to countermand. The clearest example is the sages' taxonomy of women. As noted at the outset, they simply adopted the classification imposed by Scripture in the law of women's vows (Num. 30:2–17). There, the text explicitly endorses (or perhaps establishes—this is a chicken-egg question) the autonomy of widows and divorcées by stating that no one can annul their vows (Num. 30:10). In addition references to the daughter (Num. 30:4, 17) imply that legal control over a daughter lasts only while she is *"still in her father's house by reason of her youth."* The logical inference is that daughters who have come of age are automatically emancipated. Thus, the biblical law of vows defines three categories of legally autonomous women in so unequivocal a fashion that the sages have no choice but to incorporate these into their system.

The sages might perhaps have sought a way around this problem—as they did, for instance, in requiring two witnesses to warn a suspected adulteress (thus permitting the husband later to divorce her without returning her marriage portion) or in combining Num. 30:14 with Num. 30:17 to define a wife's self-denying vow as any vow that might impair the conjugal relationship. But in both of these cases, the sages could appeal to the language of Scripture, either in context or drawn from elsewhere; here, by contrast, no such option existed, that is, they could find no proof text for rejecting the classification of women contained in the law of vows.

Furthermore, Scripture's taxonomy of women exhibits another feature—which from the sages' point of view may have further validated the biblical taxonomy—impelling the sages to adopt it despite its counterproductiveness for male economic interests. We should not underestimate the considerable aesthetic appeal of Scripture's binary logic to mishnaic sages who were independently committed to the principle of Hellenistic polarities. With the six scriptural/mishnaic categories in place, neatly forming a three-by-two grid, we should expect to find exactly what we do find, namely, that women in opposed subgroups display diametrically opposed features with respect to the main basis of the classification. Hence, if three subgroups are defined as legally dependent, it makes good sense that their opposite numbers should enjoy legal autonomy.

Autonomous women, as we saw, were treated as persons in all matters pertaining to the private domain. But this raises yet another problem: Why not treat dependent women as nonpersons—that is chattels—in *all* respects? This would surely accord with the bipolarity of mishnaic logic. Yet, as we saw, it was only in the context of male ownership of female sexuality that the sages demoted women to the status of chattel. How can we explain this fact? Here, I suggest the following reasoning on the sages' part. A woman, dependent or autonomous, remains a woman; thus perceived, she possesses many features in common with other women. Those common features will predominate in all contexts that fall outside the purpose underlying the taxonomy supplied by Scripture and adopted by Mishnah. Thus if women are persons in principle, then every woman of full age must be treated as such, with only one permissible exception: A dependent woman may receive special treatment with respect to the specific factor that motivated her initial classification of dependency—namely, her value to the man who legally owns her sexual and reproductive function.

Still another consideration may operate here. The impetus to treat women as persons over a large part of the spectrum of Israelite life (i.e., in the private domain) may stem partly from the sages' interpretation of Scripture's statement that God created man and woman alike in his image: *"And God created man in his image; in the image of God he created him; male and female he created them"* (Gen. 1:27). Although one modern scholar, Phyllis Bird, has argued convincingly that this reading of Scripture almost certainly depends on a fortuitous mispunctuation of the masoretic text,[332] the adopted reading was certainly taken very seriously. The problem of women's equality was considered not only by Jewish sages, but also by early patristic writers, who likewise experienced difficulty in coming to terms with a notion so alien to the dominant culture of the day and so much at odds with their own patriarchal stance.[333] If God indeed stated that women, like men, are created in his image, their otherness cannot be so complete as men might otherwise be free to suppose. Women share with men a common humanity. In the last analysis the otherness of women resides most obviously and undeniably in their sexual differentiation from men and in the function this serves. So, for the sages of the Mishnah, women may in that respect, but only in that respect, be viewed as Other; in all other contexts of private law, the system must—as, indeed, it does—treat them very much like men. It is only in the public domain that the sages manage to avoid this result. This they do by the simple expedient of excluding women from the separate-but-equal world of cultural creation forged by men to express, not the otherness of *women* but the otherness of *men*.

In conclusion I would urge historians to undertake the kind of detailed investigation of patriarchal systems that alone can provide solid information to confirm or refute untested assumptions and uncorroborated speculations that have marred the infant years of feminist research. As Rosaldo cogently pointed out:

> [F]eminists differ in their diagnoses of our prehistoric lives, their sense of
> suffering, of conflict, and of change. Some . . . romanticize what they imagine

was a better past, while others find in history an endless tale of female subjugation and male triumph. But most, I think, would find no cause to question a
desire to ferret out our origins and roots.[334]

Underlying Rosaldo's mild rebuke of the early feminist penchant for
speculation, sometimes in blithe disregard of demonstrable facts, is the
conviction that there is no substitute for painstaking research into historical
fact as the basis of theory. Feminist scholarship thus far has suffered from a
shortage of historicolegal studies of a kind that can elicit the concrete
information essential to the formulation of viable theories about the position of women in patriarchy.

An important exception is Gerda Lerner's *The Creation of Patriarchy*,[335]
which unfortunately appeared too late for adequate discussion here. I find
myself in substantial accord with Lerner's theoretical interpretations, in
particular with her conclusion that "it is not women who are reified and
commodified, it is women's sexuality and reproductive capacity which is so
treated."[336] As with Lerner, it was precisely when I "began to see that I
needed to focus more on the control of women's sexuality and procreativity
than on the usual economic questions" that the distinction between woman
as chattel and woman as person became stunningly clear.

This inquiry into the image and status of women in mishnaic law
constitutes one attempt to supply the lacuna perceived by Rosaldo. Most
important, it demonstrates that the position of women in the mishnaic
system was neither a romantically better past nor an endless tale of female
subjugation and male triumph. True, woman was never a complete person
in mishnaic society, but neither was she always and only a chattel.

APPENDIXES

Appendix 1. Further Illustrations of Chattel Status of Minor Daughter

(See chap. 2, "Virginity and Bride-Price," pp. 21ff.)

In one unusual case, the sages are forced to treat the question of one girl's virginity on an individual basis; but she is the exception that proves the rule. In what follows the physical situation is clear, but we have a paradox, for some girls have suffered sexual intrusion but retained (or regained) their virginity, whereas one girl innocent of sexual activity has lost her hymen by accident.

A.   [In a case where] a grown male [over nine years and a day (T. Ket. 1:2)][337] has had intercourse with a little girl [under three years and a day (T. Ket. 1:2)], or a little boy [under nine years and a day] has had intercourse with a grown female [over three years and a day],

B.   or [in the case of] a girl injured by a piece of wood [*i.e., who lost her virginity by accident*],

C.   their k^etubbah-money is two hundred **zuz**, in the view of R. Meir. [*The two girls at A are classified as virgins. In the first case of the girl's hymen is thought to have grown back, whereas in the second case a boy under nine is deemed incapable of rupturing the hymen. Both girls thus remain physical virgins, though both have suffered sexual intrusion, hence are psychologically nonvirgin. The girl at B has lost the physical signs of virginity, but is psychologically virgin because she has had no sexual experience. Meir would classify her as a virgin.*]

D.   But sages [in general] hold that the k^etubbah-money of a girl injured by accident is one *maneh* [= 100 *zuz*]. [***The majority stress the physical absence of the hymen, just as they emphasize the physical presence of the regenerated hymen in ruling the little girl at A a virgin.***]

                                                                            M. Ket. 1:3

Which of these girls qualify as virgins, and which do not? Here, as before, the sages choose to solve the case of the ambiguous virgin by reference to the girl's ultimate physical condition. They classify sexually experienced girls as virgins merely because they have retained or regenerated the hymen, whereas an inexperienced girl who lost her hymen by accident counts as nonvirgin. The puzzle here is, why do the sages apply a *physical* criterion to the girl "injured by a piece of wood" (M. Ket. 1:3B) while using in all other cases (M. Ket. 1:3A) the same *cultural* rule they employed before? Closer scrutiny suggests an answer. At M. Ket. 1:3A conventional wisdom solves the problem simply by assuming what everybody "knows." But the case at M. Ket. 1:3B is highly ambiguous. The girl claims to have lost her virginity by accident—but who knows? Where they cannot determine the "truth" by applying a conventional presumption, most sages rely on the physical criterion. Only one sage, Meir, alone gives the girl the benefit of the doubt.

Appendix 2. Exceptions to the Rule Compensating a Father for the Violation of His Daughter

(See chap. 2, "Seduction and Rape: Criminal Penalties," pp. 23ff.)

The status of the minor daughter as her father's chattel is underscored by two further exceptions to the rule of compensation to the father. The first involves a girl divorced after betrothal but before actual consummation of marriage. In such a case the bridegroom who divorces her must give the father the brideprice he has been holding in trust for the bride. Sages dispute whether a subsequent seducer or rapist need pay a fine, given that the girl's father has already recovered her marriage portion from the man who divorced her.

A.   [Concerning] a pubescent girl who was betrothed and then divorced [before consummation of the marriage], R. Yose the Galilean rules that there is no fine [payable] for her [by one who seduces or rapes her after the divorce even though she was still a virgin at that time]. [***M. Ket. 4:2 requires the divorcing fiancé to pay such a girl's marriage portion to her father, if she is still under age. As the father has thus already received a bride-price, no fine need be paid by her subsequent violator.***]
B.   And R. ʿAqiba rules that there is a fine for her, but the fine [goes] to the girl herself [rather than to her father in the normal way].

                                                                            M. Ket. 3:3

This girl's position is ambiguous. Most divorcées, even if still under age, become autonomous by virtue of the divorce (M. Qid. 1:1) and collect their own marriage portion from the divorcing husband (M. Ket. 4:2). But a girl divorced by her espoused husband before consummation has never left her father's house. Because she remains under the father's authority, it is he, not she, who collects her marriage portion from the divorcing fiancé (M. Ket. 4:2). Reasoning that a father who has already collected once cannot expect a second reimbursement for the same virgin, Yose would simply exempt the violator from the fine! He never considers the possibility of compensating the girl herself. So long as she stays in her father's house, her virginity remains his property. ʿAqiba, by contrast, reasons that because the girl remains a virgin, her subsequent violator should pay the penalty, just as he would have had to pay bride-price to her had he married her instead of raping her in these circumstances (M. Ket. 1:2B). But, agreeing with Yose that the father cannot collect twice, ʿAqiba has to award the money to the girl. The views of both sages reflect an anomaly whereby the penalty for seduction or rape continues to accrue to the father, as mandated by Scripture, even though the Mishnah's framers (apparently following a change in Israelite custom) assign bride-price to the girl herself as part of the marriage settlement.

The chattel status of the minor daughter is further highlighted by another exceptional case, that of a girl orphaned in childhood. After her father's death (which makes her technically autonomous), her mother or brother arranges her marriage. If her fiancé should divorce her prior to consummation, she reverts (though still a minor) to the autonomous state she attained when her father died. But she remains a virgin, and once more the question arises, what if some man now rapes or seduces her?

> A. [Concerning] an orphan girl who was betrothed and divorced [following her father's death and is still under age], R. Eleazar rules that one who seduces [her] is exempt [from penalty],
> B. but one who rapes [her] is liable [and the penalty goes to the girl].
>
> M. Ket. 3:6

This orphan girl differs from the girl in the preceding case in being *sui juris* before the rape or seduction occurred. Hence, Eleazar treats her as an adult. As such, her rights vary, depending on whether she was seduced by consent or raped against her will. A consenting adult has voluntarily yielded her virginity, but a rape victim is entitled to collect the fine. The significant point is that because this girl has no father and is legally autonomous, her sexuality belongs to her alone. The fine for her violation cannot go to her mother or brother, who do not own the right to profit from her virginity. The exceptional case once more proves the general rule: A minor girl's sexuality belongs to her father, and to him alone.

Appendix 3. Further Examples of Forfeiture of Marriage Portion by Women Exempted from the Ordeal

(See chap. 3, "The 'Straying Wife' as the Husband's Sexual Property," pp. 50ff.)

The sages employ the same strategy for controlling the wife's sexual conduct, with respect to other classes of women who for various reasons escape the ordeal. If a man's claim on a woman's sexuality is insufficient to subject her to the ordeal, the sages protect his interest by invoking the penalty clause. They apply it, for instance, to women who are merely prospective wives at the time of the alleged offense as well as to marriages that infringe caste guidelines. Such women are not, strictly speaking, *"under the authority of"* the husband (Numb. 5:19–20), hence cannot be subjected to the ordeal. Nonetheless, the husband may divorce these wives without paying their marriage portions (M. Soṭ. 4:1). So, too, with women exempted for various other reasons (M. Soṭ. 4:2).

A.   A betrothed woman or a widow awaiting [consummation with] her levir do not drink [*i.e., are exempt from the ordeal for the reason given at C*].

B.   But [if their prospective husbands divorce them for suspected infidelity], they do not collect [their] marriage portion.

C.   As it is stated [in Scripture], *"When a woman, being under the authority of her husband, goes astray,"* this excludes a betrothed woman and a levirate widow. [*Even though such women are expected to reserve themselves for the prospective marriage partner, his lack of authority at the time of the woman's involvement with another man precludes the use of the ordeal. Nonetheless, the sages rule that a husband who suspects his wife of such a liaison during the betrothal period may divorce her without paying her off.*]

D.   A widow [married] to a high priest, a divorcée or released levirate widow [married] to a common priest, a *mamzeret* or *neṭinah* [married] to an Israelite, or an Israelite's daughter [married] to a *mamzer* or *natin* do not [have to] drink. [*They escape the ordeal because these marriages are flawed by violation of caste guidelines; hence the husband has no true authority over them. Nonetheless, they forfeit the marriage settlement to which M. Ket. 11:6 specifically entitles them despite the flaw, should the husband divorce them on suspicion.*]

M. Soṭ. 4:1

A.   The following neither drink [the potion] nor collect their marriage portion [if divorced upon suspicion]:

B.   She who says, "I am defiled." [*She admits her infidelity rather than undergo the ordeal. Here the husband can and must divorce her without payment, for her self-confessed adultery forfeits her settlement.*]

C.   She against whom [two] witnesses have testified that she is defiled. [*Her guilt being thus proven, the ordeal becomes unnecessary.*]

D.   And she who says, "I will not drink." [*She refuses to undergo the ordeal; this is equivalent to the confession of the wife at B.*]

E.   If her husband says, "I will not make her drink" or if her husband has intercourse with her on the way [to the priest, thereby condoning her suspected infidelity], she does collect her marriage portion [even though] she does not [have to] drink.

F.   [As to women] whose husbands die before [the wives] have drunk [*i.e., there is now no husband to assert his right by bringing her before the priest, as required by Num. 5:15*],

G.   the school of Shammai rules that they may collect their marriage portions without drinking;

H.   but the school of Hillel rules that they neither drink nor collect their marriage portion [*which ordinarily accrues to a widow on the husband's death. Here, the settlement is forfeit because the question of the wife's infidelity remains in doubt, and "the burden of proof lies on the plaintiff" (M. B.Q. 3:11). In this case, the plaintiff is the widow claiming her portion, who cannot rebut her husband's accusation because it is virtually impossible to prove a negative averment, such as "I have not committed adultery."*]

M. Soṭ. 4:2

These cases, like M. Soṭ. 4:3 (p. 53), endorse the husband's right to exclusive use of his wife's sexuality. Even a wife exempt from the ordeal cannot misbehave with impunity, for she stands to lose her marriage settlement. Paradoxically, the exception whereby a husband who condones his wife's infidelity loses the right to punish her (M. Soṭ. 4:2E) proves the rule that he owns her sexuality, for it shows that he can legally acquiesce in her bestowing her favors elsewhere.[338] Interesting, too, is the dispute between schools at M. Soṭ. 4:2 F through H. Both agree that a widow cannot be subjected to the ordeal because no living man has the right to complain about her. But while Shammaites would permit this widow to collect her portion, Hillelites, by withholding it, allow the dead hand of her husband to rule her from the grave. Such is the measure of a husband's right to enforce his wife's fidelity.

Appendix 4. Husband's Right to Revoke His Wife's Nazirite Vow as Inimical to Conjugal Relations

(See chap. 3, "Wife's Vows Inimical to Conjugal Relations," pp. 54ff.)

A special kind of self-denying vow, which Scripture permits both men and women to take, is the Nazirite vow (Num. 6:1–21, discussed by the sages in tractate *Nazir*). The Nazirite devotes himself or herself to God's service for a specified period, during which he or she undertakes to abstain from wine, avoid contamination by corpses, and refrain from cutting the hair. Because the Nazirite vow is clearly self-denying (especially with respect to abstention from wine), the Mishnah's framers apply the general rule that a husband can revoke such a vow (Num. 30:14; M. Naz. 9:1), though Scripture, which sets out the law of the Nazirite in some detail, makes no such explicit provision. The sages presumably consider the Nazirite vow potentially inimical to the husband's interests, for they offer several illustrations of the scope and limits of a husband's power to revoke his wife's vow.

A.   [Concerning a man] who said, "Lo, I become a Nazirite!" and whose fellow heard [him] and said "So do I!" [and a third man said] "So do I!", all of them become Nazirites. [*By adopting the first man's words, they bind themselves in a similar fashion.*]

B. If the first [man] was released [*from his vow by a sage, as provided in*
    M. Ned. 3:1–2 for certain types of vow], all of them stand released. [*Just as*
    the first man's spoken formula sufficed to bind them all, so his release
    suffices to exonerate them all.]

C. If the last [man] was released, the last stands released; but all the others
    remain bound [*for their vows in no way depended on his*].

D. If a man said, "Lo, I become a Nazirite!" and his fellow heard [him] and
    said, "Let my mouth be as his mouth, and my hair as his hair!" [i.e., *"My*
    mouth will drink no wine, my hair will remain uncut"], lo, the latter
    becomes a Nazirite, [for he has adopted the first man's vow as his own].

E. [If a man said], "Lo, I become a Nazirite!" and his wife heard [him] and
    said, "So do I!" he can annul her vow, though his own [vow] stands.
    [*Because he vowed first, he has said nothing to endorse her subsequent*
    vow.]

F. [If the wife said,] "Lo, I become a Nazirite!" and her husband heard [her]
    and said, "So do I!" he has no power to annul [her vow]. [*His words have*
    implicitly endorsed her vow.]

M. Naz. 4:1

A. [If a man said,] "Lo, I become a Nazirite!—and thou [likewise]?"
    [*addressing his wife*], and she said, "Amen!" he can annul her vow, but his
    own [vow] stands [*as at (M. Naz. 4:1E)*].

B. [But if the wife said,] "Lo, I become a Nazirite!—and thou [likewise]?"
    [*addressing her husband*], and he said, "Amen!" he has no power to annul
    [her vow], [*for the same reason as at (M. Naz. 4:1F)*].

M. Naz. 4:2

Granting that a woman's scripturally conferred power to take the Nazirite vow is intrinsically the same as a man's, why should the Mishnah's
framers condition the validity of her vow on the husband's acquiescence?
The answer is not far to seek. In the context of vows (as we have seen) the
sages choose to interpret self-denying as denying the husband, especially if
the vow directly or indirectly affects conjugal relations. At first sight it is not
clear how the Nazirite vow (which does not preclude sexual intercourse or
aesthetic practices like bathing) can adversely affect the husband. But the
framers offer us a hint at M. Naz. 4:5, wherein they let a man revoke his
wife's Nazirite vow on the ground that he takes no pleasure in a woman he
finds repulsive or who will become unattractive by shaving her head as
Scripture requires at the end of the Nazirite term.

A. [339]*[I]f circumstances require a Nazirite wife to fulfill her vow afresh*], [her
    husband] may annul [her vow], for he has power to say, "I do not like a
    repulsive woman" (*mᵉnuwwelet*).

B. Rabbi [Judah the Prince] rules that even if her proposed hair-offering has
    been offered in cultic purity [*and she is now on the point of cutting it off*],
    he may annul [her vow], for he can say, "I do not like a shorn woman."

M. Naz. 4:5

In this unit the sages do not make clear what is meant by "repulsive
woman" (at M. Naz. 4:5A). However, subsequent commentators have

argued, based on other literary evidence, that the practices of Nazirites included abstention from sexual intercourse (to avoid even temporary cultic pollution) even though Scripture did not actually require this.[340] If so, we see once more that in the minds of the sages, a man's right to countermand his wife's Nazirite vow stems from the fact that in practice this will probably deprive him of his conjugal rights. Thus, in permitting the husband to revoke his wife's Nazirite vow, the sages employ the same principle they established earlier—a wife's self-denying vow means one that impairs the husband's sexual rights. Here again, the sexuality factor justifies his controlling her in ways that diminish her personhood. For the sages concede (M. Naz. 4:1F and M. Naz. 4:2B) the wife's intrinsic power to make a vow that binds not only herself, but also her husband—if he chooses to endorse it. Yet because this vow may impair the conjugal relationship during the period of the wife's Naziritehood, the sages insist on the husband's right to revoke it if he chooses.[341]

Appendix 5. Effect of Sexual Acquisition of a Woman on Her Caste Privileges

(See chap. 3, conclusion of "Wife's Vows Inimical to Conjugal Relations," p. 60 n. 113).

As we know, a man acquires sexual rights in a woman by performing a competent act of acquisition that creates a valid relationship of betrothal or marriage. But if the spouses are of different castes (M. Qid. 2:3), something else happens, too, depending on which of them belongs to the higher caste. In particular a lower-caste woman gains the right to partake of her new husband's caste privileges. If he is a *kohen*, the newly acquired bride at once shares his scriptural right to eat *t*ᵉ*rumah*-food, that is, food donated to the priesthood by lower-caste Israelites (Exod. 29:28). If, by contrast, the woman is of a higher caste than the man, she loses her own caste privileges because, for practical purposes, she suffers the disadvantages of her husband's lower caste. Thus, the daughter of a *kohen* is entitled as a member of her father's household to eat *t*ᵉ*rumah*-food. But if she marries a man who is not a *kohen* (Lev. 22:12), she loses this right, for she no longer belongs to a priestly family. If, however, she later returns to her father's house on widowhood or divorce from a marriage in which she bore no children, she reverts to her father's household (for this limited purpose)[342] and may once more partake of *t*ᵉ*rumah*-food (Lev. 22:13). The framers here expand the scriptural rules, specifying precisely which contacts or relationships affect the status of the *kohen*'s daughter and which do not.

A.   An unborn child [*in the womb of a* kohen's *daughter married to a nonpriestly man who has since died*]; a [nonpriestly] levir [*even though he has not yet consummated with his brother's widow, a* kohen's *daughter*]; betrothal

[of a *kohen*'s daughter to a nonpriestly man]; [marriage of a *kohen*'s daughter to a nonpriestly] deaf-mute [*whose marriage is considered valid even
though he could not recite the espousal formula*]; [consummation of marriage with] a boy aged nine years and one day [*who for caste reasons is
ineligible to marry into the priesthood but, being over nine years, is deemed
capable of having intercourse*]—

B.   [all the foregoing] disqualify [the *kohen*'s daughter from eating *t*ᵉ*rumah*],
      [*even though their acts of acquisition that disqualify her are legally imper-
      fect*].

C.   But [*if the foregoing cases were reversed, involving a* kohen *and an Israe-
      lite's daughter*] they do not qualify [her] to eat [*t*ᵉ*rumah*] [*precisely because
      their acts of acquisition are imperfect*].

D.   [*In the case of the nine-year-boy*] [this is the case even if] there is doubt
      whether he is or is not aged nine years and one day or [if there is] doubt
      whether he has produced two hairs [as a sign of puberty] or not.[343]

                                                                      M. Yeb. 7:4

A.   A rapist, a seducer, or an imbecile do not [by their intercourse with her]
      disqualify [a *kohen*'s daughter from eating *t*ᵉ*rumah* if they are not members
      of the priestly caste] nor do they qualify [her] to eat [*t*ᵉ*rumah* if they are
      members of that caste]. [*This is because they have not effectively acquired
      her in marriage; the rapist and seducer did not intend marriage, and the
      imbecile cannot form that intention. Hence the woman remains a member
      of her own family.*]

B.   However, if they are not eligible to enter [the community of] Israel, lo, these
      [men defined at A] do disqualify [her if she is a *kohen*'s daughter]. [*This is
      because she is irrevocably profaned by sexual contact with a man ineligible
      to "enter the community of YHWH," as for instance a* mamzer, *a* Moabite,
      or an Ammonite (Deut. 23:3–4)].

C.   How so [*referring to A above*]? If an Israelite has had intercourse [by force,
      or with consent, or he being an imbecile] with a *kohen*'s daughter, she may
      [nontheless continue to] eat *t*ᵉ*rumah* [*because he has not acquired her*].

D.   If he has impregnated her, she may not eat *t*ᵉ*rumah*. [The fetus's nonpriestly
      status, derived from its father, demotes the mother's status to that of Israe-
      lite].

E.   But if the fetus is cut from her womb [i.e., *not born alive*], she may [once
      more] eat *t*ᵉ*rumah* [*because she regains her priestly status when the lower-
      caste child is separated from her body*].

F.   [As for] a *kohen* who has intercourse [by force, or with consent, or he being
      an imbecile] with an Israelite's daughter, she may not eat *t*ᵉ*rumah* [*because
      the priestly man has not legally acquired her in these circumstances*].

G.   If he impregnated her, she may not eat *t*ᵉ*rumah* [*because we do not know
      whether the child will be born alive. Only the actual birth of the priestly
      child qualifies its mother to eat* t*ᵉ*rumah.*]

H.   But if she gives birth [to a son], she may eat *t*ᵉ*rumah* [*for the reason given at
      G*].

                                                                      M. Yeb. 7:5

Once more, the woman is viewed as the sexual property of a man. In
deciding what acts can negate the privileges of the *kohen*'s daughter, Mish-

nah's framers view the woman, not in her own right, but only by reference to some man who has performed an act of sexual acquisition (even merely potential, as with the levir at M. Yeb. 7:4A) in relation to her. If the act is deemed effective, she acquires the man's caste with its attendant advantages or drawbacks. This effect is produced, not by her own action, but by some man's sexual act performed with respect to her. That act is effective even where the actor is a minor, or impaired, or the lowest of outcastes. Thus, the *kohen*'s daughter can lose her priestly status through marriage, impregnation, or (sometimes) mere sexual contact with lower-caste men. The actions of a deaf-mute, or a nine-year-old boy, or the mere presence of an unborn child within her can alter her status. All that matters is that the act should have some sexually acquisitive effect.[344] Moreover, the act of an objectively inferior man suffices to disqualify the priestly woman even if the act is not technically valid. Clearly a double standard prevails here. For although a technically incomplete acquisition by a nonpriestly man serves to deprive the *kohen*'s daughter of her priestly privileges, the very same acts performed by a *kohen* with respect to an Israelite woman do not suffice to qualify the woman for priestly privileges. The imposition of this double standard treats the woman once more as nonperson. But the woman's personhood is discounted here in an even more basic way. For even the high-born *kohen*'s daughter loses her rights through the actions of men, boys, and unborn children of lower social status. That a mere fetus can deprive her of her rights shows the precarious nature of a woman's personhood in the eyes of the framers.

The Mishnah's elaboration of the rules that create or destroy a woman's connection with a priestly family goes far beyond anything found in Scripture. Why should this be so? The answer can only be this: In the cases at hand the sages contemplate the woman in the context of her sexual acquisition by a man. Their negation of her personhood in that situation comports fully with what we have already seen. The woman as sex object is perceived and treated as chattel.

Appendix 6. Further Illustrations of the Effect of Ambiguity on the Personhood of the Wife

(See chap. 3, "Ambiguity of Status: Effect on the Wife," pp. 60ff.)

A second type of ambiguity, stemming from errors in the delivery of the writ, may likewise place a woman in the hybrid category of divorced-and-not-divorced. The Mishnah develops Scripture's requirement that a husband who divorces his wife must give the writ *"into the wife's hand"* (*wenatan beyadah*, Deut. 24:1). Because the Hebrew word for hand (*yad*) can also mean jurisdiction,[345] the sages interpret the phrase as meaning "into the wife's control." Hence, the writ must be delivered to the woman in her private domain under circumstances that show she knows what is happening. Delivery at the wife's house effects a valid divorce. Improper delivery, as in the husband's house, or while the wife is sleeping and unaware, or by deceiving her about the nature of the document, fails to terminate the marriage.

A. [In the case of] one who throws a *get* to his wife while she is within her own house or in her courtyard, lo, she is [validly] divorced [*because the* get *was delivered to her private domain*].

B. If he threw it to her within his house or in his courtyard, even if he was in bed with her [at the time], she is not divorced [*because his home or yard is his domain, not hers*].

C. [But if he threw it] into her lap or into her basket, lo, she is divorced. [*These count as her private domain, even though she is in his house at the time, because a person's "four cubits" of immediately surrounding space or private possessions constitute his or her personal domain.*]

M. Giṭ. 8:1

A. If [*when handing her the* geṭ], he said to her, "Receive this writ of indebtedness" or if she found it [on the ground] behind him [and] read [it], and lo, it was her *geṭ*, it is not a [valid] *geṭ*. [It is not valid] until he says to her, "Here is thy *geṭ*." [*In both cases, he has failed correctly to state the nature of the document, hence failed to effect proper delivery.*][346]

B. If he placed it in her hand while she was asleep, [and] she awoke [and] read [it], and lo, it was her *geṭ*, it is not a [valid] *geṭ*. [It is not valid] until he says to her, "Here is thy writ of divorce."

C. If she was standing in the public domain and he threw it toward her,

D. if [it fell] nearer to her, she is [validly] divorced,

E. and if nearer to him, she is not divorced.

F. [But if the *geṭ* fell halfway [between them], she [counts as] divorced-and-not-divorced [*with the same results described at M. Giṭ. 7:3 (p. 62), that if the husband later dies childless, his brother may not perform levirate marriage with the widow (in case she is actually a divorcée and no widow) but must, nonetheless, release her from the levirate bond before she can remarry (in case she is indeed his brother's widow).*]

M. Giṭ. 8:2

These rules are mostly self-explanatory. We need consider only the equivocal case at M. Giṭ. 8:2F. As always, the sages' general preoccupation with taxonomy and their particular concern with ownership of a woman's sexuality places the wife in the worst of all possible worlds. In the cases discussed earlier, she became an innocent victim through nobody's fault. No one could know whether the sick man would die of his illness; no one could establish the precise moment of the absent husband's death. In this last case, however, her problems stem from her husband's negligent failure to deliver the *geṭ* properly. Here, the sages treat the wife even more unfairly than at M. Giṭ. 7:3–4 and M. Giṭ. 7:9F. For there, the unclarity in the woman's status resulted simply from the nature of the case; but here, the confusion is attributable directly to the husband's error. Yet it is the *wife* who loses her rights. When it comes to the formalities of divorce, then, the sages plainly treat the husband as a person and the wife as a mere object. Their horror of ambiguity concerning the woman's sexuality overrides her substantive rights of personhood. Indeed, as we saw, they sometimes go so far as to frustrate the husband's attempt to secure those very rights for her. So far as the sages are concerned, a woman is not the subject of laws; where sexuality is involved, she is their object.

Appendix 7. Husband Who Renounces Right to Control Disposition of His Wife's Property

(See chap. 3, "The Wife as Owner of Property," pp. 87ff.)

A further proof of the wife's intrinsic equality as property owner lies in the case of a husband who voluntarily renounces his right to control the disposition of his wife's property (thus restoring her unfettered power of alienation).

A. [Concerning] one who declares in writing to his [betrothed] wife, "Neither right nor claim do I have upon thy property,"

B. lo, he may [nonetheless] enjoy the usufruct [of the wife's property] during her lifetime; and if she dies [without issue], he may inherit from her.

C. If so, to what purpose did he declare in writing to her, "Neither right nor claim do I have upon thy property"?

D. [It was] so that if she should sell [it] or give [it] away, [her disposition] will stand. [*The husband here has relinquished only his right to control his wife's disposition of her property, and none of his other rights. That is, so long as she does not dispose of the property, he continues to enjoy usufruct during her lifetime and inheritance rights if she dies without issue.*]

E. [If] he declared in writing to her, "Neither right nor claim do I have upon thy property or the usufruct thereof,"

F. lo, he does not enjoy usufruct during her lifetime, but if she dies, he [still] may inherit from her. [*Once again, the husband loses only those rights he has specifically relinquished, and no others.*]

G. R. Judah rules [that] he always enjoys usufruct unless he declares in writing to her, "Neither right nor claim do I have upon thy property or the usufruct thereof, or the yield of the usufruct, without end."

H. [If] he declared in writing to her, "Neither right nor claim do I have upon thy property, or its usufruct, or the yield of its usufruct during thy lifetime or at thy death,"

I. he does not enjoy usufruct during her lifetime, and if she dies without issue, he does not inherit from her.

J. R. Simeon b. Gamaliel rules [that] if she dies without issue, he does inherit from her because he has made a stipulation contrary to what is written in the Torah, and if anyone makes a stipulation contrary to what is written in the Torah, his stipulation is void.[347]

M. Ket. 9:1

The sages do not tell us why a husband might renounce his right to usufruct or to control of his wife's property. Perhaps he gives this up in order to persuade a wealthy woman to marry him.[348] To the extent that a husband forgoes his power of administration, the wife's control over the disposition of her property revives.[349]

Appendix 8. Law of Usucaption as Inapplicable to Property of Spouses

(See chap. 3, "The Wife as Owner of Property," pp. 87ff.)

The sages consider whether to apply to the property of spouses the general rule that unchallenged use of property for a specified period leads to acquisition by usucaption. For instance, one who enjoys undisturbed usufruct of a field for three years acquires prescriptive title to that field (M. B.B. 3:1). However, the Mishnah's framers make a special exception for husband and wife. Although the law entitles a husband to the usufruct of his wife's property, the sages expressly debar him from thereby acquiring title. In reciprocal fashion the sages likewise deny a wife the right to acquire her husband's property merely by enjoying its fruits for the prescribed period.

> A. A man cannot acquire prescriptive title to his wife's property; and a woman cannot acquire prescriptive title to her husband's property.[350]
>
> M. B.B. 3:3

The framers specify no reason for this exception to the rule of usucaption by three years' undisturbed use. Commentators have suggested that it may stem from the tendency of spouses to give each other, for the sake of marital harmony, privileges not intended to establish actual legal rights.[351] But whatever its basis, the reciprocity of the rule as between husband and wife points to a measure of equality between the two when viewed purely as property owners. This illustrates once more the gulf that separates the sages' attitude to the wife as property owner from their view of a woman as the husband's sexual property. So long as the latter is not in issue, a wife remains a person.

Appendix 9. Standard of Proof in Cases Involving Wife as Sex Object and as Property Owner

(See chap. 3, "The 'Straying Wife' Revisited," pp. 91ff.)

The distinction between wife as sex object and wife as property owner appears also in the sages' rules concerning what testimony will suffice. The rules that follow confirm what we already know: Although the most tenuous evidence invokes the framers' insistence that a man divorce the suspect wife rather than continue with a woman of doubtful fidelity, they concede the insufficiency of such evidence to deprive her of her property rights.

A.   [Concerning one] who warned his wife of his jealousy, and she [subsequently] secluded herself [with the man in question], even if [her husband] heard [about this] from a flying bird, he must divorce her [for suspected adultery]; but he must still deliver her marriage portion [*because the bird is not a competent witness to deprive her of property*]. This is the opinion of R. Eliezer.

B.   [But] R. Joshua rules that [the husband is not forced to divorce her] until the women who spin by moonlight gossip about her. [*There must be at least some plausible evidence against her.*]

M. Soṭ. 6:1

A.   If a single witness said, "I saw her defiling herself," she would not [have to] drink [the potion]. [*A single competent witness suffices to prove her guilt, thus obviating the ordeal. But a single witness cannot deprive her of her money, for which purpose two are required.*]

B.   Moreover, even a male or female slave [*ordinarily ineligible to testify*] is competent [to prove her guilt and obviate the ordeal] and even [*as long as there are two of them*] to disqualify her from [collecting] her marriage portion.

C.   [But as for] her mother-in-law, and her mother-in-law's daughter, and her co-wife, and her husband's brother's wife, and her husband's daughter— these are competent, not to disqualify her from [receiving] her marriage portion, but only to exempt her from drinking [the potion]. [*These women are competent to prove her adultery, thus obviating the ordeal, but not to deprive her of her property rights in her marriage settlement.*]

M. Soṭ. 6:2

A.   If one witness says, "She is defiled," and one witness says "She is not defiled,"

B.   or if one woman says, "She is defiled," and one woman says, "She is not defiled,"

C.   she must drink. [*The evidence, either at A or at B, is equivocal; it proves nothing, but raises sufficient suspicion to invoke the ordeal.*]

D.   If one person says, "She is defiled," and two say, "She is not defiled," she must drink. [Again, the evidence raises sufficient suspicion to invoke the ordeal.]

E.   But if two say "She is defiled," and one says "She is not defiled," she need not drink. [*In this case, the testimony of two witnesses has convicted her; hence the ordeal is unnecessary.*]

M. Soṭ. 6:4

These rules illustrate the ambivalent attitude of the sages toward the suspected adulteress. On the one hand, they find the thought of her infidelity so abhorrent that they force the husband to divorce her on the merest suspicion (provided, of course, that she was previously warned, M. Soṭ. 6:1). At the same time, they require two competent witnesses before they will deprive the wife of her property. Moreover, recognizing that her own husband's kin or her co-wives may be biased against her, the sages draw the line at accepting testimony, even of two such witnesses, as a basis for depriving the wife of her marriage portion. The same reasoning underlies the sages' rejection of equivocal or refuted testimony at M. Soṭ. 6:4. When it comes to a wife's property rights, then, the law treats her as a person. Only when it comes to control of her reproductive function do the sages depart from due process.

Appendix 10. Curtailment of Levirate Law to Increase Pool of Women Eligible for Marriage

(See chap. 4, "Mishnaic Expansion of the Levirate Law," pp. 100ff.)

Sometimes the sages choose to limit, rather than expand, the scope of the scriptural levirate law, as when they exempt an extensive class of women from both levirate marriage and the requirement of ḥaliṣah release. Having seen how Mishnah's expansions of Scripture diminish the personhood of levirate widows, we might suppose that the sages' exemptions aim to enhance these widows' personhood by freeing them from the constraints of the law. Certainly the exemptions do have that effect. However, it turns out that the Mishnah's framers are not motivated by any desire to benefit women, rather, they exempt these widows for the benefit of a particular class of men, namely, the priestly caste.

The sages' preoccupation with sanctity explains their interest in matters pertaining to the priesthood, especially the priestly marriage laws. Scripture forbids a *kohen* to marry a *"woman divorced from her husband"* (Lev. 21:7). Because a levirate widow is deemed "married" to her levir even before consummation, the Mishnah treats a released widow as a divorcée. That status disqualifies her from marriage to a *kohen*. Here, the levirate widow stands in contrast to a normal widow, who may marry any *kohen* except the high priest (Lev. 21:13). This preclusion of released levirate widows along with the preemption of widows whose levirs choose to marry them creates a practical problem by depleting the pool of potential wives for *kohanim*. So the sages modify the impact of Scripture by exempting specified widows from the levirate law, obviating both the primary obligation and the secondary requirement of *ḥaliṣah*. Widows thus exempted become available for marriage into the priesthood. The Mishnah stresses the importance of levirate exemptions by opening tractate *Yebamot* with the long list of women precluded by Scripture's rules of consanguinity or affinity from marrying their levirs (Lev. 18). Then they assert that these forbidden women automatically exempt their co-wives (i.e., all other wives of the deceased) from the levirate law—even though such co-wives have no blood relationship to the levir. The forbidden women and their co-wives, freed from both the obligation of levirate marriage and the requirement of *ḥaliṣah*, thus qualify for marriage to *kohanim*.

A.   Fifteen women [who are near of kin to their levir] exempt their co-wives and the co-wives of their co-wives—and so on indefinitely—from [the legal requirement of] *ḥaliṣah* as well as from levirate union itself; and these are they:

B.   [the levir's] daughter, and his daughter's daughter, and his son's daughter; his wife's daughter, and her son's daughter, and her daughter's daughter; his mother-in-law, and his mother-in-law's mother, and his father-in-law's mother; his uterine sister, and his mother's sister, and his wife's sister, and the wife of his uterine brother, and the wife of his brother who was not [alive] during [the levir's] lifetime [*i.e., a levirate widow previously married to a far older brother of the levir, which brother had died before the present levir was born*]; and [the levir's] daughter-in-law;

C.   These women exempt their co-wives, and the co-wives of their co-wives, and so on indefinitely, from both *ḥaliṣah* and levirate union.[352]

M. Yeb. 1:1

A.   The school of Shammai permit the co-wives [of the women enumerated in M. Yeb. 1:1] to [marry] the surviving brothers,

B.   but the school of Hillel forbid [this].

C.   If [such co-wives] have performed *ḥaliṣah* [as required by Shammaites], the school of Shammai declare them ineligible for [marriage into] the priesthood [because they are classified as divorcées],

D.   but the school of Hillel [for whom the release ceremony was unnecessary, hence lacks legal significance] declare them eligible.

E.   If [the aforesaid co-wives] have consummated levirate marriage [and are subsequently widowed again], the school of Shammai declare them eligible [forremarriage into the priesthood because they were never in the category of divorcées];

F.   but the school of Hillel declare them ineligible [because they contracted a forbidden marriage, hence are "profaned women" precluded by Lev. 21:7 from marrying into the priestly caste].[353]

M. Yeb. 1:4

These rules (on the dominant Hillelite view) maximize the number of women freed from the requirement of *ḥaliṣah* and removed from the category of divorcée. Evasion of that classification keeps all these widows in the pool of potential wives for priestly men. This is certainly the motivation behind M. Yeb. 1:1. First, it is explicit in the statement in M. Yeb. 1:4D that such women are "eligible" to marry a *kohen*. Second, the Hillelites' desire to qualify these women for priestly marriages is conclusively proved by their exempting them not only from levirate marriage, but also from the release ceremony. If the main concern were simply to free these women for remarriage in general, they needed no exemption from *ḥaliṣah*. For released levirate widows, like divorcées, are precluded from remarriage only to members of the priestly caste. Furthermore, throughout the tractate, many women forbidden for various reasons to enter levirate marriage must nonetheless obtain a release.[354] A similar rule would have sufficed in M. Yeb. 1:1, but for the sages' desire to enlarge the pool of marriage partners for *kohanim*. The same motivation explains the following provisions, validating testimony that rescues a woman from a possible levirate tie:

A.[355] [As for one] who said on his deathbed: "I have sons," he may be believed [*because this statement, if accepted, prevents his wife from becoming a levirate widow*].

B.   [if he said], "I have brothers," he is not to be believed [*because this statement, if accepted, shackles the widow to a levir; moreover, unless the brothers can be located, she can never remarry, lacking a release*].

M. Qid. 3:8

For women's personhood, the outcome of the foregoing rules is somewhat ambivalent. On the one hand, the sages' action in freeing so many widows from the levirate constraint increases the personhood of these women. No longer shackled, they can remarry without a release. Moreover, their choice is not limited to nonpriests. On the other hand, this benefit to women is clearly incidental to the sages' primary purpose. Furthermore, in one sense the Mishnah treats these women as chattel even here. For these rules arbitrarily deprive them of a possible advantage. In mishnaic society some levirate widows may have actually welcomed the economic protection of compulsory marriage to their levirs. But M. Yeb. 1:1 arbitrarily removes this protection simply because of the women's value as potential wives for *kohanim*. Thus the levirate law, whether implemented or evaded, contemplates women as objects whose value consists in their sexual availability to men of one class or another. As always in that context, the system reduces women to chattel.

Appendix 11. Divorcee's Right to Freedom from Unreasonable Conditions

(See chap. 5, "The Wife's Passive Rights in the Law of Divorce," pp. 133ff.)

The Mishnah's framers will not permit the husband to ground his wife's divorce in conditions they consider unreasonable. The sages address the problem of conditional divorces, wherein a wife undertakes to perform an ongoing service that will continue after delivery of the *get*. If such a condition imposed by the husband becomes impossible to fulfill, its failure will retroactively invalidate the divorce. For a wife who has remarried in good faith, the disastrous consequences discussed earlier will ensue. The sages consider when a condition must be held to have failed and, if so, whether the divorce can nonetheless be saved.

A.   [If a husband said to his wife], "Lo, this is thy *get* on condition that thou serve my father" or "on condition that thou nurse my son":

B.   (How long must she nurse him? Two years; but R. Judah rules, eighteen months.)

C.   If [after she has begun to perform the service in question] the son dies or the [husband's] father dies [as the case may be], this remains a [valid] *get*. [*Because no time period was explicitly imposed, any degree of performance suffices and the recipient's death terminates the obligation.*]

D.   [But if the husband said], "Lo, this is thy *get* on condition that thou serve my father for two years" or "on condition that thou nurse my son for two years," and the son died or the father died [within the two years specified], or the father said [to his son], "I do not wish her to serve me"—[even] without provocation on the wife's part—this is not a [valid] *get*. [*Here, unlike the case at A through C, the wife has not satisfied the condition, which explicitly required the service to last for two years.*]

E.   But Rabban Simeon b. Gamaliel rules that in this [situation] it remains a valid *get*.

F.   Rabban Simeon b. Gamaliel made a general ruling that [in the case of] any impediment not caused by [the wife] herself, this remains a [valid] *get*. [*In the case of any ongoing condition that fails through no fault of the wife, she will not be penalized by the retroactive invalidation of her divorce.*]

M. Git. 7:6

Here, the sages address two questions. First, a condition that must continue after delivery of the *get* will be interpreted as leniently as possible (M. Git. 7:6 A and C), in order to avoid retroactive invalidation of the *get* through failure of the condition. Thus, where no length of service has been specified, any degree of performance will suffice. Second, where the husband designates a set period, the sages dispute whether a condition frustrated through no fault of the wife should invalidate the divorce. An earlier view (M. Git. 7:6D) that any failure, even beyond her control, places the divorcée in the unfortunate position of an adulteress (with all the dire consequences we know so well) is amended by Simeon b. Gamaliel M. Git. 7:6E and F), so that if failure of the condition is not the wife's fault, her divorce remains valid.

These rules reflect two aspects of a divorcée's personhood. First, a husband who offers his wife a divorce in return for her promise to perform a continuing service assumes that he can trust her; he expects her to act in accordance with a common standard of morality. Simeon's amendment at M. Git. 7:6F addresses the wife's morality more directly. He asks whether her failure to perform the promised service stems from her own fault. In assuming that the woman has sufficient responsibility to act in good faith and to expect the consequences if she cheats, Simeon perceives her as both a moral and a rational being. Second, this divorcée retains control over her status; she can preserve the validity of her divorce simply by keeping her word. Such personal control over her own life goes beyond rights assigned by others and reflects a higher level of personhood.

ABBREVIATIONS

ANET	Ancient Near Eastern Texts (Pritchard)
ʿArak.	ʿArakin
b.	ben ("son of")
AJS	Association for Jewish Studies
B.	Bavli (Babylonian Talmud)
B.B.	Baba Batra
B.C.E.	before the common era
B.M.	Baba Meṣiʿa
B.Q.	Baba Qamma
Bek.	Bekorot
Ber.	Berakot
Bik.	Bikkurim
C.E.	of the common era
Col.	Colossians
Cor.	Corinthians
Dem.	Demaʾi
Deut.	Deuteronomy
ʿErub.	ʿErubin
Exod.	Exodus
Gen.	Genesis
Giṭ.	Giṭṭin
Ḥag.	Ḥagigah
Hor.	Horayot
Hos.	Hosea
HTR	*Harvard Theological Review*
HUCA	*Hebrew Union College Annual*

Ḥul.	Ḥullin
JAAR	*Journal of the American Academy of Religion*
JBL	*Journal of Biblical Literature*
JJS	*Journal of Jewish Studies*
Josh.	Joshua
JPS	Jewish Publication Society
JTS	Jewish Theological Seminary
Judg.	Judges
Ker.	Keritot
Ket.	Ketubbot
Lev.	Leviticus
M.	Mishnah
M.S.	Maʿaser Sheni
Mak.	Makkot
Maksh.	Makshirin
Meg.	Megillah
Men.	Menaḥot
Mid.	Middot
Naz.	Nazir
Ned.	Nedarim
Nid.	Niddah
Num.	Numbers
OUP	Oxford University Press
Par.	Parah
Pes.	Pesaḥim
Ps.	Psalms
Qid.	Qiddushin
R.	Rabbi
R.H.	Rosh Hashanah
Shab.	Shabbat
Sam.	Samuel
San.	Sanhedrin
SBL	Society for Biblical Literature
Shebu.	Shebuʿot
Sheq.	Sheqalim
Soṭ.	Soṭah
S.P.C.K.	Society for the Propagation of Christian Knowledge
Suk.	Sukkah
T.	Tosefta
Tem.	Temurot
Ter.	Terumot
Tim.	Timothy
Ṭoh.	Ṭohorot
Tos.	Tosefot
Y.	Yerushalmi (Palestinian Talmud)
Yeb.	Yebamot
Zeb.	Zebaḥim

NOTES

1. The name *Mishnah* is not actually mishnaic but of later provenance. It is the Talmud's technical term for *oral tradition learned by constant repetition* and (by extension) for the legal rules found in that tradition. The Mishnah itself calls its rules *halakot,* meaning "extrascriptural laws." The Hebrew noun *mishnah* comes from the root *sh-n-y* or *sh-n-h,* meaning "to repeat." Babylonian rabbinic tradition (B. Ber. 5a) teaches that the Mishnah was given to Moses at Sinai along with the Decalogue, the Torah, the rest of Scripture, and the Gemara (talmudic commentary on the Mishnah). This notion, however, does not appear in the Mishnah proper, nor does the verb *sh-n-y* there have the technical meaning "to repeat oral tradition." (The concept of tradition from Sinai and the noun *mishnah* itself appear only in tractate *Abot,* which most modern scholars view as a later addendum to the Mishnah inserted to dogmatize the authority of the oral tradition by tracing it in an unbroken line back to the sinaitic revelation.) The notion of a Torah consisting of written and oral components (cf. the Roman concept of *leges scriptae* and *leges non scriptae*) appears in rabbinic literature for the first time in the Babylonian Talmud, which (at B. Shab. 31a) attributes the concept of two *torot* (one written, one oral) to Shammai, an eminent Jewish sage of the late first century B.C.E. The Mishnah's six divisions are called *Z^{e}ra^{c}im* ("Agriculture"), *Mo^{c}ed* ("Appointed Times"), *Nashim* ("Women"), *N^{e}ziqin* ("Damages"), *Qodashim* ("Hallowed Things"), and *Ṭohorot* ("Cultic Purity").
2. For a brilliant analysis of religion as the expression of the worldview of a social group, see Berger 1967.
3. Exod. 19:6. The Hebrew term *qadosh,* usually translated as "holy" or "sacred," actually means "set apart" from the generality of things for a specific purpose, usually of a religious nature. (cf. *muqdash,* "consecrated.")

218

4. Eliade 1959, p. 88.
5. The other is the Division of Damages, which mainly comprises rules of civil and criminal law and procedure. Between them, divisions three and four contain most kinds of laws found in any secular legal system. They include topics similar to those covered in the earliest extant manual of Roman law, the *Institutes of Gaius*, composed in the late second century C.E. at about the same time as the Mishnaic Divisions of Women and Damages. For the dating of the Division of Women, see Neusner 1980, vol. 5, pp. 198–235; for the date of Gaius, see Zulueta 1946, pt. II, p. 5.
6. The name of the first division, Agriculture, is somewhat misleading. The division actually gives the Israelite farmer and herdsman instructions about agricultural offerings due the Temple and its functionaries. These laws rest on scriptural provisions about the sacrificial cult and donations to priests, levites, and the poor. Even after the destruction of the Temple, Israelites could continue to give offerings to members of the priestly and levitical castes as enjoined by Scripture and set forth in the Mishnah. These regulations, although governing the conduct of mundane agricultural and pastoral enterprises, are primarily cultic in character.
7. Danby 1933, p. xxii, points out that "Rabbi [Judah the Patriarch, editor of the Mishnah] did not aim at promulgating the Mishnah as an authoritative, definitive legal code, a final summary of Jewish law, like the *Shulhan Arukh* of later times." On this point Danby is undoubtedly correct; however, his assertion, immediately following, that the Mishnah "was, simply, a compilation of the Oral Law as it was taught in the many rabbinical schools of his time" seems to adopt the traditional view that the Mishnah represented the form of Judaism paramount and normative in its day. Archeological discoveries, such as the Dead Sea Scrolls and the synagogue of Dura-Europos, along with the work of Jacob Neusner and others have made clear that mishnaic Judaism was only one of many competing Judaisms of its day.
8. See, e.g., Eliade 1959; Douglas 1966; Geertz 1973.
9. Some modern feminists, following the work of Simone de Beauvoir, have employed Marxist or other economic analyses to explain the development and persistence of patriarchal societies. See, e.g., de Beauvoir 1953 (1974 ed.), pp. 42–67; Rosaldo and Lamphere 1974, pp. 1–87; Kuhn and Wolpe 1978, pp. 1–10, 42–67; MacCormack 1980; O'Brien 1981; MacKinnon 1982; Meyers 1983. The work of several feminist scholars is discussed in chap. 8. An important recent work is Lerner, 1986, which appeared too late for adequate discussion in this study; see nn. 335 and 336. More recently, sociobiologists have claimed a predominantly biological basis for the evolution of sociolegal norms of sexual relationships and personal status. A useful summary of those arguments appears in Diamond 1985.
10. This exclusion of women may stem less from a deliberately calculated policy than from a general attitude toward women that seems to have pervaded ancient Near East and Mediterranean cultures of the day. Legal compilations contemporary with the Mishnah (in particular, the Roman *Institutes of Gaius* and the Indian *Laws of Manu*) as well as the writings of Philo of Alexandria show that many contemporary cultures perceived women largely as adjuncts to the lives of men and not as candidates for full membership in society, especially with respect to intellectual expressions of the culture.
11. A discussion of some current feminist theories about the evolution of the status of women in patriarchal societies appears in chap. 8.

12. The emphasis on analogy and contrast is a characteristic the Mishnah shares with Hellenistic rhetoric. Pomeroy 1975, p. 25, speaks of "the Greek mind, with its penchant for combining symmetry and alternatives." The possible influence of Aristotelian categories and Greek rhetoric on the Mishnah has been discussed by, among others, Daube 1949. See also n. 13.

13. So B. Ḥul. 79b. Jastrow, 1904/1950, vol. 1, pp. 618–19, gives "a kind of bearded deer or antelope." However, we note that in classical Greek logic the concept "goat-stag" (*tragelaphos*), "a fantastic animal represented on Eastern carpets and the like" (Liddell and Scott, 1968, p. 1567), is a standard paradigm for a hybrid and logically nonsensical category. Plato, *Republic* 6:488A, trans. Cornford 1941.

14. M. Bik. 2:8. A similar problem of classification of an *androgynos* appears in M. Bik. chap. 4. However, Danby 1933, p. 98, fn. 5, notes that this chapter is in all probability not part of the Mishnah but rather a version of T. Bik. 2:3.

15. For a full discussion of this problem, see Wegner 1988.

16. Gaius criticizes the rule of Roman law that places women under perpetual tutelage, pointing out that a grown woman has as much competence as a grown man. ". . . hardly any valid argument seems to exist in favor of women of full age being in *tutela*. That which is commonly accepted, namely, that they are very liable to be deceived owing to their instability of judgment and that therefore in fairness they should be governed by the *auctoritas* of tutors, seems more specious than true. For women of full age conduct their own affairs, the interposition of the tutor's *auctoritas* in certain cases being a mere matter of form; indeed, often a tutor is compelled by the praetor to give *auctoritas* even against his will" (Gaius bk. I, 190; trans. Zulueta 1946, pt. I, p. 61).

17. We should not assume, however, that the primary motivation of Scripture's textwriter was to create women's rights *per se*. The inheritance law, for instance, was designed mainly to keep property within the tribe, as clearly appears from Num. 36:8, an amendment to Num. 27:8.

18. The moral opprobrium attaching to extramarital sexual relations, at least between unmarried adults, rests more on Christian interpretation of the writings of Paul than on the laws of the Old Testament.

19. This study does not concern itself with slave women. For a study of the status of slaves in the Mishnah, see Flesher 1988.

20. The minor daughter must, however, be redeemed at puberty unless her purchaser marries her to himself or his son (Exod. 21:7ff.; see n. 49).

21. Scripture assigned bride-price to the father. The Mishnah's framers modify that rule by making the husband a trustee of the bride-price, which must be returned to the wife when the marriage is dissolved by death or divorce. We discuss this in more detail in connection with divorcees and widows in chap. 5.

22. See M. Nid. 5:7. The special significance of the six-month period from twelve to twelve and one-half years in the life of the minor girl is discussed later (see nn. 28 and 29).

23. See Douglas 1966; Turner 1969.

24. See Douglas 1966 (discussed in chap. 6).

25. See O'Brien 1981 (discussed in chap. 8).

26. The polygynous system of the Mishnah involves a pervasive double standard. Though a man has the *exclusive* right to his wife's sexuality, the wife's right to the husband's sexual function is never *exclusive*. She cannot legally preclude her husband from taking additional wives or having sexual relations with

unmarried women. By contrast, she can neither have more than one husband nor indulge in sexual relations with other men.

27. All translations of mishnaic texts are the author's own.

28. M. Nid. 5:6 states that the vows of a young girl become binding on her at the age of twelve years and one day. But M. Nid. 6:11 states that a girl who has grown two pubic hairs becomes liable to observe the commandments of the Torah. For practical purposes the chronological test became the rule of thumb for the time at which a girl ceases to be a girlchild (*qᵉṭannah*) and becomes a pubescent (*naʿarah*). During this second stage she remains under her father's control, yet she is independently liable on her own account to keep the dictates of Jewish law.

29. The Mishnah nowhere states that the period of pubescence (*naʿarut*) ends at twelve and one-half years. But Maimonides asserts that the period of pubescence, beginning when a girl produces two pubic hairs, ends six months later [Maimonides, *Commentary*, ad M. Ket. 3:7 (= Albeck 1958, M. Ket. 3:8)]. For purposes of practical Halakhah, the chronological age of twelve years six months and one day defines the moment at which a girl ceases to be a pubescent girl (*naʿarah*) and becomes a mature woman (*bogeret*) with full legal autonomy.

30. Although this parable appears in tractate *Niddah*, which is not part of the mishnaic Division of Women, the point it makes about the daughter's progress from dependence to autonomy echoes a principal concern of that division and thus forms an appropriate introduction to our discussion.

31. The rules at 5:7D apply equally to minor sons (M. B.M. 1:5) because they address the age, not the sex, of the child. However, D appears here only as a lead-in to E. The main point is the metaphor of the fig, symbolizing the three-stage development of the girl, in which the intermediate stage of *naʿarah* is crucial, as we shall see.

32. The Mishnah assigns no equivalent intermediate status of *naʿar* for a male child. Though both boys and girls reach majority at maturity, the special status of *naʿarah* represents the six-month period during which the father may hand over the daughter to a selected husband for consummation of the marriage. There is no equivalent period for a boy because the mishnaic father does not hand over his son to anybody in marriage. The boy must wait until he passes the age of thirteen, after which he makes his own marriage arrangements. The same attitude toward young girls as sex objects appears in the aprocryphal Ecclesiasticus (Wisdom of Ben Sira), where, indeed, it is far more pronounced than in Scripture. See Trenchard 1982, pp. 129–165. Ecclesiasticus, dating from the second century B.C.E., is closer to the time of the Mishnah than to that of the oldest scriptural texts. We may wonder whether the attitude it expresses toward young girls represents a traditional viewpoint of Semitic culture or whether it reflects the dominant culture that both in Ben Sira's day and in mishnaic times was Hellenism. Certainly there existed in Greek culture an "ancient belief that young girls were lustful." See Pomeroy 1975, p. 64, who cites Aristotle *Historia animalium* 7.1 (581b) and Aristotle *Politics* 7:14.5 (1335a).

33. The term *kᵉtubbah*, from the Hebrew k-t-b ("to write"), means simply "a (legal) document." The origins of the *kᵉtubbah*, a document unknown to Scripture, are obscure. It was already used, however, by at least one Jewish community of the fifth century B.C.E. See Yaron 1961, pp. 44–64. Traditional sources ascribe its institution to Simeon b. Shetaḥ, a sage of the first century B.C.E. (B. Ket. 82b)]. See Geller 1978.

34. *Mohar b^{e}tulin*, from the *mohar ha-b^{e}tulot* of Exod. 22:16. This technical term appears in the traditional *k^{e}tubbah* used in Jewish marriage to this day.

35. *A man marries a woman and cohabits with her. Then he takes an aversion to her and makes up charges against her and defames her, saying, 'I married this woman, but when I approached her, I found that she was not a virgin.' In such a case, the girl's father and mother shall produce the evidence of the girl's virginity before the elders of the town at the gate. And the girl's father shall say to the elders, 'I gave this man my daughter to wife, but he has made up charges, saying, "I did not find your daughter a virgin." But here is the evidence of my daughter's virginity!' And they shall spread out the cloth before the elders of the town. The elders of the town shall then take the man and flog him, and they shall fine him a hundred [shekels of] silver and give it to the girl's father, for the man has defamed a virgin in Israel. Moreover, she shall remain his wife, he shall never have the right to divorce her. But if the charge proves true, the girl was found not to have been a virgin, then the girl shall be brought out to the entrance of her father's house, and the men of her town shall stone her to death, for she did a shameful thing in Israel, committing fornication while under her father's authority. Thus you will sweep away evil from your midst* (Deut. 22:13–21).

    All quotations from Scripture are taken, unless otherwise stated, from the New JPS Torah 1962.

36. The Monday court session would require a Sunday wedding, but there might not be sufficient time to prepare this after the termination of the Sabbath on Saturday night, hence only the Thursday session is practicable.

37. Two hundred *zuz*, or fifty shekels, was the equivalent of one year's living expenses for an Israelite at the time of the Mishnah. M. Peah 8:8 makes that sum the cut-off point for classifying a man as poor for the purposes of entitlement to poor relief in an agricultural system dependent on the annual cycle of harvests (Brooks 1983, pp. 150–51). The bride-price of virgins was held in trust by the husband during the marriage for transfer to the wife on widowhood or on divorce without just cause. The widow or divorcée was thus assured of maintenance for one year following the marriage, which gave her time to find another husband if she so chose.

38. Mishnaic marriage law employs three technical legal terms: *'erusin*, here translated as "betrothal"; *qiddushin*, here translated as "espousal"; and *nissu'in*, here translated as "consummation." A girl's betrothal/espousal might take place in infancy, in which case consummation must wait until the girl reaches puberty—between twelve and twelve and one-half—when her father transfers her to the husband's domain. In postmishnaic usage (e.g., at B. Qid. 12b) *'erusin* and *qiddushin* are used interchangeably. However, the Mishnah's use of three technical terms must reflect a time when the first two denoted separate stages in the process, so I use the two English terms *betrothal* and *espousal* to preserve the difference in the mishnaic terminology. The first blessing pronounced in the marriage service (as prescribed at B. Ket. 7b) describes the bride as *'arusah* (betrothed girl), not permitted sexually to the bridegroom until he recites the formula of espousal (*qiddushin*).

39. M. Nid 5:4. "If [a girl is] younger [than three years and one day, intercourse with her] is as if one sticks a finger in an eye." Just as the finger will cause the eye to water, yet the eye will return to its former state; so the hymen of a girl under three may rupture on intercourse, but it will regenerate later (B. Nid. 45a).

40. See app. 1 for a related example.

41. Recent media discussion (in 1984-1985) of the prevalence of incest forced by fathers on young daughters in contemporary America somewhat diminishes the shock.

42. The sages deduce this by reading Exod. 22:15-16 and Deut. 22:28-29 together, as follows:

    If a man seduces a virgin who has not been spoken for, and lies with her, he must make her his wife by payment of a bride-price. If her father refuses to give her to him, he must still weigh out silver in proportion to the bride-price for virgins (Exod. 22:15-16).

    If a man comes upon a virgin who is not engaged and he seizes her and lies with her, and they are discovered, the man who lay with her shall pay the girl's father fifty [shekels of] silver, and she shall be his wife. Because he has violated her, he can never have the right to divorce her (Deut. 22:28-29).

    An ingenious study by Calum Carmichael (Carmichael 1979) attempts to relate this and many other biblical laws concerning women to ancient Hebrew myths. While persuasive at many points (especially where he illustrates the linguistic interdependence of Genesis legends and Deuteronomic legislation), Carmichael's analysis is flawed by his frequent conflation of distinct legal categories and his glossing over significant differences. Material distinctions he neglects include: seduction versus rape, harlotry versus adultery, bastardy in the common-law sense versus *mamzerut* in the technical Hebraic sense (see n. 60), wife versus concubine, and liaisons between Israelite men and foreign women versus liaisons between Israelite women and foreign men. Carmichael overlooks or ignores the existence of numerous parallels between the Deuteronomic laws he would relate narrowly to the Genesis myths and the laws of many other semitic systems (from the Code of Hammurabi down to classical Islamic law), which certainly are not dependent on the legends of Genesis. Furthermore, he tends to base his analysis on modern "Judeo-Christian" notions of sexual morality rather than on the ancient concept of women's biological function as the property of particular men, which, in my view, forms the true basis of the laws he discusses.

43. The ten Israelite castes are enumerated at M. Qid. 4:1. Strict rules governed intermarriage between castes.

44. The remainder of this unit is omitted here. The omitted cases, like those under discussion, involve the question of payment of a fine for improper sexual conduct. But the omitted cases involve a different issue (intercourse with specified women forbidden by Lev. 18) and have no direct relevance to the rape or seduction of minor daughters.

45. The remainder of this unit is omitted as irrelevant (see n. 44).

46. There is a differential in *civil damages* [but even these are payable to the father, not the girl herself (M. Ket. 3:4-5, see the next section, "Seduction and Rape: Civil Damages.")]

47. It is true that mishnaic law imposes fixed fines for many offenses, not all of a sexual nature. However, the point here is that in the cases before us we find the imposition of a fixed penalty applied across the board without reference to mitigating or aggravating factors. This clearly indicates that the sages' primary concern is the penalty payable to the girl's father for the loss of his daughter's value on the marriage market.

48. On R. Eleazar's view at M. Ket. 3:6 (app. 2), a mature *rape victim* (as opposed to one who permits a man to *seduce* her) would presumably collect the fine.

49. *When a man sells his daughter as a slave . . . [i]f she proves to be displeasing to her master, who designated her for himself, he must let her be redeemed* (Exod. 21:7-8). The sages interpret this to mean that although an Israelite girlchild may be sold as a slave, once she reaches puberty her master must either marry her [to himself or his son (Exod. 21:9)] or permit her relatives to redeem her.

50. See app. 2 for further exceptions to the rule requiring the violator to compensate the girl's father.

51. The remainder of this unit is omitted as irrelevant.

52. We cannot expect social attitudes in ancient societies to correspond precisely with our own. Nonetheless, it is fair to assume that any girl in any society at any time will feel quite differently about rape than about seduction.

53. The statement "Everything follows the social standing of the man who inflicts the disgrace and the man who suffers it," which appears in identical language in M. B.Q. 8:1, is obviously a standard formula. Nonetheless, the damage at M. B.Q. 8:1 is inflicted by one free man on another (described as "his fellow") who is the only possible referent for "the man who suffers it." Hence, there is no question of *mitbayyesh* referring to anyone but the victim himself. In the case before us, by contrast, the victim is a *girl*, yet the formula by retaining its masculine form clearly points to the girl's *father* as the injured party rather than the victim herself.

54. Granted, the same formula is used with respect to the man injured in M. B.Q. 8:1 for the purpose of assessing damages. However, there is one significant difference—the man in M. B.Q. 8:1 cannot, in fact, be sold as a slave; the girl here *can* (as long as she is under twelve years old).

55. Scripture's statements about payment of bride-price to the father occur only in the context of seduction and rape (e.g., Exod. 22:15-16; Deut. 22:28-29; Gen. 34:11-12). But those texts clearly imply that the money would go to the father even in a normal marriage situation.

56. This point is discussed in more detail in chap. 7.

57. See Wegner, 1987.

58. The verse forbids a man to marry "a woman and her daughter." In context, however, the text clearly refers to two existing women who happen to be mother and daughter, hence it cannot refer to the man's own wife and daughter. Had the original list intended to prohibit a man's daughter, the natural place to do so would have been between verses 9 and 10 of Lev. 18, where she is conspicuous by her absence.

59. The remainder of this unit, irrelevant here, is presented in our discussion of the autonomous woman.

60. Hebrew, *mamzer*, meaning the child of adultery or incest, i.e., of a sexual union that is illicit because of an impediment to marriage between the partners (owing either to the fact that the woman is legally married to someone else or to consanguinity, or affinity, between the partners). The status of *mamzer* carries with it grave disabilities, including ineligibility to marry a normal Israelite. This disqualification, based on Scripture (Deut. 23:3), retains practical importance in Jewish marriage law to this day, as evidenced by the notorious Langer case in Israel in 1971. See Abramov 1976, pp. 189-90. (It should be noted that a child born out of wedlock to two Jews who were free to marry at the time of conception is not a *mamzer*.)

61. Cf. M. Bek 7:7. "One who has married forbidden women is disqualified [from cultic activity] until he vows to derive no benefit from them [i.e., until he forswears intercourse with them]."

62. Though the Mishnah does not say so explicitly, another principal concern of its framers was the eligibility of a girl or woman to marry a *kohen* (member of the priestly caste). Levitical law forbids a priest to marry a divorcée (though he may marry a widow); and a high priest may not marry a nonvirgin (Lev. 21:7, 21:13). We know this problem was present to the mind of the editor of tractate *Qiddushin* chap. 3, for it is explicitly discussed in M. Qid. 3:12. It is important because of the need to avoid cultic pollution generated by an illicit union.

63. True, the Mishnah speaks elsewhere of a man's forgetting the details of important matters (M. Men. 13:1, 13:2, 13:6, 13:7). But there is surely a qualitative difference between a man's forgetting which offering he had planned to bring to the Temple and his forgetting which of his daughters he had promised in marriage. Even if both questions are purely hypothetical, choice of subject matter for hypothetical questions can be psychologically revealing of cultural attitudes (as we saw with the man who equated his daughter with a slave woman in M. Qid. 2:3).

64. Similar cases appear in M. Qid. 3:10-11. The same attitude underlies the case of a man who has betrothed one of five women and cannot recall which one (M. Yeb. 15:7).

65. So B. Ned. 67a; Maimonides, *Commentary, ad* M. Ned. 10:1; Danby 1933, p. 277. The mishnaic text is ambiguous, possibly due to a lacuna.

66. The *practical* difference between the status of Israelite boys and girls approximates the position in Roman law of the Mishnah's day, as outlined by Gaius: "Parents are allowed to appoint by will tutors to the children they hold in *potestas*, to males below the age of puberty, to females of whatever age, even if they be married. For the early lawyers held that women even of full age should be in *tutela* on account of their instability of judgment. . . . Males, on the other hand, are released from *tutela* when they reach puberty" (Gaius bk. I, 144, 196; trans. Zulueta 1946, p. I, pp. 49, 63). (The Israelite girl, normally married off at puberty, passes from the guardianship of her father to that of her husband.)

67. One or two statements outside the Division of Women refer by implication to the incapacity of the girlchild (along with the minor boy) to create legal effects by their actions. See, e.g., M. M.S. 4:4; M. ʿErub. 7:6. Not surprisingly, incapacity of minors of both sexes characterizes most legal systems. But apart from these references and one discussion of the vows of a girlchild (M. Nid. 5:6), the framers seem unaware of the minor daughter as anything but a sexual chattel. In the patriarchal culture of the Mishnah, we should hardly expect concern with the minor daughter to range far beyond her likely future as wife and mother.

68. I strongly suspect that this description of Yavneh as a vineyard (or grove) is a literary convention. Hellenistic culture (whose influence on the sages of the Mishnah is well attested) modeled its schools on Plato's Academy, which was named for its location in the Grove of Academe.

69. Talmudic authorities later take the view that a man is duty bound (*ḥayyab*) to maintain his sons, but they disagree on whether the maintenance of daughters is a duty (*ḥobah*) or a supererogatory pious deed (*miṣwah*). See B. Ket. 49a,b and B. Ket. 65b.

70. Both Greek and Roman cultures permitted female infanticide. See Pomeroy 1975, pp. 46, 164; Lefkowitz and Fant 1982, p. 173; Gardner 1986, p. 155. So also did pre-Islamic Arabian culture, as attested by qur'anic denunciation of the practice (suras 6:152, 16:58–59, 17:31, 81:8–9).

71. In fact, the Greek historian Hecataeus of Abdera in his brief history of the early Israelites (ca. 300 B.C.E.) goes out of his way to mention the (to him) astounding fact that Mosaic law required the Israelites to rear *all* their children (in contrast to Greek laws permitting infanticide). Stern 1974, vol. 1, pp. 29, 33.

72. The Mishnah's refusal to send the girl forth naked forms an interesting contrast with Turner's description of the treatment of persons in liminal situations in some primitive tribal ceremonies, including the ritual for curing a barren marriage in which it is customary for the spouses to be stripped naked to undergo what is perceived as a transition from death to life. Turner 1969, p. 31.

73. The few mishnaic allusions to the harlot (*zonah*) either involve a scriptural ruling on the priest's daughter who must be burnt for harlotry (Lev. 21:9) or they denote women who commit adultery. Only one passage (M. Tem. 6:2–3) speaks of a common prostitute but even then only to explain Scripture's reference to *"the hire of a harlot"* (Deut. 23:19). Nowhere do they discuss prostitution as an actual feature of mishnaic society.

74. Here, the word *na'arah* is used nontechnically to denote a girl or young woman—whether unmarried, widowed or divorced—still living in her father's house. This is clear from the context, which mentions two classes of adult women (Albeck 1958, p. 184). In the remainder of the unit, *na'arah* has its normal technical meaning of a girl aged between twelve and twelve and one-half years.

75. Here I quote the traditional translation, which is no less accurate and far more aesthetic than the New JPS Torah's *"Be fertile and increase."*

76. Later talmudic explanations (e.g., B. Yeb. 65b, which claims that the continuation of Gen. 1:28—*"and fill the earth and subdue it"*—proves that the command was directed only at the man because only men could be directed to *"subdue"* the earth) scarcely convince the modern mind, though perhaps they were persuasive in their time.

77. Had they wished, the sages could have avoided discussing the woman's role by simply relying on Gen. 35:11 (where God repeats the command to *"be fruitful and multiply"* to Jacob in the masculine singular). Their purposeful citing of Gen. 1:28 shows that they deliberately chose to make a point: that woman is not obligated despite the plural verb.

78. The Hebrew term for "acquired" (*niqneit*) comes from the verb *q-n-y*, to acquire property (usually by purchase).

79. This opening statement reminds us of a rule of Roman marriage law of the late second century (the very period of the Mishnah's creation in the Roman province of Judaea): "Of old, women passed into *manus* in three ways, by *usus*, *confarreatio*, and *coemptio*" (Gaius, bk. I, 110–113; Zulueta 1946, pt I, p. 35). As Gaius explains matters, *usus* means cohabitation for one year, explicitly called usucaption; *confarreatio* is a ceremony that includes, *inter alia*, the recitation of special formal words (if reduced to writing, they would constitute a deed or writ); *coemptio* is a "sort of imaginary sale." In this connection, we note that many rules of mishnaic law have interesting counterparts in Roman law. A detailed presentation of the rules governing women in Roman law is given by Gardner 1986. Both the similarities and the differences between the

Roman and mishnaic law of women's status are worth studying for the light they may shed on the relationship between attitudes to women and the rules patriarchal societies make to control them.

80. Espousal by deed was probably obsolete by the time of the Mishnah. It certainly had fallen into disuse by talmudic times, as emerges from the discussion at B. Qid. 9a, where the rabbis cannot identify with precision the nature of the document to which the Mishnah refers.

81. Espousal by intercourse (the only marriage ritual mentioned in Scripture) seems by mishnaic times to have become too primitive for the changing mores—perhaps because (like any legal transaction) it required the presence of two witnesses. Nonetheless, all three methods remain theoretically valid in Jewish law to this day. Hence two Jews who marry by civil ceremony alone may be deemed in Jewish law to have married by intercourse (provided there was no halakhic impediment to the union). So if partners to such a marriage subsequently become divorced, some authorities maintain that Jewish law requires the husband to give the wife a precautionary *get* (writ of Jewish divorce) before she may remarry in the Jewish rite.

82. *Ḥaliṣah* is the ceremony of unshoeing, a biblical form of divorce releasing the levirate widow from her automatic marital tie to her late husband's brother (Deut. 25:5–10, discussed in detail in chap. 4).

83. Lev. 25:45 calls the Canaanite slave a "possession" (*'aḥuzah*), which is the same term applied to real property in Lev. 27:16. Hence the Mishnah rules that such a slave may be acquired by precisely the same three modes prescribed for the acquisition of real property (M. Qid. 1:5). See also M. B.B. 3:1.

84. This equation may have been influenced by the fact that Scripture uses the same verb *l-q-ḥ* (to take) for taking a wife as for buying goods (Maimonides, *Commentary, ad* M. Qid. 1:1; Albeck 1958, p. 307). It is true that the root *q-n-y* can have a more figurative meaning when used in nontechnical contexts (see, e.g., M. Qid. 4:14 and several statements in tractate *Abot*: 1:6, 2:7, 4:11, 6:5, 6:10—though the references in *Abot* should be viewed with caution, given the prevalent view that the tractate is almost certainly of later date than the Mishnah as a whole). However, I maintain that the usage of *q-n-y* in M. Qid. 1:1 does bear the meaning of acquisition of property. Babylonian sages use also the noun *qinyan* ("act of acquisition") with reference to marriage, pointing out explicitly that since Scripture uses the same verb, *l-q-ḥ* ("to take") for taking a wife (Deut. 22:13) as for buying a field (Gen. 23:13), and since the verb *q-n-y* ("to acquire for money") is also used in reference to the field, one who takes a wife has performed an act of acquisition for money. (*qiḥah iqarei qinyan*, B. Qid. 2a). David Halivni Weiss 1964 suggests that the mishnaic use of *q-n-y* for the acquisition of wives occurs only when a marriage is tied specifically to a property transaction (e.g., a levirate marriage), hence it should not be construed to mean that the ancient Israelite bought his wife. The truth of the matter, I suggest, is not that the man bought the *whole woman*, but that the bride-price did buy his exclusive legal right to *her sexual function*. Moreover, marriage is certainly viewed as the acquisition of a wife by a husband, not the other way about. No mishnaic source even remotely suggests that in marriage a wife *acquires* a husband—even when she is portrayed as *selecting* him (e.g., M. Qid. 4:9, discussed later).

85. Moreover, M. Qid. 1:1 introduces the topic of marriage and could have directly opened the discussion of espousals in tractate *Qiddushin*, chap. 2. But in that

case the rules for acquiring the various forms of property set out in M. Qid. 1:2–5 would have no logical place in the tractate.

86. Neusner 1980, vol. 5, p. 21, suggests that this juxtaposition reflects the fact that other property transfers (e.g., dowry) usually occur when a woman changes hands. But this may not have been the primary reason. People bought and sold land, cattle, slaves, or chattels in contexts other than marriage. Most rules about contracts or property appear in the Division of Damages, in tractates *Baba Meṣiʿa* and *Baba Batra*, respectively. Either tractate could have provided a natural topical location for M. Qid. 1:2–5.

87. This distinction between Israelite bondmen and foreign slaves is established by my colleague Paul Flesher (see n. 19).

88. The Tosefta ("Supplement") is a compendium of rules expressed in mishnaic style and following the arrangement of the mishnaic material. Modern scholars believe these rules to be a later (probably third-century) supplement to the Mishnah itself. See Neusner 1977, pp. ix–x.

89. The Hebrew terms used here denote different castes of Israelites, some of whom are forbidden to intermarry with others (M. Qid. 4:1). A *kohen* is a descendant of Aaron the High Priest; this hereditary dynasty functioned as priests in the Temple at Jerusalem. A *levi* is a member of the tribe of Levi; this caste functioned as assistants to the *kohanim* in performing Temple rites. A *natin* is a descendant of the Gibeonites enslaved for Temple service by Joshua (Jos. 9:27). For the meaning of *mamzer*, see n. 60.

90. The term *geṭ* is a Hebraization of the Aramaic *giṭṭa* ("document"). The full name of the writ is *geṭ piṭṭurin* ("writ of dismissal"), but it is normally called simply a *geṭ*.

91. On the other hand, they do not permit the use of a writ that was expressly prepared with another woman in mind. See M. Git. 3:1 (discussed in chap. 5).

92. As in most disputes between the schools of Hillel and Shammai, the Hillelite rule later became the rule of Halakha (B. ʿErub. 6b). The New Testament alludes to the same controversy, recording a dispute in which Jesus may either have sided with the Shammaites (Matt. 5:31–32, taking *porneia* to mean "unchastity") or may have espoused a third position, in which *ʿrwh* has the meaning it bears in Lev. 18, namely, "incest." The latter interpretation led the Church at one point to prohibit divorce altogether, although it permitted annulment in cases where the marriage was invalidated by the subsequent discovery that the parties were within the prohibited degrees.

93. As before, the analogy between food and sex is no accident! A wife who has relations with another man becomes forbidden to her husband (M. Soṭ. 5:1). One could say that this too constitutes "spoiling his meal."

94. In fact, where the bride is of full age, the spouses' inequality is even greater in divorce than in marriage; an adult bride must freely have consented to the marriage, yet her wishes are irrelevant to its termination.

95. Only in the extreme case, where she is too demented to know what is happening, do the sages preclude her husband from divorcing her (M. Yeb. 14:1D). This special case stems not from the sages' pity for her plight, but from the fear that if left to her own devices, she may form another attachment and then be unable to produce her writ of divorce if someone questions her freedom to enter that union.

96. The remainder of the unit is omitted as irrelevant.

97. In addition, evidence external to Scripture, such as the Elephantine papyri or the *Code of Hammurabi*, indicates that ancient Near East legal systems, includ-

ing the law governing the Israelite colony at Elephantine in the fifth century B.C.E., recognized a woman's capacity to divorce her husband in appropriate cases. Yaron 1961; see n. 33.

98. Douglas 1966, pp. 35–40.

99. Heb., *shakab 'ish 'otak* (lit. has laid you).

100. Heb., *taḥat baᶜalek* ("under your husband"). New JPS Torah has: *"while married to your husband."*

101. Heb., *wayyitten 'ish bak et sheᵏobto*. New JPS Torah has: *"had carnal relations with you."* This and other standard translations all employ euphemisms that obscure the phrase's literal meaning, which is important for our present purpose.

102. Scripture itself is unclear on the point; although dubbing the wife *soṭah* ("errant") at the outset (thus implying that she has in fact offended), the text later states that the procedure applies when the husband merely suspects her but cannot prove the offense by the normal rules of evidence.

103. In scriptural idiom the word *yarek* ("thigh") is a common euphemism for the sexual organs. See, e.g., Gen. 24:9, 46:26, 47:29, Exod. 1:5, Judg. 8:30.

104. So Albeck *ad loc.*, 1958, p. 243. This rule is not found in Mishnah, but it appears at B. Ket. 60a and T. Nid. 2:7. A similar rule of pre-Islamic Arabian law prevails in Islam to this day.

105. See further examples that illustrate this point in app. 3.

106. A Nazirite vowed to let his or her hair grow (until the end of his Nazirite term, when he would cut it off and present it as an offering), to abstain from wine and liquor, and to avoid contact with corpses. The use of the Hebrew term *nazir* in postbiblical Hebrew to mean "monk" is misleading because a Nazirite did not take a vow of chastity. (But see the discussion in app. 4.)

107. The Hebrew expression *leᶜannot nefesh* found here is traditionally translated as "to afflict the soul." However, the New JPS Torah translation as "self-denial" correctly takes account of the basic meaning of *nefesh*, which in Hebrew as in other Semitic languages means self.

108. The obscure term *qonam* in mishnaic law introduces a vow. It has roughly the force of "I abjure [some specified benefit] as though it were *qorban* (an offering devoted to God)." See Jastrow 1904/1950, vol. 2, p. 1335, s.v. *"konam."*

109. The Babylonian rabbis note the Mishnah's failure to mention explicitly the effect on conjugal relations as a ground for annulment of the vow. But they conclude that the framers took for granted that the rule of Num. 30:17 (*"between a man and his wife"*) was sufficient ground in itself, whereas the self-denying character of a vow was a separate ground (B. Ned. 79B).

110. The wife's Nazirite vow is discussed in app. 4.

111. Although, as we shall see later (p. 79), the wife can likewise insist on the husband's performance of his conjugal duties toward her, the penalties imposed for his nonperformance are lower than those imposed for a wife's refusal to perform (M. Ket. 5:7)—a clear reflection of the husband's greater right in this matter.

112. Obviously the reference to other men has no application during the subsistence of her marriage, when even without making such a vow she cannot consort with any man beside her husband.

113. For a discussion of yet another context in which a man's sexual control of a woman affects her rights, see app. 5.

114. The wife's corresponding rights to conjugal visitation are discussed in detail later in this chapter, under "Reciprocity of Conjugal Rights and Duties."

115. See M. Yeb. 13:2 (discussed in chap. 2). In later times, Babylonian rabbis forbade a man to marry off his daughter until she is old enough to give an informed consent (B. Qid. 41a). But, as a medieval commentary to the Talmud points out, the exigencies of economic life dictated that a man betroth his minor daughter as soon as he can provide sufficient dowry for her in case a reversal of fortune in later years makes her betrothal more difficult. Hence the rabbinical injunction was never treated as a halakhic obligation but only as a recommendation. (Tos. *ad* b. Qid. 41a, s.v. *asur.*)

116. In drawing this conclusion, I construe the phrase *we'im raṣu* at M. Qid. 4:9 E and J to have an identical meaning, i.e., to refer in both cases to the wishes of the two men involved while ignoring those of the girl or woman, respectively. I base this construction on the exact parallelism of the language of M. Qid. 4:9 A through E with that of F through J, and also on the effect of ambiguity on the wife in similarly ambiguous cases we are about to discuss. Of course, if the woman is included among the referents of *we'im raṣu* at J, my interpretation would be wrong.

117. This is not as farfetched as it sounds. Cases abound among Jews to this day in which a married levir, barred from marrying his brother's widow by the post-talmudic ban on polygyny, refuses to release her—generally for purposes of extortion. (See n. 166.)

118. The problem of the *'agunah* ("chained wife") continues to plague Jewish women to this day. In the State of Israel, soldiers are encouraged to write their wives conditional divorces before going into battle in order to save them from this plight should the husbands go missing in action. Widows of sailors in the submarine *Dakar*, which disappeared without trace in 1968, were tied to obviously dead husbands for thirteen years (until 1981), at which time the Israeli rabbinical court finally found a way to declare the men officially dead despite the lack of eyewitness testimony.

119. The talmudic rabbis later invested Yose with such authority that wherever he differed from his colleagues, his view was accepted as the rule of Halakhah (B. 'Erub. 46b). However, we have no evidence that Yose's view prevailed in the time of the Mishnah (which mostly records anonymous consensus but sometimes cites individual opinions without indicating which prevailed in practice).

120. For further examples of the effect of ambiguity (this time in the delivery of the writ), see app. 6.

121. Two cases of purely mechanical errors in the *geṭ* or its delivery that produce similar results for the woman appear at M. Giṭ. 8:8 and 8:9.

122. Here I prefer Albeck's interpretation (1958, p. 47) to that of Danby (1933, p. 232). The latter reads this last rule in conjunction with M. Yeb. 10:1U and renders: "and a child begotten by him [namely, the levir who consummates with the supposed widow] is not a bastard." That interpretation seems unlikely because if the first husband is still alive, the child of a union between his wife and his brother is surely illegitimate (Lev. 18:16). Albeck reads the rule at M. Yeb. 10:1U disjunctively, as referring to a husband who returns and takes back the wife who was mistakenly married by his brother and subsequently begets children with her.

123. The terminology of Deut. 24:1, *wehay etah le'ish 'aḥer* ("and becomes another man's wife"), was interpreted by the sages in a very literal way. The expression *hyh l* . . . means literally "becomes the property of"—in this case, the sexual

property of the man with whom the woman has intercourse. The act of intercourse is here considered more crucial than the formalities of marriage and divorce. For this reason Deut. 24:1-4 also governs the case of the woman in M. Yeb. 10:1 who through an innocent mistake has intercourse with another man during her husband's lifetime.

124. Even if a husband mistakenly married his wife's sister while his wife remained alive (a violation of Lev. 18:18), the sages impose no penalties corresponding to those inflicted on the wife in the case at hand. At most, he would have to divorce her. (Cf. M. Yeb. 2:7 where men who mistakenly marry their levirate widows' sisters before releasing the widows are permitted to keep the sisters.) The effect of ambiguity of status on the levirate widow who remarries in the mistaken belief that she is free to do so is discussed in chap. 4

125. The ransom rule applies even in the case of a *kohen*, forbidden by Scripture to take his wife back after captivity and presumed rape (Lev. 21:7).

126. T. Ket. 4:17 specifies that this mishnaic rule applies only to minor daughters (because the father's obligation of child support ceases at majority). This rule rests on a clear assumption that the orphaned minor daughters will be married off by their mother or brothers while still minors (cf. M. Yeb. 13:1), so that the question of supporting them after they come of age will not arise.

127. The same is true in other Semitic systems. With respect to bride-price, for instance, Islamic law ordains a minimum customary sum (Schacht 1964, p. 167). Of course, a husband can always stipulate to give his bride *more* than the minimum customary entitlement (cf. additions to the bride-price, M. Ket. 5:1), but he cannot give *less* without the explicit consent of the bride or her father.

128. This important thesis is developed in Neusner 1986 (esp. vol. 5).

129. So New JPS Torah. Alternatively, "he must not *diminish*, etc." Although in context this verse refers to a concubine, the sages reasoned that a wife must possess rights at least equal to those of a concubine.

130. See Geller 1978, pp. 227ff.

131. The Aramaic formula, *mᵉzonayki u-kᵉsutayki wᵉ-sippuqayki*, is an obvious adaptation of the scriptural formula of Exod. 21:10, *shᵉ'erah kᵉsutah wᵉ-'onatah*, the precise meaning of which is discussed in n. 143.

132. A *qab* is a measure of capacity, six *qabs* equaling one *sᵉ'ah* (approximately three liters).

133. A *log* was a measure of capacity equal to one quarter of a *qab*. A *maneh* or *minah* (so Danby) was a measure of weight equal to 560 grams. (Danby 1933, app. 2, p. 798.)

134. In some versions, "a reed mattress or a rush mat."

135. A *ma'ah* was the smallest silver coin, worth one sixth of a *zuz* (Danby 1933, app. 2, pp. 797-98).

136. The remainder of this unit spells out a wife's *duties*, and is discussed in the next section, "The Wife's Matrimonial Duties."

137. Cf. B. Yeb. 44a, which advises a man to take no more than four wives to ensure that each gets to spend one sabbath per month with him.

138. "If he desires not to supply food for his slave, he is permitted [to act thus]; but if [he desires] not to supply food to his wife, he is not permitted [to act thus]."

139. M. Ket. 5:9A through C, which deals with a wife's maintenance, has just been discussed (see n. 136).

140. This was the general rule in Mediterranean cultures of antiquity. As Pomeroy points out, "working in wool was traditionally a woman's task, in Rome as well as in Greece" (1975, p. 199). She cites documentary evidence that many lower-class women in Hellenistic and Roman culture were self-employed as woolworkers, including one epitaph that stated of the deceased, "Her conduct was appropriate. She kept house, she made wool."

141. The laws of the mishnaic Division of Damages (*Neziqin*) take for granted that only men are likely to go out in public. Cultic, religious, and judicial officials in the public sphere (discussed in chap. 6), were always men. Litigation was conducted by men; and though a woman might be plaintiff or defendant in some suits (M. B.Q. 1:3), she generally was not permitted to testify (with certain exceptions discussed in chap. 5).

142. This is discussed in chap. 6. In one place (M. Soṭ. 6:1) the Mishnah speaks of women who gossip together while spinning their yarn by moonlight; elsewhere we learn that a husband may not unreasonably forbid his wife to attend wedding and funeral celebrations in the homes of neighbor women (M. Ket. 7:5). But the notion of women meeting together in organized groups for some cultural or intellectual purpose is specifically precluded by the prohibition of female commensal fellowship groups (M. Pes. 8:7).

143. The three terms appearing in the Hebrew text—*she'erah*, *kesutah*, *we'onatah* ["her food, her clothing, and her *'onah*" (? = "conjugal rights" or "cohabitation")], are all biblical *hapax legomena*, which makes their meaning difficult to ascertain. They are technical legal terms already archaic when the biblical text was edited. The first two terms are readily traceable to Hebrew roots meaning "flesh" and "covering," hence commentators agree that they signify food and clothing. But the third term, *'onatah*, spelt *'-n-t-h* in the text, presents a difficulty. The editors of the Mishnah understood the word to stem from the root *'-n-t*, meaning "time" or "season," and interpreted the word *'onah* as meaning "set time for conjugal visitation." The same general meaning can be reached by assuming that *'onah* comes from the root *'-n-h* or *'-n-y*, meaning "to have intercourse" (cf. Gen. 34:2; Deut. 22:29). However, a third possibility exists—noted by at least two medieval commentators on Exod. 21:10—that makes far more sense in terms of the rules of other legal systems in regard to a wife's entitlement to maintenance. I refer to Ibn Ezra's suggestion, in his comment on Exod. 21:10, apparently citing the opinion of the Rashbam (R. Samuel b. Meir, brother of R. Jacob Tam, whom Ibn Ezra met while on a visit to France about 1150) to the effect that "there is one who says [it means] a dwelling house." [See comments of Ibn Ezra and the Rashbam, *ad* Exod. 21:10, in *Miqra'ot Gedolot* (*Exodus*), pp. 92–93.] A rule that requires a husband to supply a wife with food, clothing, and shelter would seem natural enough to Ibn Ezra, living as he did in a Muslim environment and no doubt acquainted with the rule of Islamic law (itself based on pre-Islamic Arabian custom) that requires a husband to provide his wife with *ma'kul*, *malbas*, *maskan* (food, clothing, and lodging, see Schacht 1964, p. 167). More interesting is his citing the opinion of a French rabbi—who lived in a land of Christendom uninfluenced by any knowledge of Islam—that *'onah* means "dwelling house," from the root *'-w-n*, meaning "to dwell." But the view of the Mishnah's framers that *'onah* denotes a wife's minimum quota of sexual intercourse produces the interesting result that in Jewish law, unlike other legal systems, intercourse has always been considered a wife's *right* rather than merely her *duty*, an interpreta-

tion that explains the interesting provisions of M. Ket. 5:6. We note that the Septuagint (dating from c. 300 B.C.E.) likewise translates *ʿonah* by the Greek *homilia*, meaning "intercourse." For completeness, we note that the new JPS Torah translation suggests (at p. 136, fn. b) that *ʿonah*, in fact, means "ointments," as in analogous provisions in other ancient Semitic codes, e.g., the *Code of Hammurabi*, sec. 178, (Pritchard 1950, *The Ancient Near East*, vol. 1, p. 159). However, the linguistic formula used in those provisions does not correspond precisely to the biblical formula, a fact that detracts from the plausibility of the suggestion and has led to its rejection.

144. A similar notion of reciprocity and complementarity is found in Islamic law, a system in which the rules of family law and personal status closely resemble mishnaic and talmudic rules. The relationship between the spouses is expressed by the terms *nafaqa* ("maintenance") and *iḥtibas* ("obedience"), the former term connoting the husband's obligation toward the wife and the latter term her obligation toward him. The high degree of correspondence between the rules of Jewish (mishnaic/talmudic) and Islamic family law is discussed in my article on the status of women in Jewish and Islamic marriage and divorce law (Wegner 1982a).

145. The sages' methods of compulsion are discussed in a later section dealing with the divorcée. (See pp. 135–37.)

146. The Hebrew *ha-maddir* is ambiguous. It may mean that the husband vows what follows or that he forces his wife to vow what follows.

147. The sages give no reason for the thirty-day grace period. Babylonian rabbis explain that in this short time the husband's vow will not become public knowledge and embarrass the wife (B. Ket. 70b).

148. Danby renders, "If a man vowed to abstain from [sexual intercourse with] his wife should she taste a certain fruit. . . ." The Hebrew *ha-maddir 'et 'ishto* could possibly bear that meaning, but the context of these units taken as a whole makes my rendering more plausible.

149. The Tosefta claims that if the husband precludes his wife from such social intercourse, people will refuse to attend her own mourning rites, thus depriving her of an important personal dignity (T. Ket. 7:5).

150. The remainder of this unit, which deals with a levirate widow's right to reject union with a repulsive levir, is discussed in chap. 4.

151. This and other rulings of Admon recorded in tractate *Kᵉtubbot* (chap. 13), represent the mishnaic equivalent of equity, a system developed in medieval England to mitigate the rigors of the common law. As with equity, the underlying rationale is the notion that people are not objects of law, but human beings deserving of humane consideration. Admon's ruling expresses the view that a woman is a person too.

152. A minor girl with an entitlement to property (whether by inheritance or otherwise) cannot claim this until she comes of age (M. Ket. 6:6). This rule explains why a father does not enjoy usufruct of the minor daughter's property (M. Ket. 4:4, discussed earlier)—the daughter herself does not, properly speaking, own the property before she comes of age.

153. The Babylonian rabbis understood this very well, for they permitted a wife whose earnings exceed the husband's cost of maintaining her to opt out of working for him in return for maintenance and to keep her earnings instead (B. Ket. 58b, *'eini nizzonet wᵉ'eini ʿosah*).

154. I present only the central portion of M. Giṭ. 5:6, the rest is irrelevant here.

155. In this connection we note that in Anglo-American law, it was not until the late nineteenth century that husbands lost control of their wives' property.

156. Further cases on the wife as property owner will be found in app. 7 and app. 8.

157. Further cases on this point will be found in app. 9.

158. See app. 4. Albeck 1958, p. 374, in a supplementary comment on M. Naz. 4:5, explains why the term m^e*nuwwelet* ("repulsive") used there can hardly refer merely to abstention from wine (as assumed by the talmudic rabbis and later commentators) as well as why it is plausible to suppose loss of consortium is at stake here.

159. Lev. 18:16 (*Do not uncover the nakedness of your brother's wife*) was interpreted by Jewish and Christian exegetes alike to preclude such a marriage even after the husband's death. The prohibition formed the basis of Henry VIII's argument for the annulment of his marriage to Catherine of Aragon, the widow of his older brother Arthur. Pope Clement VII's refusal to agree to the annulment precipitated Henry's break with the Roman Church and inaugurated the English Reformation.

160. This is particularly important if the man who wants to marry her happens to be a *kohen* (a member of the priestly caste) because a *kohen*, more than all other Israelites, must conform with Scripture's restrictions on his choice of marriage partners (Lev. 21:7ff.), lest he impair the sanctity of his caste.

161. The child will bear the name of the deceased but is not actually perceived as "his seed"—unlike the case of Tamar in Gen. 38. This point is brought out by Epstein's careful exposition of the successive stages of evolution of the levirate law (Epstein 1942, pp. 77–114). However, the technical differences between the three versions of the institution that appear in Gen. 38, Ruth 3–4, and Deut. 25 are not material to the present discussion, since the mishnaic law bases itself squarely on the Deuteronomic version. In context, the word *ben* in Deut. 25:5 almost certainly meant son, specifically, and did not include daughter. Nothing in the mishnaic law suggests a broader meaning. Later, when the levirate law fell into disfavor because of social change, the Talmud and other sources interpreted it to become operative only if the deceased left neither a son nor a daughter. This interpretation was possible because of the ambiguity of the word *ben*, which at least in the plural, *banim*, sometimes means children generally without regard to their sex. This more liberal interpretation was one among many efforts to reduce the impact of the much disliked biblical rule.

162. The Latin term conveniently distinguishes husband's brother from sister's husband, whereas the English term *brother-in-law* does not. The Hebrew terms for *husband's brother* and *brother's wife* are *yabam* and y^e*bamah*, respectively.

163. We note the discrepancy between the agnatic levirate law and the laws of inheritance as set out in Num. 27:8–9, which make a man's brothers his heirs only when he lacks daughters as well as sons. These two laws stem from different sources; the inconsistency need not bother us here. Probably the levirate law suited a nomadic lifestyle, with its greater emphasis on the propagation of sons for the clan than on territorial claims (land was not subject to private ownership), whereas in the settled agricultural lifestyle of the Israelites after the conquest of Canaan, the nuclear family and lineal inheritance assumed greater prominence. (See Mace 1953, pp. 95–117.) A settled society would be apt to produce a legal amendment of the type found in Num. 27:8 read together with Num. 36:8 that permits daughters to inherit but restricts the marriage of heiresses to their own clan or tribe.

164. Islamic law knows a form of divorce called *khul‛* (from the same root as *ḥaliṣah*, so Gesenius 1949, p. 283, s.v. *ḥ-l-ṣ*). The Islamic ceremony, based on ancient Arabian law, takes its name from the fact that the husband there "divested" himself of his wife by symbolically removing (*kh-l-‛*) his shoe. Cf. Ruth 4:7–8, wherein Ruth's nearest kinsman divests himself of his right to take her along with the rest of her husband's property by removing his shoe. This, however, should not be confused with the mishnaic levirate law as the term for removal of the shoe in Ruth 4:7–8 is not *ḥ-l-ṣ* but *sh-l-p*.

165. Carmichael 1977, in an ingenious interpretation, claims that the body language of the ritual symbolizes the sexual connotations of the levirate law. The woman's spitting at the levir, for instance, symbolizes his refusal to inseminate her.

166. *Ḥaliṣah* is still required today to release a Jewish woman for remarriage if her husband dies without issue and leaves a brother. Even if such brother is already married, he must still release his sister-in-law. The requirement has led to documented cases of serious abuse in the form of extortion by unscrupulous levirs. (See Abramov 1976, p. 185.)

167. Niditch 1979.

168. The remainder of this unit is omitted as irrelevant.

169. The remainder of this unit is omitted as irrelevant.

170. Further mishnaic modifications of the scriptural levirate law, all designed to maximize the use of women's reproductive function, appear in app. 10.

171. We defer analysis of the last part of the unit (M. Ned. 10:6 G and H) for our discussion of the levirate widow as person.

172. I present only that portion of M. Yeb. 14:4 (= Danby 1933, M. Yeb. 14:7) that is relevant here.

173. Lest this scenario be thought farfetched, we note that this very case occurred in the State of Israel in 1967. A deaf-mute married levir was willing but unable to release his brother's widow. The chief rabbis circumvented the difficulty by requiring the levir to take the widow (permissible in Jewish law, which technically permits polygyny), spend the night with her at a hotel, and then divorce her the next day. (This was legally possible because divorce requires only a document, not a declaration. Note also that levirate union, unlike marriage, does not require *qiddushin*, so that the inability of the deaf-mute to recite that formula was irrelevant here.) To ensure the man's execution of the divorce, the rabbis previously made him sign an agreement to pay the woman substantial support until he divorced her. (See Abramov 1976, p. 184).

174. The purpose of levirate marriage is to produce a son in the name of the dead man. A sterile woman obviously cannot achieve this, hence she is barred from marrying the levir.

175. The Mishnah curiously ignores Scripture's clear directive permitting a new husband to annul after marriage his bride's vows made during the betrothal period. Obviously Scripture's ruling on this point offends the sages' Hellenistic taxonomy. Instead, they prescribe the joint procedure outlined in M. Ned. 10:4 (discussed in chap. 2), whereby father and husband act together before the girl is transferred.

176. Gaius, writing in the middle of the second century C.E., says tutelage of women resulted from the view of "the early lawyers" that even women of full age should be in guardianship for that reason: *"Veteres enim voluerunt feminas, etiamsi perfectae aetatis sint, propter animi lævitatem in tutela esse"* (emphasis added). Zulueta translates: For the early lawyers held that women even of full

age should be in *tutela* on account of their instability of judgment." (Gaius, bk. I, 144; de Zulueta 1946, pt. I, p. 49). No equivalent rule appears in mishnaic law, but rabbis of the Babylonian Talmud refer to women as "unstable" (lit. light-minded) in a Hebrew expression that looks like a literal translation of the Latin, namely *nashim da'atam qallah* (*qallut = levitas*; *da'at = animus*). See B. Sab. 33b; B. Qid. 80b.) Whether this terminology was an independent development or was influenced by Roman law is beyond the scope of the present study, but I am strongly inclined to the latter view because the Hebrew formula sounds strangely stilted and looks like a clumsy attempt to render a Latin abstraction into a concrete Hebraism.

177. In strict accuracy, we note that the Mishnah subdivides minor daughters into two groups: the *q'tannah* (under twelve) and the *na'arah* (between twelve and twelve and one-half). For present purposes, however, that distinction is unimportant.

178. The sages also state the corollary: A man cannot give his adult daughter in marriage. We derive this from the case of the man who gives his "daughter" in marriage without specifying which daughter. He throws all his minor daughters into doubtful marital status through ambiguity. But those of his daughters who have come of age are unaffected (M. Qid. 3:8) because a man cannot legally give in marriage a daughter who has attained majority (M. Qid. 2:1).

179. See notes 28 and 29.

180. Although the text uses the Hebrew term *'ebed* for foreign slave and Hebrew bondman alike, I translate the first as "slave" and the second as "bondman" to reflect the distinction between Israelite bondmen and Canaanite slaves drawn in Flesher 1988.

181. Gaius inveighs against this practice as unreasonable (bk. I, 190; Zulueta, pt I, p. 61). However, he mentions a statutory exception, the *ius liberorum*, whereby women who had borne three or more children did attain autonomy following the enactment of the *Lex Julia et Papia Poppæa* in 18 B.C.E. and 9 C.E. (Gaius, bk. I, 145, 194; Zulueta, pt. I, pp. 49, 61.) This suggests that Roman culture shared the mishnaic view that a woman's most important function was the production of children. Adequate performance of that function was rewarded by emancipation when the woman had served her socially approved purpose.

182. In the story of Samson (Judg. 13:2ff.), it is not Samson's father but an "angel of the Lord" who makes this decision.

183. On the wife's inability to affect the status or rights of her husband, as contrasted with the husband's power to affect the status or rights of his wife, see also the discussion of M. Ned. 11:12 in chap. 3 and M. Qid. 3:8 in app. 10.

184. The Mishnah gives no reason for barring women from testifying, but the Babylonian Talmud suggests sociocultural reasons: A woman's place is in seclusion at home (B. Shebu. 30a, interpreting an obscure passage in Ps. 45:14), not exposed to public view and possible insults in a courthouse (B. Git. 46a).

185. Heb., *hinuma*. So Albeck 1958 (p. 92), note to M. Ket. 2:1. Danby 1983 (p. 246) adopts the Babylonian Talmud's explanation of *hinuma* as a bridal litter (B. Ket. 17b) but notes the possible connection to Gk. *hymenaios* ("bridal song").

186. Those listed as ineligible to testify include such dubious characters as diceplayers, usurers, pigeon-flyers, and traffickers in sabbatical-year produce.

187. Curiously, the Mishnah's framers seem to ignore the possibility of collusion between these two women, whereby one hand may be washing the other.

188. From the expression *te'agenah* occurring at Ruth 1:13 (from which the modern Hebrew *'ogen*, anchor, is likewise derived).
189. The remainder of the unit is omitted for brevity as the point is already made.
190. See nn. 117, 118.
191. The remainder of the unit is omitted as irrelevant.
192. The remainder of the unit is omitted as irrelevant.
193. Two further instances of female agents are the bondwoman, in M. Ter. 3:4, appointed by her master as his agent to donate *terumah* ("heave-offering") to the priest (in accordance with Num. 18:8ff. and Deut. 18:4), and the bondwoman, in M. M.S. 4:4, appointed by her master to redeem the second tithe (in accordance with Deut. 14:22ff.)
194. Socrates said of a wife who had mastered the science of economics (housekeeping) that she displayed "a masculine mind" (Xenophon, *Oikonomia* 9–10.1).
195. Although the feminine form *henwanit* appears only here, the masculine form *henwani* is used routinely in the Mishnah to denote a man who keeps a stall in the marketplace or some other place readily accessible from the public domain (see, for instance, M. B.Q. 6:6, M. Ned. 11:2).
196. We note that Jastrow translates *henwanit* as found in M. Ket. 9:4, by "saleswoman" rather than "stallkeeper" (Jastrow 1904/1950, vol. 1, p. 481, sv. *henwani*), perhaps to imply that the wife sold goods from the house. On the other hand, Pomeroy points out that in classical Athenian culture, although generally women did not go to market even to buy food (a chore performed by men, in part, to protect women from the hazards of the marketplace), poorer women sometimes worked outside the home "as vendors, selling food or what they had spun or woven at home" (Pomeroy 1975, pp. 72–73). Under imperial Rome, likewise, it was common for women to work outside the home (ibid., pp. 200–201).
197. In like fashion the sages specify that a woman, just as a man, is bound by the laws inculpating a person who swears a rash oath and then fails to keep it (M. Shebu. 3:7, 10) or a vain oath asserting an evident untruth or impossibility (M. Shebu. 3:8, 11).
198. We discussed the first part of this unit at the beginning of chap. 5.
199. The first part of this unit is omitted as irrelevant.
200. The legal power of intention in mishnaic law is discussed at length in Eilberg-Schwartz 1986a).
201. For a similar curb on the husband's power to limit the wife's freedom after the divorce, see app. 11.
202. At M. Git. 7:5, for instance, they may have wished to give a bankrupt husband who can no longer maintain his wife, or who has mortgaged his wife's property to a third party (despite her lien on it), a legal means of getting himself off the hook. A wife might well agree to the proposed arrangement to free herself for remarriage to someone who can afford to support her.
203. Cases where Jewish wives have invoked American law to declare a husband in contempt (and impose a jail sentence) for refusing to implement a prenuptial agreement to deliver a *get* if the spouses ever obtain a civil divorce raise knotty constitutional questions. Does the First Amendment, forbidding excessive entanglement of state and religion, preclude American courts from forcing a man to do something that his religious authorities have ordered but are powerless to enforce? At the time of writing, this question has not yet reached the U.S. Supreme Court.

204. We noted earlier a special kind of Islamic divorce known as *khul*. That procedure closely resembles the procedure in M. Giṭ. 7:5 in that a faultless wife who desires release can agree to forgo all or part of her marriage portion in return for the husband's granting her a divorce. (See n. 164).

205. If this turns out to be the case, she may not remarry until the child is born and the husband must support her throughout the period of pregnancy and lactation.

206. Instructive here is the case of the Prophet Muḥammad's first wife, the wealthy widow Khadija. Though both pre-Islamic Arabian law and Islamic law permitted polygyny, Muḥammad took no additional wives during her lifetime. It is reasonable to surmise that his dependence on her largesse may have been a factor in the situation. After her death, the prophet married a total of twelve other women.

207. Generally a party needs two witnesses to support or rebut a claim. However, M. Shebu. 7:1 provides that a hireling who sues a householder for wages due and is met with the householder's assertion that he has paid him must swear an oath in rebuttal of that assertion. M. Shebu. 7:4 provides that where one of two joint plaintiffs is not competent to testify (so that the testimony of the competent plaintiff does not suffice to prove their joint case), the competent plaintiff may swear to his claim on oath to compensate for the insufficiency of testimony.

208. See app. 4 for a discussion of the relevance of the Nazirite vow to conjugal relations.

209. Goitein 1978, pp. 346–53.

210. The other exception is Lev. 21:2, wherein the mother precedes the father in the list of close kin for whom a member of the priestly caste may cultically defile himself by contact with their corpses.

211. We should bear in mind that the mishnaic system is not representative of all forms of Judaism flourishing in its day. See, for instance, Brooten's work on inscriptional evidence for women's communal leadership roles in Graeco-Roman Jewish communities of the first six centuries of the Christian era (Brooten 1982).

212. Cults like that of Dionysus, in which women constituted most of the worshippers, were private rather than public forms of worship (Kraemer 1979). Moreover, the appeal of such cults precisely to the marginal and liminal elements in society symbolized a "motif of the reversal of normal states and judgments" whose social function was to affirm and legitimate the normal social order in which men occupied themselves with cultural matters like religion, whereas women stayed at home. Kraemer further notes that "women possessed by Dionysus are compelled to abandon, at least temporarily, their domestic obligations of housework and childrearing in favor of the worship of the god."

213. Even when women held a semblance of power in ancient religions, this was often more apparent than real. For instance, the Delphic Oracle, though spoken through a woman, was interpreted by a male priest. Moreover, it is highly significant that vestal virgins (as their title implies) had to give up their normal female function of childbearing in return for the right of active participation in the cult. Indeed, a vestal virgin found to have had sexual relations was punished by being buried alive.

214. The sole exception appears in the ritual of the suspected adulteress (Num. 5:11–31); but in that special case, it is the *priest* who must *"bring her forward and*

have her stand before the LORD" as part of the ordeal—not a voluntary act of the woman.

215. Exactly what this scriptural expression implies, beyond its use as a technical term for entry into the precincts of the Sanctuary, is beyond the scope of this study. See, however, Rabin 1930, *"Lifnei YHWH," Tarbiz,* vol. 23, pp. 1–8.

216. We speak here of sacrifice for cultic purposes (as opposed to secular slaughter of animals for food, which the Mishnah apparently permits a woman to perform, M. Ḥul. 1:1). However, if a woman has in fact ritually slaughtered a beast, its use is permitted *ex post facto* to avoid economic loss (M. Zeb. 3:1).

217. The Babylonian rabbis (B. Pes. 91a) and Maimonides (*Mishneh Torah: Laws of Passover Sacrifice*) interpret the Mishnah to forbid a fellowship of women and slaves combined or of children and slaves combined (for fear of various kinds of licentious conduct) but to permit a fellowship consisting of women alone. But the mishnaic text is distinctly ambiguous, and we must be circumspect in relying on later interpretations of the original meaning of an earlier text.

218. Patriarchal cultures and modern societies emerging from them have tended to perceive fellowship as a male institution, in part because it involves a public assembly, whereas women were expected to remain secluded at home, making a fellowship of women difficult or impossible in practice. Meeks points out that although first-century Greek women sometimes joined men's clubs, "apart from associations of priestesses there is little evidence for all-women's [*sic*] clubs." Meeks 1983, p. 24.

219. In this regard, we note the Deuteronomist's connection of the paschal sacrifice with the cultic pilgrimage to the Temple at Jerusalem (Deut. 16:2, 17) and the fact that Mishnah, following Scripture, exempts women from pilgrimage (M. Ḥag. 1:1, discussed later in this chapter). Stein 1957, discussing the influence of the Greek symposium on the form of the Passover Haggadah, points out that, just as with the classical Greek symposium, women take no part in the Seder liturgy and there is only one scenario (at B. Pes. 116a) where the sages contemplate women joining in the table talk: "The wise son asks his father (about the laws of Passover), and if he is not wise, the wife asks her husband." B. Pes. 108a states that even though women are obligated to drink the four cups of wine "because they participated in the miracle of the Exodus," a woman is not required to recline at the table like men unless she is a lady of high standing (*'ishshah ḥashubah*). The Palestinian Talmud (Y. Pes. 37b), by contrast, makes reclining obligatory for women regardless of social class. But it is clear that women generally, though present, did not participate actively in the discussions at the Seder celebration.

220. Only the relevant portion of this unit is given here.

221. Economic motivation overrides other considerations in a number of rules validating cultic acts performed by women. For instance, M. ʿArak. 1:1 permits a woman to vow the scripturally prescribed valuation of a human being or animal to the Temple, even though Lev. 27:1 specifically mentions only a *man* as making such donations. To invalidate her vow would deprive the priesthood of revenue. Likewise, M. Zeb. 3:1 validates the use of a beast ritually slaughtered by a woman; to rule otherwise would render the carcass unfit for sacrifice or private consumption, causing serious economic loss. In general interpreters of Scripture defined "men" arbitrarily—either to include or to exclude women, depending on what suited the exegetes' perception of societal needs.

222. *1. When you enter the land that the LORD your God is giving you as a heritage, and you possess it and settle in it, 2. you shall take some of every first fruit of the soil, which you harvest from the land that the LORD your God is giving you, put it in a basket and go to the place where the LORD your God will choose to establish his name. 3. You shall go to the priest in charge at that time and say to him, "I acknowledge this day before the LORD your God that I have entered the land that the LORD swore to our fathers to assign us." 4. The priest shall take the basket from your hand and set it down in front of the altar of the LORD your God. 5. You shall then recite as follows before the LORD your God: "My father was a fugitive Aramean. He went down to Egypt with meager numbers and sojourned there; but there he became a great and very populous nation. 6. The Egyptians dealt harshly with us and oppressed us; they imposed heavy labor upon us. 7. We cried to the LORD, the God of our fathers, and the LORD heard our plea and saw our plight, our misery and our oppression. 8. The LORD freed us from Egypt by a mighty hand, by an outstretched arm and awesome power, and by signs and portents. 9. He brought us to this place and gave us this land, a land flowing with milk and honey. 10. Wherefore I now bring the first fruits of the soil which You, O LORD, have given me." You shall leave it before the LORD your God and bow low before the LORD your God. 11. And you shall enjoy, together with the Levite and the stranger in your midst, all the bounty that the LORD your God has bestowed upon you* and your household. (Deut. 26:1–11, emphasis added.)

223. If, however, a woman had chosen to give the shekel as a supererogatory offering, this was *ex post facto* acceptable (M. Sheq. 1:5)—no doubt for the same reasons discussed in n. 221.

224. As the Talmud notes (B. Qid. 33b–34a), the Mishnah's framers, in fact, depart from this global exemption in several cases. For instance, eating unleavened bread on Passover is a time-contingent positive precept that women must perform, but study of Torah is not time-contingent, yet women are excluded from this, as discussed later.

225. Similar exclusions appear at M. Men. 9:8 and M. Par. 12:10.

226. More surprising, no explanation is offered by the rabbis of the Talmud who comment on the rule nor by the most important later exegetes of Mishnah (Maimonides) and Talmud (Rashi). The earliest source to offer a rationale is the fourteenth-century commentator Abudarham, who states that God exempted women from certain precepts so as to free them to attend to their husband's needs. (*Sefer Abudarham* 1340/1950, pt. III, "The Blessing over [fulfilling] the Commandments."

227. Obviously my statement imports a value judgment. But as it is primarily the life of mind and spirit that raises man above the beasts, I believe it is a value judgment that must have been made in all times and places by most persons of both sexes. Hence it is fair to assume that any culture that effectively excludes women from those aspects of life has deprived at least some women of something they may have ardently desired.

228. The Mishnah obligates women to recite certain prayers in private. However, by not counting her in the *minyan* (quorum of ten required for public prayer), the sages psychologically discourage her from making a special point of attending public worship. Men, by contrast, being eligible for the quorum, can derive the satisfaction of having performed a *miṣwah* (pious deed) if they leave their work

to make up a prayer quorum—which at least provides some compensation for economic loss suffered by interrupting their work for that purpose.

229. As T. Ber. 6:18 explains, this is why the Jewish male blesses God daily for not making him a gentile, a slave, or a woman. Rashi, commenting on the same rule, adds that, like a slave, a woman is not subject to Jewish religious duties because "a wife is also a bondwoman to her husband, like a slave to his master," apparently implying that the first duty of slaves and women alike is to their earthly rather than their heavenly master. (Rashi *ad* B. Men. 43b, foot of page, s.v. *haynu ishshah*.) See also Sefer Abudarham, n. 226.

230. For excellent discussions of this problem, see Berman 1973, Sigal 1975, and especially Biale 1984.

231. The menstruant must make various inspections at times specifically related to her period and must visit the ritual bath seven days after cessation, the commandment to separate *hallah* accrues when the dough is prepared, and the light must be kindled shortly before nightfall.

232. See n. 233.

233. This fact was already noted by the rabbis of the Babylonian Talmud, who discuss it at great length (B. Qid. 33b–36a). Moreover, as Maimonides points out: "By *all* [positive precepts accruing at a set time], the Mishnah means *most*. But concerning positive precepts that do or do not bind women there is no general rule. Rather they have been [individually] transmitted in the oral law, and are well-known matters. For instance, we know that eating unleavened bread on the first night of Passover, and rejoicing on festivals, and participating in *haqhel* [the assembly of the Israelite people held every seven years to hear the Torah, Deut. 31:12], and praying the *T^efillah* prayer, and lighting the *Hanukkah* lamp and the Sabbath lamp, and reciting *Qiddush* on Sabbaths and festivals—all these are positive precepts to be performed at a set time, yet every one of them is incumbent on women. And conversely, the commandment to be fruitful and multiply, and to study Torah, and to redeem the firstborn male, and to wage war against Amalek—all these are positive precepts not tied to a set time, yet women are exempt from them." (Maimonides, *Commentary ad* M. Qid. 1:7.)

234. The remainder of this unit is omitted as irrelevant.

235. The remainder of this unit is omitted as irrelevant.

236. On its face this mishnaic rule apparently excludes adult women of a man's own household from joining with him to make up the quorum of three (e.g., a man with two wives). But we should bear in mind that a polygynous man probably kept his wives in separate establishments and ate with them separately rather than together. (Islamic law likewise recommends this as the ideal norm.)

237. According to later authorities, there is no objection to women's forming their own quorum for grace (B. Ber. 45b). This, however, is the only context in which the talmudic rabbis validate a women's fellowship group.

238. In this regard we note that the qur'anic rule (Sura 33:35) exhorting Muslim men and women alike to observe four out of the five primary duties of Islam (declaration of faith, prayer, almsgiving, fasting) conspicuously omits the fifth obligation (pilgrimage) from the list, probably because women were not required to participate in the *hajj*. The pilgrimage, alone of the "five pillars of Islam," necessitates travel in the public domain; thus the Qur'an did not see fit to make it incumbent on women. Interestingly, the Babylonian Talmud speaks of a wife who "made a pilgrimage to the Temple even

though her husband forbade it" (B. Ned. 23a). This demonstrates that in Judaism, as in Islam, women are merely exempted, not totally excluded from the pilgrimage.

239. Generally women are explicitly excluded along with minors, slaves, and imbeciles. Maimonides takes the silence here to mean that a woman is, in fact, eligible to read the Book of Esther. (*Commentary ad* M. Meg. 2:4).

240. The beginning of this unit is omitted as irrelevant.

241. See Sigal 1975, p. 238.

242. Most of this unit is omitted as irrelevant.

243. Because "Israelites are not suspected of such conduct" (T. Qid. 5:10; B. Qid. 82a). So Albeck 1958, *Nashim*, note to M. Qid. 4:14, p. 329.

244. The remainder of this unit is omitted as irrelevant.

245. Analogously, the Qur'an (Sura 24:31) requires women to veil themselves in the presence of all men except near kinsmen, eunuchs, and slaves (i.e., they might remain unveiled in the company of those precluded by law, custom, or some other circumstance from having sexual relations with them).

246. Werblowsky 1982, p. 125.

247. Hebrew, *tiflut*. Jastrow vol. 2 1904/1950 (p. 1687), translates this term as "obscenity," commenting, "because the laws concerning sexual aberrations may excite her sensuality."

248. Joshua's views on this subject seem to support (or perhaps account for) the talmudic tradition that he eked out a meager living working at home as a smith or charcoal-burner (B. Ber. 28a).

249. The Babylonian Talmud (B. Qid. 29bff.) offers a lengthy argument to justify excluding women from the study of sacred texts. The argument turns out to be pure casuistry, based on juggling with the vocalization of Deut. 11:19. (See Biale 1984, pp. 31ff., for a good exposition of this passage.) Nonetheless, Maimonides later treats the exclusion of women from Torah study as an established rule.

250. Derogatory remarks about the evils of consorting with women appear in tractate *Abot* (at M. Abot 1:5): "Do not converse much with women . . . he that converses much with women causes evil to himself and neglects the study of Torah, and his end is to inherit Gehinnom." Although these sentiments obviously support my argument that women are excluded from study because men fear their sexuality, I have chosen not to include them in the study because there are strong reasons (based on scholarly analysis of the tractate's style and contents) for believing that tractate *Abot* is a later addition to the Mishnah rather than a contemporaneous document. If so, it would be anachronistic to ascribe its sentiments to the framers of the Mishnah proper, consistent though they are with what we have seen.

251. Cultic impurity bears no relation to modern notions of dirt and cleanliness. In the mishnaic system, only those bodily fluids that Scripture enumerates as sources of cultic contamination give cause for concern. These happen to include menstrual blood and other genital discharges, but not (for instance) urine or feces, which to our way of thinking may seem far more "dirty" than an emission of blood. For a convincing anthropological explanation of the menstrual and related taboos in primitive societies see Douglas 1966/1980, especially pp. 1–40, 129–158. See also Eilberg-Schwartz 1986b.

252. Indeed, the rules are so detailed as to have prompted an early Muslim tradent to preface his collection of the Islamic rules about menstruation with the follow-

ing comment, "Some say that Allah first sent menstruation among the Children of Israel." (al-Bukhari, al-Ṣaḥiḥ, vol. 1, headnote to Title 6, "Menstruation," trans. Houdas and Marcais, 1903-1914.)

253. The problem of the man as cultic contaminant is dealt with in tractate *Zabim*, "Men who suffer genital emissions." But after the destruction of the Temple, those rules lost all practical significance.

254. It is fair to note that a man who incurs cultic impurity, whereby he may convey contamination, is likewise perceived as a polluting object as well as a person who must take steps to eliminate the problem. However, in the case of a man, the problem is generally occasional, whereas the woman becomes a polluting object on a regular basis for almost half of every month.

255. The remainder of this unit is omitted as irrelevant.

256. Berman 1973 (p. 16) points out that although Jewish law does not require a woman to marry or procreate, the sages left this as her only viable life-option.

257. Maim. *Commentary ad* M. Hor. 3:7.

258. The plural form *b^enei yisra'el* ("Children of Israel") is an eponymous generic term that implies no judgment of inferior status—on the contrary, it suggests the equality of all Israelites as descendants of a single ancestor. In any case it refers to the people of Israel at large, semantically including both male and female. *Bat yisra'el*, by contrast, denotes an individual Israelite female. Other biblical terms, such as *ben adam* ("son of man," "mortal") or *bat ṣion, bat y^erushalayim* ("daughter of Zion, daughter of Jerusalem") are not properly comparable with mishnaic Hebrew. But even if they were, *ben adam* is effectively a generic, applying equally to male and female, whereas the other two terms are affectionate diminutives or pet names. The fact that a pet name expresses affection does not obviate its belittling connotation. The very use of the term *diminutive* for such epithets makes its own point. (An analogous confusion results when men who "put women on a pedestal" in order to keep them there claim that this elevates women's status above that of men.)

259. The term *yisra'elit* does appear in Tosefta, e.g. at T. Soṭ. 5:4. However (as the headnote to Kasovsky's Concordance to the Tosefta makes clear), the thrust there is *to distinguish females of the Israelite caste from females of the priestly or levitical castes*. In other words the context involves no direct contrast between Israelite *females* (of whatever caste) and Israelite *males*. This, in fact, supports my argument, for it indicates that terms underscoring the legal subordination of women become relevant only when it is necessary to consider the woman in her relationship to males of her own caste.

260. More than one hundred such references occur in the Mishnah; several appear in the present study. In context, most usages are contrasting a woman of the Israelite caste with a woman belonging to some other caste (e.g., when discussing the effect of marriages between the Israelite and priestly castes, M. Ter. 6:2, 7:2). But the term *bat yisra'el* clearly bears the generic sense of "Jewish woman," corresponding to *yisra'el* for "Jewish man," just as *bat kohen* ("daughter of a priest")—routinely used for a woman of the priestly caste regardless of her age—corresponds to *kohen*, the designation for a male of the priestly caste. The significant point is that the term *ben yisra'el* simply does not exist as a designation of personal status. To us (though not, perhaps, to the Mishnah's framers), the demeaning effect of being defined always and only as someone's daughter is self-evident.

261. Neusner 1981a, pp. 187ff. Neusner's term *analogical-contrastive* connotes, for mishnaic law, what English common law calls the process of "analogy and distinction."

262. Ibid., p. 190.

263. A classic formulation quoted by de Beauvoir is Engels's claim that when private property appears on the scene, "master of slaves and of the earth, man becomes the proprietor also of woman." (de Beauvoir 1953 (1974 ed.), p. 60.)

264. We are reminded of the assertion, frequently voiced in our own society, that a gang-rape victim "asked for it" simply by "being there." See Tong 1984, pp. 100–104; Brownmiller 1975, p. 433.

265. Niditch 1979 rightly characterizes the prostitute as a liminal character in Israelite society, in part owing to the anomaly of her being an unmarried nonvirgin. This would account for the sages' aversion to the subject, so far as concerns Israelite harlots, who are subject to opprobrium in light of the moral strictures about harlotry (Lev. 19:29). However, Niditch's claim that Rahab is accepted because prostitution has somehow become "institutionalized" in Israelite society misses an important point. Rahab was not an Israelite. As many mishnaic rules make clear, non-Israelites are routinely assumed to adhere to a lesser standard of morality. Niditch's "special class of women who can play the harlot without being condemned" is simply the class of foreign women.

266. See Smith 1978, pp. 292–93, 309, "Map is not territory—but maps are all we possess."

267. Douglas 1966, pp. 41–57.

268. Shaye J. D. Cohen 1985, pp. 46–48. Cohen offers a brilliant analysis of the origins of the matrilineal principle in mishnaic law. (See M. Qid. 3:12.) Cohen's theory that this represents an adaptation of the rules of *connubium* in Roman law is utterly convincing.

269. Soler 1979, p. 30.

270. As pointed out in chap. 1, level of personhood depends on the balance between an individual's entitlements and obligations. That many systems assign women fewer rights than men does not mean that women are not persons, but only that their level of personhood is lower than that of men.

271. De Beauvoir 1953 (1974 ed.), pp. xxvii–xxviii.

272. The anomalous character of woman in the Mishnah is discussed by Neusner 1979, pp. 96–97, citing the work of Simone de Beauvoir and Michelle Zimbalist Rosaldo on woman as anomaly.

273. "[A]n anomaly is an element which does not fit a given set or series; ambiguity is a character of statements capable of two interpretations. But reflection on examples shows that there is very little advantage in distinguishing between these two terms in their practical application. Treacle is neither liquid nor solid; it could be said to give an ambiguous sense-impression. We can also say that treacle is anomalous in the classification of liquids and solids, being in neither one nor the other set." (Douglas 1966, p. 37.)

274. The affinities between the talmudic and Islamic laws of women's status are far greater than is generally realized. See Wegner 1982a, pp. 1–33.

275. A subtle distinction appears here. Unlike the case of the wife who mistakenly remarried, the sages cannot override the rights of personhood of the merely *suspected* adulteress. Whereas in the earlier case it is *certain* that she has had sexual relations with another man, in the present case her husband *cannot prove this*. (If he could prove it, she would be subject not to the ordeal, but to a trial for adultery.)

276. M. Giṭ. 9:8 achieves nothing if the husband persists in his refusal. One Israeli husband has spent twenty-six years in jail for contempt, while his wife remains shackled to him. See also n. 203 on an aspect of this problem in contemporary America.

277. Lévi-Strauss 1978, pp. 22–23, cited in MacCormack and Strathern 1980, p. 2. See also Turner 1969, p. 106.

278. For anti-Semite and Jew, see Sartre 1946 (trans. 1948), pp. 40–41.

279. Neusner 1979a, pp. 96–97, citing the work of de Beauvoir and Rosaldo.

280. Douglas 1966, pp. 3–4.

281. As Douglas 1966 has pointed out, although anomaly and ambiguity are not synonymous, the practical applications tend to be the same. See n. 273.

282. Douglas further points out, "There are several ways of treating anomalies. Negatively, we can ignore, just not perceive them, or perceiving them we can condemn. Positively we can deliberately confront the anomaly and try to create a new pattern of reality in which it has a place. It is not impossible for an individual to revise his own personal scheme of classifications. . . . But cultural categories are public matters. They cannot so easily be subject to revision." (Douglas 1966, pp. 38–39.)

283. Pomeroy 1975, p. 25. See n. 12.

284. See text to nn. 13–15 and Wegner 1988.

285. Børreson 1968/1981, pp. 26–29.

286. Neusner 1981b, pp. 270–71.

287. The other prime source of such contamination, intercourse with a menstruant, was thought so basic to cultic pollution that the Mishnah's framers placed the tractate on menstruants in the Division of Cultic Purity rather than in the Division of Women.

288. See, e.g., I Cor. 11:2–16, 14:34–35; Col. 3:18–19; I Tim. 2:9–15.

289. The first woman Reform rabbi was ordained in 1972, the first woman Reconstructionist rabbi in 1973, and the first woman Conservative rabbi in 1985.

290. Loewe 1966, a pioneering study of women in Judaism. Many other references appear in the bibliography. Recent surveys of the field appear in Heschel 1983, Biale 1984, and Umansky 1985.

291. Ozick 1979, reprinted in Heschel 1983, pp. 120–51, at p. 122.

292. Ozick 1979, in Heschel 1983, p. 126.

293. Greenberg 1981, p. 6.

294. Thus the ban on polygamy ascribed to Grershom of Mainz in the eleventh century was a direct response to the establishment of Christian hegemony in Europe, and many improvements in Jewish women's position in divorce law in medieval Islam represented responses to specific amendments to Islamic law, an analogous theocratic system based on almost identical principles of jurisprudence. On the general similarity of Islamic and talmudic law, see Wegner 1982c.

295. Biale 1984, p. 266.

296. Plaskow 1983, in Heschel 1983, pp. 223–33.

297. Geertz 1973, pp. 87–125.

298. Turner 1969, pp. 94–130.

299. Neusner 1979a, pp. 96–97.

300. Umansky 1982, pp. 114–15, 116.

301. Umansky 1983, p. x.

302. Fiorenza 1984, p. xiii.

303. Baskin 1985.

304. Ibid., p. 8.

305. Rosaldo 1974, pp. 23–24, emphasis added.
306. Baskin 1985, pp. 9–10, citing Neusner 1979, pp. 92–93.
307. Brooten 1980.
308. Baskin 1985, p. 10.
309. Compare, e.g., the German usage of such titles as Frau Professor or Frau Doktor to designate not a woman professor or doctor but merely the *wife* of a man who follows the calling in question.
310. Kraemer 1985. See also Shaye J. D. Cohen 1980.
311. Ortner (1974), pp. 72–73.
312. Ibid., p. 73.
313. Ibid., p. 69.
314. Ibid., p. 69, emphasis added.
315. MacCormack and Strathern 1980, p. 9, fn. 7.
316. Lévi-Strauss 1966/1984, p. 128.
317. MacKinnon 1982, pp. 515, 516.
318. Kuhn and Wolpe 1978, pp. 56, 57.
319. Ibid., p. 46.
320. De Beauvoir 1953 (1974 ed.), pp. 63–67.
321. Ibid., p. xxxiii.
322. Aristotle (trans. Balme, 1972), *De generatione animalium*, 775a.
323. It appears in the patristic writings of Augustine and later reappears in Aquinas. See Børreson 1968/1981, pp. 29, 159.
324. Baer 1970, pp. 14–35.
325. Wegner 1982b, pp. 562–63.
326. Evans-Pritchard 1965, p. 55.
327. Rosaldo and Lamphere 1974, pp. 1–15, 17–42; Ortner 1974, pp. 67–87.
328. The relevance of this to the current political and social controversy over a woman's right to abortion should not be overlooked. The insistence of the self-styled "right-to-lifers" (who totally ignore the right of mother and family to a decent quality of life) that their opposition rests on the concept of the fetus as a person almost certainly masks ulterior (perhaps subconscious) motives of the kind just outlined.
329. O'Brien 1981, pp. 93–139.
330. We note, however, that the Talmud (B. Ket. 58b, 65b) insists that this rule applies only up to the equivalent of the husband's cost of maintaining his wife and that the surplus is actually the property of the wife.
331. Meyers 1983. See also Sanday 1974.
332. Bird 1981. The text was neither vocalized nor punctuated until the early centuries of the Christian era.
333. Børreson 1981, pp. 93–139.
334. Rosaldo 1980, p. 391. These observations were published shortly before their author's death in a climbing accident. The death of Michelle Zimbalist Rosaldo was a grievous loss to the coterie of feminist theoreticians. To heed her statement on the need to "ferret out" the origins and roots of women's current status in Western society would constitute a fitting tribute to the work so tragically cut short.
335. Lerner 1986.
336. Ibid., p. 8. (Cf. n. 84 and accompanying text.)
337. For the purposes of this rule, the Tosefta defines a "grown male" as any male over nine years and one day, on the assumption that a younger male cannot achieve erection and penetration.

338. We bear in mind that condonation is possible only in the case of merely *suspected* infidelity. If adultery is *proven*, the law (following Deut. 24:1–4) precludes the husband from taking his wife back.

339. Only the final portion of the unit is given here.

340. Albeck 1958, p. 374 (supplementary comment on M. Naz. 4:5) explains in detail why *mnwwlt* can hardly refer merely to abstention from wine (as assumed by the rabbis of the Talmud and later commentators) and why it is plausible to suppose loss of consortium is at stake here.

341. We recall that the wife, though powerless to prevent her husband from following an occupation that renders him obnoxious to her, has a theoretical right to release from the marriage by divorce, without forfeiture of her marriage portion, if the husband's malodorous occupation makes sexual intercourse unbearably repugnant to her. (M. Ket. 7:10, discussed in chap. 3.)

342. In general (as we know) a widow or divorcée is legally autonomous and does not revert to membership in her father's household. The special mishnaic provisions involved here obviously depend on a specific scriptural rule governing the daughter of a priest (Lev. 22:13).

343. The remainder of the unit is omitted as irrelevant.

344. The only exception here is the case of intercourse with a man who for caste reasons is unacceptable to the community of Israel. Here, even though the act of intercourse does not acquire the woman, the pollution is considered so great that she must forfeit her priestly privileges anyhow.

345. Cf. Latin *manus*, the Roman law term for a husband's authority over his wife.

346. The insistence that the husband state orally, "This is thy writ of divorce," indicates that the written document, although required, constitutes mere evidence that the man has made the essential oral declaration. If so, mishnaic law would comport with other Semitic systems, such as Islamic law, in which the oral declaration constitutes the act of divorce. We note that the Aramaic papyri from Elephantine include no divorce documents, but several of the marriage documents refer to the contingency of divorce, which is explicitly described as occurring by oral declaration of either spouse. As Yaron points out (1961, pp. 54–55), there is absolutely no evidence that the Jews of Elephantine required a writ of divorce. The requirement of a writing, in mishnaic and later Jewish law, apparently rests explicitly on the scriptural directive *"and he writes"* in Deut. 24:1.

347. In fact, a husband's right to inherit from his wife rests on no scriptural foundation, but first appears in M. B.B. 8:1.

348. Such arrangements may have been quite common. A poor man marrying a wealthy woman might give up other rights too, e.g., his right to take additional wives. The Prophet Muḥammad, a poor man, who at twenty-five married a wealthy widow of forty under pre-Islamic Arabian law (in which the rules of property and personal status closely resemble those of mishnaic and talmudic law) may have voluntarily given up his right to take additional wives. Certainly he took none until Khadija's death, after which he married polygamously a total of twelve other women.

349. According to Simeon b. Gamaliel (M. Ket. 9:1), this flexibility is subject to one constraint: Where Scripture has decreed a particular right, that right cannot be abrogated even by its beneficiary. Simeon thinks (absent any proof text) that a husband's right to inherit from his wife stems from the Torah; but sages in general do not take this view.

350. I present only the relevant portion of the unit.
351. See, for instance, Maimonides, *Commentary, ad* M. B.B. 3:5; Albeck 1953/1963, *N^eziqin, ad* M. B.B. 3:3.
352. The remainder of the unit is omitted as irrelevant.
353. The remainder of the unit is omitted as irrelevant.
354. See M. Yeb. 1:2, 2:1, 2:2, 2:3, 3:1, 3:2, 3:4, 3:6, 3:8, 3:9, 4:8, 6:4.
355. The remainder of the unit is omitted as irrelevant.

BIBLIOGRAPHY

Abramov, S. Zalman. *Perpetual Dilemma: Jewish Religion in the Jewish State.* London: Associated Univ. Presses, 1976.

Abudarham, David b. Joseph. *Sefer Abudarham* [Seville, 1340]; A. J. Wertheimer, ed. publisher, *Abudarham ha-Shalem.* Jerusalem: Wertheimer, 1950.

Albeck, Ḥanokh. *Shishshah Sidrei Mishnah: Seder Nashim.* Tel Aviv: Devir, 1958.

———. *Shishshah Sidrei Mishnah: Seder Neziqin.* Tel Aviv: Devir, 1963.

Aristotle. *De generatione animalium.* Trans. D. M. Balme. Oxford: Clarendon, 1972.

Baer, Richard A., Jr. *Philo's Use of the Categories Male and Female.* Leiden: Brill, 1970.

Baskin, Judith. "The Separation of Women in Rabbinic Judaism." In Yvonne Haddad and Ellison Findly (eds.), *Women, Religion, and Social Change,* pp. 3-18. Albany, N.Y.: SUNY Press, 1985.

Beauvoir, Simone de. *The Second Sex (Le Deuxième Sexe,* 1949; trans. H. M. Parshley, 1953). New York: Vintage, 1974.

Berger, Peter. *The Sacred Canopy: Elements of a Sociological Theory of Religion.* Garden City, N.Y.: Doubleday, 1967.

Berman, Saul. "The Status of Women in Halakhic Judaism." *Tradition* 14:2 (1973), 5-28.

Biale, Rachel. *Women and Jewish Law.* New York: Schocken, 1984.

Bird, Phyllis. "Male and Female, He Created Them: Gen. 1:27b in the Context of the Priestly Account of Creation." *HTR* 74 (1981), 129-59.

Blackman, Philip. *Mishnayoth,* vol. 3, *Order Nashim.* London: Mishnah Press, 1953.

Børreson, Kari Elisabeth. *Subordination and Equivalence: The Nature and Role of Woman in Augustine and Aquinas* [1968]; trans. Charles H. Talbot, Washington: Univ. Press of America, 1981.

Brooks, Roger. *Support for the Poor in the Mishnaic Law of Agriculture: Tractate Peah.* Chico, Calif.: Scholars Press, 1983.

Brooten, Bernadette. *Women Leaders in the Ancient Synagogue.* Chico, Calif.: Scholars Press, 1982.

Brownmiller, Susan. *Against Our Will: Men, Women and Rape.* New York: Simon and Schuster, 1975.

al-Bukhari, Muḥammad. *al-Jamiᶜ al-Ṣaḥiḥ* [ca. A.D. 850]. Trans. O. Houdas and W. Marcais as *El-Bokhari, Les Traditions Islamiques,* 5 vols. Paris: 1903–1914.

Carmichael, Calum. "A Ceremonial Crux: Removing a Man's Sandal as a Female Gesture of Contempt." *JBL,* 96 (1977), 321–36.

——. *Women, Law, and the Genesis Traditions.* Edinburgh: Edinburgh Univ. Press, 1979.

Cohen, A. *The Babylonian Talmud, Seder Nashim (ed. I. Epstein): Soṭah. Translated into English with Notes, Glossary and Indices.* London: Soncino, 1936.

Cohen, Boaz. *Jewish and Roman Law. A Comparative Study.* New York: Jewish Theological Seminary, 1966.

Cohen, Shaye J. D. "The Origins of the Matrilineal Principle in Rabbinic Law." *A.J.S. Review,* 10 (1985), 19–53.

——. "Women in the Synagogues of Antiquity." *Conservative Judaism,* 34 (1980), 23–29.

Daiches, Samuel, and Slotki, Israel W. *The Babylonian Talmud, Seder Nashim (ed. I. Epstein): Kethuboth. Translated into English with Notes, Glossary and Indices.* London: Soncino, 1936.

Danby, Herbert. *The Mishnah. Translated from the Hebrew with Introduction and Brief Explanatory Notes.* Oxford: Oxford University Press, 1933.

Daube, David. "Rabbinic Methods of Interpretation and Hellenistic Rhetoric." *HUCA,* 22 (1949), 239–62.

Diamond, Jared. "Everything *Else* You Always Wanted to Know About Sex." *Discover* 6 (April 1985), 70–82.

Douglas, Mary. *Purity and Danger.* London: Routledge and Kegan Paul, 1966.

Eilberg-Schwartz, Howard. "An Anthropological Approach to the Menstrual Taboo in Judaism." In Eilberg-Schwartz, *Excursions in the Anthropology of Ancient Judaism.* Indiana Univ. Press (forthcoming).

——. *The Human Will in Judaism: The Mishnah's Philosophy of Intention.* Chico, Calif.: Scholars Press, 1986.

Eliade, Mircea. *The Sacred and the Profane.* New York: Harcourt Brace, 1959.

Epstein, Louis M. *Marriage Laws in the Bible and Talmud.* Cambridge: Cambridge Univ. Press, 1942.

Evans-Pritchard, E. E. *The Position of Women in Primitive Societies and other Essays in Social Anthropology.* London: Faber and Faber, 1965.

Falk, Ze'ev W. *Jewish Matrimonial Law in the Middle Ages.* Oxford: OUP, 1966.

Fiorenza, Elisabeth Schüssler. *In Memory of Her: A Feminist Theological Reconstruction of Christian Origins.* New York: Crossroad, 1984.

Firestone, Shulamith. *The Dialectics of Sex: The Case for Feminist Revolution.* New York: Bantam, 1975.

Flesher, Paul V. *Oxen, Women or Citizens? Slaves in the System of the Mishnah.* Atlanta: Scholars Press for Brown Judaic Studies, 1988 (forthcoming).

Freedman, H. *The Babylonian Talmud, Seder Nashim (ed. I. Epstein): Kiddushin. Translated into English with Notes, Glossary and Indices.* London: Soncino, 1936a.

———. *The Babylonian Talmud, Seder Nashim (ed. I. Epstein): Nedarim. Translated into English with Notes, Glossary and Indices.* London: Soncino, 1936b.

Gardner, Jane F. *Women in Roman Law & Society.* Bloomington: Indiana Univ.
Press, 1986.

Geertz, Clifford. *The Interpretation of Cultures.* New York: Basic Books, 1973.

Geller, Markham J. "New Sources for the Origins of the Rabbinic Ketubah."
HUCA, 49 (1978), 227–45.

Gesenius, F. H. W. *Hebrew-Chaldee Lexicon to the Old Testament.* Trans. Samuel
P. Tregelles. Grand Rapids, Mich.: Eerdmans, 1949.

Goitein, Shelomo Dov. *A Mediterranean Society: The Jewish Communities of the
Arab World as Portrayed in the Documents of the Cairo Geniza,* 4 vols.
Berkeley: Univ. of California Press, 1967–1983.

Goodwater, Leanna. *Women in Antiquity: An Annotated Bibliography.* Metuchen,
N.J.: Scarecrow Press, 1975.

Greenberg, Blu. *On Women and Judaism.* New York: JPS, 1981.

Haddad, Yvonne, and Findly, Ellison, eds. *Women, Religion and Social Change.*
Albany, N.Y.: SUNY Press, 1985.

Haughton, G. C., ed. *Manav Dharma Shastra, or the Institutes of Manu: Code of
Hindu Laws,* 4 vols. New Delhi: Cosmo, 1982.

Hauptman, Judith. "Images of Women in the Talmud." In Ruether, *Religion and
Sexism,* pp. 184–212. New York: Simon and Schuster, 1974.

Heschel, Susannah, ed. *On Being a Jewish Feminist.* New York: Schocken, 1983.

Hyman, Paula. "The Other Half: Women in the Jewish Tradition." *Conservative
Judaism,* 26 (1972), 14–21.

Janeway, Elizabeth. *Man's World, Woman's Place: A Study in Social Mythology.*
New York: Dell, 1971.

Jastrow, Marcus. *A Dictionary of the Targumim, the Talmud Babli and Yerushalmi,
and the Midrashic Literature.* 2 vols. New York: Judaica Press, 1904, repr.
1950.

Kasowski, Ch. J. *Otsar l^eshon ha-Mishnah* (Concordance to the Mishnah). Jerusalem: Masada, 1956–60.

———. *Otsar l^eshon ha-Talmud* (Concordance to the Talmud). Jerusalem: Ministry
of Education and Culture, Government of Israel, 1954–1982.

———. *Otsar l^eshon ha-Tosefta* (Concordance to the Tosefta). Jerusalem: JTS, 1961.

Klien, B. D. *The Babylonian Talmud, Seder Nashim (ed. I. Epstein): Nazir. Translated into English with Notes, Glossary, and Indices.* London: Soncino, 1936.

Koltun, Elizabeth, ed. *The Jewish Woman.* New York: Schocken, 1976.

Kraemer, Ross. "Ecstasy and Possession: The Attraction of Women to the Cult of
Dionysus." *HTR* 72 (1979), 55–80.

———. "A New Inscription from Malta and the Question of Women Elders in the
Diaspora Jewish Communities." *HTR* 78 (1985), 431–38.

Kuhn, Annette, and Wolpe, Anne-Marie, eds. *Feminism and Materialism: Women
and Modes of Production.* London: Routledge and Kegan Paul, 1978.

Lefkowitz, M. R., and Fant, M. B. *Women's Life in Greece and Rome.* Baltimore,
Md.: Johns Hopkins Univ. Press, 1982.

Lerner, Gerda. *The Creation of Patriarchy.* New York: Oxford Univ. Press, 1986.

Lévi-Strauss, Claude. *Myth and Meaning.* London: Routledge and Kegan Paul,
1978.

———. *The Savage Mind (La Pensée Sauvage,* 1962; trans. 1966). Chicago: Chicago
Univ. Press, 1984.

Liddell, Henry George, and Scott, Robert. *A Greek-English Lexicon*, 9th ed. Oxford: Clarendon, 1968.

Lieberman, Saul. *The Tosefta. According to Codex Vienna, with Variants from Codex Erfurt, Genizah Mss. and Editio Princeps (Venice, 1521). The Order of Nashim I. Yebamot, Ketubbot, Nedarim, Nazir.* (New York: Rabinowitz, 1967); *II. Soṭah, Giṭṭin, Qiddushin* (New York: Rabinowitz, 1973.

Loewe, Raphael. *The Position of Women in Judaism.* London: SPCK, 1966.

MacCormack, Carole P. "Nature, Culture and Gender: A Critique." In MacCormack and Strathern (eds.), *Nature, Culture and Gender*, pp. 1–24. Cambridge: Cambridge Univ. Press, 1984.

MacCormack, Carole P., and Strathern, Marilyn, eds *Nature, Culture and Gender.* Cambridge: Cambridge U.P., 1980.

Mace, David R. *Hebrew Marriage.* New York: Philosophical Library, 1953.

MacKinnon, Catherine. "Feminism, Marxism, Method and the State: An Agenda for Theory." *Signs*, (1982), 515–47.

Meeks, Wayne. *The First Urban Christians.* New Haven: Yale Univ. Press, 1983.

Meyers, Carole. "Procreation, Production, and Protection: Male-Female Balance in Early Israel." *JAAR*, 51 (1983), 569–93.

Moses b. Maimon (Maimonides). *Mishnah im Perush HaRambam* (Commentary on the Mishnah), 3 vols., trans. from Arabic to Hebrew by Yosef Qafaḥ. Jerusalem: Mossad HaRav Kook, 1963.

———. Mishneh Torah (Code of Jewish Law). Jerusalem: Mossad HaRav Kook, 1956–68.

Netter, Shlomo Zalman, ed. *Ḥamishah Ḥumshei Torah, Miqra'ot Gᵉdolot.* Jerusalem: Sefer Pub. Co., n.d.

Neusner, Jacob. *A History of the Mishnaic Law of Damages*, 5 vols. Leiden: Brill, 1985.

———. *A History of the Mishnaic Law of Women*, 5 vols. Leiden: Brill, 1980.

———. *Judaism: The Evidence of the Mishnah.* Chicago: Univ. of Chicago Press, 1981.

———. *Method and Meaning in Ancient Judaism.* Chico, Calif.: Scholars Press, 1979a.

———. *Method and Meaning in Ancient Judaism. Second Series.* Chico, Calif.: Scholars Press, 1981.

———. *New Perspectives on Ancient Judaism*, vol. 1. Lanham, Md.: Univ. Press of America, 1987.

———. *The Tosefta. Translated from the Hebrew. Third Division: NASHIM. The Order of Women.* New York: Krav, 1979b.

———. *The Tosefta. Translated from the Hebrew. Sixth Division: TOHOROT. The Order of Purities.* New York: KTAV, 1977.

Niditch, Susan. "The Wronged Woman Righted: An Analysis of Genesis 38." *HTR* 72 (1979), 143–149.

O'Brien, Mary. *The Politics of Reproduction.* London: Routledge and Kegan Paul, 1981.

O'Flaherty, Wendy Doniger. *Women, Androgynes and Other Mythical Beasts.* Chicago: Univ. of Chicago Press, 1980.

Ortner, Sherry. "Is Female to Male as Nature is to Culture?" In Michelle Z. Rosaldo and Louise Lamphere, eds., *Women, Culture, and Society*, pp. 67–87. Stanford, Calif.: Stanford Univ. Press, 1974.

Otwell, John T. *And Sarah Laughed. The Status of Women in the Old Testament.* Philadelphia: Westminster Press, 1977.

Ozick, Cynthia. "Notes Toward Finding the Right Question." *Lilith*, no. 6 (1979). Reprinted in Susannah Heschel (ed.), *On Being a Jewish Feminist*, New York: Schocken, 1986. pp. 120-51.

Pickthall, Mohammed Marmaduke. *The Meaning of the Glorious Koran. An Explanatory Translation*. New York: New American Library, n.d.

Plaskow, Judith. "The Right Question is Theological." In Susannah Heschel (ed.), *On Being a Jewish Feminist*. New York: Schocken, 1983, pp. 223-33.

Plato, *Republic*. Trans. Francis MacDonald Cornford. Oxford: Clarendon, 1941.

Pomeroy, Sarah B. *Goddesses, Whores, Wives, and Slaves. Women in Classical Antiquity*. New York: Schocken, 1975.

Pritchard, James B. *The Ancient Near East*, vol. 1, *An Anthology of Texts and Pictures*; vol. 2, *A New Anthology of Texts and Pictures*. Princeton, N.J.: Princeton Univ. Press, 1958 and 1975. (Cited as Pritchard, *ANET*)

Rabin, Nehemiah. *"Lifnei YHWH," Tarbiẓ*, vol. 23 (1930), pp. 1-8.

Rabinowitz, Louis I. "Levirate Marriage and Ḥaliṣah." *Encyclopaedia Judaica*, vol. 11, pp. 122-31.

Rosaldo, Michelle Z. "The Use and Abuse of Anthropology: Reflections on Feminism and Cross-Cultural Understanding." *Signs* 6, (1980), 391.

Rosaldo, Michelle Z., and Lamphere, Louise, eds. *Women, Culture, and Society*. Stanford, Calif.: Stanford Univ. Press, 1974.

Ruether, Rosemary Radford, ed. *Religion and Sexism. Images of Women in Jewish and Christian Traditions*. New York: Simon and Schuster, 1974.

Sanday, Peggy R. "Female Status in the Public Domain." In Michelle Z. Rosaldo and Louise Lamphere, eds., *Women, Culture, and Society*, pp. 189-206. Stanford, Calif.: Stanford Univ. Press, 1974.

———. "Towards a Theory of the Status of Women." *American Anthropologist*, 75 (1973), 1682-1700.

Santillana, David. *Istituzioni di Diritto Musulmano Malichita*, vol. 1: Rome: Anonima Romana Editoriales, 1926; vol. 2: Rome: *Istituto par l'Oriente*, 1938.

Sartre, Jean-Paul. *Anti-Semite and Jew*. Trans. George G. Becker. New York: Schocken, 1948.

Schacht, Joseph. *An Introduction to Islamic Law*. Oxford: OUP, 1964.

Sigal, Phillip. "Male Chauvinism in the Halakhah." *Judaism*, 24 (1975), 226-44.

Simon, Maurice. *The Babylonian Talmud, Seder Nashim (ed. I. Epstein): Giṭṭin. Translated into English with Notes, Glossary and Indices*. London: Soncino, 1936.

Slotki, Israel W. *The Babylonian Talmud, Seder Nashim (ed. I. Epstein): Yebamot. Translated into English with Notes, Glossary and Indices*. London: Soncino, 1936.

Smith, Jonathan. *Map Is Not Territory: Studies in the History of Religions*. Leiden: Brill, 1978.

Soler, Jean. "The Dietary Prohibitions of the Hebrews." *New York Review of Books*, June 14, 1979, pp. 24-30.

Stein, S. "The Influence of Symposia Literature on the Literary Form of the Pesaḥ Haggadah." *JJS*, 8 (1957), 13-44.

Stern, Menaḥem. *Greek and Latin Authors*. vol. 1, *on Jews and Judaism. Edited with Introductions, Translations and Commentary, From Herodotus to Plutarch*; vol. 2: *From Tacitus to Simplicius*. Jerusalem: Israel Academy, 1974 and 1980.

Tong, Rosemary. *Women, Sex, and the Law*. Totowa, N.J.: Rowman and Allenheld, 1984.

The Torah. The Five Books of Moses. A new translation of The Holy Scriptures according to the Masoretic Text. Philadelphia: JPS, 1962. (Cited as New JPS Torah)

Trenchard, Warren. *Ben Sira's View of Women.* Chico, Calif.: Scholars Press, 1982.

Trible, Phyllis. *God and the Rhetoric of Sexuality.* Philadelphia: Fortress, 1978.

Turner, Victor. *The Ritual Process.* Ithaca, N.Y.: Cornell Univ. Press, 1969.

Umansky, Ellen. "Feminism and the Reevaluation of Women's Roles Within American Jewish Life." In Yvonne Haddad and Ellison Findly (eds.), *Women, Religion, and Social Change,* pp. 477-94. Albany, N.Y.: SUNY Press, 1985.

———. *Lily Montagu and the Advancement of Liberal Judaism.* New York: Mellen, 1983.

———. "(Re)imaging the Divine." *Response,* 13 (1982), 110-19.

Wegner, Judith Romney. "Dependency, Autonomy and Sexuality: Woman as Chattel and Person in the System of the Mishnah." In Jacob Neusner, *New Perspectives on Ancient Judaism,* vol. 1, pp. 89-102. Lanham, Md.: Univ. Press of America, 1987.

———. "The Image of Woman in Philo." In Kent H. Richards (ed.), *SBL 1982 Seminar Papers,* pp. 551-63. Chico, Calif.: Scholars Press, 1982b.

———. "Islamic and Talmudic Jurisprudence: The Four Roots of Islamic Law and Their Talmudic Counterparts." *American Journal of Legal History* 26 (1982c), 25-71.

———. "The Status of Women in Jewish and Islamic Marriage and Divorce Law." *Harvard Women's Law Journal,* 5 (1982a), 1-33.

———. "Tragelaphos Revisited: The Anomaly of Woman in the Mishnah." *Judaism* 37 (1988), 160-172.

Weiss, David Halivni. "The Use of *qnh* in Connection with Marriage." *HTR,* 57 (1964), 244-47.

Werblowsky, R. J. Z., "Women . . . and Other . . . Beasts" or "Why Can't a Woman Be More Like a Man." *Numen* 29 (1982), 124-31.

Yaron, Reuven. *Introduction to the Law of the Aramaic Papyri.* Oxford: OUP, 1961.

Zulueta, Francis de. *The Institutes of Gaius,* 2 vols. Oxford: OUP, 1946.

INDEX

wife's household duties, 75–76, 151–52
wife's property rights, 87–91
wife's rights of due process, 91–93
wife's right to divorce with $k^e tubbah$, 80–84
wife's right to maintenance, 74–75
wife's vows inimical to conjugal relations, 54–60
Wolpe, Anne-Marie, 192
Woman
as anomaly, 175–80
as autonomous, 114–44
biological function of, 5
as chattel, 6, 7–8, 13, 41–70, 99–109, 170, 171
as dependent, 20–39, 40–96, 97–113
disqualification from leadership roles, 153–56
does not "come before YHWH," 146–48
economic function of, 5, 127
exclusion from public domain, 145–67
exemption from certain religious duties, 153–56
as imperfect man (Aristotelian view), 193
intellect of, 8, 121, 127, 154
as man's enabler, 154
morality of, 8, 121, 126–27
as person, 6, 7–8, 13, 70–95, 109–12, 172–75
as Self and as Other, 8, 197
as sexual distraction, 148, 166
sexual morality of, 159–62
as source of cultic pollution, 148, 155, 162–65

"woman's place," vii, 3, 12, 150–53, 183–86
"women's precepts," 155
Women, Division of. *See* Mishnah, Division of Women
Worship
communal, 6, 157
private, 157, 189

Xenophon, 237 n.194

Yabam (levir), 98, 234 n.162. *See also* Levir
Yaron, Reuven, 247 n.346
Yavneh. *See* Grove of Yavneh
Yahweh, 4, 147, 157
Y^e bamah (levirate widow), 98, 99, 103, 234 n.162. *See also* Levirate widow
Y^e bamot, tractate ("Levirate Widows"), 98, 212
Yentl, v
Yibbum (levirate union), 101. *See also* Levirate marriage law
Yoḥanan b. Baroqa, R. (early 2nd cent. c.e.), 41–42, 120
Yoḥanan b. Nuri, R. (early 2nd cent. c.e.), 48
Yoḥanan b. Zakkai, R. (late 1st cent. c.e.), 54
Yose [b. Ḥalafta], R. (mid-2nd cent. c.e.), 29, 30, 56, 62, 64, 67, 74, 81, 95, 148, 250 n.119

Ziqqah, levirate bond, 98. *See also* Levirate marriage law